STUDIES IN LEGAL LOGIC

Law and Philosophy Library

VOLUME 70

STUDIES IN LEGAL LOGIC

by

JAAP HAGE
University of Maastricht,
The Netherlands

Springer

A C.I.P. Catalogue record for this book is available from the Library of Congress.

ISBN 1-4020-3517-9 (HB)
ISBN 978-1-4020-3517-3 (HB)
ISBN 1-4020-3552-7 (e-book)
ISBN 978-1-4020-3552-4 (e-book)

Published by Springer,
P.O. Box 17, 3300 AA Dordrecht, The Netherlands.
www.springeronline.com

Printed on acid-free paper

Printed in the Netherlands.

CONTENTS

CHAPTER 2: LAW AND COHERENCE

CHAPTER 3: REASON-BASED LOGIC

CHAPTER 4: COMPARING ALTERNATIVES

CHAPTER 5: RULE CONSISTENCY

CHAPTER 6: WHAT IS A NORM?

CHAPTER 7: LEGAL STATICS AND LEGAL DYNAMICS

CHAPTER 8: DIALECTICS IN ARTIFICIAL INTELLIGENCE AND LAW

CHAPTER 9: LEGAL REASONING AND LEGAL INTEGRATION

If you want to swim against the current, don't blame the river.
(Alleged text of a Chinese fortune cookie)

INTRODUCTION

This book is based on a number of papers that I (co-)wrote after finishing *Reasoning with rules*. Those papers were published in heterogeneous journals, conference proceedings, or not at all yet. In my own experience they are united by a common theme, namely the role of logic in the law.

In the first chapter I distinguish two ways of looking at logic. One way, which has been the dominant view during the 20th century, is to interpret logic ontologically, namely as the theory of what *must* be true, given the truth of a number of sentences. The relation between logic and ontology becomes clear if we pay attention to the fact that logic aims at finding general characteristics of arguments that make them good ones. Traditionally an argument is said to be good (in the sense of 'valid'), if its conclusion must be true given the truth of the premises. Logical research is devoted to the discovery of argument forms in which the premises necessitate the truth of the conclusion. A major, if not the only, source of such necessary inference steps is provided by necessary relations between states of affairs. If either P or Q is the case, and P is not the case, then it must be so that Q is the case. This is a necessary relation between states of affairs which is reflected in the truth values of sentences, and this relation justifies the derivation of Q from $P \vee Q$ and $\sim P$.

This example leans strongly on propositional logic, but it is possible to find other necessary connections between states of affairs that are less well accounted for in traditional logic. For instance, if the conditions of a rule are satisfied and there is no exception to this rule, the rule conclusion is attached to the state of affairs that satisfies the rule conditions. This is a necessary connection between states of affairs (satisfaction of the rule conditions, absence of exceptional circumstances, the rule conclusion), and this connection justifies derivation of the rule conclusion. Logic studies necessary relations between states of affairs (ontology), translates them into necessary relations between truth values of sentences, and exploits them to identify good arguments.

According to the other view, logic deals with the question under which circumstances we can *rationally accept* the conclusion of an argument on basis of the argument's premises. On this view, the emphasis is on the role that logic plays when we deliberate whether to accept, for instance, a belief or a principle. When logic is seen in this way, the relation between logic and epistemology becomes clear. Both disciplines deal with the *justification* of beliefs, or – better – acceptances.[1] It may even be argued that there is essentially one discipline, which deals with justified acceptance and is somewhat artificially subdivided into a part that focuses on arguments by means of which acceptances are justified and a part that focuses on the kind of premises by means of which acceptances can be justified.[2]

Both views of logic have their value and seem to me to be compatible with each other. Logic as I see it is strongly interwoven with both epistemology and ontology. The interrelations between logic, epistemology and ontology are a recurring theme in the chapters of this volume, which explains the choice of the title 'Studies in Legal Logic'.

The fact that the book is based on a number of papers that were in part published before and that were written with different audiences in mind, explains some peculiarities. One is that there is some overlap between different chapters. This overlap was necessitated by the wish to make the original papers, and the chapters based upon them, understandable by themselves. Another one is that the development of my thoughts in time has caused minor, and sometimes only seeming, inconsistencies between the chapters. For instance, Reason-based Logic is presented in chapter 9 as a non-monotonic logic, while in chapter 3 (which was written later) I emphasize that the non-monotonic aspect of Reason-based Logic is less important. A third peculiarity that I want to mention is that some chapters (in particular 7 and 8) were originally written with the AI and Law community in mind as the intended audience, which explains that chapter 8 discusses computer implementations of reasoning systems, while the most part of the book is directed at an audience of legal, and sometimes even general philosophers.

1 See chapter 2, section 2, for an explanation of this replacement of beliefs by acceptances.

2 This view on the relation between logic and epistemology was inspired by Toulmin (1958, 253f.)

In the first chapter, *Law and Defeasibility*, I try to take a step back from the attempts to develop non-monotonic logics for defeasible reasoning in the law, and address the question what precisely the phenomenon is that we aim to capture by means of these special logics. My answer to this question, that we aim to capture the defeasibility of justification, leads to a view of logic according to which logic deals with *justification* of conclusions on basis of premises, rather than with guaranteeing the *truth* of the conclusion given the truth of the premises. Briefly stated, the development of logics for defeasible reasoning presupposes a re-definition of the traditional object of logic. Besides this general point about the nature of logic, I also argue that legal reasoning involves defeasibility in an essential way, although not all forms of legal reasoning do so.

Law and Defeasibility was presented in earlier forms at a meeting of JURIX (the Dutch-Flemish research group on Law and Computer Science) in Amsterdam 2003, and at a special workshop at the IVR 2003 conference in Lund. I would like to thank the participants in these meetings for their valuable comments. The chapter in (almost) its present form has been published in a special issue of the Artificial Intelligence and Law journal, devoted to papers of the aforementioned special workshop (Hage 2003 LD). This special issue also contains a review of the paper by Bulygin (Bulygin 2003).

The step from logic towards epistemology that was hinted at in the first chapter, is taken completely in the second chapter, *Law and Coherence*. The purpose of this chapter is to show the crucial importance of coherentism for the law. It is not meant to develop criteria to judge the coherence of the law or theories about the law. Although the chapter formulates a criterion for coherence, this criterion is much too abstract to be put to practical use.

In chapter 2, two versions of legal coherence are distinguished. According to one of them, the law is coherent if it is based on a single starting point, or - at least - as few different starting points as possible. The other one holds that (a theory about) the law is coherent if it is part of a coherent theory of everything. This latter notion of coherence is an adapted version of coherence as used in epistemology. I argue that the law *must* be coherent in this second, epistemic sense, and that it *may* be coherent in the first sense, but only if this fits in a coherent theory of everything. In the course of my argument, I develop the already mentioned version of an epistemic coherence theory, which I call integrated coherentism. The main findings of the chapter are used to argue why much of Raz's criticism of coherentism in the law is unfounded. The central theme of this chapter was also addressed by a paper in Ratio Juris (Hage 2004).

In the third chapter, *Reason-based Logic*, not published before, I step away from the abstract philosophical issues dealt with in the first two chapters, and offer an updated version of Reason-based Logic, the logic for legal reasoning developed in, amongst others, my *Reasoning with Rules*.[3] The new version of Reason-based Logic differs in at least three aspects from the earlier version. First, the logic has been simplified somewhat, to make it more accessible. Second, the emphasis on its being a non-monotonic logic has been removed. And finally, the presentation of the logic has been adapted to the underlying philosophy of logic that there is no sharp boundary between logic and domain knowledge. As a consequence, I present first a kind of basic version of the logic, which only deals with reasons and their balancing. The logic of legal rules is the subject of the second part of the chapter and is presented as an extension of basic Reason-based Logic, based on necessary connections between states of affairs in the legal domain.

Part of the motivation to present a new version of Reason-based Logic was that a reshuffling of some basic concepts of the logic was needed to use Reason-based logic for comparative reasoning. Comparative reasoning is the topic of the fourth chapter, *Comparing Alternatives*, which was not published before. In this chapter I present another extension to basic Reason-based Logic, this time to make it possible to compare alternatives qualitatively, on basis of the sets of reasons that plead for and against them. I show how this method of qualitative comparison of alternatives can be used to deal with legal theory construction, legal case based reasoning and legal proof. The extension of Reason-based Logic which is necessary to make it deal with comparative reasoning, greatly increases the possibilities of this logic in comparison to the version described in *Reasoning with Rules*.

In the fifth chapter, *Rule Consistency*, the idea is developed that a set of rules is consistent if and only if it is not possible that the conditions of all the rules are satisfied and the conclusions of these rules are incompatible. One of the complications dealt with is that rules are also factors that determine whether it is possible that the conditions of all the rules are satisfied and whether the conclusions are incompatible. The chapter can be seen as an illustration of a theme of this book that there is no sharp boundary between logic and domain knowledge. Rules are treated as domain knowledge when they are evaluated on their consistency, and as (part of) logic when they are used to determine which states of affairs are compatible. Precursors of this chapter have been published in the proceedings of the JURIX 1999 conference, in Law and Philosophy and in Information and Communications Technology Law (Hage 1999 (RC), 2000 (RC) and 2000 (CRN)).

The organizing theme of *What is a norm?*, the sixth chapter, is that the term ‘norm’ stands for so many different things that it is better abandoned.

[3] Hage 1997 (RwR). See also Verheij 1996 and Hage 1996.

The body of the chapter consists of discussions of some theories of what norms are, in particular the command theory and the theory that norms are deontic facts. In my opinion, the main value of the chapter lies in the conceptual distinctions it makes between orders, commands, rules, descriptive counterparts of rules and deontic facts, and its discussion of speech acts as means to create law. The chapter also contains a discussion of the moderately idealistic background (in the sense of ontological idealism) that underlies much of this work. *What is a norm?* has not been published before. Some of the implications of this chapter for deontic logic have been described in Hage 1999 (MNDL).

The ontological theme of chapter six is continued in the seventh chapter *Legal Statics and Legal Dynamics*. It elaborates the idea that the law consists of static and dynamic connections between states of affairs. These connections, causation and constitution, are analyzed in some detail and are related to, amongst others, MacCormick and Weinberger's institutional theory of the law[4], rights as legal status, and to juristic acts as means to modify the law. This chapter is based on a paper that I co-wrote with Bart Verheij (Hage and Verheij 1999). I want to thank Bart and Elsevier, the publisher of the original paper, for their permission to adapt the paper for the present volume. Obviously, I take the full responsibility for the changes made.

Chapter 8. *Dialectical Models in Artificial Intelligence and Law*, is based on a presentation that I gave at a workshop related to Royakker's defense of his thesis.[5] It discusses the several uses to which dialogs and dialectics are put in logical theory and the analysis of legal reasoning. Apart from a systematic overview of the field, the chapter offers a theory about the relation between dialogs, dialectics and (legal) justification. It also elaborates the idealistic theme of chapter 6.

The chapter is a slight reworking of Hage 2000 (DM). Thanks go to Ronald Leenes, Arno Lodder and Bart Verheij for many discussions about legal dialogues that inspired the ideas presented here, to Tom Gordon for pointing out some weakness in the purely procedural view of the law which I hope have been overcome, to José Plug for suggesting many improvements in the formulation and to Henry Prakken and an anonymous referee of the Artificial Intelligence and Law Journal for suggesting many additional improvements.

After the paper on which this chapter is based was published, much relevant new material has been published. I do not have the impression,

4 MacCormick and Weinberger 1986.

5 Royakkers 1996.

however, that this material necessitates modification of the main argument line of this chapter and therefore I only mentioned some of the more recent publications, without striving for completeness.

Chapter 9, *Legal Reasoning and Legal Integration*, illustrates how the theoretical work of, in particular, the chapters 3 and 4, can be put to practical use. It contains an elaborate argument why case-based reasoning does not necessarily give a legal decision maker more leeway than rule based reasoning. By means of this argument it is argued why Legrand's view that a uniform civil law code cannot lead to uniform private law, is based on a wrong premise. This chapter is a slightly modified version of Hage 2003 (LRLI). I want to thank Jan Smits for valuable comments that made it possible to clarify some obscure parts in the argument of this chapter.

Writing a book is much easier with the help of others. In this connection I want to thank the Law Faculty of the University of Maastricht for providing me with a working environment that made my research possible. Several persons have so much influenced my thinking on the topics of this work that it is impossible to point out precise passages that have benefited from my discussions with them. First and foremost in this connection are my former near colleague Bart Verheij, who is in the above indicated sense co-author of (but not co-responsible for) several chapters, and Aleksander Peczenik who helped me make the return from Law and AI to (legal) philosophy in general. Henry Prakken and Giovanni Sartor have provided me since the beginnings of the nineties with intellectual challenges, helpful comments and an ongoing discussion from which I profited very much. Later on, Carsten Heidemann has come to fulfill a similar role, especially with regard to ontological idealism. Bob Brouwer, Jan Sieckmann, Jan Wolenski, Eugenio Bulygin and Arend Soeteman and an anonymous reader for Springer have, directly or indirectly, given comments on (parts of) this book from which I learned a lot. Most thanks, however, go to my wife Loes and my daughter Suzanne, for providing me with a pleasant home where I could write.

Chapter 1

LAW AND DEFEASIBILITY

1. INTRODUCTION

During the last few decennia quite a bit of literature has been published about so-called defeasible reasoning in the law.[1] Nevertheless, the question what this defeasibility precisely amounts to has received scarce attention.[2] Intuitively, the defeasibility of legal reasoning is a characteristic of the law or of legal reasoning and its understanding would be an understanding of what goes on in the law. Logical systems, such as non-monotonic logics, would only be means to capture a phenomenon that exists independently of these systems.

Recently, the question whether legal reasoning is really defeasible has been raised with some urgency.[3] It seems therefore time to pay systematic attention to the nature of defeasibility in general and to the relevance of defeasibility for the law in particular. Another topic that deserves attention is whether the analysis of legal reasoning, assuming that it is defeasible, requires the use of some non-monotonic logic. It has recently been argued that it does not.[4]

The structure of this chapter is as follows: First I will try to pin down the notion of defeasibility and in that connection I will distinguish between five

1 E.g. Raz 1975, Gordon 1986, Schauer 1991, MacCormick 1995, Prakken and Sartor 1997 and 2004, Verheij 1996, Hage 1997 Prakken 1997 and Brozek 2004.

2 One exception is Prakken and Sartor 2004.

3 Bayón 2001.

4 Soeteman 2003.

kinds of defeasibility, namely ontological, conceptual, epistemic, justification, and logical defeasibility. The second step is to investigate whether the law, legal knowledge, legal reasoning, or legal justification, is defeasible in one of these distinguished senses of defeasibility. The answer will be affirmative. Given this affirmative answer, I will address the question whether legal reasoning, where it is defeasible, should be analyzed by means of a so-called non-monotonic logic. Again, the answer will be, cautiously, affirmative.

2. KINDS OF DEFEASIBILITY

Although it is often argued that legal reasoning is defeasible, it is seldom specified what this alleged defeasibility amounts to. The first step in filling this gap is to distinguish defeasibility from non-monotonicity.

2.1 Non-monotonicity and defeasibility

Monotonicity and non-monotonicity are characteristics of systems of (formal) logic. A system of logic is monotonic, if and only if it is such that if a set of sentences S' is a superset of S, the set of conclusions C' that follow according to this logic from S' is a superset of the set C of conclusions that follow from S. A system of logic is non-monotonic if and only if it is not monotonic.

As can be seen from these definitions, monotonicity and non-monotonicity are characteristics of logical systems and have as such little to do with the law or with legal reasoning, or even with reasoning in general. Possibly a non-monotonic logic is useful to model legal reasoning, because legal reasoning is defeasible in a sense that is still to be specified. But even then the non-monotonicity of the logical system is something else than the defeasibility of the reasoning that is modeled by means of it.[5]

[5] Non-monotonicity as a characteristic of logical theories and defeasibility are not always well distinguished. For instance, Hage (1997 RwR, 4) calls the phenomenon that additional information can make a conclusion underivable which would be derivable in the absence of this information, the defeasibility of arguments. Prakken and Sartor (2004) adduce the non-monotonicity of common sense reasoning to illustrate what they call inference-based defeasibility. The very notion of inference-based defeasibility already presupposes that defeasibility has something to do with arguments, instead of what these arguments aim to capture, namely justification.

2.2 Ontological and conceptual defeasibility

'Defeasibility' was originally a technical legal term, standing, according to Collins English Dictionary, for the capability of an estate or an interest in land of being defeated, or – what boils down to the same thing – being rendered void. In his paper The ascription of responsibility and rights, Hart extended the use of this notion to all concepts that have the property that there are a number of conditions of application, but also one or more circumstances that, if they occur, end the prima facie applicability of the concept.6 The concept of a contract is a typical example. A contract that has come into existence after an offer and acceptance can be invalidated if one of the parties invokes a defeating condition, such as fraudulent misrepresentation, or undue influence. In this connection it is crucial that the defeating conditions are actually invoked; the mere fact that they occurred is not sufficient to defeat the contract. Therefore, defeaters are to be distinguished from ordinary conditions for the existence of a contract, which do not need explicit invocation.

For the understanding of this kind of defeasibility it is also crucial that the defeat of the contract has retro-active force.[7] If defeat would operate *ex nunc*, there would merely be a change in the facts: before the defeat the contract was valid and after the defeat it is invalid. Such a change in the facts is a very common phenomenon and there is no need to have a special concept - defeasibility - to denote it. For instance, if an open door is closed, the door was open before the event and it is closed afterwards. It would be rather peculiar to say that the fact that the door was open has been defeated by the event that the door was closed.

The case of a defeated contract is special, because of the retro-active force of the defeat. As long as the contract is not defeated, it is valid, but as soon as it has been defeated, it is considered to have been invalid all of the time. This is a rather uncommon phenomenon and deserves for that reason the special name of defeasibility. Since this kind of defeasibility concerns the retro-active change of the *facts* and not our beliefs about the facts, I propose to call it *ontological defeasibility*.

In his discussion of defeat in *The ascription of responsibility and rights* Hart connected defeat not so much to facts as to concepts. Concepts such as '(valid) contract' would be defeasible because they cannot be adequately characterized without reference to the conditions that would defeat their

[6] Hart 1949.

[7] The importance of retro-active force that distinguishes defeat from merely a change in the facts was not emphasised by Hart in his *Ascription*.

applicability. One may introduce a special term, *conceptual defeasibility*, for the defeasibility of concepts, although in my opinion it is not very elucidating to connect defeasibility to particular concepts, rather than to the phenomena denoted by these concepts.

2.3 Epistemic and justification defeasibility

Most, if not all, of our beliefs are amenable to revision. Some changes in the set of all our beliefs occur spontaneously, for instance because of sensory perception, or because we forget things that we used to know. Other changes are generated by the insight that beliefs should rationally be accepted or rejected, given what else we believe. This insight may lead us to accept new beliefs that should rationally be accepted, or to abandon beliefs, because they should rationally be rejected. It is possible to call the revisability of our beliefs 'defeasibility'[8] and I will use the term *epistemic defeasibility* for this kind of defeasibility.

In my opinion epistemic defeasibility as a separate notion is not very interesting, because it is merely another term for a phenomenon that is already known as revisability. Moreover, the revisability of beliefs is a psychological phenomenon, which has as such only indirectly to do with reasoning or logic. For this reason I will further ignore epistemic defeasibility.

There is, however, another kind of defeasibility, closely related to and easily confused with[9], epistemic defeasibility, which is more interesting. We accept some of our beliefs because it is *justified* to accept them given our other beliefs. For instance, we believe that John is punishable, because we both believe that John owns pornography and that owning pornography is punishable. If we stop believing that owning pornography is punishable, the belief that John is punishable loses its justification. The same holds if we acquire the beliefs that Johns owns pornography purely for scientific issues and that owning pornography for scientific issues is not punishable. To say it differently, the belief that John is punishable, which used to be justified given the original belief set, is not justified anymore given the new belief set. I will call this kind of defeat, which results from changes in the beliefs that underlie another belief, *justification defeat*.

[8] See, for instance, Pollock 1995, 40. Bayón 2001 argues that this kind of defeasibility is the only kind that is relevant for the law.

[9] Brozek 2004, 33, for instance, shifts easily from the operation of one's cognitive system under defeasible rules (epistemic defeasibility) to the defeasible justification of beliefs (justification defeat).

Normally if one's beliefs are not justified anymore, one abandons them, which means that epistemic defeat is a natural consequence of justification defeat. But this does not always happen. An exception would for instance be that one does not realize the impact of the changes in one's belief set and consequently does not (yet) make the rationally required changes. Moreover, sometimes new beliefs are acquired, or old beliefs are lost, without justificatory reasons for it. Justification defeat and epistemic defeat apparently not always go hand in hand and – next to their conceptual difference – this is a reason to distinguish them well.

2.4 Justification defeat and defeasible reasoning

There is a close connection between justification defeat and the defeasibility of reasoning. Many arguments are used to justify their conclusions. This means that the person who adduces such an argument, if sincere, intends to show by means of the argument that its conclusion is justified. If, on the arrival of new information, the conclusion turns out not to be justified anymore, the original argument by means of which the conclusion was justified, loses its force. *In this sense*, it may be said that the argument turned out to be defeasible too. Notice that on this interpretation, the defeasibility of the argument is the result of the defeasibility of the justification that was given by means of the argument and not the other way round. Defeasibility is not primarily a characteristic of arguments, but of justification.

2.5 Absolute and relative justification

From the kinds of defeat that I distinguish, justification defeat has the strongest relation to the non-monotonicity of some systems of logic. This is particularly clear when justification defeat occurs because of additions to one's belief set.[10] If the belief that John is punishable is not justified anymore because of the additional beliefs that that Johns owns pornography purely for scientific issues and that owning pornography for scientific issues is not punishable, this is quite similar to the phenomenon that a valid argument from a set of premises becomes invalid if more premises are added. The justificatory relation between a belief set and a particular belief corresponds to the derivability relation between a set of premises and a possible conclusion from these premises.

[10] That justification defeat also occurs when beliefs are taken out of one's belief set was pointed out to me by Carolus Grütters.

In this connection it is important to distinguish between two senses in which a belief may be said to be justified, name absolute and relative justification. Absolute justification is a status of beliefs that is like truth, in the sense that it can be passed from the premises to the conclusion of a good argument. I am not aware of attempts to give an account of what absolute justification amounts to, but the following may serve to provide such an account.

A belief is absolutely justified if either

- it is justified by itself,

or

- it is justified relative to a set of beliefs that are themselves absolutely justified.

This is a recursive definition, because it refers again to absolute justification. This recursion must 'bottom out' somewhere, if the definition is not to be circular. Moreover, the only place where it can bottom out is on beliefs that are justified by themselves. I have strong doubts, however, whether the idea of a belief that is justified by itself, makes sense. A belief can be true, or false, depending on whether the facts are as the belief holds they are. I cannot see, however, what it would mean that a belief is justified, unless in the sense of being justified relative to other beliefs that justify it, that is in the sense of relative justification. To state it bluntly, in my opinion the idea that a belief is justified in itself does not make sense and since the notion of absolute justification depends for its sense on that of being of being justified in itself, the idea of absolute justification is in my opinion without sense itself.

The more interesting notion is that of relative justification.

A belief is justified relative to a set of beliefs, if and only if it is rational to accept this belief if one accepts (all beliefs in) the belief set.[11]

Where absolute justification, would the notion have made sense, would be like truth, relative justification is more like validity. A relatively justified belief 'follows' from the belief set, but whether the beliefs in the belief set are themselves correct, remains open.

[11] In this chapter I treat justification as a relation between beliefs. This is a bit narrow and in chapter 2, I treat justification as a relation between 'acceptances', where acceptances include beliefs amongst other 'things', such as rules, principles and values.

Justification defeat concerns the question whether a belief is justified relative to one's belief set, *where the contents of the belief set are not specified.* It occurs because of changes in the belief set, which make that a belief that was justified relative to the old belief set is not justified anymore relative to the new belief set. It cannot occur with respect to a specified set of beliefs, because a belief is either justified relative to a particular set, or not, but it is not possible that is first justified relative to some belief set and later not justified anymore relative to this same set.[12]

For instance, if P's belief set contains the beliefs that thieves are punishable and that John is a thief and nothing else that is relevant, P is justified to believe that John is punishable. That is so, because the belief that John is punishable is justified relative to the beliefs that John is a thief and that thieves are punishable (and P's other, irrelevant, beliefs). If, at a later stage, P comes to believe that John acted under force majeure and that those who acted under force majeure are not punishable, P's belief that John is punishable has lost its justification. The belief that John is punishable is not justified relative to the beliefs that John is a thief, that thieves are punishable, that John stole under force majeure and that acts performed under force majeure are not punishable. Clearly, the newly acquired beliefs have no impact on P's being justified in his beliefs before the acquisition of these new beliefs. They have influence on P's being justified in the light of all his beliefs, because the set of all P's beliefs has changed and the justification of the belief that John is punishable has changed with it. Justification defeasibility has to do with this phenomenon, that a change and - most interesting - an increase in one's total set of beliefs, may bring about that the justification of a particular belief (in the light of everything else that one believes) disappears.

Defeasible reasoning is sometimes described as reasoning with *incomplete knowledge*. However, a direct consequence of the analysis presented above is that justification defeat is not a consequence of incomplete knowledge. With regard to the issue whether a belief is justified relative to some particular belief set, the information cannot be incomplete. All the relevant information is by definition included in the belief set. This information is sufficient to decide whether a belief is justified *relative to this belief set*, although it may be insufficient to decide whether the belief is true.

[12] This is liable to exception for the case that one modifies the logic by means of which justified beliefs are derived from what else one believes. The exception can be avoided if the notion of a belief set is replaced by the broader notion of an acceptance set. An acceptance set includes everything that one accepts, including beliefs, rules, principles and – in this connection particularly relevant - standards for reasonable inference. More about acceptance sets in chapter 2.

Because justification defeasibility deals with relative justification and not with truth, incomplete information does not play a role in connection with justification defeat.

2.6 Logical defeasibility

Sometimes the notion of defeasibility is also used in connection with conditionals (logical operators) and with rules. A conditional $p \rightarrow q$ can be said to be defeasible if one or more of the following are the case:

1. if $p \rightarrow q$ is true, then it is not necessarily the case that $p \ \& \ r \rightarrow q$ is true (no 'strengthening of the antecedent'[13]);
2. if both $p \rightarrow q$ and p are true, then it is not necessarily the case that q is true;
3. if both $p \rightarrow q$ and p are true, then it is not necessarily the case that q can be derived validly (where validity is taken in a broader sense than deductive validity, because otherwise this third possibility would coincide with the second).

A rule 'if conditions then conclusion' can be said to be defeasible if it is not necessarily the case that if its conditions are satisfied, the conclusion holds.[14]

Both the defeasibility of conditionals and of rules is defined in connection with logical systems in which defeasible conditionals and rules operate. The defeasibility that is at stake is not primarily a phenomenon outside logic that can be modeled by means of some logical theory, but rather an aspect of some logical theories. For this reason I will disregard these kinds of 'logical defeasibility' as phenomena that are less interesting for understanding the defeasibility of the law or legal reasoning.

More generally, it seems to me that in the discussions about defeasibility in connection with the law, the intended kind of defeasibility – if there is a clear intention at all - is mostly justification defeasibility.[15] For this reason I

[13] Cf. Alchourrón 1993.

[14] Prakken and Sartor 1996.

[15] Prakken and Sartor (2004) distinguish three aspects of defeasibility in the law, namely inference-based defeasibility, process-based defeasibility and theory-based defeasibility. In section 3.1 I will say more about process-defeasibility.

If my view that justification defeasibility is the relevant notion in the law is correct, the distinction between inference-based defeasibility and theory-based defeasibility collapses, because in both cases the issue at stake is whether it is justified to hold one (inference-based defeasibility) or more (theory-based defeasibility) beliefs in the light of what else one believes.

will confine my discussion of law and defeasibility in the rest of this chapter to justification defeasibility.

3. IS LEGAL REASONING DEFEASIBLE?

The next question to deal with is whether justification defeat plays a role in legal reasoning. This question should be answered affirmatively if there is *some* role for justification defeat in legal reasoning. It is not necessary that all legal reasoning is justification defeasible. In the following subsections, I will discuss three reasons why legal reasoning might be defeasible.

3.1 Justification defeat and the burden of proof

At least some legal conclusions can turn out to be unjustified in the light of new information that was not taken into account in drawing them. Let me give two examples. The first example concerns the division of the burden of proof. Suppose that Violet speeded and is prosecuted. If the prosecutor succeeds to prove the speeding and nothing else happens, the judge is justified in her conclusion that Violet is punishable. However, if Violet defends herself by pointing out that her child was seriously ill and that she speeded under force majeure to bring her child in time to the hospital, acceptance of this defense by the judge would take the justification of this conclusion away. In other words, the information that Violet acted under force majeure functions as a justification defeater for the conclusion that Violet is punishable for speeding. The division in the burden of proof between Violet and the public prosecutor is explained by the fact that the defense of Violet functions as a defeater of the justification of punishability provided by the prosecutor. If the absence of force majeure would have been a normal condition of punishability, the public prosecutor would have born the burden of proof that there was no force majeure.

It is also possible to give a different interpretation to the example. Bayón has pointed out that the division of the burden of proof can also be explained by means of procedural rules that allow a judge to convict a defendant if a

---

Brozek 2004 takes deontic defeasibility as the central notion (p. 205). His examples of deontic defeasibility (p. 27) include some that have nothing specifically deontic about them. I suspect that Brozek uses the expression 'deontic defeasibility' for all defeasibility in which legal rules play a role. In my terminology this would be logical defeasibility.

transgression was proved, while force majeure was not proved.[16] Under this interpretation, which focuses on procedural aspects rather than on the question whether the conclusion that the suspect is punishable is justified, no defeat seems to be at stake.

Arguably, however, justification defeat plays a role under this interpretation of the burden of proof too, although only as explanation of the procedural rules. There are procedural rules which indicate under which circumstances a judge can - or even ought to - convict a suspect. In my opinion, these rules reflect the circumstances under which a judge is justified in believing that the suspect is punishable.[17] By default a judge is not justified in assuming that somebody is punishable (presumption of innocence). Therefore it must be proved that the suspect committed a fact that is punishable. When this has been proved, the judge is pro tanto justified to believe that the suspect is punishable. However, if it has also been proved that there was a ground of justification the belief that the suspect is punishable is not justified anymore.[18] For this reason the procedural rules only allow the judge to convict a suspect if it was proved that he committed a crime and if it was not proved that there was a ground of justification. The references in the procedural rules to proof, rather than to fact, are signs that some form of defeasible reasoning plays a role, although the use of the procedural rules itself may be non-defeasible.[19]

[16] Bayón 2001. Another alternative analysis is given in Brozek 2004, 29. Brozek points out that it is possible that the shift in the burden of proof is meant to allow an opponent of an argument to attack one of the argument's premises.

[17] It seems to me that where Prakken and Sartor (2004) distinguish process-based defeasibility as one of three aspects of defeasibility in the law, they have this characteristic of legal procedures in mind.

[18] Obviously this does not mean automatically that a conviction of a suspect becomes unjustified when, after the conviction, new facts appear that make it clear that there was a ground of justification. It is a matter of the law and not of logic or general theory of justification, how such situations should be dealt with. Obvious as this may be, it has no implications for what I wrote about the role of justification defeat in explaining procedural rules.

[19] In general defeasibility plays a role when conclusions are not based on which facts obtain, but on which facts have been proved. Facts about the past do not change, but beliefs about the past, including what has been proved about the past, tend to evolve in the course of time. As a consequence, beliefs that are based on what was proved are liable to lose their justification if relevant facts that did not count as proved before, come to count as been proved.

3.2 Justification defeat and the context of discovery

Even if the distribution of the burden of proof is disregarded, there is evidence that justification defeat plays a role within legal reasoning. It is not uncustomary to distinguish two 'phases' in legal reasoning that leads to a solution for a particular concrete case.[20] In the second phase, sometimes called the context of justification[21], first order justification[22], or internal justification[23], the legal consequence of a particular case is presented as the outcome of a deductively valid argument. The major premise of this argument is a (universally quantified) material conditional with a generic case description as its antecedent and the corresponding legal consequence as its consequent. The minor premise is the description of (the relevant facts of) the case at hand. The first phase, labeled as the context of discovery[24], second order justification, or external justification, consists of a series of (one or more) arguments in which the truth (or validity) of the major premise of the first argument is established.

The idea behind this distinction between two phases is that legal judgments must be universalizable. If some case has a particular legal consequence, all cases that are similar in all relevant aspects should have similar legal consequences. The major premise in the context of justification specifies both which aspects of the case are relevant for the legal consequence that is attached to it and what this legal consequence is. In the rest of this chapter, I will refer to such a premise as a *case-legal consequence pair* (CLCP). The CLCP is a specification of what the law is for cases like the one at stake. The first phase of the argument is to determine the contents of this CLCP.

If legal reasoning is conceptually divided into two phases along the lines sketched above, the context of justification in which the CLCP is applied to the case at hand can be represented as a form of deductive reasoning and justification defeat plays no role in it. If the conclusion of this second phase

[20] The quotes around 'phases' are to recognise that the two phases are not always separated in time, but are rather two logically distinguishable aspects of legal reasoning. See in this connection also Wolenski 1979.

[21] Bayón 2001 and Soeteman 2003, implicitly.

[22] MacCormick 1978, 101f.

[23] Alexy 1978, 273.

[24] The context of discovery can be taken in at least two ways. One way is to see it merely as a psychological process, the contents of which are not interesting, which leads to a hypothesis that can possibly be justified in the legitimation phase. The other way is to see it as a phase of non-deductive reasoning. Only on this interpretation of the context of discovery can it be equated with external, or secondary justification and can it be seen as a kind of justification at all. Presently, I take the context of discovery in this second sense.

would be incorrect, the same counts for the CLCP. Justification defeat, if it plays a role in the law, should be looked for in the first phase, that of discovery.[25]

It seems obvious to me that justification defeat plays a role in the context of discovery. Let me first return to the example of Violet who was found guilty of speeding, but who was nevertheless not punishable because a ground of justification was present. The conclusion that Violet is not punishable for speeding can be legitimated by the following deductive argument:

CLCP:	Precisely those who have speeded and did not have a ground of justification for speeding are punishable for speeding.
Case facts:	Violet speeded, but had a ground of justification for doing so.
Therefore:	Violet is not punishable for speeding.

The context of discovery in this connection consists of one or more arguments that end up in the CLCP of the deductive argument above. The first step in this context might be that there exists a rule that makes speeding punishable and that therefore those who have speeded are punishable for speeding. Pro tanto, the belief that those who have speeded are punishable for speeding is justified. However, if grounds of justification and their effects are taken into account, this belief loses its justification. Instead one is pro tanto, namely in the light of both the rule that makes speeding punishable and the rule(s) about grounds of justification, justified in the belief that precisely those who have speeded and did not have a ground of justification for speeding are punishable for speeding. Apparently, justification defeat plays a role when two or more rules are combined into a CLCP.

Let me now mention the second example of justification defeat, which not only illustrates how justification defeat plays a role in the context of discovery when several legal rules are combined into a single CLCP, but also how facts about the non-legal world play a role in this connection. Suppose that in a particular country, say Taxopia, taxes on vehicles are raised. Vehicles are categorized according to their weights, with a certain amount of taxes specified for each category. For this purpose, three pieces of legislation are drafted. The first piece introduces the taxes on vehicles. It also empowers the government to develop a system of categories by means of which vehicles can be categorized. The second piece of legislation, made by the government, introduces this system. Moreover, the Minister of

[25] This view is shared by Bayón 2001, Soeteman 2003 and Brozek 2004, 134.

Finance is empowered to make decrees by means of which certain amounts of tax are attached to the categories in which vehicles are subdivided. The Minister exercises this power in the third piece of legislation. Since in Taxopia, even more than in many other countries, taxes are a means of making policy, it is decided by means of a fourth piece of legislation that the vehicle taxes for cars are increased with 20%. So Taxopia ends up with four pieces of legislation, three of which regulate the taxes of vehicles in general and the fourth of which deals especially with taxes on cars and refers for the amount of the additional tax to the general regulation about vehicles, to which it makes an exception by increasing the tax.

The description of the tax law of Taxopia as presented above followed the (main) lines of the legislation, that is, of the legal sources. It is also possible to represent the same law in the form of CLCPs by identifying a number of case types and to specify for every type its fiscal consequences. These case types should ideally be mutually exclusive and together exhaust all legal possibilities.[26] Suppose, for instance, that the legislation distinguishes five categories. The first one is essentially occupied by bicycles and other non-motorized vehicles. The second one is occupied by small motorized vehicles, such as most motorcycles and mopeds. The remaining three categories are essentially occupied by various sizes of cars, but also contain some heavy weight motorcycles, tractors etc. Since not all vehicles in the last three categories are cars, the vehicles in the three categories must for tax reasons be divided into vehicles in the categories 3-5 that are cars and vehicles in the categories 3-5 that are not cars. So we end up with eight sets of vehicles, each with its own amount of vehicle tax. The sets are taken such that all members of each set have the same fiscal consequences, while it is not possible to join two or more sets without members of the same set having different fiscal consequences.

In this connection it is important to notice that the amount of sets does not only depend on the legislation, but also on other facts in the world. It is, for instance, important to know whether there are any other vehicles than cars in the categories 3-5, or whether there are cars in the categories 1 and 2. Moreover, the number of distinguishable sets may change without changes in the legislation, for instance because heavier motor cycles are built, thereby introducing non-cars in category 5.

Let us call the first way to describe (part of) a legal system description by sources and the second way description by CLCPs. If we only have a description by sources, legal reasoning, which is then *reasoning by sources*,

[26] This approach is inspired by the treatment of generic cases in Alchourrón and Bulygin 1971, chapter II, which may be consulted for a more precise presentation.

involves a process of theory construction in which all the rules that have impact on the case at hand must be considered, interpreted and if necessary combined. This process, which may be identified with the context of discovery, involves defeasible reasoning, because taking a new rule into consideration may bring about that a CLCP which was justified in the light of the sources that were originally taken into consideration is not justified anymore. The same counts if new beliefs about the world (about which vehicles there are and which of them are cars) are taken into consideration. For instance, if the special rule about cars is taken into consideration, the general CLCP about vehicle taxes loses its justification.

If we have a set of CLCPs, we can justify legal decisions in concrete cases by pointing to their generic cases and the legal consequences attached to them. Ideally (when the CLCPs are exhaustive and mutually exclusive) it is not possible that a concrete case falls under more than one relevant[27] CLCP, so it is not necessary to look any further as soon as the relevant CLCP has been found. Reasoning *with* CLCPs, which might be identified with the context of justification, is non-defeasible. Reasoning *about* the CLCPs however, the context of discovery is justification defeasible.

It is noteworthy that it is also possible to justify the legal solution for a particular case directly by means of defeasible reasoning by sources. It is not necessary to formulate a general CLCP first and then subsume the case under it. It may be necessary that for every case with its legal solution a CLCP should exist, but from this necessity it does not follow that this CLCP must play a role in the justification of the solution for this case. The arguments in the context of discovery that lead to the justification of a CLCP can be reformulated (by instantiating them) to the effect that they lead immediately to the solution for the case at hand. If this approach is taken, the argument that leads to the solution for the concrete case is completely subject to justification defeat.

It seems clear that defeasible reasoning plays a role in the law, but this does not imply that all legal reasoning is defeasible. We have seen that it is possible to split legal justification into two phases, the first of which, the phase of discovery, contains defeasible reasoning, while the second phase, that of justification, consists of deductive and therefore non-defeasible reasoning. I have briefly argued, however, that this division can be circumvented by letting the phase of discovery deal directly with the legal consequences of the concrete case at hand. If this approach is taken, the only kind of reasoning that is necessary is defeasible. Therefore my conclusion

[27] Relevant in the sense that the legal consequence of the CLCP in question deals with the issue at stake.

would be that in the law we can both encounter defeasible and non-defeasible reasoning, but that it is not well possible to replace the defeasible part by non-defeasible reasoning, while it is, at least in a number of cases, possible to skip the non-defeasible part.

3.3 The defeasibility of legal rules

A third reason why legal reasoning might be defeasible is based on the assumption that legal rules are defeasible in the sense that it is possible to find implied exceptions that can often not be specified in advance. This assumption is broadly shared.[28] Bayón nevertheless has a problem with it, because in his opinion it is not a necessary characteristic of legal rules that they are thus defeasible. A legal system might make it impossible to allow exceptions to rules, even if they are over-inclusive, or if some relevant principle was not taken into consideration in drafting the rule. I will discuss Bayón's problem with the view that legal rules are defeasible by means of an example.

Probably like other legal systems, the Dutch law has a regulation for the transfer of movable property by a non-owner to a third party who acted in good faith. The legal problem that this regulation must deal with results from a conflict between at least two interests. One interest is that of the owner of the property that was transferred, who wants to remain owner. The other interest is that of the party who acted in good faith and expected to become owner of the transferred property. The Dutch regulation (sections 3:84-86 of the Civil Code) balances these two interests, with the effect that under some circumstances the third party becomes owner of the property, while under other circumstances the original owner remains owner, anyway for a period of three years. The interests of smooth commerce also played a role in the way the topic was regulated.

Let us assume that the regulation of the Civil Code strikes for normal cases a right balance between the conflicting interests. Suppose, however, that the regulation does not work well for some exceptional cases and that if the balance would have to be struck anew for those cases, another outcome would have resulted. One argument for the defeasibility of legal reasoning would be that the regulation provides a good outcome under normal circumstances, but that it should not be applied under particular exceptional circumstances. For instance, for some cases the regulation may protect the

[28] Bayón 2001 gives a number of references in footnote 21. These include Alexy 1996, 88/9, Sartor 1995, 120f. and Prakken 1997, 47/8. He might also have included Hage 1997 (RwR), 106f.

third party in good faith and for these cases the argument that leads to the conclusion that this third party has become the new owner, is prima facie correct. However, given new information to the effect that exceptional circumstances are present, this conclusion is not desirable anymore.

There are two extreme ways to deal with exceptional cases in which rules give 'wrong' solutions for cases. One extreme way is to ignore the rule and fall back on the principles underlying the rule and all other principles that might turn out to be relevant and compute the best outcome on the basis of all relevant principles. On this approach, the presence of the rule does not make any difference, because the rule is only applied if its outcome agrees with the outcome of the underlying principles. The rule is then superfluous next to the principles; it is merely a 'rule of thumb'.[29] The other extreme way is to apply the rule, without any regard to whether its outcome is correct in the light of the relevant principles. On this 'entrenched' model[30], the applicability of a rule makes principles that deal with the case at hand superfluous.

By describing the two mentioned ways as extremes, I suggested that a middle road is possible. This middle road is to take applicable rules as the starting point in legal decision making, but to leave the possibility open to deviate from the rule's outcome if this is desirable in the light of the relevant principles. Whether this possibility to deviate should be used, does not only depend on the balance of the relevant principles, but also on the facts that deviation from the rule diminishes legal certainty and that it negatively affects the legislator's authority. Both facts are reasons not to deviate from the rule. The amount of weight that is attached to the applicability of a rule as an *independent* reason for the rule's conclusion determines whether this middle road runs closer to the first, or to the second extreme.[31]

Bayón is right when he supposes that it is a matter of the law whether exceptions to rules are possible. It is imaginable that there are legal systems which do not allow exceptions to any rule. However, I do not know any such a system and I wonder whether Bayón knows any. He does not give an example and I think that there is no such an example. There are very good reasons why a legal system should sometimes allow exceptions to rules and the account given by Schauer of the over-inclusiveness of rules provides a good enough insight in why that is so.[32] Probably the possibility mentioned

[29] Schauer 1991, 77, but see also 104f.

[30] Schauer 1991, 52. See also Raz 1975, 73, who writes that mandatory norms are exclusionary reasons.

[31] This way to deal with rules is at least similar to what Schauer calls *rule-sensitive particularism*. See Schauer 1991, 97 and the literature mentioned there.

[32] Schauer 1991, 31f.

by Bayón of a legal system that does not allow exceptions to rules is a mere theoretical possibility.

Is such a mere theoretical possibility not enough to conclude that it is not a logical matter whether rules are amenable to exceptions? Logic deals with what is logically necessary and the theoretical possibility of a legal system that does not allow exceptions to rules suffices to show that the possibility of exceptions is not logically necessary. At least, that is what might be argued.

Before answering this question, I want to point out that if rules are defeasible, this does not mean that every rule must have an actual exception in one or more cases. It does not even mean that most rules have actual exceptions in one or more cases. It merely means that for every rule it is in theory possible that there is, or will be, some case in which an exception to the rule should be made. Only if this theoretical possibility does not exist, rules are not defeasible. This holds not only for rules in general, but also for any particular rule. A particular rule is not defeasible if it is not even in theory possible that in some case an exception should be made to this rule. Defeasibility does not require the existence of such exceptions in actual cases and not even that one can imagine a case in which such an exception would exist. Lack of imagination does not show a rule to be non-defeasible. Non-defeasibility can only been shown if it follows from constraints imposed on the logical behavior of rules. Unless a legal system adopts the extreme entrenched model of rule application for some, or all of its rules, the constraints on the logical behavior of rules that might cause them to be indefeasible are lacking. I do not know a legal system that has adopted the extreme entrenched model for any of its rules.

If there is no actual legal system in which rules are non-defeasible and if it is implausible that such a system could actually exist, is it then logically necessary that rules are defeasible? Or must we make the stronger demand that it is not even imaginable that such a system exists? Asking the question shows the futility of attempts to answer it. When a necessity becomes a logical necessity is a matter of convention, or of pragmatism. Is it useful to treat some knowledge as unrevisable or should we treat as mere 'domain knowledge'?[33] In the case of legal rules, I think that it is useful to assume that the defeasibility of rules is a necessary characteristic, which deserves study separate from the study of positive law. This means that in my opinion, Bayón's objection does not cut ice and that the defeasibility of legal rules provides a third reason why legal reasoning is defeasible.

[33] I argued for this Quinean perspective on (legal) logic in (Hage 2001 LL).

4. DOES LEGAL REASONING REQUIRE NON-MONOTONIC LOGIC?

The next question to deal with is whether we need a non-monotonic logic to represent the phenomenon that a belief that is justified in the light of the set of beliefs B1, is not justified in the light of belief set B2, which has resulted from B1 by making one or more changes to it. Before continuing on this path, I want to discard some issues. First I want to ignore changes involving replacement of one belief by another belief. These changes can be decomposed into abandoning the old belief and adopting the new belief. As a consequence the only changes that remain to be discussed are the abandonment of old beliefs and adoption of new beliefs.

Second I want to deal briefly with the abandonment of old beliefs. We do not need a non-monotonic logic to deal with this phenomenon. Deductive logic is very well capable to represent that a belief that was justified on the basis of some set of premises is not justified if one or more of these premises are given up. A conclusion that follows deductively from a set of premises does not necessarily follow deductively from every subset of these premises. If 'being justified' is (wrongly) taken in the sense of 'deductively following from', a conclusion that is justified by a set of premises needs not be justified anymore if one or more of these premises are dropped.

Therefore the only case that needs special consideration is when a belief that was justified in the light of belief set B1 is not justified anymore in the light of belief set B2 which is a proper superset of B1. This case is quite similar to the characterization of the non-monotonicity of logical system L by saying that S is according to L derivable from B1, while it is not derivable from B2. Justification defeasibility deals with the relation 'is justified by', between a belief set and a belief, where non-monotonicity deals with the relation 'is derivable from', between a set of sentences and a sentence. At first sight, therefore, there is much to say for logically representing justification defeat by means of a non-monotonic logic. Nevertheless some authors have objected to this approach and it is worthwhile to look into their reasons for protesting.

4.1 Alchourrón's criticism of non-monotonic logic

Non-monotonic logics were developed to deal with the defeasibility of arguments, both inside and outside the law. However, it may be argued that such logics are not useful, or even based on confusion. The idea that the use of non-monotonic logics is based on confusion, namely the confusion between logic and belief revision, was advanced by Alchourrón. I will present his argument by means of a legal example.[34]

Alchourrón approaches the idea of defeasibility from the phenomenon of defeasible conditionals. His basic idea is that a defeasible conditional is a conditional that holds under 'normal' circumstances. The defeasibility of the conditional that if somebody is a thief, he is punishable, would boil down to it that thieves are punishable under normal circumstances. Suppose that the conditional that thieves are punishable does not hold for thieves under twelve years old. One way to deal with this is to use a non-monotonic logic, under which the argument from 'John is a thief' to 'John is punishable' is not valid if John is under twelve. Another way to deal with the same phenomenon is to refine the false belief that thieves are punishable into the belief that thieves of twelve years and older are punishable. From the point of view of what is derivable, this belief revision boils down to the same thing as using a defeasible conditional. And the question then arises what the gain of the defeasible conditional is. In this connection Alchourrón writes[35]:

> *... when someone has to accomplish the task of representing incomplete knowledge ... he will be confronted with the following dilemma. Either use conceptually strong sentences (general conditionals) with many interesting consequences and assume all the dangers involved and hence be ready to revise the premises as often as needed; or use the conceptually weaker defeasible conditionals which will be almost completely secure, at the price of losing most (if not all) of the interesting conclusions. We have to choose between the quiet darkness of Paradise or the risky lights of daily life.*

It seems to me that two points should be noted in connection with Alchourrón's criticism. The first point is that it is indeed possible to deal with defeasibility logically by means of deductive logic in combination with belief revision.[36] Non-monotonic logics are not necessary to handle defeasibility.

This brings me to the second point, namely that it is matter of pragmatics whether one should prefer a non-monotonic logic to a deductive logic in combination with belief revision. Possibly there is no preference that holds universally. Given the quoted passage, Alchourrón had (at least amongst

[34] The following is based on Alchourrón 1993, 69f.

[35] Alchourrón 1993, 83.

[36] If a conclusion C follows defeasibly from a set of premises P, it follows deductively from P plus two additional premises, namely the premises that there are no special circumstances and that if P and there are no special circumstances, C is true. Defeat can then be dealt with by removing the belief that there are no special circumstances.

others) scientific theory construction in mind, when he expressed his preference for belief revision above non-monotonic logic. If one takes the purpose of scientific theory construction as to give precise descriptions of law-like connections, Alchourrón's preference for belief revision is understandable, because the use of a non-monotonic logic only masks the incorrectness of the theory that can only be applied defeasibly. For instance, Newtonian mechanics is – in a sense - wrong, because it only gives the right outcomes when small velocities are involved. However, even when dealing with scientific theory construction, one might prefer relatively simple laws with a restricted scope of application[37] and consequently the use of a non-monotonic logic to model law application. This might be better than working with universally applicable laws that buy their broad scope of application at the cost of a highly complex content (e.g. the more complex content of relativistic mechanics). The question that needs to be addressed in this connection is whether the nature of legal justification would lead to a preference for belief revision, or for the use of a non-monotonic logic.

4.2 Soeteman on legal justification

Soeteman precisely gives the necessary type of argument for belief revision and against the use of a non-monotonic logic.[38] In his opinion real justification must always be based on a deductively valid argument. He writes:

> *... as long as an argument cannot be analyzed deductively, the conclusion is not warranted. As long as an argument is not reconstructed as deductively valid an alternative conclusion is still possible and the conclusion therefore is not completely justified.*

Moreover, Soeteman emphasizes that such a 'complete justification' is of the greatest importance in law, because of the weighty consequences of legal judgments. His point is that legal conclusions, because of their importance, must be completely justified and that a conclusion is only completely justified if an alternative conclusion is impossible.

There are several things that may be said about this argument. First, it may be highly desirable that legal conclusions are beyond any doubt, but conclusions beyond any doubt are seldom to be reached within human affairs. Therefore, the demand for such indubitable conclusions might be a demand for the impossible. Obviously, we should strive for the best, but I

[37] Compare in this connection what Toulmin writes about Snell's law. (Toulmin 1953, 57f.)
[38] Soeteman 2003.

will argue that the use of a non-monotonic logic does not interfere with this endeavor.

The second thing that can be said regards the premises of justifying arguments. Non-monotonic logic can, according to Soeteman, only justify a conclusion under the presupposition of a normality hypothesis. Without this hypothesis, the argument is unconvincing. Therefore such a normality hypothesis should be part of the premises. If the normality hypothesis is added to the premises, the argument becomes deductively valid and the conclusion has become unavoidable for those who accept the premises. For instance, the argument that John is a thief, that, barring exceptions, thieves should be punished and that therefore John should therefore be punished, is defeasible, but can be analyzed deductively by adding the premise that in John's case there is no exception to the rule that thieves should be punished.

There are three objections that can be raised against this approach. The first objection is that if one wants to use logic to model justification, logic has the task to answer the question whether acceptance of some belief is justified in the light of one's other beliefs. These other beliefs are in this connection fixed. If a normality hypothesis N is added, the question has changed. It is not anymore whether conclusion C is justified in the light of belief set B, but whether C is justified in the light of B + N.

Second, it is not a viable strategy to make additions to a set of premises, in order to make a conclusion that seems to be justified in the light of what is accepted, follow deductively. The conclusion would only be justified if the additional premise is true. However, the truth of this premise can often only be established if one knows whether the conclusion is true Whether the conclusion is true is usually precisely the issue at stake.

Take the argument that John is punishable because he is a thief and because, in general, thieves are punishable. It is given that John is a thief and that, in general, thieves are punishable and the function of the argument is to establish whether John is punishable. The question that logic must answer is whether it is rational to accept that John is punishable, given that he is a thief and that in general thieves are punishable. Because the justification of this conclusion on basis of these premises is defeasible, one might want to add the normality hypothesis to the premises, to make the argument deductively valid. However, the only way to make certain that the normality hypothesis is true is to establish that John is punishable indeed.[39] Since it is precisely the point of the argument to establish that John is punishable, it makes little

[39] This would only be different if there were an exhaustive list of all exceptional circumstances.

sense to include a normality hypothesis in the premises that presupposes the truth of the conclusion.

My general point here is that logic often plays a role in contexts in which the available premises do not allow the deduction of the conclusion. The demand that the premises are completed to make them entail the conclusion makes logic useless in these contexts, because the truth of the additional premises cannot be established independent of the truth of the conclusion. It will not do to state that the argument presupposes these premises nevertheless. What the argument presupposes is that the premises provide *sufficient support* for the conclusion to make it *rational to accept* the conclusion on the basis of the premises. This presupposition concerns the rationality of belief change, not the truth of one or more premises.

The third argument against Soeteman's approach, according to which a defeasible argument is replaced by a deductively valid argument with an additional (normality) hypothesis, is that it moves the cause of uncertainty from the validity of the argument to the truth of the additional premise. The deductive justification of the judge's conclusion has been achieved, but the certainty of the conclusion has not become any stronger, because the possible reasons why John should after all not be punished remain the same in both cases. If there is a ground of justification, this is handled under deductive logic by the falsity of the premise that there is no exception to the rule that thieves are punishable. Under a non-monotonic logic it is handled by making an exception to the rule that thieves are liable to be punished. It seems, therefore, that the difference between deductive logic with an uncertain premise and non-monotonic logic with certain premises does not make a difference. The use of non-monotonic logic does not increase uncertainty in comparison to deductive logic in combination with dubitable premises.

One might argue, however, that there is a difference, because the judge that uses deductive logic must establish that there is no exception to the rule before he can punish John. If he would use a non-monotonic logic, he would, on the contrary, be free to disregard the presence of a possible exception as long as this presence has not been argued.

Such an argument would assign logic a too important role, however. Logic as such cannot determine the investigatory tasks of a judge. Under a non-monotonic logic just as well as under a monotonic logic, the judge may have the task to gather all information that might be relevant for his judgment. If this information includes that there is an exception to the rule that thieves should be punished, the verdict under the use of a non-monotonic logic will be the same as under the monotonic logic, namely that John should not be punished.

More generally, the logical formalism that one chooses for the analysis of legal justification needs not have any influence on the outcome of legal judgments. Everything that can legally be accomplished with the use of deductive logic together with belief revision can also be accomplished with the use of a non-monotonic logic and vice versa. Therefore, the undeniable importance of legal justification need not have any impact on the choice of the logic by means of which legal decision making is analyzed. Which logic one uses is a matter of pragmatics and - as I have argued in the first part of this section – non-monotonic logic is prima facie the obvious candidate to deal with justification defeat.

4.3 The nature of logic

Although non-monotonic logic is prima facie the obvious candidate for the logical analysis of justification defeat, there is still a lot of resistance against this kind of logic. One possible explanation of this phenomenon is that non-monotonic is not considered as a 'real' logic at all. The criticism of Alchourrón discussed in section 4.1 seems to illustrate this. To deal with such criticisms, I will pay some attention to the nature of logic.

The function of logic lies in the evaluation of arguments. In an argument, one or more reasons are adduced to support the acceptance of a conclusion. Two questions arise in this connection: are the statements that mention the reasons true and - assuming that these statements are true - is it rational to accept the conclusion? The function of logic is traditionally taken to provide standards with the help of which the second of these questions can be answered.

Formulated thus, the function of logic is quite broad. Logic would, for instance have the task to answer the question whether it is rational to accept the conclusion that John is punishable, on the assumption that John is a thief. More precisely, the question of rationality can be formulated as whether it is more rational to accept the conclusion as true, to reject it as false, or to postpone judgment, under the assumption that the premise is accepted as true.

In comparison to this broad function, modern logic has been restricted in at least two ways. Firstly, the scope of logic has been minimized by removing everything that might be seen as domain knowledge out of the realm of logic by treating it as 'content', while logic is taken to deal with the 'form' of arguments only. Secondly, the standard for acceptance of an argument's conclusion has become that the conclusion must be true, given the truth of the premises, thereby declaring arguments that provide their conclusion with less support as invalid. To state it more briefly, logic has been restricted to deductive logic.

There is, however, no necessary connection between rational acceptance and deduction. In fact, the very existence of justification defeat presupposes that there may be circumstances that a belief is justified relative to a belief set, even though it does not follow deductively from this set. Restricting logic to deductive logic has the disadvantage that it excludes induction, abduction and many forms of practical reasoning[40] from logical evaluation, or condemns them to invalidity, namely if measured by deductive standards. This disadvantage is avoided if logic is taken as *the study of standards for rational acceptance*. On this view, logic deals with arguments in the sense of sentences adduced to support the acceptance of some other sentence.

Deductive logic as the study of necessary relations between the truth values of sentences has *as such* nothing to do with what we should rationally believe. It only provides data (q must be true if both p→q and p are true) that may be considered relevant for a theory of rational belief (revision). The following quotation from a paper by Israel illustrates the point[41]:

> *The rule of modus ponens is, first and foremost a rule that permits certain kinds of syntactical transformations on (sets of) formally characterized syntactic entities. (Actually, first and foremost, it is not really a rule at all; it is "really" just a two-place relation between on the one hand an ordered pair of well-formed formulas and on the other hand, a well-formed formula.) .... adherence to a set of deductive rules of transformation is not a sufficient condition for rational belief; .... Real rules of inference are rules (better: policies) guiding belief fixation and revision.*

If one adheres to this view of logic, the use of non-monotonic logic rests on confusion with regard to the nature of logic. This confusion is that one tries to make logic do what it was not meant to do, namely make it provide standards for the evaluation of holding beliefs on the basis of other beliefs. However, if one adopts the broader view of logic as standards for rational acceptance, it is precisely the purpose of logic to provide such 'policies for belief fixation and revision'. More or less the same point can be made by pointing out that on the deductive view logic deals with truth and with relations between truth values of sentences. On the broader view, logic deals with justification.

On the deductive view, logic is essentially monotonic. If a conclusion must be true given a set of premises, this same conclusion must still be true

[40] I take practical reasoning here both in the sense of real life reasoning (as opposed to, for instance, philosophical and mathematical reasoning) and in the sense of normative reasoning.

[41] Israel 1980. I replaced the abbreviation 'wff' with 'well-formed formula'.

given even more premises. The monotonicity of deductive logic follows immediately from the deductive nature of the logic. Moreover, the notion of truth with which deductive logic deals, is, metaphorically speaking, itself monotonic. If a sentence is, given a number of facts, true, it cannot become false in the light of even more facts.[42]

If logic deals with justification, things become completely different. Justification is by definition relative, namely relative to the premises on which the justification is based. A judgment that is justified by a set of premises is *justified relative to these premises*.[43] If the set of premises is changed, the justification relative to the old set of premises does not amount to justification relative to the new set of premises, not even if the new set is an extension of the old set. Just as truth is, metaphorically speaking, monotonic, justification is, metaphorically speaking, non-monotonic. Logic according to the broad view deals with justification and is therefore essentially non-monotonic.

The only reason I can think of to prefer deductive logic is that one believes, as Israel does, that only deductive logic is 'real' logic and that, for instance, justification has nothing to do with logic as such, but at most with one use logic is put to. It does not make much sense to have a discussion about the proper meaning of the word 'logic', so I will not argue that Israel's view is wrong. Instead I would like to say that a tool to evaluate whether a conclusion should rationally be accepted in the light of what else one believes, whether it is called 'logic' or something else, should not have the property of monotonicity.

5. CONCLUSION

In this chapter I have tried to answer three questions, namely what defeasibility is, whether it occurs within the law and whether we need a non-

[42] This may be different in contexts where truth is identical to being justified and the law might be such a context. In Hage 2004 (see also chapter 2 of this work) I adopt the theory that the law is what the best (justified) theory about the law says it is. If this view is correct, the 'monotonicity of truth' does not hold.

[43] This should not be confused with the false view that the conclusion of a justificatory argument runs that this conclusion is justified relative to the premises. That the justification of a conclusion is always relative, does not mean that justified conclusions are themselves relativised. The relativity is presupposed, rather than stated.

A similar point might be made with regard to value judgements (and all judgments based on the application of some standard). Every value judgment is relative to a standard, but the judgment itself is in general not relativised to this standard.

monotonic logic to deal with defeasible legal reasoning. My conclusions were that it is possible to distinguish several kinds of defeasibility, but that the most interesting kind for our purposes is justification defeat. Justification defeat is the phenomenon that a conclusion that is justified in the light of one belief set is not justified in the light of another belief set (which is a superset of the former).

Justification defeat plays a role in the law, both in the division of the burden of proof and in the context of discovery in which CLCPs are formulated that can be used in deductive justification of legal conclusions.

Non-monotonic logics almost mimic justification defeat (if 'is justified by' is replaced by 'is derivable from') and they are therefore very useful for the logical analysis of justification defeat. It is, however, always possible to replace these logics by a combination of deductive logic and belief revision. Under some circumstances this might be useful, but despite Soeteman's argument to the contrary, legal justification seems not to fall under these circumstances.

Chapter 2

LAW AND COHERENCE

1. INTRODUCTION

In the last few decennia, coherence theories have gained substantial popularity in the law.[1] These theories hold that the law is a coherent whole, or that legal judgments are justified if they fit in a coherent theory of the law.

The subject of coherence in the law has been approached in different ways. On the one hand there are coherence theories for the law that find their inspiration not only in jurisprudence, but also and perhaps mainly in epistemology. The work of Peczenik might be treated as representative for this approach.[2] In his *On Law and Reason*, Peczenik writes that

- legal reasoning is supported by reasonable premises

and that

- a premise is reasonable if and only if:
  - it is not falsified, and
  - the hypothesis is not to a sufficiently high degree corroborated that this premise does not logically follow from a highly coherent set of premises.[3]

1 See for instance MacCormick 1978, Dworkin 1986 and Peczenik 1989. A general overview can be found in Kress 1996.

2 Peczenik 1989, Alexy and Peczenik 1990, Peczenik 1997 and Peczenik and Hage 2000.

3 Peczenik 1989, 158.

In this way, Peczenik connects legal justification to coherentism. The next question is when a set of premises, a theory, is coherent. The first step of the answer is that 'the more the statements belonging to a given theory approximate a perfect supportive structure, the more coherent the theory'. Several theories about this supportive structure are possible in the eyes of Peczenik, but he goes on to describe one of them in terms of ten factors including the number of supportive relations between elements of the theory, the length of the supportive chains, whether there exists a connection between the supportive chains and whether the elements of the theory reciprocally justify each other. Some of these factors contain subfactors and many of them merely have a prima facie status.[4]

Concerning the relevance of coherence for the law, Peczenik first refers to MacCormick according to whom justice would require that legal justification is embedded in a fairly coherent system. This is a normative/evaluative argument why the premises of legal justification should belong to a coherent theory. However, Peczenik also takes a second road. He writes that 'If the norm- or value-system in question is more coherent, then there exists a prima facie reason that it is correct'.[5] On this approach, coherence is evidence for correctness and this fits well in an epistemic view of coherence.

On the other hand, there are coherence theories that look for their inspiration mainly to jurisprudence. Dworkin's theory of law as integrity is a good example of this approach. According to Dworkin:

> *The adjudicative principle of integrity instructs judges to identify legal rights and duties, so far as possible, on the assumption that they were all created by a single author – the community personified – expressing a coherent conception of justice and fairness ... According to law as integrity, propositions of law are true if they figure in or follow from the principles of justice, fairness, and procedural due process that provide the best constructive interpretation of the community's legal practice.*[6]

When he argues for adoption of law as integrity, Dworkin does not refer to epistemological theories, or to factors that might play a role in epistemology too, but to typical normative considerations by arguing that 'a community of principle, which takes integrity to be central to politics, provides a better defense of political legitimacy than the other models [of community].' In arguing for law as integrity, Dworkin deals with legal philosophical issues

[4] Peczenik 1989, 160f. and Alexy and Peczenik 1990.

[5] Peczenik 1989, 177f.

[6] Dworkin 1986, 225.

such as the duty to obey the law and the right of the government to use collective force. It seems, at least at first sight, that when Dworkin discusses law as integrity, he is dealing with another issue than Peczenik when he argues that legal justification must start from a coherent theory.

In his paper *The relevance of coherence*, Raz distinguishes between two variants of coherentism, the epistemic one and the constitutive one.[7] Given this distinction, Peczenik's approach to coherence in the law would, at least to a large extent, be based on the epistemic variant of coherentism, while Dworkin's approach would be an example of constitutive coherentism. As we will see in section 7, Raz believes that the epistemic variant of coherence is essentially flawed, not only in connection with the law, but in general. For legal coherentism this would not be problematic, however, because in Raz's view coherence in the law would be constitutive. In contrast to Dworkin, however, Raz sees only a limited role for constitutive coherence in the law.

In this chapter I will argue for a coherentist theory of justified acceptance that I will call *integrated coherentism*. Integrated coherentism is a theory of justified acceptance and fits as such in the domain of epistemological theories. Nevertheless I will argue that this theory is - given some assumptions about the nature of social reality – also a theory of the law. This means that I reject in connection with the law the distinction between epistemic and constitutive coherentism. Moreover, I will argue that integrated coherentism plays a central, rather than a limited role, in the law.

2. JUSTIFICATION

Epistemic coherentism is a theory about the justification of, usually, beliefs. Its plausibility depends amongst others on what one takes justification to be. In this connection it is important to distinguish between what justification is and the standards by means of which justification is measured. In this section I will briefly deal with the nature of justification, without saying much about the standards that should be used for justification.

Justification can be looked at from at least three angles. The first one is from the object of justification. For instance, is a particular act or belief justified? The second angle is the person who is justified in, for instance, holding a belief, or performing some act. The third angle is the auditorium for which the justification takes place. A judge who motivates his judgment justifies this judgment for, in the first place, the process parties, and in the

[7] Raz 1994 (RC).

second place the (legal) community that has vested decision making powers in him. I discuss these three angles in turn.

2.1 Acceptances

At first sight there are many things that can be justified, such as acts, decisions, policies, rules, beliefs and states of affairs. On closer inspection, everything that can be justified turns out to depend somehow on decision making. For instance, acts can be justified to the extent that they are potentially the outcome of decision making (intentional acts); policies and rules can be adopted and abandoned, respectively abrogated and all of these are the outcomes of decisions. The same counts for beliefs, which can also be adopted and abandoned deliberately. And, finally, states of affairs can be justified to the extent that they are the outcome of decision making, or can be changed intentionally.

The view of justification that I will present here as a presupposition of what follows does not deal with all objects of justification, but is broader than merely a theory about the justification of beliefs. Its topic is the justification of 'acceptances' in general and it treats a belief as one kind of acceptance. I will use the term 'acceptance' as a catch-all for everything, with the exception of behavior[8] that is amenable to justification. An acceptance is something that is actually accepted; 'things' that are amenable to acceptance are called 'potential acceptances'. Potential acceptances include:

- beliefs ('London is the capital of the United Kingdom'),
- practical judgments ('I should review this paper tomorrow'),
- plans ('I will take the plane to Bologna next Saturday').
- rules ('One ought to drive on the right hand side of the road'),
- values ('Truth is to be promoted'),
- logical standards ('If $P \rightarrow Q$ and P are both true, Q must be true'), or
- guidelines for belief revision ('If two acceptances are incompatible, the one that was more recently required should be abandoned').

An acceptance may be said to be justified if it is right. The precise form of rightness depends on the nature of the acceptance. Right beliefs are true; right logical standards lead to conclusion that, given the premises are better accepted than rejected or suspended; right rules are those rules that lead to

[8] Legal decisions (e.g. convict the suspect) can both be seen as behavior, in which case it is not amenable to acceptance and as a judgement about what should be done (the suspect should be convicted), in which case it is a potential acceptance.

the goal for which they were adopted (in case of rules that were adopted for some purpose). Whether an acceptance is right depends on the facts and on standards that make these facts relevant for the kind of rightness in question. In the case of beliefs, for instance, the standard is whether the belief is true and therefore the rightness of the belief that it is raining depends on this standard and the fact that it is raining. Given this standard, the belief that it is raining is justified if it is in fact raining.

Two things are noteworthy about this last example. First, that the rightness of a belief does not depend on one's other beliefs. It depends on the facts in the world, not on the beliefs about these facts. However, the standard for the rightness of beliefs, that right beliefs are true ones, is not a matter of fact, but depends on the person or group that uses standards for the rightness of beliefs. (A belief might also be considered to be right if it is in accordance with the text of a holy book, even if it were false.)

The second thing to note is that being justified as a characteristic of acceptances is redundant next to the already existing characteristic of being right. Being justified is nothing else than being right. For this reason I prefer to stick with rightness and to ignore the notion of being justified as a characteristic of acceptances. The only reason I mention it is that being justified in the sense of rightness sometimes seems to play a role in discussions about justification.[9]

2.2 Internal personal justification

Instead of asking whether a particular acceptance is justified, it is possible (and makes more sense) to ask whether a person is justified in accepting something. Is the judge justified in holding the suspect guilty? Is Amnesty International justified in accepting the goal to free as many as possible political prisoners? By asking these questions, the emphasis is on the persons (or personified organizations) that accept something, not on what is accepted. That is why I call justification from this point of view *personal justification*.

[9] For instance, Chisholm (1989, 8) writes that 'The term "justify" in its application to a belief, is a term of epistemic appraisal: it is used to say something about the reasonableness of that belief'. On this view, being justified is a characteristic of the belief.

Audi (1998, 163) writes about the inferential transmission of justification as if being justified is a characteristic of beliefs that can, just like truth, be transmitted from the premises to the conclusion of an argument.

See also the discussion of 'absolute justification' in chapter 1, section 2.5. It seems to me that the notion of 'absolute justification' only makes some sense in connection with the justification of acceptances in the sense of rightness.

There are two perspectives on personal justification. The one perspective is that of the person who asks himself 'Am I justified in accepting this?' This is, for instance, the question of the judge who is wondering whether the evidence is sufficient to convict the suspect. The second perspective is that of the spectator, who wonders whether some other person is or was justified in accepting something. The legal commentator, for instance, may ask whether the legislator was justified in his judgment that this bill should be passed. To make the discussion of these two perspectives more convenient, I will dub the first perspective 'internal personal justification' and the second perspective 'external personal justification' and abbreviate them to *internal*, respectively *external justification*.[10]

Suppose that P believes, and has no reason to doubt, that it is raining. Suppose, moreover, that P must make up his mind whether the streets are wet. Going by his best knowledge[11], P should come to the conclusion that the streets are wet and in this sense he is justified in his belief that the streets are wet. However, the reason for P to believe that the streets are wet is not that he believes that it is raining, but rather (the fact) that it is raining. In terminology of Haack[12], it is the *content* of what P believes, not his belief *state*, which is relevant for his internal justification. Whether P is internally justified in holding a belief (or, in general, accepting something) depends on, one the one hand, the facts and, on the other hand, the standards that P uses (and is justified in using) to assign relevance to the facts.

Now suppose that in fact it is not raining. Then P is not internally justified to believe that the streets are wet, for his reason to believe this is that it is raining, while in fact it is not. However, if we ask, from the external point of view, whether P is justified in his belief that the streets are wet, the answer must be affirmative. Assuming that P was both justified (but not right) in believing that it is raining and in adopting the inference rule[13] that the streets may be taken to be wet if it is raining, the best thing P could do is to adopt the belief that the streets are wet. Apparently, there is a difference between internal and external justification, because where for internal justification the facts are relevant, for external justification (justified) beliefs about the facts are relevant. The same point can again be made in terms of

[10] Notice that the notions of internal and external justification as used here differ from Alexy's use of them. Cf. Alexy 1978, 273 and chapter 1, section 3.2 of the present work.

[11] For the sake of argument, I assume that it would not be rational to invest time and energy to acquire additional information.

[12] Haack 1999.

[13] In this chapter I use the expression 'inference rule' for what Toulmin (1958) called a 'warrant', not for inference rules in the sense in which they occur in systems of formal logic.

the distinction between belief contents and belief states: belief contents are relevant for internal justification, belief states for external justification.

That this difference between internal and external justification is legally relevant, is illustrated by the following Dutch case.[14]

> X was suspected of hiding two dangerous kidnappers. For this reason the police raided his house, causing damage in the course of action. At the end, it turned out that the suspicion was false, although at the moment that the police decided to raid the house, it was justified. X sued the government for the damages. The government defended itself by adducing that the raid was justified, given the information that was at the time available to the police. The Dutch Supreme Court convicted the government to pay for the damages, however, because the police behavior was only prima facie justified, but turned in the end out to have not been justified. Apparently, the government used the external notion of justification, while the Supreme Court used the internal notion.

Both from the internal perspective, when a person is wondering whether to accept something, and from the external perspective, when the question is raised from the outside whether a person is justified in accepting something, the relevant facts to go by are this person's internal states.[15] When I wonder whether the streets are wet, my decision should depend on the fact whether the streets are wet, but I can only 'access' this fact through my belief that the streets are wet. This belief may be false, but the best thing I can do about this is to check it ... by means of my other beliefs (and standards). The same counts for the standards involved. These standards are not given with the facts, but are adopted (accepted) by the person using them. They may be wrong, but the best thing to do about this is to check them by means of my other standards and beliefs.

It turns out that personal justification is necessarily relative, namely relative to the internal states of the person for whom the justification holds. This does not mean that the justified acceptances are themselves relativized. If I am justified in my belief that the streets are wet, this justification is relative to what else I accept, but this does not mean that I believe that 'the streets are wet, assuming the rightness of my other acceptances'. I believe that 'the streets are wet' and this belief is justified (or not) relative to the rest of my acceptances. Personal justification is inherently relative in this sense.

[14] HR 26 januari 1990, NJ 1990/794.

[15] In section 2.3 I will discuss the objection that the right standards are not up the person, but are 'independently' given.

2.3 Justification for an audience

If one attempts to justify something in front of an audience, one should present this audience with an argument that will probably convince it. This means that the premises from which this argument starts should be accepted by the audience.[16] If one wants to convince an audience that P was justified in accepting something, this will be much easier if the beliefs and standards on which P's acceptance is based are accepted by the audience too.

This holds in particular with regard to the standards. Suppose that P believes that the streets are wet and bases this belief on the fact that it is raining and on the standard (inference rule) that if it is raining, the streets are wet. Suppose, moreover, that the members of the audience live in a country where all streets are roofed and that they are not familiar with countries in which this is not the case. For such an audience, it may seem that P is not justified in his belief that the streets are wet, because he uses a wrong standard. The reason is that the audience replaces a standard that P is justified in accepting by a standard the audience is justified in accepting. In the eyes of the audience, the right (misleadingly called 'justified') conclusion cannot be that the streets are wet. However, if P was justified in his acceptance of the inference rules 'if it is raining, the streets are wet', P is justified in his conclusion that the streets are wet too, even if this conclusion is unjustified (that is: wrong) in the eyes of the audience.[17]

2.4 Broad coherentism

The view adopted above, that all justification is relative to the internal states of the person who is justified, is a so-called *internalist* theory of justification.[18] An internalist theory of justification holds that the justifiability of holding a belief (or - more generally – of something that one

[16] This was emphasised by Perelman and Olbrechts-Tyteca (1969, 23f.)

[17] We will encounter a more realistic example of this fallacy in section 7.

[18] The distinction between internalist and externalist epistemological theories should not be confused with the internal and the external perspective on justification. The former distinction deals with the issue whether only mental states play a role in the justification of beliefs. The latter distinction concerns the issue whether justification is dealt with from the perspective of a reasoning person, or from the perspective of an external observer who evaluates this reasoning. If my view of the internal perspective is correct, namely if facts rather than beliefs about facts play a role from the internal perspective, this perspective presupposes an externalist epistemological theory. The external perspective presupposes on my view an internalist epistemological theory.

accepts) is a function of our internal states. An externalist theory denies this.[19]

In traditional epistemology, which focuses on knowledge of the physical world, it is customary to distinguish between internalist theories that assign a privileged status to some acceptances and internalist theories that do not. Acceptances with a privileged status are considered to need no justification, or are taken to be justified in themselves, whatever that may be. The obvious candidates for acceptances with a privileged status are beliefs based on sensory perception. These beliefs are in some theories assumed to guarantee contact with the external world and provide the foundations on which the building of other acceptances is erected. Such theories are called 'foundationalist'.[20]

Internalist theories that do not assign a privileged status to some acceptances usually assume that the justification of acceptances rests on coherence with other acceptances. Therefore these theories are called *coherence theories*. Notice that coherence theories in this sense are defined in contrast to foundationalist theories. I will call coherence theories that do not pose additional demands on their contents, *coherence theories in the broad sense*. Coherence theories in this broad sense are by definition internalist theories of justified acceptance that do not assign a privileged status to a particular set of acceptances.

A subset of the coherence theories in the broad sense may be called *strict coherence theories*. These strict theories demand that a justified (in the sense of coherent) set of acceptances exhibits a particular structure of mutual support between its elements. An interesting issue for discussion then becomes what this structure of mutual support would be.[21]

19 Pollock and Cruz 1999, 22f. Their wordings suggest, however, that they intend their distinction to apply to the justifiability of beliefs themselves (justifiability in the sense of rightness), rather than the acceptance of these beliefs.

20 Some foundationalist theories assign a special status to some acceptances because they are assumed to be incorrigible, without necessarily being based on sensory perception. See Alston 1992.

21 Such a discussion can be found in, amongst others, Alexy and Peczenik 1990. See also Bracker 2000.

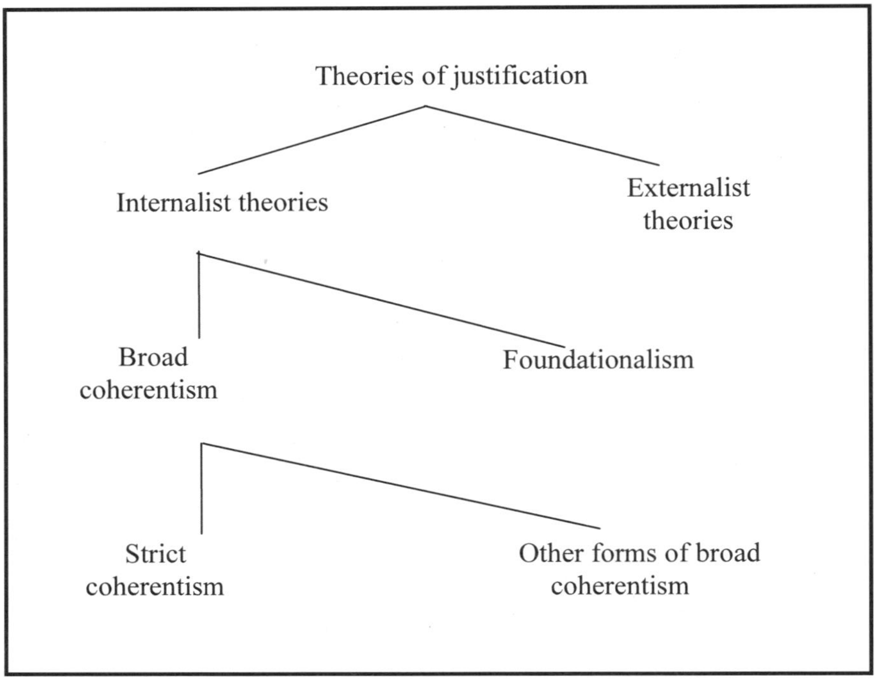

In the following, I will deal with justification from the external perspective. Then, given the relative notion of justification adopted above, a theory of justified acceptance must be internalist and consequently either foundationalist or coherentist in the broad sense. The distinction between foundationalist and coherentist theories is not as strict as might seem at first sight, however.[22] In particular a theory may assign a privileged status to some of its elements, but base this status on reasons derived from other parts of the theory. For instance, one can have a theory that holds that perceptive states provide us - under suitable circumstances - with reasons why what we perceive is true, while these perceptive states themselves are not in need of any justification.[23] This theory would assign a privileged status to perceptive states (they need no justification), but does this for reasons based upon the rest of the theory. Such reasons might for instance be that, under suitable circumstances, perception provides us with a reliable picture of the world. These reasons have themselves no privileged status and need justification in the sense that they are part of a coherent theory. Such a theory would be

[22] This is also extensively argued in Haack 1993, 13f.
[23] Cf. Haack 1999.

coherentist in the broad sense, because the privileged status of perceptive states is not a priori given with this epistemological theory, but depends on the actual contents of the theory that is developed within a framework which as such does not assign a privileged status to any element. In a sense, however, the theory would also be foundationalist, because the perceptive states end up with a privileged status.

The crucial difference with a straightforward foundationalist theory is that in the variant under discussion here, the privileged status of perceptive states is not given with the theory of epistemic justification as such, but merely with the contents of one particular theory about the world, which fits in a broadly coherentist theory of epistemic justification. This distinction, between on the one hand the postulates of a theory of epistemic justification as such and on the other hand the contents of a theory about the world that fits within such an epistemic theory, is crucial for the understanding of integrated coherentism.

3. MUTUAL SUPPORT

When coherentism is at stake, it is generally taken to be more specific than merely epistemic internalism without privileged acceptances. A fashionable view of coherentism runs that a theory is coherent if it is consistent and comprehensive, and if its elements mutually support each other.[24] Let us assume for a while that the notions of consistency and comprehensiveness are unproblematic and focus on the idea that the elements of a comprehensive theory mutually support each other. The question that must be answered then is what this mutual support involves.

3.1 Deductive support

A simple view of support would be that an element of a theory is supported by the rest of the theory if it can be deduced from the rest. Let us call this view the deductive support theory. That the deductive support theory is unattractive becomes clear from a simple example:

[24] See, for instance, Bracker 2000, 166/7.

Theory 0

1. The butler murdered Lord Hard.
2. The butler had a motive.
3. The butler murdered Lord Hard and the butler had a motive.

The elements 1 and 2 of this theory together deductively support element 3, while element 3 deductively supports both the elements 1 and 2. This small theory would therefore be coherent in the narrow sense (strong mutual support). However, it is not a very interesting form of support, because element 3 merely repeats the elements 1 and 2.[25] Although the triviality of the support relation may be less plain if the deductive chains between the elements of a theory are longer, deductive support between elements of a theory will always be trivial in the sense illustrated by the example above, because deductively valid inferences are in general reformulations of information contained in the premises of the argument.[26]

Another problem with deductive support is that it can only be applied to theories that contain only elements with truth values. Deductive validity of arguments is defined in terms of the truth values of the premises and the conclusion. Although rule and principle applying arguments superficially seem to be of the same form as some kinds of deductively valid arguments, this appearance is deceptive, if only because rules and principles lack truth values.[27] Therefore, if coherentism is to be applied to legal theories too, the support relation must not be confined to deductive support only.

It turns out that the mutual support needed for a coherent theory cannot be deductive support.[28] But what else can it be? Let us look at a theory of coherence that was elaborated by Thagard cum suis, according to which coherence is a form of constraint satisfaction.

[25] Cf. also Alexy and Peczenik 1990, note 5.

[26] This was already pointed out forcefully in Toulmin 1958, 123f. See also my discussion of the container metaphor of reasoning in Hage 1997 (RwR), 245f.

[27] This subject is too complex to go into details here. The interested reader is referred to Hage 1997 (RwR), 78f.

[28] Other objections against what he calls 'coherence as implication' are formulated in Lehrer 2000, 100/101.

3.2 Coherence as constraint satisfaction

In a number of publications[29], Thagard developed the theory of knowledge as constraint satisfaction. In Thagard and Verbeurgt 1998, this theory of coherence is summarized as follows:

- Elements are representations such as concepts, propositions, parts of images, goals, actions, and so on.
- Elements can cohere (fit together) or incohere (resist fitting together). Coherence relations include explanation, deduction, facilitation, association, and so on. Incoherence relations include inconsistency, incompatibility and negative association.
- If two elements cohere, there is a positive constraint between them. If two elements incohere, there is a negative constraint between them.
- Elements are to be divided into ones that are accepted and ones that are rejected.
- A positive constraint between two elements can be satisfied either by accepting both of the elements or by rejecting both of the elements.
- A negative constraint between two elements can be satisfied only by accepting one element and rejecting the other.
- The coherence problem consists of dividing a set of elements into accepted and rejected sets in a way that satisfies the most constraints.

Let me illustrate this theory by means of an example from the field of judicial proof. Suppose that Lord Hard was found in his room, murdered by means of a knife. The butler was seen entering Lord Hard's room. Moreover, the butler had a motive to murder Lord Hard, because his Lordship had seduced the butler's daughter Harriet. However, the butler has a phobia for knives, which makes it less probable that he killed the Lord with a knife. Lady Maureen, Lord Hard's wife, had a motive for murder too, because knowing of the seduction, she suffered from heavy jealousy. The butler is accused of heaving murdered the Lord and the issue at stake is whether he actually murdered the Lord.

In order to depict the constraints between the different beliefs that play a role in this case, I will number them:

1. The butler was seen entering Lord Hard's room.
2. Lord Hard seduced the butler's daughter.
3. The butler had a motive to murder Lord Hard.
4. The butler had a phobia for knives.

[29] Amongst others: Thagard 1992, Thagard and Verbeurgt 1998 and Thagard 1999.

5. Lady Maureen was jealous with regard to the Lord.
6. Lady Maureen butler had a motive to murder Lord Hard.
7. Lady Maureen murdered Lord Hard with a knife.
8. The butler murdered Lord Hard with a knife.

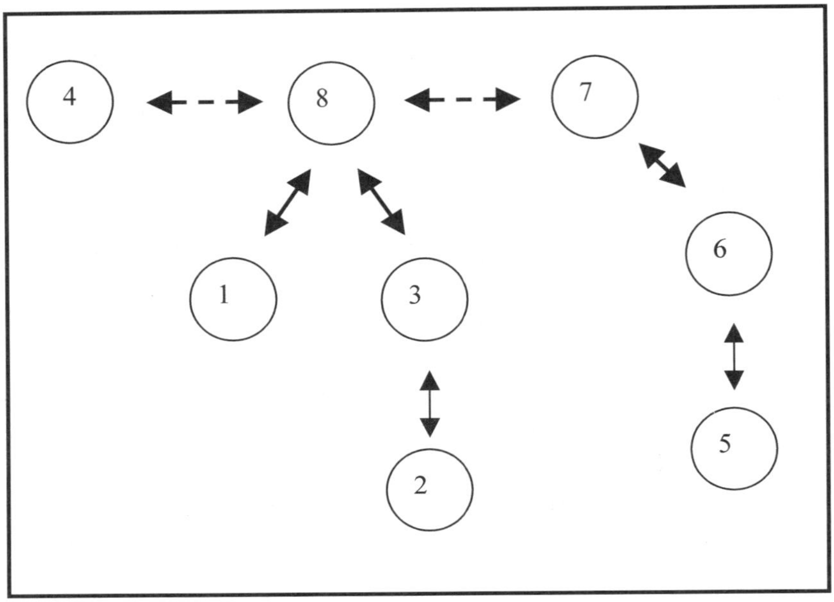

The circles in this picture represent the possible beliefs in a theory about the murder case. The double-headed arrows represent constraints between these beliefs. Arrows with a closed line represent positive constraints; arrows with a dotted line represent negative constraints. Initially the beliefs 1, 2, 4 and 5 have a positive status. By repeatedly increasing the status of the beliefs that are positively connected to another belief with a positive status, or negatively connected to a belief with a negative status and decreasing the status of the other beliefs, in the end an equilibrium results.[30] This equilibrium divides the beliefs into two categories, beliefs with a positive status, which are accepted and beliefs with a negative status, which are rejected. The resulting theory is coherent, because the beliefs and disbeliefs mutually support each other.

This theory of coherence as constraints satisfaction has several advantages. First it leaves the nature of the elements in a coherent set open.

[30] I am implicitly applying the connectionist treatment of the network of beliefs, that Thagard applies in his publications. More on this approach can be found in Rumelhart and McClelland 1986, or in modern introductions to artificial intelligence or cognitive science.

This makes it possible for the theory to deal with elements that have no truth value, such as rules, principles and values and even concepts and parts of images. For application in the law, it is crucial that a coherence theory can deal with elements that are not bearers of truth values.

Second the theory gives a precise specification of what counts as support. Support is a positive constraint and negative support is a negative constraint. This would still be rather vague, were there not the third advantage of coherence as constraint satisfaction, namely that it can be interpreted in terms of neural nets (connectionism) and that there are algorithms available for computing coherence.

Coherence as constraint satisfaction is a promising version of a coherence theory. Nevertheless I think that the theory in the version presented above should be rejected as a theory of legal coherence, if only because an acceptable coherence theory should treat the support relations between the elements as elements of the theory.

Let me return to Lord Hard's case to illustrate what I mean and consider the relation between the belief that the butler was seen entering Lord Hard's room and the belief that the butler murdered Lord Hard. At first sight there is a positive constraint between these two beliefs. But what to think of the case in which one also believes that Harriet saw Lord Hard alive and well after her father, the butler, left his room? If Harriet saw Lord Hard after her father left the Lord's room, the link between the belief that the butler was seen entering Lord Hard's room and the belief that the butler murdered Lord Hard loses its force. So the presence of this link is negatively connected to the belief that Harriet saw Lord Hard alive after her father left his room. This connection between the belief that Harriet saw the Lord and the constraint between the beliefs about the butler entering the room and murdering the Lord, should be part of the theory.

More theoretically this means that one would like positive and negative constraints to be treated as elements of the theory. Moreover, it should be possible to have positive and negative constraints, not only between beliefs mutually, but also between beliefs and constraints. This is illustrated by the following figure in which constraints are depicted as boxes on lines. It shows how there can be a constraint between a belief and a constraint:

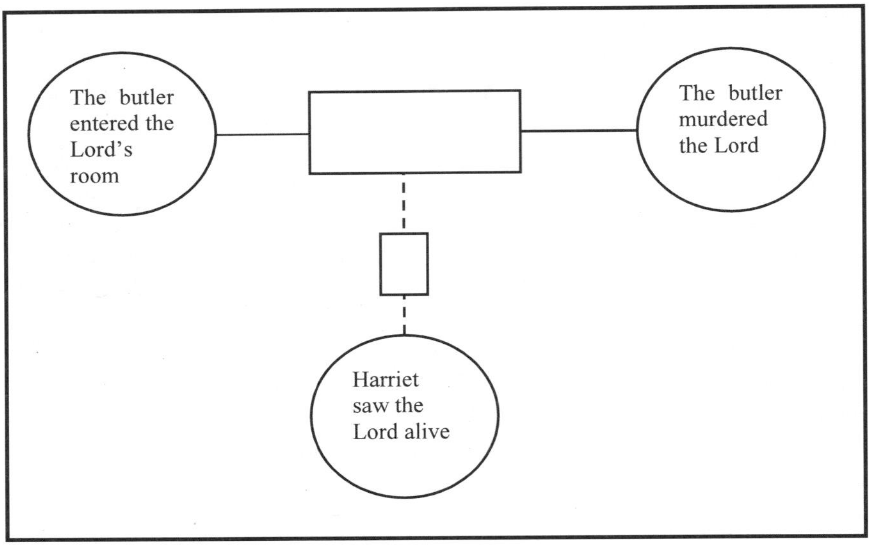

4. A CASE STUDY

Before proposing an alternative for Thagard's theory of coherence as constraint satisfaction, I want to pay some more attention to the example of the murder upon Lord Hard. One of the things I want to illustrate is how the pursuit of coherence almost automatically leads to making the theory more and more comprehensive. That is why I will start with a very small theory:

Theory 1

1. The butler had a motive to murder Lord Hard.
2. The butler was seen entering Lord Hard's room.
3. The butler murdered Lord Hard.

Let us assume that neither one of these sentences is above doubt. For instance, the person who was seen entering Lord Hard's room might have been somebody else. It is understandable that the butler had a motive (revenge for the seduction of his daughter by Lord Hard), but the butler might have been unmoved by such all too human passions. And finally, it is not certain that the butler murdered Lord Hard, although it is made probable by the evidence. Although none of the sentences is above doubt, they mutually support each other and together they seem to form a coherent theory.

4.1 Contributive reasons

The question that must be answered now is what the nature of this support is, since it is not deductive support. The support offered by deductively valid arguments is that the conclusion of such arguments must be true if the premises are true. A weaker notion of support is that of a contributive reason for (believing) a conclusion.[31] The presence of such a reason makes the conclusion more believable than it was without the reason. There is, however, no guarantee that the conclusion is true if a contributive reason for this conclusion obtains. A contributive reason may in itself be strong enough to justify belief in the conclusion if there are no counter reasons present, but this needs not be the case. For instance, the mere fact that the butler had a motive for murdering Lord Hard is not sufficient to believe that he actually committed the murder. The same counts for the contributive reason that the butler was seen entering Lord Hard's room. Let us assume, however, that, taken together, these two contributive reasons justify the conclusion that the butler murdered Lord Hard.

The presence of contributive reasons, no matter how many, does not guarantee the truth of the conclusion for which they plead. It does not even guarantee that the belief in the conclusion is justified, because whether such a belief would be justified does not only depend on the reasons pleading for the conclusion, but also on the reasons pleading against it. Suppose, for instance, that Lord Hard would have died soon anyway and that the butler would have inherited a pretty amount of money from the Lord, an inheritance which he would loose if it were discovered that he committed the murder. This would be a contributive reason against the conclusion that the butler murdered Lord Hard. There may be even more contributive reasons against this conclusion, for instance that the Lord was murdered by means of a knife and that the butler had a phobia for knives. Whether a conclusion is justified on the basis of contributive reasons depends on the balance of the contributive reasons for this conclusion and the contributive reasons against it.[32]

[31] Here I assume that the reasons are all reasons for believing a conclusion. The distinctions between reasons for belief, reasons for acting and constitutive reasons is discussed in Hage 1997 (RwR), 59f.

[32] There are even more complications because some facts make that other facts that would normally be reasons for or against a conclusion lose their reason giving force, or change the relative weight of reasons. I will ignore these logical details here.

4.2 Missing links

Given the notions of contributive reasons for and against a conclusion, the second example can be given a more thorough analysis. The fact that the butler had a motive to murder Lord Hard is a contributive reason for the conclusion that he committed the murder.

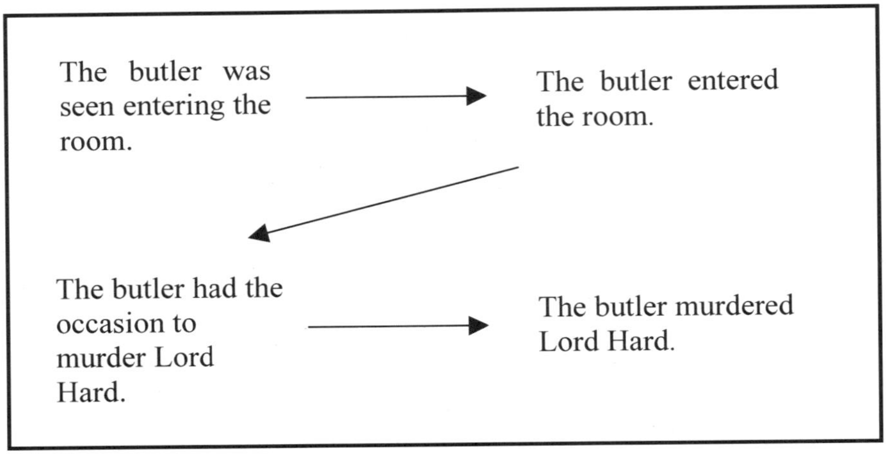

The same holds for the relation between the fact that the butler was seen entering Lord Hard's room and the conclusion that the butler murdered the Lord, but there are some complications here. The mere fact that the butler was *seen* entering Lord Hard's room is hardly a reason why the butler murdered Lord Hard. It is, however, a reason to believe that the butler in fact entered the room. And this fact is in turn a reason to believe that the butler had the occasion to murder the Lord. It is this last fact that is the immediate reason to believe that the butler murdered Lord Hard.[33]

If we compare this chain with the small theory of our example, we find that the second and third link of the chain are missing in the theory. Suppose that somebody believes the theory, but suspends belief in the second and the third link of the chain, or - even worse – believes their negations. Would we then still say that the theory is coherent? The support relation between the second and the third sentence of the theory is lost and with it the coherence of the theory. The lesson to draw is that theory 1 as such is not very

[33] There are other ways to construct a chain of reasons leading to the conclusion that the butler murdered Lord Hard. The crucial point here is not *which* chain of reasons is made, but rather *that* a chain is made.

coherent, but that it is part of a larger and more coherent theory that includes the second and the third link of the chain:

Theory 2

1. The butler had a motive to murder Lord Hard.
2a. The butler was seen entering Lord Hard's room.
2b. The butler entered the room.
2c. The butler had the occasion to murder Lord Hard.
3. The butler murdered Lord Hard.

4.3 Connections as elements of the theory

This elaboration of theory 1 illustrates how a coherent set of beliefs has a tendency to become more comprehensive. But there is more to come. Suppose that somebody holds the beliefs of theory 2, but did not believe that there is any connection between the elements of this set. Would we then say that his belief set was coherent? Presumably not. The coherence of the set lies in the assumed connection between the elements. The belief in sentence 3 should be based on the beliefs in the sentences 1 and 2c. This assumption of relevance is not a factual belief as expressed in the sentences 1, 2a-c and 3, but should nevertheless somehow be part of the coherent theory, because its denial or even suspension of the assumption makes the theory incoherent. Theory 2 therefore naturally expands to the more coherent

Theory 3

1. The butler had a motive to murder Lord Hard.
2a. The butler was seen entering Lord Hard's room.
2b. The butler entered the room.
2c. The butler had the occasion to murder Lord Hard.
3. The butler murdered Lord Hard.
4a. 1 expresses a contributive reason for believing 3.
4b. 2a expresses a contributive reason for believing 2b.
4c. 2b expresses a contributive reason for believing 2c.
4d. 2c expresses a contributive reason for believing 3.
4e. 3 expresses a contributive reason for believing 1, (2a, 2b) and 2c.

This is the occasion to make an important observation, namely that a theory not only contains independent beliefs, but also the links between these beliefs. The theory itself indicates that some of its elements are supported by other elements and the other way round.[34] It is characteristic for the theory of integrated coherence that will be exposed in section 5 that the relations between the elements of a theory are not determined by rules or standards outside the theory, but are parts of the theory itself.

4.4 Abstract reasons as elements

Theory 1 turns out to have been not so coherent after all, because it needed expansion to theory 3. However, even additional expansion is necessary, because reasons do not stand by themselves. If some concrete fact is a reason for a particular conclusion, similar facts are normally reasons for similar conclusions. Another way to say the same thing is that reasons can be generalized. The result of such a generalization is an abstract reason that a fact like the current reason is in general a reason for a conclusion like the current conclusion. In the present case, for instance, one abstract reason would be that if somebody has a motive for murdering somebody else, this is a reason to believe that the former person murdered the latter. Such an abstract reason is not a statement which is true or false independent of the person for whom, or group within which it holds, but rather something which is accepted or not. Since concrete reasons can be generalized into abstract reasons and since it is incoherent to accept that a particular fact is a reason for accepting a conclusion without accepting the corresponding abstract reason[35], theory 3 must be expanded to make it include the abstract reasons underlying the concrete reasons expressed in the sentences 4a-4b:

Theory 4:
1. The butler had a motive to murder Lord Hard.
2a. The butler was seen entering Lord Hard's room.
2b. The butler entered the room.
2c. The butler had the occasion to murder Lord Hard.
3. The butler murdered Lord Hard.
4a. 1 expresses a contributive reason for believing 3.

[34] It may seem that a theory need not specify the logical relations between its elements and that this job can be left to logic. This overlooks, however, that logic is not something that is given independent of one's beliefs. Even a generally accepted form of logic, such as for instance predicate logic, presupposes a theory of what can validly be derived from what and such a theory requires acceptance just like one's beliefs. See also section 5 and - more generally - chapter 1.

[35] That this is incoherent presupposes a theory about the 'logical' behavior of concrete reasons, in particular that they can be generalised into abstract reasons. Such a theory should be part of a larger coherent theory. For the purpose of the present example, I simply assume that such a theory is already accepted.

4b. 2a expresses a contributive reason for believing 2b.
4c. 2b expresses a contributive reason for believing 2c.
4d. 2c expresses a contributive reason for believing 3.
4e. 3 expresses a contributive reason for believing 1, 2a, 2b and 2c.
5a. If somebody has a motive to murder somebody else, this is a contributive reason to believe that the former person murdered the latter.
5b. If something was seen happening, this is a contributive reason to believe that this actually happened.
5c. If somebody entered the room of a murdered person, the former person had the occasion to murder the latter.[36]
5d. If somebody had the occasion to murder somebody else, this is a contributive reason to believe that the former person murdered the latter.
5e. If a conclusion of a reason to believe is true, this is a reason to believe the reason for this conclusion.

In particular the abstract reason formulated in 5e is interesting, because it underlies so-called abductive arguments.[37] If a fact would explain the occurrence of another fact, the occurrence of this other fact is in turn a reason to believe the explaining fact. The strength of this reason depends on the availability and the plausibility of other explanations. If the murder on Lord Hard would be explained better by the theory that his wife killed him out of jealousy, the fact that Lord Hard was murdered provides little support for the beliefs that the butler had a motive and that the butler was seen entering Lord Hard's room.[38] So the coherence of theory 4 presupposes a belief that there is no better explanation for the murdering of Lord Hard than the facts stated in the sentences 1 and 2a-2c. This belief in turn presupposes beliefs about other possible explanations of the murder of Lord Hard and standards for the comparison of the plausibility of different explanations.

Clearly theory 4 is still in need of expansion. In particular it does not take possible reasons against the conclusion that the butler murdered Lord Hard into account. Drawing the conclusion that the butler committed the murder

[36] This principle does not sound convincing, which illustrates that the argument needs to be elaborated further than this paper allows place for.

[37] Abductive arguments are arguments of the following form:
Facts like P tend to cause facts like Q.
A fact like Q occurred.
Therefore: a fact like P occurred.

[38] These two beliefs may nevertheless be true. In the indicated circumstances they only receive little support from the fact that Lord Hard was murdered.

presupposes the balancing of reasons for and against this conclusion, which asks not only for a decision about the relative weight of the reasons, but also for a judgment about the presence of all reasons for and against the conclusion. Most notably it presupposes that one has not only balanced the reasons for a conclusion against the reasons against in ones theory, but also that all relevant reasons are already part of the theory. In other words, the theory must contain all the reasons concerning a conclusion, including their relevance and their relative weight. Further elaboration of the theory would require more space than this chapter allows. Moreover, the elaboration would probably presuppose still other beliefs, principles or standards which should then be added to the theory and which would in turn presuppose other beliefs, etc ….

5. CONCLUSIONS FROM THE CASE STUDY

What does the above sequence of theories illustrate? First and foremost, I think, why coherent theories, in the strict sense of coherence, must be comprehensive.[39] The elements of a small theory can only support each other if other elements are also accepted. This means that these other elements should also be part of the total belief set. Moreover, the additional elements lead to again other elements, etc …. Comprehensiveness is not only an additional requirement for coherent theories in the broad sense next to strict coherence, but rather a presupposition of strict coherence. The support relation between the elements of a belief set is weakened, if not destroyed, if the belief set does not also contain additional elements.

This is especially clear from the abduction principle which will be part of most theories. The abduction principle depends for its application on the absence of other, more plausible explanations of the phenomenon that is explained by some reason. Application of the induction principle therefore requires a view of which alternative explanations are available and a theory of what makes one explanation more plausible than another explanation. Effectively this means that application of the abduction principle presupposes a theory about the nature of explanation and a theory about all

[39] This point was also stressed by Sosa 1989, who argues that narrow reflective equilibrium, restricted to coherence within a particular domain, ‘must be supplemented by wider reflection, at least to the point where we are satisfied that there is no other domain relevant to the topic under consideration’ and to which he adds in a footnote that a domain could rarely, if ever, lie in total epistemic isolation.

facts that would provide possible alternative explanations and about their relevance.

The second point illustrated by the above sequence of theories is that the pursuit of a coherent theory is a never-ending enterprise. Every addition to an existing theory is a potential occasion to make new additions. In the end, a coherent theory would be a theory of 'everything'. Theories of everything are not realistic and the same counts for ideal coherent theories. In the practice of real life reasoning, the pursuit of coherence functions as a device for local belief revision. By pointing out that a theory in its present version is not coherent, one can move the holder of the theory to amend it, either by deleting elements from it, or by adding new elements. The result of such a change will never be a completely coherent theory, but if everything goes well, it is a more coherent theory. Coherence is not a characteristic that real theories can possess, but rather a *correctional device* to be used in the never-ending process of updating and (hopefully) improving existing theories.[40]

The insight that coherence is a correctional device is also important for another reason. A common objection to coherence theories is that they cut knowledge of from reality. If beliefs are only tested against other beliefs, the influence of reality on our beliefs would be lost.[41] This objection would be effective if all beliefs in one's stock of beliefs were there on a voluntary basis. However, we hold many of our beliefs spontaneously and sometimes even unconsciously. Think for instance of beliefs based on sensory perception. If one sees a chair, this will normally lead to the belief that there is a chair. This belief is presumably the direct consequence of seeing the chair, but it is not based on some reason, such as the reason that one believes to see a chair.

These spontaneous beliefs play a role in the construction of a coherent belief set. On the assumption that they somehow derive from reality, they guarantee that the contact between a coherent set of beliefs and reality is not completely lost.[42] It should be noted, however, that the assumption that spontaneous beliefs 'somehow' derive from reality does not imply that these spontaneous beliefs are always true, or even that they are justified. Spontaneous beliefs are merely 'there' and play a role in the construction of

40 This dynamic aspect of the pursuit of coherence is also mentioned by Bender 1989 (CJK), 8.

41 Discussions of this objection can be found in Moser 1989, Pollock and Cruz 1999, 74/5 and Haack 1993, 26f.

42 If one does not assume that spontaneous beliefs somehow derive from reality, it is unclear how any epistemological theory might salvage the relation between one's beliefs and reality.

a coherent theory. It will often occur that they are abandoned during the process of construction.

In this connection the famous metaphor of Neurath gives a good indication of the role of coherence.[43] According to this metaphor, 'we are like sailors who must rebuild their ship upon the open sea'. We start with a pre-existing body of spontaneous beliefs that is modified in order to make it coherent. Moreover, the process of modification never ends, if only because the entrance of new spontaneous beliefs never ends as long as one is able to perceive.[44] Coherence is a correctional device, a goal pursued in the processing the body of our beliefs.

The third point that I want to emphasize and which I already mentioned in connection with Thagard's theory of coherence as constraint satisfaction, is that the connections between the elements of a theory, the constraints in Thagard's theory, are themselves part of the theory in question. A coherent theory is in accordance with constraints that are part of the theory themselves.[45] This third point is the crucial one for the theory of integrated coherence: the support relations between the elements of a theory are not defined outside the theory, but are part of the very theory. It can also be made by stating that in integrated coherence, logic is part of the coherent theory and not something outside of it. In this way, a kind of Quinean holism is incorporated into the theory of integrated coherence.[46]

[43] Neurath 1932/3.

[44] Probably the process of modification would even continue if there were no new input, but this remains a matter of speculation because we do continuously receive input of new beliefs.

[45] The idea that a theory sets itself the standards that it must satisfy is an extrapolation of the idea that a belief set also contains meta-beliefs. Cf. the discussion of meta-beliefs in Bender 1989 (CJK).

[46] Cf. Quine 1953 and 1986.

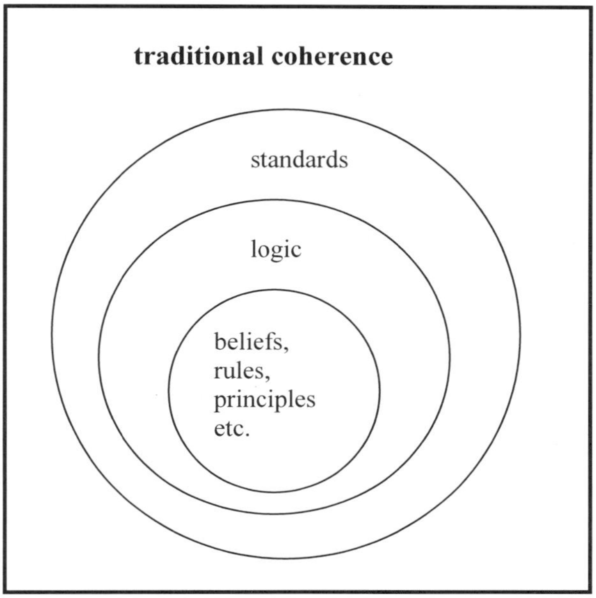

In a traditional coherence theory, the real theory consists of beliefs about the world and possibly rules and principles. Next to this theory there is a logic that defines which logical relations exist between the elements of the theory, what follows from the theory and what is inconsistent with it. And finally there is a substantive set of standards that define what a good theory is and, if these standards refer to coherence, what coherence in a theory amounts to. In integrated coherence the logic and the standards for a good theory are considered to be part of the theory itself. Outside the theory is only the minimal standard that a good theory satisfies its own standards.[47]

[47] Notice, by the way, that this opens the possibility that the standards that a theory contains for good theories do not refer to coherence. In that case, a 'coherent' theory in the sense of this paper would not be coherent. This possibility does not worry me, because, given the nature of the human cognitive apparatus, it would surprise me if some actual 'coherent' theory would not also include some version of a coherence theory of knowledge. And if it did, I have no problem with giving up the name 'integrated coherentism'.

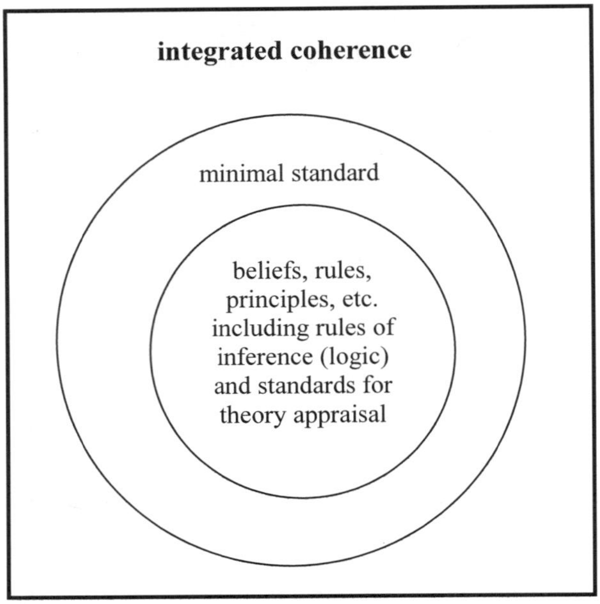

6. INTEGRATED COHERENTISM

After the preparatory work of the previous sections, I will use this section to sketch the outlines of the theory of integrated coherence.[48] The most basic notion is that of a theory. A theory is a set of acceptances plus perceptive states.[49] I assume that these acceptances and perceptive states determine what it is rational to believe, what standards should rationally be accepted, what it is rational to reject and about which potential acceptances one should

[48] The theory of integrated coherence as sketched in this section has parallels with argument-based semantics as discussed in Dung 1995, Prakken and Vreeswijk 2001 and Verheij 2003 (DL).

[49] Haack 1993, 29 argues, to my opinion convincingly, that not only the contents of beliefs, but also perceptive states (such as 'I see a chair') can be reasons for or against adopting or maintaining acceptances.

Haack continues to draw the - in my opinion false – conclusion that not all justification is a logical matter. She draws this conclusion from the fact that perceptive states, which are obviously not propositions, play a role in justification. Her error seems to me to be that she overlooks that even where descriptive sentences are used in arguments, the logical role (that of reasons) is played by the *facts* expressed by these sentences. A similar logical role can also be played by the *fact* that one is in a certain perceptive state.

suspend one's judgment because it is neither rational to accept them, nor rational to reject them.

At some moment in time, a theory might contain elements that should rationally be accepted, elements that should rationally be rejected and 'neutral' elements. The idea of integrated coherence is that the theory should be modified such that the elements that, according to the (rest of the) theory, should rationally be rejected are removed from it (the counterpart of the traditional demand of consistency), while elements that rationally should be accepted, but which are not yet part of the theory, should be added to it (the counterpart of logical closure). Neutral elements that are part of the theory remain in it, while neutral elements that are not part of the theory remain outside. In this connection the question which (potential) elements should rationally be accepted or rejected is answered solely on the basis of those elements of the theory that should not rationally be rejected. *A coherent theory is then a theory that contains all potential elements that should rationally be accepted according to its own elements and that does not contain any elements that should rationally be rejected according to (the rest) of its elements.*

A theory specifies which elements should be accepted or rejected relative to its own elements. To this extent the standard for coherence is integrated in the theory. A minimal standard must be external, however, namely that a coherent theory should satisfy its own standards for a good theory.

Integrated coherentism does not refer to mutual support as a standard for coherence. What counts as mutual support and the extent to which this kind of mutual support increases the quality of a theory are issues that are left to the theory itself. It might therefore be the case that an integratedly coherent theory consists of elements that lend little mutual support to each other. However, the demands that a coherent theory contains all those elements that should rationally be accepted according to itself and should not contain any elements that should rationally be rejected according to the theory itself, almost certainly guarantee a substantial degree of mutual support because all elements that are part of the theory because of these demands will be supported by other elements. Moreover, if the theory contains something like the abduction principle[50], which is very plausible if the theory is the outgrowth of a spontaneous human belief set, many supported elements of the theory will in turn support the elements that support them.

[50] What holds for the abduction principle also holds for a principle that allows induction. I will leave induction outside the scope of this paper, however.

7. THE RELATIVITY OF JUSTIFICATION

In the remainder of this chapter, the implications of integrated coherentism for legal justification will be traced. I will use Raz's criticism of coherence theories in the law as starting point for my discussion. In his paper *The Relevance of Coherence*, Raz formulates fundamental criticism against all forms of epistemic coherentism.[51] Remember that coherence theories are internalist, meaning that they only deal with mental states of persons to determine which acceptances are justified *for these persons*.[52] Justification is consequently a personal matter; acceptances are justified for a particular person and not in general, whatever 'general justifiedness' might mean. Raz does not object to this person-relatedness of justification, but points out that some of the mental states[53] of a person may be acquired in an unreliable way, for instance through prejudice or superstition. According to Raz coherence with such wrongly acquired mental states would not lead to justification. Consider, for example, a person who is influenced by a self-acclaimed prophet, who has written a book of 'revelations' containing a peculiar vision of the world and of moral and epistemic standards. The most important epistemic standard is that the book of revelations in question contains answers to all questions. If the acceptances of this person are taken as input set, the resulting coherent set may be weird in the eyes of non-believers.[54]

The justification of a particular acceptance is ideally based on a coherent acceptance set to which this particular acceptance belongs. This coherent set must be the outcome of a correction process that started from a number of spontaneous acceptances. Raz's criticism boils down to it that not every set of spontaneous acceptances can lead to a coherent set that justifies its contents. In particular if the original set of spontaneous acceptances contains irrational elements, the resulting coherent set would not justify its elements.

The crucial question in this connection is which standards should be used to determine whether the spontaneous acceptance set contains irrational elements. Should this be determined by means of standards in the coherent set that is the outcome of this spontaneous set, or by means of different, 'objective' standards? If the rationality of the input set should be measured

[51] Raz 1994 (RC).

[52] Later in this section I will retract this claim somewhat.

[53] Raz writes about beliefs. For reasons exposed in section 2.1 I prefer to broaden the set of entities that are considered for justification to acceptances in general.

[54] Some non-believers may be so optimistic to think that even coherent sets based upon such 'irrational' input sets would turn out to be 'rational' after all, because such 'irrational' input sets are even irrational according to themselves and would become 'rational' after correction by their own standards.

against standards in its resulting coherent set, Raz's argument misses the point. In the final coherent set, the resulting acceptances are rational according to the standards in the set itself. If the input set contained irrational elements, these elements have been filtered out in the resulting coherent set and the original mistakes have been corrected. If some elements were not filtered out, they turned out to be not irrational after all.

Presumably, however, Raz meant to say that the rationality of the input set should be measured against independent standards. The crucial question then becomes what these independent standards would be. Raz mentions a few, such as that beliefs should not result from prejudice or obstinacy. These seem to be good standards, but who is to be the judge of that? If these standards are part of the coherent acceptance set, the effects of prejudice and obstinacy will be filtered out in the coherent set. If the standards are not part of the coherent set, where stems their justification from, then?

The only sensible answer seems to be that they are generally accepted. Moreover, if they are to be good standards, they should not only happen to be generally accepted, but should also be rationally generally accepted. Or, to put it in coherence terminology, they should be part of a coherent set of generally accepted acceptances. Formulated thus, it becomes clear what Raz's problem is. Justification according to 'our common epistemic vocabulary' is not a personal matter, but a matter of standards that are broadly accepted, or – probably even better - correct. What would seem to be justified because it belongs to a personal coherent acceptance set, may be unjustified because it does not belong to a more broadly acceptable or even correct coherent set.[55]

I can be brief about the 'objective' or 'correct' standards. Standards are by their very nature not true or correct in the sense of solely dependent on an independent reality. They can be reliable and there can be very convincing reasons to adopt them, but they are never true or correct in the sense that they are somehow given independent of acceptance. They can be justified, but this justification is necessarily relative to other standards that are not true or correct in the sense considered here. The best that can be obtained are standards that (rightly) have received broad acceptance.

The question then seems to be what the correct standards for justification are. Are they the standards which are part of a coherent personal acceptance set, or are they the standards that belong to a coherent acceptance set which

[55] More complex constructions are also imaginable. One might construct a coherent acceptance set on the basis of spontaneous *personal* beliefs and spontaneous *social* standards. The result would be a coherent set based on a hybrid of personal and social input. Such a set might even better capture what is commonly called justified than a coherent set based on purely social acceptances.

resulted from what was commonly accepted? Asking the question is already giving most of the answer. Apparently two different versions of justification are involved. One deals with the question what a particular person is justified in accepting. The other deals with the issue what is acceptable according to common standards. These different versions of justification are not a reason against coherence theories of justification, but rather a reason to relativize justification not so much to a person, but to an acceptance set, leaving the question open whether they are the acceptances of a person or a group. An acceptance may then be justified for a particular person or for a social group, such as physical scientists or lawyers. It makes no sense to ask the question whether a particular acceptance is justified in abstract. All justification is relative, and the criticism that what is justified according to a particular coherent acceptance set is not 'really' justified seems to overlook this point.

8. THE BASE OF COHERENCE

The first line of criticism adduced by Raz against coherentism in the law, which I discussed in the previous section, was directed against epistemic coherentism in general. The second line of criticism deals with constitutive coherentism in the law, the view that the content of the law is determined by coherence. In his discussion of constitutive coherence in the law, Raz points out that any coherent theory presupposes something that must be made coherent and Raz calls this the 'base'. In the previous section we already encountered this base as the input set for a coherent acceptance set and in section 5 the role of the base was mentioned as reason why coherent theories need not be disconnected from reality. From this correct observation concerning the necessity of a base, Raz concludes that 'even according to coherence accounts, coherence is but one of at least two components in any theory of law'.[56]

In a sense this is right. The base plays a role in determining the coherent acceptance set that stems from it. But if this observation is the first step towards the conclusion that if a legal judgment is to be justified, the base from which it was ultimately derived should be justified (or correct) too, it is misleading. The base that functions as input to this process is irrelevant for the justification on basis of the coherent acceptance set that resulted from it. A particular acceptance is justified relative to an acceptance set, if this acceptance set is coherent and if the acceptance is an element of it. The base

[56] Raz 1994 (RC), 289.

from which the coherent acceptance set stems may *determine* the contents of this set, but has no role in the *justification* of an acceptance.

Nevertheless, Raz's text suggests that he wants to take the misleading road of assigning the base of an acceptance set a role in the justification of the acceptances that are part of it. He considers the possibility that the base would contain all possible legal propositions, including the principle of maximizing happiness and the categorical imperative. We might then end up, according to Raz, with a morally perfect set of propositions, but not with a theory of the law. Raz sees this as a reason why we should only include objective legal propositions in the base.

I would prefer a different road, namely not to confine the base to only legal (or moral) propositions, but to make it contain all propositions. Then it would also include propositions about what counts as law and what counts as morality and propositions concerning the proper demarcation of law and morality. The resulting coherent acceptance set would then presumably contain a theory about the relation between law and morality and if this theory would be a positivist one, it would assign the principle of the maximization of happiness and the categorical imperative to the realm of morality and declare them irrelevant (or only slightly relevant) for the contents of the law. What Raz sees as a danger of placing too many (and in particular the wrong, moral) acceptances in the base is in my opinion a danger of placing too few acceptances in it. If the acceptances of the base include all acceptances, the role of individual elements of the base in determining the coherent output set is less important than Raz assumes and that is the reason why the base is not an independent factor in determining the justification of legal judgments.

The difference between integrated coherentism and Raz's view becomes even more prominent when we look into the question to what extent the base is 'transitory'. Under a transitory base, Raz understands a base 'which provides a starting-point on which some coherence-maximizing procedure is applied, leading eventually to a discarding of the base'. Raz mentions Rawls' theory of reflective equilibrium as an example of a theory that uses such a transitory base. According to Raz, a transitory base is not suitable for law and adjudication and nobody has ever suggested such a view of law. The prima facie plausibility of Raz's view is that if the whole base were overthrown by the coherent acceptance set that results from it, the law according to this coherent set would have nothing to do with the law as we actually know it and can therefore not sensibly be called 'law' at all. It should be noted, however, that a truly comprehensive acceptance set would presumably contain a subset about semantics, including a theory of reference. If this theory holds that words like 'law' refer directly to certain phenomena, e.g. the contents of legislation and court decisions, and that these phenomena are therefore necessarily part of what we refer to by the word 'law'[57], the coherent acceptance set could not contain a subset that is completely different from what we actually call law. However, this does not show that there cannot be a transitory base for the law, but only that, given certain boundary conditions amongst which a particular semantic theory, the base that is in theory transitory will in fact not be overthrown.

Let me add an example to illustrate why Raz is wrong. Suppose that somebody has a base that includes the rule of recognition that all rules made by the government according to procedure P (P-rules) are rules of law and that there are no other legal rules. The same base contains the beliefs that the rules 1-10, which are not P-rules, are legal rules. The base does not contain any other purely legal beliefs, but it does contain a belief about the proper role of government within society and that his role includes that it can exclusively make authoritative guidelines for behavior within society. Moreover, this belief is firmly embedded in a political philosophy, which is in turn embedded in a view of the world as a whole and the role of human beings in it. The purely legal part is inconsistent and should be modified. Given the way it is embedded in a total view of the world, the rule of recognition is not the best candidate for removal and therefore the belief that the rules 1-10 are legal rules will be sacrificed in making the set coherent. This means that more than 90% of the legal beliefs should be given up, because they are badly embedded in the rest of non-legal knowledge.

Although lots of possibly relevant details, including details about semantics, are lacking, I believe that an account like the above of what acceptance revision might entail is not unrealistic and that would go to show that Raz's idea that a legal base cannot be transitory, is wrong. In general, it is my opinion that precisely because Raz considers the base of a coherent theory of the law as a base theory *of the law* and consequently in isolation of the rest of one's acceptances, he assigns the base a far too important role in determining whether a particular legal judgment is justified.

9. AUTHORITY VERSUS COHERENCE?

Another line of criticism that Raz formulated against coherentism in the law has to do with the authority of law makers. According to Raz, the law is a set of standards that guide conduct and judgments about conduct. These standards emerge from the activities of authoritative institutions. Consequently, the law reflects the intentions of its makers and the reasons

[57] Cf. Kripke 1972, Putnam 1975 (MM) and Stalnaker 1997.

they had for making the law as they did. This means that the contents of the law are, at least in part, determined by politics and given the vagaries of politics, 'there is no reason to expect the law to be coherent'.

Before considering whether this criticism really affects coherentism in the law, I want to draw the reader's attention to what might be an underlying motive of Raz's attack on coherentism. The real issue at stake might be to what extent legal decision makers have leeway to frame their decisions as seems best to them and to what extent they are bound by a law that is independent of the way they see it. This discussion can be focused on the specific question to what extent the law is determined by its sources and amongst these in particular the sources that involve explicit decision making. To frame the question (overly) simply: Who makes the law, legislators or judges who must decide new cases? The more a judge is allowed to see the law as part of a coherent whole, the more leeway he seems to have to (re)construct the law as seems fit to him. The issue of coherence is then just a way to discuss the degree in which legal decision makers are bound by the law and in particular by legislation and case law.[58] I do not want to take sides in this discussion. Instead I want to show that different positions in it can be accommodated in a framework of integrated coherentism.

A normative system can be coherent in content, but also in origin.[59] A typical example of a system that is coherent in content is utilitarianism. There is one ultimate moral principle, to strive for the greatest happiness of the greatest number, and the rest of morality is merely elaboration of this ultimate principle on the basis of factual circumstances. A typical example of a system that is coherent in origin is a legal system as envisaged by Kelsen. There is one basic norm, which determines who are competent to make new law. The law consists precisely of those norms that are made on the basis of this basic norm. What these norms are is again a matter of factual circumstances. The law is determined by which persons or organizations that were directly or indirectly made competent by the basic norm and by what they decided. The crucial difference with systems that are coherent in content is that in systems that cohere in origin, the contents of

[58] It is not unusual to reframe this old discussion in fashionable terminology. It is for instance also possible to formulate it as a discussion about whether the law, or legal reasoning, is defeasible. The more defeasibility, the more leeway for legal decision makers, it might seem. See in this connection for instance Bayón 2001. In my opinion, this connection between defeasibility and freedom of legal decision making is just as misguided as the connection between judicial freedom and broad coherentism.

[59] This distinction was inspired by Kelsen's distinction between static and dynamic normative systems. See Kelsen 1960, 198.

the law are, at least partly, determined by new decisions. These decisions need not be coherent in content, as Raz correctly pointed out.[60]

A system that is coherent in origin need not be coherent in content and vice versa. If this is what Raz wanted to point out with his argument, he was right. It seems, however, that he meant to say more in two respects. He apparently adduced the point of several sources of law as an argument against coherentism in general. That would be a mistake, because the coherence of law might in Kelsenian vein be constructed as coherence of origin instead of content. Moreover, he seems to assume that the fact that the contents of legal decisions need not be coherent implies that the content of the law is not coherent. That would only follow on a view according to which the contents of the law are by and large determined by the contents of these decisions. Such a view is certainly defendable, but depends on a particular view how the law is to be constructed. An alternative view would be that the contents of these decisions should be considered as input to a process of (re)construction that leads to a system that is coherent in content.[61]

Let us take a step back from the discussion about the proper role of authoritative legal decisions in the construction of the law. The position one takes in this discussion will be influenced by one's views about the relation between the law and state authorities and between law and politics.[62] Integrated coherentism requires that ones politico-philosophical views in this respect cohere with one's views about the room for legal decision makers to make the law coherent in content. It is compatible with different views about the proper kind of coherence (origin or content) in constructing the law. It is even compatible with rejection of both content and origin coherentism concerning the law.

The discussion whether the law should be constructed coherently and if so on the basis of content or origin, deals with another form of coherentism than the broad version defended in this chapter. It puts stronger demands on the way law should be constructed than merely that the theory of the law is part of a coherent acceptance set as defined in section 5. In fact it is a discussion whether the law should be coherent in the strict sense and what

[60] It may intuitively be attractive to say that a system that is based on one single starting point, no matter whether it concerns content or origin, is for that reason coherent. However, the presence of a single starting point has more to do with simplicity than with coherence. I do not see why a system with several starting points that are suitably delimited in their sphere of operation should be less coherent. In this chapter, I will not develop this issue any further, however.

[61] Cf. Peczenik and Hage 2000.

[62] The discussion about coherentism between Dworkin and Raz clearly illustrates this point.

such strict coherence should look like (criteria for strict coherence). All answers in this discussion, including non-coherentist ones, are compatible with integrated coherentism, at least if one makes one's position in this discussion broadly coherent with one's other views, including especially those concerning the relation between the law and politics.

Raz's argument against constitutive coherentism seems to presuppose that the discussion about legal coherence can be treated independently of the rest of one's acceptance set. By treating the discussion as a local one, it seems that the argument based on different sources of authority can be adduced as an argument against coherentism in general. By taking a step back from this discussion and seeing it in the context of a broader discussion (a step toward global coherence), one can see why Raz's argument does not affect broad coherentism, but only one specific and local variant of strict coherentism, namely *content* coherence of the *law*.

10. CONCLUSION

The foundation of this chapter is a theory of justification. According to this theory a justification is an argument why something should be accepted rather than rejected, given what else is accepted. Coherentism as a theory about justification is, given the above definition necessarily internalist. Justification is justification of acceptances on the basis of acceptances and perceptive states. There are two variants of internalist theories of justification, namely foundationalist and coherentist, which seem to be mutually exclusive and jointly exhaustive. On closer inspection, however, it turns out that foundationalism can be incorporated in a broad form of coherentism and that broad coherentism is the single convincing theory of justification as it was defined. This broad form of coherentism merely holds that acceptances are to be justified by means of other acceptances and that none of them is a priori justified.

If one takes a closer look at the way coherentism functions in the practice of justification, it turns out that there is a natural tendency of acceptance sets to become more and more comprehensive, but also that a completely coherent set is an unattainable ideal. The pursuit of coherence functions in practice as a correctional device by means of which incoherent acceptance sets can be improved. The unattainable ideal is a completely coherent set, a set that contains all acceptances that it should contain according to the standards contained in the set itself and does not contain anything that according to these standards should be rejected.

A broadly coherent acceptance set may, but need not, demand that some part of it, for instance the part dealing with the law, is coherent in a more strict way. If it does, this demand should be broadly coherent with the rest of the complete acceptance set. Moreover, the standards for this more strict form of coherence should also cohere in the broad sense with the rest of the acceptance set as a whole. Theories as those of Dworkin (law as integrity) and Raz (merely a limited role for local coherence) can be seen as competing precisely on the issue whether and how the law should be constructed as coherent in a more strict sense. An argument that it should not be constructed as strictly coherent, should not be interpreted as an argument against broad coherentism, however. It is rather the case that such an argument should fit in a broadly coherent theory of everything.

Chapter 3

REASON-BASED LOGIC

1. REASON-BASED LOGIC AS AN EXTENSION OF PREDICATE LOGIC

'Traditional' logics such as propositional and predicate logic sketch a one-sided picture of what goes on in real life reasoning. Arguments of the form 'modus ponens' have a dominant place in this picture. Other forms of reasoning, such as arguments based on balancing reasons, can only with some ingenuity be modeled in these logics. Since such arguments play an important role both in the law and in practical reasoning in general, it is attractive to have a logic at one's disposal that can deal with arguments based on the balancing of reasons for and against a conclusion.[1] *Reason-based Logic* (RBL) is such a logic.

One way to look at RBL is as a logic that is dedicated to practical (legal and moral) reasoning, with special attention to entities that function prominently in these types of reasoning, such as rules and principles. This is the way in which RBL was introduced in my *Reasoning with Rules*.[2] Another way to look at it, which I want to emphasize here, is as an extension of predicate logic. First order predicate logic is included in RBL and RBL adds to predicate logic a number of linguistic elements and axioms that deal with reasons. The 'philosophy' behind this second way of looking at RBL is

[1] Cf. Alexy 2003.

[2] The version of Reason-based Logic described in Hage 1996 can for the present purposes be equated with the version of *Reasoning with Rules*.

that there is no sharp boundary between logic and domain theory[3] and that a logic can be extended or limited, according to one's needs. RBL is in this view an extension of predicate logic that can be used for special reasoning tasks, in particular tasks in the fields of moral and legal reasoning. Moreover, according to this same philosophy, RBL can naturally be extended to deal with kinds of reasoning that cannot well be handled by its more limited versions. This means that there is no canonical version of RBL. The central function of RBL is to deal with reasons and their logic, but otherwise the logic can be limited to a core or extended to an apparatus with baroque pretensions. According to this same philosophy, logics are to some extent determined by the domains in which they are used, which means that their nature is to some extent established on the basis of empirical research. Logic is not completely a priori and logical theories are subject to changes that result from new insights, although not to the same degree as empirical theories.[4] The logic presented in this chapter is a relatively limited version of RBL that deals with contributive reasons and rules, but not with, for instance, goals and deontic predicates. In chapter 4 the logic is elaborated to deal with the comparison of alternatives.

The picture below represents the relation of the different versions of RBL to, on the one hand, predicate logic and, on the other hand, domain knowledge. The borderlines between basic RBL, an extended version of RBL, and domain knowledge are dotted to indicate that they are not very sharp.

In *Reasoning with Rules*, RBL was presented as a non-monotonic logic. However, I have come to think that the non-monotonic aspect of RBL is less central to it than I originally thought it was. Therefore I will deviate from my earlier approach here and mainly discuss a monotonic version of RBL. First I will present the language of RBL, by adding some extensions to the language of predicate logic and formulate a number of axioms that come on top of those of predicate logic. These axioms describe the logical behavior of the extensions to the language. There is no need for special RBL inference rules, because the inference rules of predicate logic suffice for the monotonic version of RBL.

[3] This theme is elaborated in Hage 2001 (LL).

[4] Partly for this reason, the version of RBL developed here differs in a number of aspects from the versions developed in earlier work, in particular in Hage 1996 and Hage 1997 (RwR), which - by the way – also differed amongst each others. The different versions of RBL reflect (slightly) different views of the logic of legal reasoning.

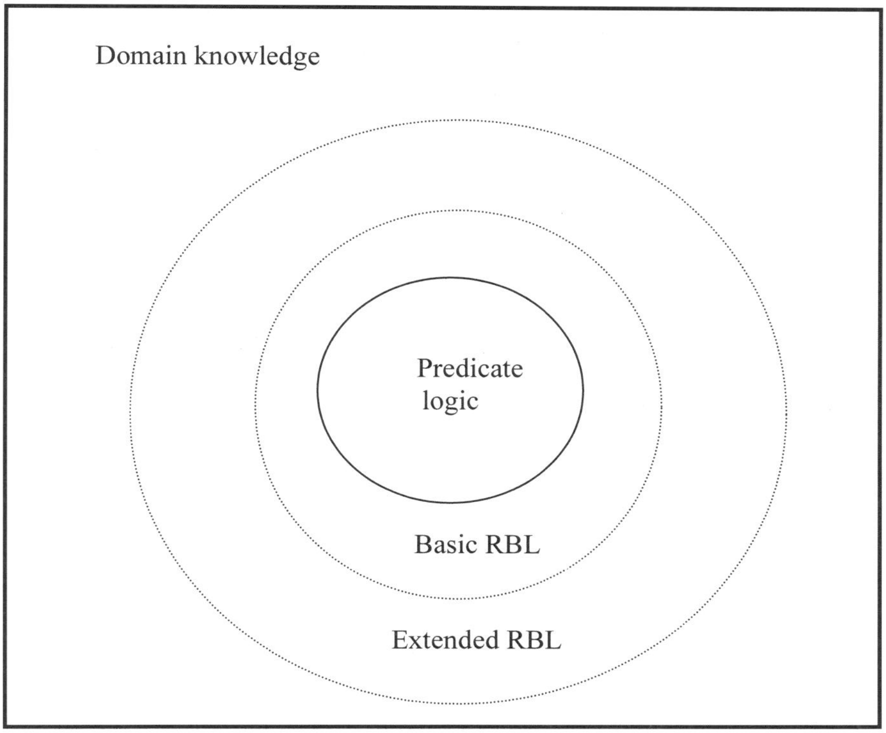

There will be no 'real' inference rules for the non-monotonic version of RBL. The idea behind the introduction of inference rules is that they allow constructive proof steps that lead from a set of premises to valid consequences from these premises. If a logic is non-monotonic, this constructive approach does not work, because non-monotonic logics base the logical consequences of a theory on the theory as a whole and what follows from it (exceptions should not be *derivable*). This means that the very idea behind the use of inference rules does not work for a non-monotonic logic, unless the purpose of derivation is changed. If the conclusions from a set of premises need not be true anymore given the truth of the premises, there is room for constructive inferences rules. However, the application of these rules does not lead to necessarily true conclusions, but to conclusions that are justified relative to the premises.[5] In section 7 I will give an informal indication of the different ways in which justification and justification defeat can be modeled.

[5] See chapter 1, section 2.3.

I will not describe a formal semantics for RBL. The semantics for the monotonic version of RBL would be the semantics of predicate logic with the additional constraint on the interpretation function that all the axioms of RBL (which define the special language elements) should be true in all models.[6]

In the following sections, I will first discuss a basic version of RBL (sections 2 to 4). Then follows an important extension to this basic version, namely a way in which RBL can deal with (legal) rules. In an appendix I will indicate the main differences between the present version of RBL and the version described in *Reasoning with Rules*.

2. THE LANGUAGE AND ONTOLOGY OF RBL

One important way in which RBL is an extension of predicate logic is that its language is an extension of the language of predicate logic. The extension consists mainly in a number of dedicated predicates, relations and function expressions that play a logical role in RBL. In this and the following sections, these extensions are introduced in an explanatory context. The first conventions concern a specification of the language for predicate logic that will be used:

- All constants for relations, predicates and sentences without a subject-predicate structure start with an uppercase letter.
- All function expressions, individual constants and variables start with a lowercase letter, except individual constants and variables that denote or stand for states of affairs. These start with an asterisk (*), followed by a lowercase letter.
- The constants ∀, ∃, ~, &, ∨, → and ≡ stand for the universal and the existential quantifier, negation, conjunction, inclusive disjunction, the material conditional and equivalence, respectively.
- Variables are *italicized*.

2.1 Sentences, states of affairs and facts

RBL presupposes a rich ontology. Next to the 'ordinary' physical things, it also assumes several kinds of immaterial entities, including states of affairs and sets of individuals (in particular sets of reasons). States of affairs are

[6] I have presented a semantics for RBL along these lines in Hage 1997 (RwR), 223f. See also chapter 5 in which model theoretic semantics is given for rule logic.

what is expressed by sentences with truth values.[7] For instance, the sentence 'It's raining' expresses the state of affairs that it is raining. Some states of affairs *obtain* in the world; these are called *facts*. A sentence that expresses a fact is *true*. False sentences express *non-facts*, namely states of affairs that do not obtain.

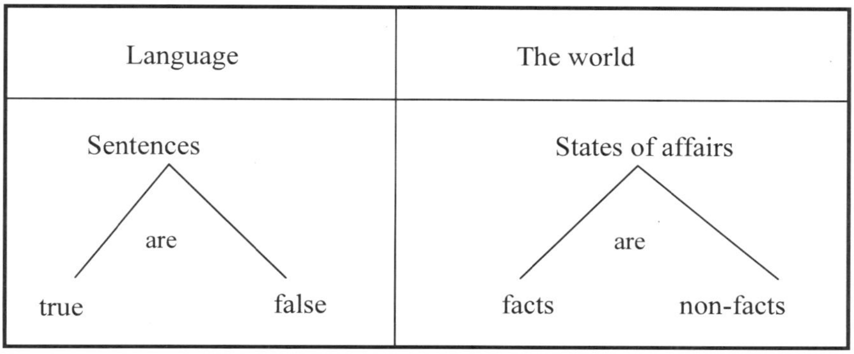

In most declarative sentences it is possible to distinguish one or more terms that denote entities in the world. Next to these terms there will be a predicate expression by means of which something is said about the denoted entities. For instance, in the sentence 'John walks' the word 'John' denotes John and the word 'walks' is used to say something about John. In the sentence 'Jane gave the book to the father of Mary' the expressions 'Jane', 'the book', 'Mary' and 'the father of Mary' denote, while 'gave … to' indicates the relation between the three denoted entities. The expression 'the father of Mary' is a so-called function expression. It denotes the father of Mary, but it also contains the term 'Mary', which denotes Mary.

Logicians call the entities about which a sentence is (logical) *individuals* and the expressions used to refer to them *terms*. Terms should be distinguished from full sentences. Sentences have truth values, terms not. Even function expressions, although they contain a reference to an individual, have no truth values. The reason for this is clear: function expressions denote individuals; they do not state anything. So, there is, from a logical point of view, a fundamental difference between sentences and

[7] The clause 'with truth values' is meant to exclude non-descriptive sentences, such as commands, but also descriptive sentences that have terms on referential positions that have no object of reference, such as 'The king of France is bald'. Cf. Strawson 1950.

terms. Sentences have truth values; they do not denote.[8] Terms, on the contrary, have no truth values, but denote.

By assuming the existence of states of affairs, this clear distinction between on the one hand terms and individuals and on the other hand sentences and truth values, is blurred somewhat. Sentences no longer only have truth values, they can also be treated as terms that denote the states of affairs expressed by them. This happens, for instance, in sentences that deal with so-called propositional attitudes, such as 'Mary beliefs that John walks'. Taken by itself, the sentence 'John walks' has, in its quality of a sentence, a truth value, but as content of a propositional attitude it denotes the state of affairs that John walks.[9]

In RBL the distinction between the two functions of sentences is made explicit by syntactical means. The state of affairs expressed by sentence `S` is *typically* denoted by the term `*s`. In this way, a term that typically denotes a state of affairs indicates by its internal structure which state of affairs it denotes. Since states of affairs are logical individuals, they can also, non-typically, be denoted by other terms. For instance, the state of affairs `*it's_raining` can also be denoted by the term `*a`. In that case the sentence `*a = *it's_raining` is true.[10] In general the following translation holds between sentences and the terms that typically denote the states of affairs expressed by these sentences:

- If `S` is a sentence and if `s` is the string that results if all the uppercase letters at the beginnings of the atomic sentences that are part of `S` are replaced by lowercase sentences, then `*s` typically denotes the state of affairs expressed by `S`.
- If `*s` is a term typically denoting a state of affairs and `S` is the sentence that results if all the lowercase letters at the beginnings of terms denoting atomic states of affairs are replaced by uppercase letters, then `S` expresses the state of affairs denoted by `*s`.

8 Frege, however, assumed that sentences denoted truth values. Cf. Geach and Black 1980, 62f.

9 There are lots of complications here. For instance, the sentence 'Mary beliefs that John walks' might be interpreted as expressing a three-place relation between Mary, John and walking, rather than as a two-place relation between Mary and the state of affairs that John walks. See in this connection Quine 1956. For the present purposes I only assume that it is sometimes useful to treat sentences as denoting states of affairs and that sentences in their function of terms should syntactically be distinguished both from sentences in their function of expressing states of affairs and from terms which do not express states of affairs.

10 The convention that terms denoting states of affairs start with an asterisk is also used for terms and variables that non-typically denote states of affairs.

Some examples:

- If `It's_raining` expresses that it is raining, then `*it's_raining` denotes the state of affairs that it is raining.
- `*it's_raining & there_is_a_storm` denotes the (compound) state of affairs that it is raining and there is a storm.
- `*gives(john, mary, wedding_ring)` denotes the state of affairs that John gives Mary the wedding ring.
- `*∀x(thief(x) → punishable(x))` denotes the state of affairs that all thieves are punishable.
- `*obtains_longer(*age(john, 6), *age(kim, 6))` denotes the state of affairs that John has been 6 years old during a longer time than Kim has been 6 years old. Notice that this state of affairs is about other states of affairs, which is reflected in the re-occurrence of asterisks in the term denoting the state of affairs.
- If `*rescued(tarzan, father_of(jane))` denotes the state of affairs that Tarzan rescued Jane's father, then `Rescued(tarzan, father_of(jane))` expresses this same state of affairs. Notice that the first letter of the function constant `father_of` remains lowercase in the sentence, because it is part of a term.

Variables for states of affairs start with an asterisk too. For instance, the following sentence expresses that Jane believes everything that John believes:

`∀*s(Believes(john, *s) → Believes(jane, *s))`

If a sentence is true, the state of affairs expressed by it obtains.[11] RBL has in this connection a dedicated predicate constant `Obtains/1`, which operates on terms that denote states of affairs. The relation between the truth of a sentence and the state of affairs expressed by this sentence is rendered by the following axiom of RBL[12]:

Definition obtains:

`∀*s(Obtains(*s)) ≡ S`

[11] Notice that the obtaining of a state of affairs is not identical to its existence. The point of having states of affairs next to facts is that it is possible for a state of affairs not to obtain. The state of affairs that does not obtain must 'exist', because otherwise the statement that a particular state of affairs does not obtain would have a non-referring subject term. Those who object against this extended use of the notion of existence may consider to replace this notion in connection with non-obtaining states of affairs with the Meinongian notion of subsistence. Cf. Lambert 1995.

[12] This definition presupposes that the state of affairs *s is typically denoted by the term '*s'.

2.2 Abstract states of affairs

States of affairs are either abstract or concrete. An abstract state of affairs can be realized (instantiated) in different ways. For instance, the abstract state of affairs that somebody gives something to somebody else is realized by the concrete state of affairs that John gives Mary a book, but also by the concrete state of affairs that Russia gives the Netherlands a collection of drawings.

Abstract states of affairs are denoted by a term for a state of affairs that contains at least one free variable. For instance:

- `*rescued(tarzan, y)` denotes the abstract state of affairs that Tarzan rescued somebody. Notice that this expression is a term that denotes a state of affairs. In particular it should be distinguished from the sentence `(∃y)Rescued(tarzan, y)`, which expresses (rather than denotes) the concrete state of affairs that there is a person that Tarzan rescued and from the term `*(∃y)Rescued(tarzan, y)`, which denotes this last concrete state of affairs.
- `*gives(x, a_book, y) & (x ≠ y)` denotes the abstract state of affairs that somebody gives a book to somebody else.

Concrete states of affairs can instantiate abstract ones. A concrete state of affairs `*s` instantiates an abstract state of affairs `*s'`, if and only if there is some substitution i such that the term that typically denotes `*s` is the result of uniformly substituting all variables in the term that typically denotes `*s'` by constants according to i.

In this connection the function `instantiation/2` is relevant. The first parameter of this function is an abstract state of affairs and the second an instantiation. Its value is the concrete state of affairs that results from replacing all free variables in the first parameter by constants according to the instantiation of the second parameter. For instance:

`*s = instantiation(*s', i)`

Whereas states of affairs can be both abstract and concrete, facts are always concrete.

3. REASONS

3.1 Kinds of reasons

The central notion in Reason-based Logic is that of a reason. There are several kinds of reasons, which have in common that they are facts which are relevant for other facts. These other facts are called the *conclusions* of these reasons.[13]

One use of 'reason' occurs in sentences like 'The reason why the string broke was that it was under a too high tension'. In this context a reason is relevant for its consequence because it is a cause. Next to reasons in the sense of causes, it is possible to distinguish between reasons why something is the case (constitutive reasons), reasons to believe and reasons for action. For instance, the facts that P owns so many dollars and that nobody else owns more, are (together) the constitutive reason why P *is* the richest person in the world. That X read in the newspaper that P owns so many dollars is a reason for X *to believe* that P is the richest person in the world. That P is the richest person in the world is a reason for journalist Y *to interview* him. Unlike reasons in the sense of causes, constitutive reasons, reasons to believe and reasons for action[14] can be adduced in arguments which lead to the conclusion that something is the case (constitutive reasons and reasons to believe) or that something should (not) be done. In this way reasons can play a role in reasoning. By mentioning facts that are reasons, one can reason for a particular conclusion.

RBL deals with constitutive reasons, reasons why something else is the case. This 'something else' can take many different forms. There can, for instance, be constitutive reasons why:

1. John is a thief
2. Thieves are punishable.
3. Victoria is smarter than Isis
4. This is a beautiful picture
5. It is reasonable to believe that the butler killed Lord Hard
6. Jane ought to repay her loan.
7. One should give to the poor.

[13] Reasons are discussed extensively in chapter 2 of Hage 1997 (RwR).

[14] I take reasons for action here in the sense of guiding (or normative) reasons, not that of motivating (or explanatory) reasons. For the difference between these two kinds of reasons, see Raz 1975, 15f., Smith 1994, 94f. and Redondo 1999, 1f.

As the examples 5-7 illustrate, constitutive reasons include reasons to believe and reasons to act. By treating reasoning about what to do as reasoning about what ought to be done, or what should be done and by treating reasoning about beliefs as reasoning about what it is rational to believe, these kinds of reasoning can be dealt with by means of RBL.

3.2 Decisive reasons

RBL distinguishes between *contributive reasons* and *decisive reasons*. Decisive reasons are concrete reasons[15] that determine their conclusions. If a decisive reason for a conclusion obtains, the conclusion also obtains. For instance, the facts that there are two horses and four cows and no other animals are together a decisive reason why there are six animals.

It makes no sense to weigh decisive reasons against other reasons. If there are contributing reasons that collide with a decisive reason, the decisive reason wins by definition, so there is no need for weighing. If there would be colliding decisive reasons, this would make their conclusions incompatible. Since there cannot be incompatible states of affairs, there cannot be colliding decisive reasons either, and sentences that express colliding decisive reasons are therefore inconsistent.

RBL has a dedicated predicate constant `Dr/2` to express that a fact is a decisive reason for some other fact. For instance, the following sentence expresses that the fact that John is older than Derek is a decisive reason why Derek is younger than John:

```
Dr(*older_than(john, derek),
  *younger_than(derek, john))
```

Because all concrete reasons are facts, it holds as an axiom of RBL that:

Decisive reason is fact:

```
∀*a(∃*b(Dr(*a,*b)) → Obtains(*a))
```

Moreover, because a decisive reason guarantees that its conclusion obtains, it holds as an axiom that:

Conclusion decisive reason obtains:

```
∀*b(∃*a(Dr(*a, *b)) → Obtains(*b))
```

From these two axioms and the definition of the predicate `Obtains` it follows that

```
∀*a*b(Dr(*a,*b) → (A & B))
```

[15] The distinction between concrete and abstract reasons is discussed in section 3.5.

3.3 Contributive reasons

Just like decisive reasons, contributive reasons are concrete reasons. In opposition to decisive reasons, contributing reasons do not determine their conclusions by themselves. There can both be contributing reasons that plead for, and contributive reasons that plead against a particular conclusion. Assuming that there are no relevant decisive reasons, it is the set of *all* contributing reasons concerning a particular conclusion, both the reasons pro and con, which determines whether the conclusion holds.

For instance, if somebody breaks the window of somebody else's house in order to save a child from the house that is burning, the question whether this behavior is lawful depends on the relative weight of two contributing reasons. One reason is that the behavior was an infringement of somebody else's property. This reason pleads *against* the lawfulness of the behavior. The other reason is that the act was necessary to save a human life. This reason pleads *for* the lawfulness of the behavior. If these two are all the relevant reasons, they determine together whether the behavior in question was lawful.

RBL has a dedicated predicate constant `Cr/2` to express that some fact is a contributive reason for some state of affairs. For instance the following sentence expresses that the fact that John is a thief is a contributive reason why he is punishable:

```
Cr(*thief(john), *punishable(john))
```

There can also be contributive reasons against a conclusion. To avoid the necessity of a special predicate constant for the expression of contributive reasons against a conclusion, these *con-reasons* are expressed as if they were *pro-reasons* for the negated conclusion. For instance, the fact that the weather report predicted sunshine is a contributive reason against the conclusion that it will be raining:

```
Cr(*prediction_sunshine, *~rain)
```

Because all concrete reasons are facts, it holds as an axiom of RBL that:

Contributive reason is fact:

$\forall *a(\exists *b(\mathrm{Cr}(*a, *b)) \rightarrow \mathrm{Obtains}(*a))$

3.4 Weighing contributive reasons

A crucial aspect of contributive reasons is that *they have to be weighed* (or *balanced*; I use these words interchangeably) against contributive reasons pleading in a different direction. To avoid misunderstandings, I want to stress that this weighing is not a psychological process. It does not even need to be accompanied by a psychological process. From a logical point of view it does not matter what goes on psychologically. The only thing that matters is that somehow information must be available that indicates which set of reasons outweighs the other set. This information needs not be available in advance to guide a decision making process; it can also be the outcome of such a process. From the logical point of view, information about the relative weights of the sets of reasons is merely a presupposition of a valid argument in which a conclusion is drawn from contributive reasons for and/or against this conclusion.

To formalize this kind of argument, RBL needs function constants to denote sets of reasons. The function constant `r⁺/1` denotes the set of all contributive reasons pleading for a conclusion, while `r⁻/1` denotes the set of all contributive reasons pleading against a conclusion.

If `*a` denotes a concrete state of affairs, then `r⁺(*a)` denotes the set of all contributive reasons pleading for *a:

Definition set of contributive pro-reasons:

`r⁺(*a)= {*s | Cr(*s,*a) is true}.`

`r⁻(*a)` denotes the set of all contributive reasons pleading against *a:

Definition set of contributive con-reasons:

`r⁻(*a)= {*s | Cr(*s, *~a) is true}.`

For example, `r⁺(*rain)` denotes the set of all reasons why there will be rain, while `r⁻(*rain)` denotes the set of all reasons why there will not be rain.

Contributive reasons need to be weighed. Psychologically, this weighing often boils down to taking a decision which set of reasons outweighs the other set. However, as already stressed, from the logical point of view the only thing that matters is that information about the relative weight is needed as a premise in a valid argument.

The information which set of reasons outweighs the other set is expressed in so-called *weighing knowledge*. RBL has a dedicated relation constant to express weighing knowledge: $>_{\texttt{conclusion}}/2$, which operates on sets of reasons. For instance, the sentence

$\{\texttt{*prediction\_sunshine}\} >_{\texttt{*rain}} \{\texttt{*cloudy, rain\_yesterday}\}$

expresses that the set containing the single reason that sunshine was predicted by the weather forecast, with regard to the conclusion that it will rain, outweighs the set containing the reasons that it is cloudy and that it rained yesterday. Often the subscript of the `Outweighs`-predicate is superfluous because the context makes it clear for and against which conclusion the reasons plead. Then the subscript is omitted.

If the contributive reasons pleading for a conclusion outweigh the contributive reasons pleading against it and there is no decisive reason against this conclusion, the conclusion holds:

Outweighing pro-reasons:

$$\forall *s(r^{+}(*s) > r^{-}(*s) \ \& \ \sim\exists *x(\mathrm{Dr}(*x, *\sim s)) \rightarrow \mathrm{Obtains}(*s))$$

If the contributive reasons pleading against a conclusion outweigh the contributive reasons pleading for it and there is no decisive reason for this conclusion, the negation of the conclusion holds:

Outweighing con-reasons:

$$\forall *s(r^{-}(*s) > r^{+}(*s) \ \& \ \sim\exists *x(\mathrm{Dr}(*x, *s)) \rightarrow \mathrm{Obtains}(*\sim s))$$

3.5 Abstract reasons

If a particular fact is a reason for some conclusion, similar facts will normally be reasons for similar conclusions. Suppose, for instance, that the fact that the weather forecast this morning predicted that it will rain this afternoon is a reason to assume that it will rain this afternoon. In that case, the fact that in the morning the weather forecast predicts rain will in general be a reason to assume that it will rain that afternoon. Similarly, being a thief is an abstract contributive reason for being punishable, because the fact that some particular person is a thief, is normally a contributive reason why this person is punishable. This phenomenon, that concrete reasons are instantiations of more abstract ones, has become known, especially in ethical theory, as the universalizability of reasons.[16] [17]

In RBL, all contributive reasons are assumed to be instantiations of abstract reasons.[18] RBL has a dedicated predicate constant `Ar/2` to express that some abstract state of affairs is an abstract contributive reason for some

[16] Cf. Hare 1981, 107f.

[17] In my 1996 and 1997 (RwR), I hardly paid attention to abstract reasons and instead wrote about (the validity of) principles. This may have created the wrong impression that these principles would possess some kind of independent status apart from that some type of fact tends to be a reason for some type of conclusion. (e.g. as so-called 'legal principles'.) To avoid this impression, I discuss this topic here in terms of abstract and concrete reasons.

[18] Decisive reasons are considered to be instantiations of rules, about which more in section 7

(other abstract) state of affairs. For instance the following sentence expresses that being a thief is a contributive reason for being punishable:

```
Ar(*thief(x), *punishable(x))
```

The universalizability of contributive reasons is expressed by the following axiom of RBL:

Universalizability of contributive reasons:

```
∀*r,*c(Cr(*r,*c) →
  ∃*r',*c',i(Ar(*r',*c') &
   *r = Instantiation(*r',i) &
    *c = Instantiation(*c',i)))
```

If some fact instantiates an abstract contributive reason for some abstract conclusion, this fact is normally a concrete contributive reason for the relevant instantiation of the abstract conclusion. For instance, if

```
P(a) & Ar(*p(x), *c(x))
```

is true, then

```
Cr(*p(a), *c(a))
```

will *normally* also be true.

Sometimes instantiations of abstract reasons are not contributive reasons. This happens in particular if there is a reason why a kind of fact that is normally a reason for some conclusion should not be taken into consideration. Take the following example: John has promised his mother in law to visit her on Sunday afternoon. After the promise, he finds out that there will be a unique concert by his favorite artist that same afternoon. Normally, John would have to balance the obligation stemming from the promise against his desire to visit the concert in order to decide what he should do. John happens to find out, however, that his mother in law will have other visitors too that afternoon, while she gave him the impression that she would be all alone if John would not visit her. Knowing this, John does not feel bound by his promise anymore and there is no need to balance reasons in order to decide what to do. The only relevant reason is the unique concert and because of this reason John decides to visit the concert.[19]

[19] Another example is that some contributive reason for a conclusion has already been taken into account in an applicable rule. Then the rule determines which conclusion holds and the contributive reasons that went into the rule are not taken into consideration anymore.

This topic is discussed extensively by Raz (1975, 35f.) under the heading of 'exclusionary reasons' and by Schauer (1991, 38f.) under the heading of 'entrenchment'. See also Hage 1997 (RwR), 110f. about rules and 'replacing reasons'.

When the step from an abstract reason to its instantiation as contributive reason is not valid, we say that the abstract reason is *excluded*. The language of RBL uses the predicate constant `Excluded/2` to express such an exclusion. Its parameters are the relevant instantiations of the abstract reason and its conclusion. For instance, if `Ar(*p(x), *c(x))` is true, `Excluded(*p(a), *c(a))` expresses the lack of relevance of this abstract reason for the instantiation of *x* by `a`. If an abstract reason is not excluded, its instantiation by a state of affairs that obtains is a contributive reason:

Instantiation of abstract reason:
Let `*ip` be an instantiation of `*p` under some substitution of the variables in `*p` and let `*ic` be the instantiation of `*c` under the same substitution of variables. Then it holds that:

```
Ar(*p, *c) & Ip & ~Excluded(*ip, *ic) → Cr(*ip, *ic)
```

The exclusion of abstract reasons illustrates a phenomenon that occurs more often, namely that states of affairs of a particular type only obtain if there are special reasons for it. Such abstract states of affairs may be called *reason-based states of affairs*.[20] In general an abstract state of affairs is reason-based if its instantiations can only obtain if either there is a decisive reason for it, or the contributive reasons pleading for it outweigh the contributive reasons pleading against it:

Definition reason-based states of affairs:
Let `*as` denote an abstract state of affairs and let `*s` be an instantiation of `*as`. Then it holds that

```
∀*as(Reason_based(*as) ≡
   ∀*s(Obtains(*s) →
      ∃*r(Dr(*r, *s)) ∨ r⁺(*s) > r⁻(*s)))
```

[20] Another example of a reason-based state of affairs is the state of affairs that an actor is obligated to perform some kind of behavior. There are no obligations without reasons. Cf. Hare 1963, 30f.

Exclusion reason-based:
The abstract state of affairs that an abstract reason is excluded is reason-based.

Reason-based(*excluded(*r, *c))

3.6 Weighing knowledge

Weighing knowledge is in general contingent, but there are two exceptions concerning the empty set. An empty set of reasons is normally[21] outweighed by any non-empty set and it does not outweigh any set. This is expressed by the following axioms of RBL:

Empty set of con-reasons in principle outweighed by non-empty set of pro-reasons:

$\forall *c(\mathrm{Ar}(*r^-(*c) = \emptyset \ \& \ r^+(*c) \neq \emptyset, \ *r^+(*c) > r^-(*c)))$

Empty set of pro-reasons in principle outweighed by non-empty set of con-reasons:

$\forall *c(\mathrm{Ar}(*r^+(*c) = \emptyset \ \& \ r^-(*c) \neq \emptyset, \ *r^-(*c) > r^+(*c)))$

Empty set of con-reasons does not outweigh any set of pro-reasons:

$\forall *c(*r^-(*c) = \emptyset \rightarrow \sim(r^-(*c) > r^+(*c)))$

Empty set of pro-reasons does not outweigh any set of con-reasons:

$\forall *c(*r^+(*c) = \emptyset \rightarrow \sim(r^+(*c) > r^-(*c)))$

4. REASONING WITH CONTRIBUTIVE REASONS

To give the reader an impression how reasoning with contributive reasons can be modeled in RBL, I will give an example. One of the more common situations when contributive reasons must be weighed is when deciding what to do. Suppose, for instance, that a public prosecutor is wondering whether she should prosecute Johnny, who is a thief, but also a minor of only 12

[21] There are situations where single reasons do not allow the derivation of the conclusions for which they plead. For instance the fact that the suspect has a motive for committing the murder is a reason to believe that this suspect was the murderer. However, this reason is in itself not sufficient, even in the absence of counter reasons, to draw the conclusion that the suspect committed the murder. Situations like these are exceptions to the principle that any non-empty set of reasons outweighs the empty set.

years old. The fact that Johnny is a thief is a reason to prosecute, but the fact that he is only 12 years old is a reason not to prosecute. This dilemma can be formalized in terms of contributive reasons for and against the conclusion that the public prosecutor should prosecute Johnny:

```
Should_do(public-prosecutor, prosecute(johnny))
```

In this connection two abstract reasons play a role. One is that the public prosecutor should prosecute thieves:

```
Ar(*thief(x),
  *should_do(public-prosecutor, prosecute(x)))
```

The other relevant abstract reason is that the public prosecutor should not prosecute minors:

```
Ar(*minor(x),
  *~should_do(public-prosecutor, prosecute(x)))
```

It both holds that

```
Thief(johnny)
```

and that

```
Minor(johnny).
```

Moreover, I will assume that the two relevant abstraction reasons are not excluded in this case[22]:

```
~Excluded(*thief(johnny),
  *should_do(public-prosecutor, prosecute(johnny)))

~Excluded(*minor(johnny),
  *~Should_do(public-prosecutor, prosecute(johnny)))
```

Given this information, it is possible to derive that

```
Cr(*thief(johnny),
  *should_do(public-prosecutor, prosecute(johnny)))

Cr(*minor(johnny),
  *~should_do(public-prosecutor, prosecute(johnny)))
```

To balance the reasons for and against the conclusion that Johnny should be prosecuted, all relevant reasons should be available. What we have in fact is

[22] This assumption receives further discussion in section 7

one reason for prosecuting and one reason against. We must assume that there are no other relevant reasons[23]:

```
r+(*should_do(public-prosecutor, prosecute(johnny)) =
   {*thief(Johnny)})

r-(*should_do(public-prosecutor, prosecute(johnny)) =
   {*minor(Johnny)})
```

To draw a conclusion whether the public prosecutor should prosecute, information is needed about the relative weight of these sets of reasons:

```
{*minor(johnny)} > {*thief(johnny)}
```

The (set consisting of the single) fact that Johnny is a minor outweighs the (set consisting of the single) fact that he is a thief (regarding the conclusion that he should be prosecuted).

Given this information, it is possible to derive that the contributive reasons pleading against prosecution outweigh the contributive reasons for prosecution:

```
r-(*should_do(public-prosecutor,prosecute(johnny))) >
    r+(*should_do(public-
prosecutor,prosecute(johnny)))
```

To continue, we also need the information that there are no decisive reasons concerning the issue whether the public prosecutor should prosecute Johnny[24]:

```
~∃*r(Dr(*r,
   *should_do(public-prosecutor,prosecute(johnny))))

~∃*r(Dr(*r,
    *~should_do(public-prosecutor,prosecute(johnny))))
```

Given the absence of decisive reasons, this leads to the conclusion that the public prosecutor should not prosecute Johnny:

```
~Should_do(public-prosecutor, prosecute(johnny))
```

23 Again, this assumption receives further discussion in section 7
24 This assumption receives further discussion in section 7 too.

5. RULES

The way RBL deals with rules does not imply a theory about the logical behavior legal rules. It is best considered as a modeling tool that is more or less suitable to deal with legal phenomena. To what extent legal rules should be modeled as RBL-rules depends on how one sees the logical behavior of legal rules. However, the logic of rules in RBL was inspired by a particular view of rules as authoritative decisions about how to deal with types of cases. This view has been exposed by Raz, who stated that mandatory rules are exclusionary reasons and by Schauer, who considers rules to be 'entrenched generalizations'.[25]

5.1 The representation of rules in RBL

Rules are usually assumed to have a conditional structure. They consist of a condition part and a conclusion part and the point of rules is that if their conditions are satisfied, their conclusions obtain. In RBL rules are treated as logical individuals, denoted by a function expression. (Something like: the rule with conditions `a` and conclusion `b`.) RBL has a dedicated function constant that has rules as its values: ⇒`/2`. Both the first parameter and the second parameter are terms denoting abstract states of affairs. The first parameter stands for the rule conditions, the second for the rule conclusion. For instance, the following term denotes the rule that thieves are punishable:

`*thief(`*x*`)` ⇒ `*punishable(`*x*`)`

[25] Raz 1975, 73f. and Schauer 1991, 47.

Rules are not considered to be sentences (nor, in general, linguistic entities) and in RBL the expressions that denote rules are used as terms. As a consequence, rules have no truth values. But like ordinary entities, they exist in time, have characteristics and stand in relations to other entities, including other rules. Moreover, it is possible to formulate rules about rules. The following term denotes the rule (of recognition) that rules made by the legislator are valid[26]:

```
*rule(r) & made_by(the_legislator, r) ⇒ *valid(r)
```

5.2 Rule application

Traditionally reasoning with rules is analyzed as arguments of the form Modus Ponens: If the rule conditions are satisfied, the rule conclusion follows from the rule and the description of the facts. Lawyers sometimes say that the facts of a case are subsumed under the rule and for this reason the traditional model may be called the *subsumption model*.[27]

The logic of rule application under RBL is somewhat different from this subsumption model. If a rule applies (is applied) to a case, the conclusion of the rule holds for this case. In terms of reasons, we might say that the application of a rule to a case is a decisive reason for the rule conclusion to hold. For instance the application to John of the rule that thieves are punishable is a decisive reason for the conclusion that John is punishable.

RBL has a dedicated predicate constant to express that a rule applies: `Applies/1`. The parameter of `Applies` is the relevant instantiation of the rule formulation. For instance, the following sentence expresses that the rule that thieves are punishable applies (John is a thief):

```
Applies(*thief(john) ⇒ *punishable(john))
```

[26] One of the major advantages of treating rules as logical individuals is that this facilitates reference to rules and consequently the representation of rules about rules. When rules are treated as full sentences, rules about rules should be formulated in a meta-language, with all complications that result from that. For instance, the following argument is hard to formalise in most logical languages:

- All rules made by the legislator are valid
- The legislator made the rule that thieves are punishable
- John is a thief
- Therefore: John is punishable

[27] This subsumption model of rule application is correct if rules are interpreted as case-legal consequence pairs, as described in chapter 1, section 3.2. The logic of rule application that is described here, is better adapted to rules as analyzed in chapter 6, section 8.

When a rule applies to a case, this is a decisive reason for the rule's conclusion:

Consequence applies:

`∀*iconds,*iconc(Dr(*applies(*iconds ⇒ *iconc),`
`*iconc))`

Obviously, only existing rules can apply to a case. In RBL the predicate `Valid/1` is used to represent the validity of rules, which is taken to be the way in which rules exist. The parameter of this predicate is a term denoting an (uninstantiated) rule. For instance:

`Valid(*thief(x) ⇒ *punishable(x))`

Because application presupposes validity, the following holds:

Application presupposes validity:
Let `ir` denote an instantiation of the rule `r`. Then

`∀r,ir(Applies(ir) → Valid(r))`

Whether a rule applies, depends in RBL normally[28] on a balance of reasons for and against application. In particular, a rule can only apply if the reasons for application outweigh the reasons against application. This means that whether the rule that thieves are punishable applies, depends on both the contributive reasons pleading for application and the contributive reasons against application and therefore *not merely on whether the rule conditions are satisfied*. In this respect the RBL-model of rule application differs considerably from the traditional subsumption model. The crucial differences between the RBL-model and the subsumption model are that the RBL-model

1. allows reasons against the application of a rule that collide with reasons for application and
2. does not state which facts count as reasons for application nor as reasons against application.

Although the reason-based model as described above does not specify which facts count as reasons for and against application of a rule, there are very plausible ways to elaborate this model. I will discuss three of such elaborations, which will be formalized as RBL-axioms.

[28] An exception, dealt with in section 5.3 is that there is a decisive reason against application of the rule.

5.3 Applicability as a contributive reason to apply a rule

The first extension is the assumption that if the facts of a case satisfy the conditions of a rule – to be abbreviated as that the rule is *applicable* to the case - this is a *contributive* reason why the rule applies.[29] RBL has a dedicated predicate constant to express that a rule is applicable: `Applicable/1`. The parameter of `Applicable` is the instantiation of the rule formulation that is satisfied by the case facts. For instance, the following sentence expresses that the rule that thieves are punishable, is applicable (John is a thief):

`Applicable(*thief(john) ⇒ *punishable(john))`

A rule is applicable to a case, if the facts of this case satisfy the rule conditions. Moreover, it may be debated whether hypothetical, rather than actually existing rules can be applicable. In the present formalization, it is assumed that applicability presupposes validity.

Applicability of a rule:
Let `*iconds` denote an instantiation of the abstract state of affairs `*conds` and let `*iconcl` denote the instantiation of the abstract state of affairs `*concl` under the same substitution. Then it holds that:

$$\forall *iconds, *iconcl(\text{Applicable}(*iconds \Rightarrow *iconcl) \equiv \\ \text{Iconds} \ \& \ \exists *conds, *concl(\text{Valid}(*conds \Rightarrow *concl)))$$

If a rule is applicable, this is a contributive reason why this rule applies:

Applicable and Applies:

$$\forall r(\text{Ar}(*\text{applicable}(r),\ *\text{applies}(r)))$$

This relation between the applicability and the application of a rule looks similar to the subsumption model, but there is a crucial difference, because on the subsumption model, the applicability of the rule is a *decisive* reason to apply the rule. What does this difference mean?

First, it means that even if a rule is applicable, there may still be reasons against applying the rule, reasons which may, but need not, outweigh the applicability of the rule as a reason for application. This might, for instance, be the case if application of the rule would be against the purpose of the rule.

Second, it means that there can be a decisive reason against application of the rule and such a decisive reason by definition brings about that the rule does not apply, even if it is applicable. A decisive reason against application

[29] Notice that the applicability of a rule is not the same as its application. The very point of the RBL-model is that applicability is merely a contributive reason for application.

of an applicable rule obtains normally when another rule with an incompatible conclusion is also applicable to the case and this second rule has precedence over the first rule. For example, in Dutch rental law, the rules concerning the rent of business accommodations are sometimes in conflict with the general rules about rent and if such a conflict occurs, the more specific rules concerning the rent of business accommodations have precedence over the general rules about rent. The applicability of a rule that has precedence over another rule is normally a decisive reason against applying the latter rule.

Third, the first elaboration of the reason-based model of rule application means that if a rule is applicable and there exists therefore a contributive reason for applying the rule and there is no reason, either contributive or decisive, against application, the rule applies and its consequence is attached to the case.[30] *This is the normal situation and in this situation the reason-based model and the subsumption model of rule application lead to the same results.* It is this kind of situation that has lent some plausibility to the subsumption model, because the shortcomings of that model are not relevant in the normal situation.

5.4 Non-applicability as a contributive reason against application

The second elaboration of the reason-based model of rule application is that if a rule is not applicable to a case, this is a contributive reason against applying the rule to this case:

Non-applicability:
`∀r(Ar(*~applicable(r), *~applies(r)))`

At first sight this extension seems superfluous, because if a rule is not applicable, there seems to be no reason for applying it, so the issue of application seems not to arise at all. The relevance of the second extension only becomes clear in the light of the third elaboration of the reason-based model of rule application.

This third elaboration is that there can be other reasons for applying a rule than only the applicability of the rule in question. The reason-based model itself does not specify what these other reasons might be; it only leaves the possibility open that there are other reasons for application. The

[30] This is an application of the principle that any non-empty set of reasons for a conclusion outweighs the empty set of reasons pleading against this conclusion. See section 3.6.

obvious role of this possibility to apply a rule when it is not applicable is to allow *analogous application* of a rule.[31]

If a rule applies to a case, although its conditions are not satisfied by that case, the condition part of the rule remains uninstantiated in the parameter of the Applies-predicate. If, for instance, the rule that thieves are punishable is applied analogously to a case of almost-theft (which is not possible in many legal systems), this can be expressed formally as

`Applies(*thief(x) ⇒ *punishable(john))`

If there is a contributive reason to apply a rule analogously, this reason must be weighed against the non-applicability of the rule and possible other contributive reasons against application. Whether the rule in the end applies, depends on the balance of all contributive reasons pleading for and against application.

When a rule is applicable and nevertheless not applied, it is said that there is an exception to the rule. Exceptions have no special role in the present version of RBL[32], but nevertheless a definition comes in helpful:

Definition rule exception:
`∀r(Exception(r) ≡ Applicable(r) & ~Applies(r))`

If there is an exception to a rule, then either the reasons against application outweigh the reasons for application, or there is a decisive reason against application.

6. REASONING WITH RULES

The RBL model of rule application is somewhat more complicated than the simple deductive model according to which rule application is represented as an argument of the form Modus Ponens. To illustrate the differences, both with the deductive model and with reasoning with principles, I will use more or less the same example as in section 4. The case deals with a thief, Johnny, who is a minor. First I disregard the fact that Johnny is a minor and discuss the simple situation in which the rule that thieves are punishable is applied to Johnny's case. Then I take another rule into consideration, namely the rule

[31] A more extensive discussion of analogous rule application can be found in Verheij and Hage 1994 and in Hage 1997 (RwR), 118f.

[32] In Hage 1996 and 1997 (RwR), I used the Excluded-predicate more or less for what I now call exceptions.

that minors are not punishable and the example becomes an example of rule conflict.

There are two other interesting cases, namely when there are contributive reasons not to apply the rule that thieves are punishable and when this rule might be applied analogously. Because the treatment of these two cases under the present version of RBL is not very different from the ways in which they are treated under RBL as presented in *Reasoning with Rules*, I refer the interested reader to that work.[33]

6.1 Simple rule application

The case at issue can be represented by the following premises:

```
Thief(johnny)
```

and

```
Minor(johnny)}
```

The validity of the rule that thieves are punishable is represented by:

```
Valid(*thief(x) ⇒ *punishable(x))
```

The facts of the case instantiate the rule conditions and as a consequence it is possible to derive that:

```
Applicable(*thief(johnny) ⇒ *punishable(johnny))
```

and

```
Cr(*applicable(*thief(johnny) ⇒ *punishable(johnny)),
    *applies(*thief(johnny) ⇒ *punishable(johnny)))
```

We have derived one contributive reason why the rule that thieves are punishable applies in Johnny's case. What we need, however, are the sets of all reasons pleading for and against application of this rule and weighing knowledge that tells us which one of these sets outweighs the other set. The case facts do not provide us with this information and there are three ways to deal with this 'problem'. One is to be content with the outcome that nothing relevant can be derived. This is obviously the wrong 'solution', because we should be able to derive that Johnny is punishable – at least if we disregard that he is a minor. The second way is to add information to the case, to the effect that there are no reasons why the rule that thieves are punishable

[33] Hage 1997 (RwR), 187f. and 191f.

should not be applied. The third way is to assume this information by default. In both cases, we can derive that:

```
r⁺(*applies(*thief(johnny) ⇒ *punishable(johnny))) =
    {*applicable(*thief(johnny) ⇒ *punishable(johnny))}
```

and

```
r⁻(*applies(*thief(johnny) ⇒ *punishable(johnny))) = ∅
```

Then we can apply the weighing knowledge that, by default, any non-empty set outweighs the empty set of reasons and draw the conclusions that

```
Applies(*thief(johnny) ⇒ *punishable(johnny))
```

and

```
Punishable(johnny)
```

6.2 Rule conflicts

Let us now consider the rule that minors are not punishable, the validity of which is represented by:

```
Valid(*minor(x) ⇒ *~punishable(x))
```

If the rule that thieves are punishable would be disregarded, treatment of this rule analogous to that of the rule that thieves are punishable would lead to the conclusion that Johnny is not punishable. Apparently the joint application to Johnny's case of the rules that thieves are punishable and that minors are not punishable leads to inconsistency.

Rather than accepting this inconsistency, the law deals with such cases by means of conflict rules, that specify which of two conflicting rules precedes. One such conflict rule says that the more specific rule precedes the more general one. Arguably the rule that minors are not punishable is more specific than the rule that thieves are punishable.[34] Instead of representing the argument from specificity to precedence, I will directly represent the precedence of the rule about minors to the rule about thieves in Johnny's case as follows:

[34] Arguably, but not from a logical point of view. One needs legal knowledge to see that the rule about minors is meant to make an exception to general rules about punishability and is *in that sense* more specific. Apparently specificity is a conclusion, rather than a premise of precedence.

```
Precedes(*minor(johnny) ⇒ *~punishable(johnny),
 *thief(johnny) ⇒ *punishable(johnny))
```

Because precedence makes only sense in case of applicable rules (if the rules would not both be applicable, the precedence issue would not arise), the applicability of the precedence relation presupposes the applicability of the rules for which this relation holds. Therefore the following might be added as an axiom to RBL:

Precedence implies applicability:

```
∀*cond1,*conc1,*cond2,*conc2 (
   Precedes(*cond1 ⇒ *conc1, *cond2 ⇒ *conc2) →
    Applicable(*cond1⇒*conc1) &
      Applicable(*cond2 ⇒*conc2))
```

If some rule has precedence over another rule, this is in general a decisive reason[35] not to apply the last rule:

Effect of precedence:

```
∀r1(Valid(*∃r2(precedes(r2, r1)) ⇒ *~applies(r1)))
```

Given this axiom, it follows from the precedence of the rule about minors over the rule about thieves that the rule that thieves are punishable does not apply. As a consequence, only the rule that minors are not punishable applies and the conclusion that follows is that Johnny is not punishable (because he is a minor).

7. REASON-BASED LOGIC AS A NON-MONOTONIC LOGIC

The examples in the sections 4 and 6 illustrated amongst others that many reasoning tasks presuppose information that is often not explicitly available. This includes information about all the reasons for or against a particular conclusion and about possible exceptions to rules. For practical purposes this lack of explicit information is seldom problematic, because we are often willing to draw conclusions in the absence of relevant information and

[35] I represent this decisive reason by means of the validity of a rule, rather than by means of a material conditional. The difference is that there cannot be exceptions to material conditionals, while rules can have exceptions. Notice that this possibility of exceptions does not conflict with the fact that a decisive reason determines its conclusion. If there is an exception to the rule underlying the decisive reason, this means that *there is no decisive reason*, not that the decisive reason does not determine its conclusion.

remain prepared to withdraw these conclusions again if what we assumed to be the case (e.g. that there are no other relevant reasons than the ones already taken into account) turns out to be incorrect. In other words, for practical purposes we work with default assumptions and recognize that the conclusions based on these assumptions are justified only to the extent that these assumptions are correct.

The question how this kind of reasoning 'by default' can be implemented in a system of logic is quite challenging, because there is no obvious way in which we tend to deal with defeasible reasoning. For instance, we can take a default assumption to be true until:

- the contrary was actually proven (possibly according to some specific procedure),
- the contrary is provable (according to some logic),
- the contrary was actually accepted (for whatever reasons),
- or until it is more reasonable to accept the contrary (given as yet unspecified standards for rationality).

All of these different variants would lead to different logics and all of them have at least something to speak for them. Probably all of these variants on defeasibility play a role in actual reasoning practices. In this book I will not attempt to develop one or more of such logical systems. Instead I will confine myself to pointing out that the phenomenon to be captured by a logic for defeasible reasoning is that an acceptance that is justified relative to a particular acceptance set, need not be justified relative to another acceptance set. This means that the notion of validity that is at stake is that of justified acceptance, not that of necessary truth of the conclusion given the truth of the premises. Because the phenomenon to be captured is justification relative to the premises of the argument, the only information that has to be taken into account to judge the acceptability of the conclusion is the information given in the premises. All other information is irrelevant. This means that the only reasons to be taken into account are the reasons that 'follow' from the premises of the argument and that there are no 'unexpected' decisive reasons or contributive reasons. Because the exclusion of abstract reasons is reason-based, the absence of unexpected reasons means that there are no unexpected exclusions either.

Even the insight that there can be no relevant 'unexpected' reasons does not suffice to overcome the problem that reasoning with contributive reasons is global. With this I mean that the conclusions based on the balancing of contributive reasons must be based on *all* the reasons that 'follow' from the premises and not merely some of them. One or more arguments that establish the presence of one or more reasons can by themselves not establish that these reasons are all the relevant reasons. Somehow one must have disposal over the sets of all reasons that 'follow from' the premises and that plead for and against a particular conclusion. Reasoning *within* the formalism of a logical system cannot lead to this kind of information. To obtain all relevant reasons, one must resort to reasoning *about* the logical system.

Instead of trying to develop a metalogical theory about RBL by means of which can be proven which reasons follow according to RBL from a particular set of premises, I propose to deal with the defeasibility of conclusions in RBL by means of a dialectical setting. If somebody shows that there is a reason for a conclusion, the conclusion is provisionally justified. His opponent can take this justification away by producing a reason against this conclusion. The proponent can then either argue for weighing knowledge according to which his reason is stronger than the reason adduced by the opponent, or he can produce additional reasons, etc.[36]

[36] These ideas have been elaborated in Hage e.a. 1994 and in Lodder 1999. See also chapter 9.

APPENDIX

The present version and presentation of RBL differs in several main aspects from the version described in *Reasoning with Rules* (RwR). I will briefly mention them in turn.

RBL AS A FLEXIBLE EXTENSION OF PREDICATE LOGIC

In RwR I presented RBL as a non-monotonic logic that was especially made to deal with rules, principles, goals and reasons. Here I presented RBL as an extension of predicate logic with only one special characteristic, namely that it deals with (reasoning with) reasons. The parts that deal with rules, principles, goals and with the comparison of alternatives (see chapter 4), can be added in the form of additional axioms. This style of presentation reflects the underlying philosophy that there is no clear boundary between pre-formal logic and domain knowledge and that it is a matter of choice which parts of a domain are considered as sufficiently fixed to treat them as logically necessary and incorporate them in a system of formal logic.[37]

RBL AS A MONOTONIC LOGIC

RBL is presented here as a monotonic, even a deductive, logic. The special needs of the legal domain which ask for a non-monotonic logic (see chapter 1, section 4) are delegated to an unspecified dialectical setting within which the present version of RBL can function.[38]

REPLACEMENT OF PRINCIPLES BY ABSTRACT REASONS

In RwR, principles took a central place. If a principle is valid, its instantiated conditions would normally be a (contributive) reason for its instantiated conclusion. In the present version of RBL, principles are replaced by abstract reasons. My main motivation for doing so, is that abstract reasons play an important role in arguments in which alternatives are compared (see chapter 4), and that these abstract reasons could not easily be modeled by means of principles. On the other hand, the operation of principles can well be described in terms of abstract reasons.

[37] Cf. Hage 2001 (LL).
[38] See also chapter 8.

RELATION BETWEEN APPLICABILITY, APPLICATION AND EXCEPTIONS TO RULES

In RwR, a rule would be applicable if its conditions are satisfied and if it is not excluded. Applicability would then be a (contributive) reason why the rule ought to be applied. In the present version of RBL, the technical notion of applicability is used as shorthand for the satisfaction of the rule conditions. The notion of exclusion does not play a role anymore in connection with rules (but it does in connection with abstract reasons). Moreover, in the present version I use the notion of an exception to a rule. Exceptions do not play a real role in reasoning with rules, however. They are merely a name for the phenomenon that a rule is applicable, but nevertheless not applied.

ABSENCE OF DEONTIC NOTIONS

In RwR the logic of rules was described in deontic terms. Applicability would be a reason why the rule *ought to be* applied. For the sake of logical simplicity, I have dropped this deontic element. I still believe, however, that the peculiar phenomena connected to the deontic element of reasoning with rules that I described in RwR (deontic collapse and deontic inflation; see RwR 205) are interesting and in need of explication.

Chapter 4

COMPARING ALTERNATIVES

1. RIGHT AND BETTER

When your old car has broken down and you must decide which brand your new one should be, your main problem will probably not be of a logical nature. Nevertheless, if you have to make a choice between for instance a Mercedes, a Volvo, and a Porsche, the logic underlying the decision is interesting. Each brand of car has advantages and disadvantages, and rational decision making requires a form of balancing these (dis)advantages. The easiest case would be if there were a common scale against which all brands could be measured, because then the only 'logic' involved would be to pick the brand with the highest score. However, when this method is not available, other ways to rationalize the decision making process must be looked for.

Another way to deal with this kind of question is to transform it into the issue whether one should buy a particular brand of car, for instance a Volvo. Logically this would boil down to balancing the reasons for and against buying a Volvo. It is well imaginable that if the question is framed this way, the reasons for buying a Volvo outweigh the reasons against buying one. It is, however, equally well imaginable that in a similar way the reasons for buying a Mercedes outweigh the reasons against buying one, and that the reasons for buying a Porsche outweigh the reasons against buying a Porsche. If the decisions are taken as independent from each other, one might well end up with buying three cars! What we need to know is not merely whether it is *right* to buy a particular brand of car, but whether it is *better* to buy a Mercedes, a Volvo, or a Porsche.

Obviously the decisions are not independent from each other, and one way to deal with this is to treat every reason for buying a Porsche as a reason against buying a Mercedes and against buying a Volvo. On this approach, the mutual dependence between the decisions is taken into account and a decision to buy one particular brand of car is implicitly a decision not to buy a car of one of the other brands.[1]

This is a viable way to deal with the issue, as long as the number of alternatives is limited. If the number of alternatives is large, the situation becomes problematic, because every reason to buy a particular brand of car becomes a reason against buying a car of any other brand. Apart from the complexity this leads to, it is unrealistic, because some reasons to buy a particular brand of car will also be reasons pleading for other brands. For instance, one reason to buy a Mercedes is that it is a safe car. This would also be a reason to buy a Volvo. Another reason to buy a Volvo might be that it fits with the image that one wants to create. This same reason might also plead for buying a Porsche. A reason against buying a Volvo would be that it is less suitable for car racing, and this reason pleads also against buying a Mercedes. And so on …

A more attractive way would be to collect for each brand of car the reasons pleading for it and the reasons pleading against it. Every brand that has stronger reasons pleading against it than for it, can be disregarded. The remaining brands should be compared. If brand A is in some respects better than brand B, and in no respect worse, brand A is preferable to brand B and brand B can be disregarded. It is well possible that this process of elimination leaves only alternative over, and then the decision can be taken purely on basis of qualitative reasoning. If more than one alternative remains, additional decision making is necessary.

2. QUALITATIVE COMPARATIVE REASONING

Suppose that one must choose between buying a Volvo and a Mercedes. A Volvo has two reasons pleading for it, namely that it is a safe car, and that there is a Volvo dealer next door. It has the disadvantage that it is an expansive car. A Mercedes is also expensive, but has (in the example) only one advantage, namely that it is a safe car. There happens to be no Mercedes dealer in the neighborhood. Under these circumstances, everything that pleads for a Mercedes also pleads for a Volvo, but a Volvo has an additional

[1] This approach is taken in Brewka and Gordon 1994 and in Gordon and Karacapilidis 1997.

reason pleading for it, namely the availability of a dealer nearby. Moreover, a Volvo and a Mercedes have the same reason pleading against it, namely that they are expensive. It seems, therefore, that a Volvo is preferable to a Mercedes. This is a reasonable conclusion, even in the absence of any information concerning the (relative) weights of the reasons that the cars are safe, that there is a Volvo dealer nearby, and that the cars are expensive. Analogously it is reasonable to conclude that a Mercedes is preferable to a Porsche, if a Mercedes and a Porsche have the pro-reason in common that they are German cars (for those who like German cars), and they also share the con-reason that they are expensive, while a Porsche has the additional disadvantage that it liable to be stolen. In general alternative A is preferable to alternative B if either:

1. the set of reasons pleading for A is 'stronger' than the set of reasons pleading for B, while the set of reasons pleading against A is not 'stronger' than the set of reasons pleading against B; or
2. the set of reasons pleading against B is 'stronger' than the set of reasons pleading against A, while the set of reasons pleading for B is not 'stronger' than the set of reasons pleading for A; or
3. both 1 and 2 hold.

2.1 Comparing reason sets

Until now, the examples dealt with the qualitative comparison of *alternatives* in terms of reasons pleading for and against them. It is also possible to apply qualitative comparative reasoning to *sets of reasons*. These sets can be compared qualitatively with regard to their relative 'strength'.

In the above characterization of when one alternative is preferable to (better than) another alternative, I placed the word 'stronger' between quotes, because the notion of strength involved needs to be elaborated. In the examples, I implicitly assumed that supersets were 'stronger' than their subsets, but intuitive as this may be at first sight, it ignores that individual reasons have a dimension of weight and that this dimension may interfere with the sheer number of reasons. For instance, if a Volvo is much more expensive than a Mercedes, its additional expensiveness might be more important than the presence of a dealer nearby, with as consequence that a Mercedes might be preferable to a Volvo, even though a Volvo has more reasons pleading for it.

Moreover, the suggestion that the same reason can plead for or against several alternatives is somewhat misleading. It may seem that their safety is a reason that pleads both for buying a Volvo and a Mercedes, but on closer examination the concrete reason for buying a Mercedes is that *a Mercedes* is a safe car, while the reason for buying a Volvo is that *a Volvo* is a safe car. Buying a Mercedes and buying a Volvo share the abstract pro-reason 'being a safe car', but they do not share concrete reasons.[2] However, the actual reasons for buying these cars are the concrete reasons, not the abstract ones. I will deal with this issue in terms of 'similar reasons', concrete reasons that instantiate the same abstract reason. For instance, that a Volvo is a safe car is as reason similar to the reason that a Mercedes is a safe car.

The issue of weights has also to do with this distinction between abstract and concrete reasons, because the weights of reasons are attached to concrete reasons. This means that the concrete reason that a Mercedes is a safe car may have a different weight than the concrete reason that a Volvo is a safe car. One might argue that abstract reasons have a dimension of weight too and that concrete reasons inherit this weight 'by default'. In this case, the reason that a Mercedes is a safe car would by default have the same weight as the reason that a Volvo is safe car. Let us assume that this is correct, but nevertheless it may occur that similar reasons in a concrete case have different weights and that this interferes with the number of reasons pleading for and against alternatives. Only if the weights of the similar reasons are identical, the strengths of two sets of reasons can be compared qualitatively by means of the numbers of their elements.

The last point can also be turned around: if two sets of reasons have similar elements, their relative strengths can be compared on the basis of the weights of their elements. For instance, if both a Volvo and a Mercedes have one reason pleading for them, namely that they are safe cars, the relative strength of these unitary sets is determined by the weights of these reasons. For instance, if a Mercedes is safer than a Volvo, the weight of the reason that a Mercedes is a safe car is by default bigger than the weight of the reason that a Volvo is a safe car. Then the set of reasons consisting of the reason that a Mercedes is a safe car is 'stronger' than the set of reasons consisting of the reason that a Volvo is a safe car.

2.2 Degrees and probabilities

The same example also illustrates a different point, concerning the relation between the 'degree' in which a fact obtains, and the weight of the reason that this fact constitutes. Let me be more concrete. A Mercedes is not just safe or not safe, but it is safe to a certain degree. In a similar way it is expensive to a certain degree. Some kind of facts – one might call them

2 Abstract and concrete reasons are discussed in chapter 3, section 3.5.

'dimensions'[3] – do not just obtain or not obtain, but they obtain in degrees. If such facts are concrete reasons, the weights of these reasons will normally depend on the degree in which these facts obtain. If car A is more expensive than car B, which is also expensive, the fact that car A is expensive is a stronger reason against buying car A than the fact that car B is expensive is a reason against buying car B.

A similar phenomenon occurs in connection with probabilities. Reasons pleading for and against alternatives, especially when these alternatives are lines of action, often will concern the consequences of adopting the alternatives. These consequences have a certain degree of probability and an attractive consequence will lead to a stronger pro-reason if the probability of this consequence is higher. Similarly, an unattractive consequence will lead to a stronger con-reason if the probability of this bad consequence is higher.[4]

As these examples illustrate, the dimension of weight of reasons can be used to reflect two other dimensions of reasons, namely the degree in which the reason-giving facts obtain and the probability of their consequences.

2.3 The 'logic' of comparison

If two 'similar' sets (sets that contain similar reasons) have more than one element, they can only be compared qualitatively on basis of the weights of their reasons if all the differences in weight work in the same direction. Suppose, for instance, that a Volvo and a Porsche have the same pro-reasons, namely their social status and their suitability for holiday purposes. If a Volvo is both better for status and for holiday purposes, the set of pro-reasons for a Volvo is by default stronger than the set of pro-reasons for a Porsche. But if a Volvo is better for holiday purposes, but a Porsche better for social status, the sets of reasons cannot be compared qualitatively, at least not without additional information.[5]

The above can be generalized as follows. Each alternative in a set of alternatives has one (possibly empty) set of reasons pleading for it (the pro-reasons) and one (possibly empty) set of con-reasons. Two alternatives can be compared by pair wise comparing the sets of pro- and con-reasons. For this purpose the relations stronger, weaker and equal are used. A set of reasons can be stronger than, weaker than, or equal to another set. These

[3] This is the term used by Ashley 1990 and 1991. See also Bench-Capon and Rissland 2001, about the relevance of these dimensions.

[4] This is a familiar theme from decision theory. See for instance Keeney and Raiffa 1993, 5f.

[5] However, see section 9.

three relations are mutually exclusive. They are not exhaustive, however, because in some cases sets of reasons cannot be compared qualitatively.

Given these relations between sets of reasons, it is sometimes possible to establish on logical grounds, without additional decision making, which of two alternatives, if any, is preferable to the other. If the two alternatives are called A and B, and the relevant sets of reasons pleading for and against A and B are called Pro-A, pro-B, con-A and con-B, it holds that:

Alternative A should be preferred to (is better than) alternative B (and then B is worse than A) if (but not necessarily only if):

- Pro-A is stronger than pro-B, and con-B is either equal to or stronger than con-A; or
- Pro-A is equal to pro-B, and con-B is stronger than con-A.

Alternative A is equal to alternative B if (but not necessarily only if) both:

- Pro-A is equal to pro-B, and
- Con-A is equal to con-B.

If either

- Pro-A is stronger than pro-B, while con-A is stronger than con-B, or
- Pro-A is weaker than pro-B, while con-A is weaker than con-B, or
- Pro-A and pro-B, or con-A and con-B cannot be compared qualitatively

then it is not possible to establish *on the above mentioned grounds* which alternative is better than the other, or whether the alternatives are equal to each other.[6]

Sometimes it is possible to determine on logical grounds whether a set of reasons is stronger than, weaker than, or equal to another set. In this connection two aspects of these sets are taken into account, namely:

1. whether one set is a proper (similar-)superset of the other, or - in other words - whether one set contains all similar elements of the other and then some more, and
2. whether one or more of the reasons in one of the sets weigh more than the similar reasons in the other set.[7]

[6] It may nevertheless be possible to establish a ranking between alternatives by means of additional decision making.

[7] As described above, the degree in which a reason (a dimension) obtains, is taken into account via the weight of the reason.

A set is stronger than another set (and the other set is weaker) if (but not necessarily only if):

- it is a proper (similar-) superset of the other and none of its reasons weighs less than the similar reason in the other set (if there is such a similar reason); or
- all its elements are similar to elements of the other set and the other way round, none of its reasons weighs less than the similar reason in the other set, and at least one of its reasons weighs more than the similar reason in the other set.

A set is equal to another set if (but not necessarily only if):

- all its elements are similar to elements of the other set and the other way round; and
- all of its reasons have the same weight as the similar reasons in the other set.

2.4 Weak Transitivity

Often two sets of alternatives will not be comparable on logical grounds alone. Then additional decision making is necessary to establish which one is better. For instance, if a Volvo is a safer car then a Porsche, but a Porsche is better for one's social status, and these are the only relevant reasons, it is not possible to establish on logical grounds which brand is better. Suppose that a decision is made that a Volvo is better than a Porsche. Suppose, moreover, that a Mercedes is just as safe as a Volvo and is even better for one's social status, and there are no other relevant reasons, then it is possible to determine on logical grounds that a Mercedes is better than a Volvo. Since it has been established by decision making that a Volvo is preferable to a Porsche, it seems rational to assume that a Mercedes must, in the absence of special circumstances, be better than a Porsche too.

This can be generalized as follows: If alternative A is better than alternative B and if C is better than A, then, *by default*, C will be better than B too. Another way to say this is that the better than relation is *weakly transitive*. The weakness of the transitivity consists in the defeasibility of the application of transitivity. Analogously, the equal to-relation between alternatives is also weakly transitive.

Weak transitivity does not only hold for the better and worse than relation as applied to alternatives, but also for the stronger than, weaker than, and equal to relations as they hold between sets of reasons. For instance, if a Mercedes and a Volvo are both reliable and save cars, while the Volvo is safer, but the Mercedes is more reliable, the sets of pro-reasons for a

Mercedes and a Volvo cannot be compared purely on logical grounds. If it is decided that the pro-reasons for a Mercedes are stronger than those for a Volvo and if it is somehow (maybe on purely logical grounds) established that the pro-reasons for a Lexus are stronger than those for a Mercedes, it can by default be derived that the pro-reasons for a Lexus are stronger than those for a Volvo.

The theory of Qualitative Comparative Reasoning (QCR) formulated above is formalized and made more precise in the sections 8f. But first I will illustrate how QCR can be put to use in three important fields of legal reasoning, namely those of legal theory construction, case based reasoning, and of legal proof.

3. THEORY CONSTRUCTION

In a series of papers[8], culminating in his book *Law's Empire*, Dworkin has developed an intuitively attractive picture of legal theory construction. This picture recognizes three stages in constructing the law.[9] The first stage, the so-called pre-interpretative stage, consists of a preliminary identification of the rules, standards and (generalized) decisions that make up the law. In this connection one might think of an inventory of the rules and standards that can be found in statutes, cases and doctrinal literature. The second, interpretative, stage consists of an identification of the principles (including values and policies) that underlie (in the sense of explain), or are part of the legal phenomena identified in the first stage. The rules etc. identified in the first stage are to be seen as means to realize the principles identified in the second stage, but they are not necessarily the best way to realize them. The purpose of the third, reforming, stage is to formulate (relevant parts of) the set of rules, including (generalized) decisions of cases, that best realizes the principles identified in the second stage.

Abstracting a little from Dworkin's analysis, it is possible to distinguish within a theory of the law three subsets of elements. The first subset consists of the sources of the law, with a prominent place for legislation and for individual cases as decided by the judiciary. The second subset consists of the principles, policies, rights and values that underlie and form the inspiration for the law. And finally there is the law as a set of generic cases,

[8] The papers in question are in particular the paper 'Hard Cases', included in Dworkin 1978 and the papers in part two (Law as interpretation) of Dworkin 1985.

[9] Dworkin 1986, 65f.

with the legal consequences attached to them by the law.[10] Henceforth I will call the first subset the *legal sources*[11], the second subset the *legal goals*[12], and the third set the *normative system*.[13]

In the process of legal theory construction, the legal sources determine a rough first account of the normative system based upon them. This prima facie normative system forms, so to speak, the set of data that the theory must explain. As in empirical theories, it is possible that some of the data must be disregarded if they do not fit in the best theory that can be constructed from them. By means of inductive and abductive reasoning, a set of goals can be identified as underlying the prima facie version of the normative system. Given these goals it is possible to devise a normative system that realizes them best, and given such an ideal normative system, it is possible to devise an adapted set of sources (new legislation or decisions in upcoming cases) by means of which such an ideal normative system is realized.

Ideally, the new sources should deviate as little as possible from the actual sources that function as input to the theory[14], because a good theory of the law should be a theory of the *law as it actually is* and not merely a theory of ideal law. Yet, the goals underlying the law are also part of the law and the normative system should also reflect them. Obviously there is a certain tension here, and it depends on ones legal-philosophical disposition how the balance between the actual sources and the legal system that is ideal in the light of the principles underlying the sources is struck.[15]

Graphically the development of the relations between the three subsets of a legal theory can be depicted as follows:

[10] Cf. the discussion of CLCPs in chapter 1, section 3.2.

[11] Legal sources in the sense intended here are not statutes or case law in general, but individual regulations and individual cases.

[12] Notice that these goals include a broad spectrum of legally relevant entities, such as (human) rights, legal principles and policies. For the present purposes these different entities are all lumped together.

[13] The use of the expression 'normative system' for generic cases with their legal consequences was inspired by the use of this expression in Alchourrón and Bulygin 1971.

[14] Where case law is concerned it is not even possible to change the existing body of case law. Old case law can at most be discarded as outdated by new case law or legislation.

[15] This issue is discussed in more detail in chapter 2, section 8f.

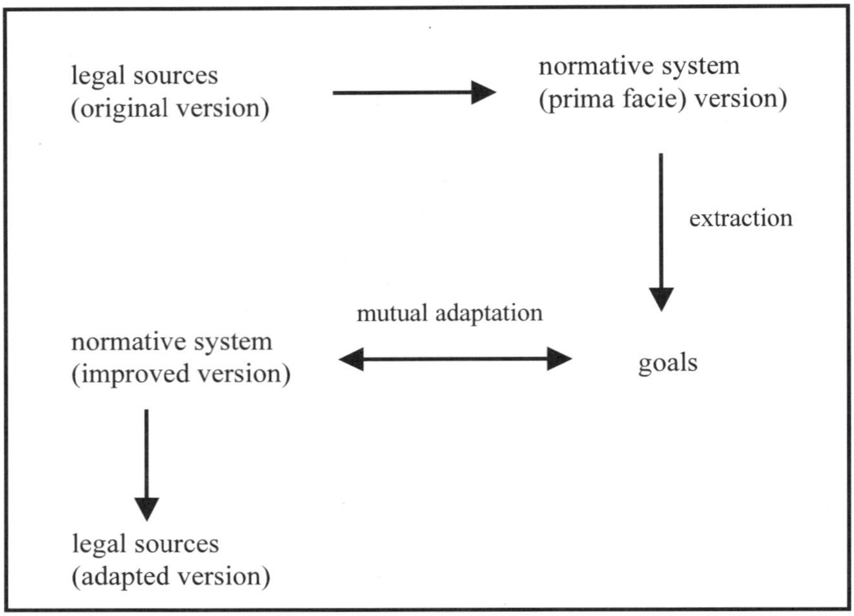

4. COMPARING SOLUTIONS FOR A CASE TYPE

One aspect of the mutual adaptation of sources, principles and normative system is the determination of the ideal normative system, given a particular set of goals. Let us have a look at an extended example that illustrates the reasoning about whether a particular solution for a type of case should be part of the theory (should rationally be accepted) given the set of goals that are included in the theory in question. The example consists of variations on the so-called Lebach-case, which was made familiar by Alexy.[16]

The standard case runs as follows: A person, let us call him E, who was condemned for abduction and subsequent murder of his victim, is released from prison after ten years. A tabloid journal jumps on this news and uses the occasion to publish an article on the dangers of abduction in general. The article is illustrated with a photograph of E just after his release. E attempts to prevent circulation of the journal.

The judge who must decide this case should balance two goals. One goal is the freedom of the press; the other is that one should respect other persons' privacy. Let us assume that the judge decides that in cases like this, privacy protection outweighs freedom of the press.

[16] Alexy 1979 and 1996.

Now let us change the case a little bit by adding the fact that the news that E was to be released was given to the press on the condition that no photographs would be taken. This forms an additional reason against publication of the article, because the effects of the offence are even enlarged by publishing the photo that was illegally taken. As a consequence the decision that it is not allowed to publish photographs of recently released prisoners if the potential publisher undertook the obligation not to take photographs at all, has even more support and is in this sense better.

It is possible to think of another change in the case which leads to a different conclusion. As yet, the question whether the released prisoner objects to the publication has not been taken into consideration yet. It was tacitly assumed that he did object, but this needs not be the case, in particular not if he were to be compensated financially for the publication. A solution to the effect that publication is only allowed with explicit consent of the person concerned, would take a new goal into consideration, namely personal autonomy. This solution would have the pro- and the con-reasons of the first one, presumably with the same weights, but would have an additional pro-reason because it is supported by the goal of autonomy. As a consequence, the last solution is better than the first one.

A similar argument can be made for the case that a potential decision has similar reasons pleading for it as the old decision, but that the reasons pleading against it are a strict subset of the reasons pleading against the old decision. This would be illustrated by the case in which the tabloid journal has contracted with E that no publication of his photograph would be made. It is arguable that the freedom of the press is not infringed by a prohibition that was voluntarily undertaken by the journal. Since the freedom of the press was a reason against the prohibition, the balance of reasons is moved towards the prohibition if this con-reason is taken away. As a consequence the solution that publication is prohibited if the potential publisher has voluntarily undertaken the obligation not to publish, has even stronger support than the original prohibition.

It is possible that a set of reasons is strengthened by adding new reasons to it, but also by strengthening the reasons that occur in it. This is illustrated by the solution that not only forbids publication of the photograph, but also prescribes that the photograph is destroyed. This solution provides better protection of privacy and is therefore better than the simple prohibition.[17]

A similar argument can be made for the case that one or more of the reasons pleading against the new decision are weaker than the corresponding

[17] Arguably, this solution would infringe the property right of the journal, but for the sake of the example, this complication is ignored.

reasons pleading for the old decision. For instance, a solution that allows publication of photographs, as long as the persons on the photographs are not recognizable, makes a smaller infringement on the freedom of the press, while the protection of the privacy remains the same. Such a solution would therefore be better than a mere prohibition of publishing photographs.

The findings from the discussed examples can be summarized in the following global guidelines for the comparison of possible solutions for a type of case:

- A solution for a case that promotes a goal should pro tanto be adopted.
- A solution for a case that detracts from a goal should pro tanto be rejected.
- If a solution for a case promotes the more important goal and detracts from the less important goal, it should pro tanto be adopted.
- If a solution for a case detracts from the more important goal, and promotes the less important goal, it should pro tanto be rejected.
- If a solution for a case promotes a goal to a large extent, this is pro tanto a stronger reason to adopt this solution than if it only minimally promotes the goal.
- If a solution for a case detracts from a goal to a large extent, this is pro tanto a stronger reason to reject this solution than if it only minimally detracts from the goal.

These guidelines demonstrate how the comparison of solutions for case types, given a set of goals, can be constructed in the form of QCR.

5. COMPARING GOAL SETS

It is not only possible to compare competing solutions for a type of cases in the light of a given set of goals, it is also possible to compare competing sets of goals in the light of a given normative system, that is in the light of a set of actual case solutions. To show how this can be done, I must briefly return to the justification of case solutions on the basis of a set of goals.

Given a set of goals, the solution for a particular case will promote some (zero or more) of these goals, detract from some other goals, and will be neutral with regard to the rest. Every goal that the solution for this case promotes, provides a reason for (the rightness) of the solution for this case, while every goal from which the solution detracts, provides a reason against this solution. Whether the solution for a case is right all things considered depends on the balance of these reasons. If the reasons why the solution is right (the pro-reasons) outweigh the reasons why the solution is wrong (the con-reasons), the solution is *right*. If the balance of reasons goes the other direction, the solution is *wrong*. If the reasons pro and con a solution are more or less in balance, the solution of the case is *indifferent*.

To make a decision about the rightness of the solution for a case, we must balance reasons and most often this will just be a matter of decision making. Such decisions about the relative weight of (sets of) reasons are expressed by what I will call *weighing knowledge*. Such weighing knowledge becomes also part of a theory of the law and I will include it in the goal part of the theory.

Improvements in the goal part of a theory can take three forms, then. One is by making modifications in the set of goals by adding new goals or removing old ones. The second is by making changes in the relative importance of the goals and the third consists of changes in the weighing knowledge. The issue to be dealt with is under what conditions one of these changes is an improvement in the goal part of the theory.

Given a set of case solutions, it is possible to compare competing sets of goals (including relative importance and weighing knowledge) qualitatively. Every set of goals qualifies some of the actual case solutions as right, others as indifferent, and the rest as wrong. A set of goals A represents the actual case solutions better than another set B, if at least one of the actual case solutions is better in the light of A than it is in the light of B, while no actual solution is worse in the light of A than it is in the light of B. In other words, a change in the goal part of a theory is an improvement if at least one of the actual case solutions has changed from wrong into indifferent or right, or from indifferent into right, while no actual case decision has moved down one or more categories. If a solution that turns out to be wrong is seen as a reason against the goal set in the light of which this solution is wrong and if a right solution is seen as a reason for the goal set, this way of comparing goal sets qualitatively is an application of the general technique of QCR described above.

6. CASE-BASED REASONING AS A FORM OF COMPARATIVE REASONING

Cases can be used in legal reasoning in several ways. One way, prevalent in the civil law tradition, is to extract a kind of rule from a decided case, and use this rule like other rules stemming from other legal sources. Another way is to use the case as a point of reference for an argument by analogy, or an e contrario argument. By pointing out an analogy between the old case and a new case, it is possible to argue that the decision taken in the old case should also be taken in the new case. Or, by pointing out a crucial difference between the old case and a seemingly similar new case, it is possible to distinguish the cases and to argue that there is no reason to copy the old decision in the new case, or even a reason to take a different decision.

The argument in which an analogy is drawn between two cases, in order to argue that the decision of the one case should be copied in the other case, can well be interpreted as a form of comparative reasoning. The way to do this is to compare cases with respect to their suitability for being decided in a particular way. If the old case was a suitable case for the decision that was actually taken in it, and the new case is just as suitable or even more suitable for such a decision, there is a reason to take this decision in the new case too. If the new case is less suitable than, or not well comparable to, the old case, this reason to decide the new case like the old one is lacking.

An example can illustrate this point. The following case was decided by the Dutch Supreme Court[18]:

Caustic soda case

Employees of a community centre placed a bag with household refuse along the street, in order to be taken away by the cleansing department. Unknown to the employees, the bag held a container with caustic soda. A cleaner put the bag into the dustcart and due to some malfunctioning of the cart's mechanism, part of the caustic soda was swept into his face, as a consequence of which he suffered serious damages to his eyes. The cleaner sued the operator of the community centre for the damages.

Even though the employees of the community centre were unaware of the presence of caustic soda in the bag, their behavior was held to be negligent. The court assumed a duty of care not to place a container with an unknown liquid in it, only protected by a cardboard box and a plastic bag, along the street to be taken away by the cleansing department, unless one has good reasons to assume that the liquid is not dangerous, or keeps the bag under control and warns those who want to handle the bag for its possibly dangerous contents.

Somewhat later the following case was brought before the Supreme Court[19]:

Yew case

Defendant's garden bordered on plaintiff's meadow, on which plaintiff held two horses. The meadow was fenced off by means of netting. Defendant had a heap of waste in his garden, near to plaintiff's meadow, on which he deposited a yew tree. Plaintiff's horses ate from the yew and died as a consequence. (Yew is poisonous for horses.) Plaintiff sues

[18] HR 8-1-1982, NJ 1982, 614.
[19] HR 22-4-1994, NJ 1994, 624.

defendant for the damages. Defendant argued that he neither knew nor should have known that the yew was poisonous for horses.

In both cases the defendant created a dangerous situation to which plaintiff fell victim. Moreover, in both cases the risk for defendant was quite high, while the costs defendant had to make to avoid the danger were low. And, finally, the cases have in common that defendant was not aware of the danger he created. Given these similarities, it is well arguable that the cases should have similar decisions and that therefore defendant in the second case should be held negligent as well.

This is not what actually happened, however. The Dutch Supreme Court held that in the yew-case, defendant was not expected to know that yew is poisonous for horses. Under these circumstances, defendant was not held negligent. Apparently there is a legally relevant difference between - on the one hand - card boxes with an unknown content and - on the other hand - yew. In connection with card boxes with an unknown content, one should assume that the content may be dangerous, unless there are positive indications to the contrary, while in connection with yew, one does not have to take possible risks into account. This difference may be summarized by saying that in the caustic soda case the creation of the danger was recognizable, while in the yew-case the creation of danger was not recognizable. By pointing out this difference, the cases can be distinguished, with the result that in the one case defendant was held negligent, and in the other case he was not held negligent.

Let us look at both lines of argument in terms of comparative reasoning. I will start from the assumption that both cases are similar. In the following table, the columns labeled with a plus-sign contain the reasons that plead for negligence, while the columns labeled with a minus-sign contain the reasons against negligence.

Caustic Soda case			Yew case	
decision: defendant was negligent			decision: ??	
+	-		+	-
defendant created a dangerous situation to which plaintiff fell victim			defendant created a dangerous situation to which plaintiff fell victim	
it was easy and cheap to avoid the danger			it was easy and cheap to avoid the danger	
the potential damages were high			the potential damages were high	
	defendant was not aware that he created a danger			defendant was not aware that he created a danger

Since both cases have similar reasons pleading for and against the decision that defendant was negligent, they are prima facie equally suitable to support this decision. This would be different if the reasons in both cases had different weights. In the absence of evidence why this would be the case, one can work with the default assumption that similar reasons in different cases have equal weights. On this assumption, the cases are *equally suitable* to support the decision that defendant was negligent. In combination with the fact that in the caustic soda case defendant was actually held negligent, this is a reason why defendant should be held negligent in the yew case too.

Suppose, presumably counterfactually, that in the yew case the potential damages were even higher than in the caustic soda case. Then the reason based on the amount of damages in the yew case has a bigger weight than the similar reason in the caustic soda case. On the assumption that all other similar reasons have the same weights in both cases, the Yew case is then even *more suitable* for assuming negligence than the caustic soda case. *A fortiori* it then holds that there is a reason to assume negligence in the yew case, given that there was such a reason in the caustic soda case.

Let us now have a look at the cases from the point of view of the Dutch Supreme Court, who found that in the caustic soda case, defendant should have taken the possible danger into account, while in the yew case this was not the case.

Caustic Soda case			**Yew case**	
decision: defendant was negligent			**decision: ??**	
+	-		+	-
defendant created a dangerous situation to which plaintiff fell victim			defendant created a dangerous situation to which plaintiff fell victim	
it was easy and cheap to avoid the danger			it was easy and cheap to avoid the danger	
the potential damages were high			the potential damages were high	
	defendant was not aware that he created a danger			defendant was not aware that he created a danger
defendant should have been aware that he created a danger				

On this reading of the cases, the caustic soda case has one reason to assume negligence that was lacking in the yew case. In all other respects the cases are similar. On this reading, the caustic soda case is more suitable for the assumption of negligence than the yew case. As a consequence the reason to decide the cases similarly that was present in the first reading of the cases, is lacking on this second reading.

Notice that this reason (based on similarity of the cases) would still be absent if the reasons pro negligence in the yew case would weigh more than the similar reasons in the caustic soda case, for instance because the potential damages were higher in the yew case. Then both cases would in one respect be more suitable for the assumption of negligence than the other case, and that makes comparison by means of qualitative reasoning impossible.[20]

As the above example illustrates, at least some form of case-based reasoning can be interpreted as a special case of QCR, namely as the comparison of cases with respect to their suitability for a particular solution. Obviously, theory construction is also relevant in connection with cases. When case-based reasoning is used as a technique, the solution is kept fixed, and cases are compared with regard to their suitability for *this solution*. When theory construction is used as a technique, a case is kept fixed as a point of reference, while solutions are compared with regard to their suitability for *this case*.

These two techniques can also be combined. Given a particular case, it is possible to compare possible solutions with regard to their suitability. When a particular solution has been adopted as, given the available information, the best one, it is possible to compare actual and hypothetical cases with regard to their suitability for this solution. In this way the best solution for one type of case can be transferred to other cases, thereby broadening the theory of the law that is under construction.

7. QUALITATIVE COMPARATIVE REASONING AND LEGAL PROOF

QCR can also play a role in connection with legal proof. If there are several competing accounts of the facts about a case, these accounts can be compared with regard to how well they fit the evidence. I cannot go deep into this issue here, but let me illustrate it by means of an example.

Suppose that Lord Hard was found in his room, murdered by means of a knife. The butler was seen by John, the Lord's son, when the butler allegedly entered Lord Hard's room at about the estimated time of the killing. Moreover, the butler had a motive to murder Lord Hard, because his Lordship had seduced the butler's daughter Harriet. However, there is also a witness, the gardener, who testifies that the butler was in the garden at the estimated time of the murder.

[20] At least, in the absence of additional relevant information.

There is also another suspect, the chamber maid Dorothea, who also had a motive to murder the Lord, because she had a relationship with the Lord before he fell in love with Harriet, and she suffered severely from jealousy. Dorothea was also seen by John when she allegedly entered Lord Hard's room at about the estimated time of the killing. The problem is, however, that Dorothea has an alibi too in the person of a visiting grocer who delivered some goods to Dorothea at the time in question.

Schematized, the two competing theories have the following reasons pleading for and against them:

The butler committed the murder			**The maid committed the murder**	
+	-		+	-
motive			motive	
witness that the butler had the opportunity			witness that the maid had the opportunity	
	alibi			alibi

At first sight the two theories are equally good. However, if the information is added that the gardener is the butler's brother, the value of the butler's alibi becomes considerably less. It may be assumed that if the gardener is the butler's brother, he may have lied about the presence of the butler in the garden at the estimated time of the murder. In terms of reasons, it may be said that the butler's alibi as a reason against the theory that he committed the murder, has less weight than the alibi of Dorothea, which was based on a more reliable witness. (I represented this in the above schema by giving the butler's alibi a smaller font.) Assuming that the motives of the butler and of Dorothea were equally strong (had the same weight) and that the testimony of John was equally reliable with regard to the butler and the maid, the theories that the butler killed the Lord and that the maid killed him are equally strong in pro-reasons. However, the theory that the butler committed the murder is weaker in con-reasons than its competitor and should therefore be preferred (in the absence of additional information).

Obviously, a similar result can be achieved by removing one of the reasons why the maid committed the murder. If John did not see the maid enter Lord Hard's room, the theory that the maid killed Lord Hard is worse than the theory that the butler killed, even if we disregard the fact that the butler's alibi was provided by his brother.

In general, competing theories about what happened in a concrete case can be compared in terms of sets of reasons pleading for and against them. These reasons will (at least partly) be based on pieces of evidence that must be explained by the theory.

A piece of evidence that is explained provides a pro-reason for the theory. The better the explanation, the stronger the pro-reason. A piece of evidence is explained marginally if its existence is compatible with the theory. It is explained better if its existence is a plausible consequence of the theory, and it is explained still better if the truth of the theory necessitates its presence. For instance, the theory that the butler killed Lord Hard explains the testimony of John, because this theory explains why the butler entered the Lord's room, and thereby that John could see the butler entering the room, and thereby that John testified that he saw the Lord entering this room. The explanation would even be better if the theory entailed that John had to (instead of merely could) see the butler entering the room.

A pro-reason also becomes stronger if the evidence it explains is more reliable. If, for instance, John held a grudge against the butler, the pro-reason for the theory that the butler was the murderer would be weaker than it actually is.[21]

A piece of evidence that the theory fails to explain and that requires explanation[22] provides a con-reason for a theory. The more remarkable the lack of explanation, the stronger the con-reason is. What was written in connection with pro-reasons about the strength of the reasons holds *mutatis mutandis* also for con-reasons.

[21] This can also be accounted for by the observation that there is another explanation for John's testimony which makes the explanation by the theory that the butler killed the Lord less plausible.

[22] Not all facts of a case need to be explained by a theory about a case that is necessarily incomplete. However, some facts of a case are remarkable and seem to require a special explanation. It is these facts that lead to counterevidence for theories that do not explain them.

8. COMPARING SETS OF REASONS

Qualitative comparative reasoning as described above deals with the comparison of sets of reasons. It is therefore possible to use Reason-based Logic (RBL) the logic that was specially developed for reasoning with reasons to formalize the above account QCR. To this purpose, another extension of RBL is developed.[23]

SIMILAR STATES OF AFFAIRS AND REASONS

Sets of reasons that plead for the 'same' conclusion in different cases do not really contain the same reasons, but only reasons that are 'similar' to each other. The following definitions deal with similarity.

<u>Similar states of affairs</u>

Two concrete states of affairs are said to be similar, if and only if they are instantiations of the same abstract state of affairs:

```
∀*s1,*s2(Similar(*s1,*s2) ≡
∃*s3,i1,i2(s1 = instantiation(*s3, i1) &
  *s2 = instantiation(*s3, i2)))
```

Notice that identical states of affairs are also similar states of affairs.

<u>Similar reasons</u>

Analogous to the definition of similar states of affairs, two contributive reasons are similar, if and only if they are both instantiations of the same abstract state of affairs, and their conclusions are also similar states of affairs. Formally:

```
∀*a1,*a2(Similar_reasons(*a1, *a2) ≡
  ∃*c1,*c2(Cr(*a1,*c1) & Cr(*a2,*c2) &
    Similar(*a1,*a2) & Similar(*c1,*c2)))
```

23 In chapter 3 the basic version of RBL was exposed and extended to deal with the logic of rules.

Similar reasonsets

Sets that consist of pair wise similar reasons are called similar reason sets:

```
∀a,b(Similar_reasonsets(a, b) ≡
  ∀*s1((*s1 ∈ a) →
     ∃s2((*s2 ∈ b) & Similar_reasons(s1, s2))) &
  ∀*s2((*s2 ∈ b) →
     ∃s1((*s1 ∈ a) & Similar_reasons(s1, s2))))
```

Similar superset

Given the notion of similar reasons, it is also possible to define the notion of a ‘similar superset’. A similar superset is like a proper superset, with the difference that all elements of the subset must have a *similar* reason in the superset. Formally:

```
∀a,b(Similar_superset(a, b) ≡
   ∀*s2((*s2 ∈ b) →
      ∃*s1((*s1 ∈ a) & Similar_reasons(*s1,*s2))) &
   ∃*s3 ((*s3 ∈ a) &
      ∀*s4((*s4 ∈ b) → ~Similar_reasons(*s4,*s3))))
```

Similar subset

A similar subset is like a proper subset, with the difference that all elements of the subset must have a *similar* reason in the superset. Formally:

```
∀a,b(Similar_subset(a, b) ≡
   ∀*s2((*s2 ∈ a) →
      ∃*s1((*s1 ∈ b) & Similar_reasons(*s1,*s2))) &
   ∃*s3 ((*s3 ∈ b) &
      ∀*s4((*s4 ∈ a) →  ~Similar_reasons(*s4,*s3))))
```

By means of the notions of a similar reason set, a similar superset and a similar subset it is possible to overcome the problems connected with the fact that the sets that must be compared do not contain identical, but merely ‘similar’ reasons.

Another issue that must be dealt with is that of comparing sets of reasons on their weights. The idea to be captured is that if a set contains a similar reason for every reason in the other set, while from each pair of similar reasons, the reason in the former set does not have a smaller weight than its counterpart in the latter set, while at least one reason has a bigger weight than its counterpart, the former set is *stronger in individual weight* than the latter.

Weight

The first step to take in this connection is to define a function that maps reasons on their weights. Let `*r` be a contributive reason for conclusion `*c`. Then `weight(*r,*c)` denotes the weight of `*r` as a contributive reason for `*c`.

Two similar reasons have in principle the same weight. This can be expressed as follows:

```
Ar(*cr(*r1,*c1) & cr(*r2,*c2) &
  similar(*r1,*r2) & similar(*c1,*c2),
    *weight(*r1,*c1) = weight(*r2,*c2))
```

`>/2 and </2`

The second step is to assign a second meaning to the relations `>/2` and `</2`.[24] These relations hold between the weights of two reasons if and only if the weight of the first reason is bigger, respectively smaller than the weight of the second reason. For instance:

```
weight(*r1,*c1) > weight(*r2, *c2).
```

Comparable reason sets

The third step is to define the relation *stronger in individual weight*, which can hold between sets of reasons. These sets must either both contain reasons that plead for a similar conclusion, or reasons that plead against a similar conclusion. I will call such sets *comparable reason sets*.

```
∀s1,s2(Comparable_reasonsets(s1,s2) ≡
  ∃*c((s1 ⊆ r+(*c) & s2 ⊆ r+(*c))) ∨
    (s1 ⊆ r-(*c) & s2 ⊆ r-(*c)))
```

$>_w$/2

The relation *stronger in individual weight* ($>_w$/2)holds between two comparable reason sets, if and only if from the reasons which the two sets *have in common* at least one reason of the first set weighs more than the corresponding reason from the second set, while the opposite is not the case.

[24] The first meaning is that of the outweighs-relation that holds between sets of contributive reasons for and against the same conclusion. Cf. chapter 3, section 3.4.

Formally:

```
∀s1,s2((s1 >w s2) ≡

  Comparable_reasonsets(s1,s2) &

  ∃*r1,*r2,*c1,*c2(
     Cr(*r1, *c1) & (*r1 ∈ s1) &
     Cr(*r2, *c2) & (*r2 ∈ s2) &
     Similar_reasons(*r1, *r2) &
     (weight(*r1,*c1) > weight(*r2,*c2))) &

  ∀*r3,*r4,*c3,*c4(
     Cr(*r3, *c3) & (*r3 ∈ s1) &
     Cr(*r4, *c4) & (*r4 ∈ s2) &
     Similar_reasons(*r3, *r4) →
        ~(weight(*r4,*c4) > weight(*r3,*c3))))
```

$<_w/2$

The relation *weaker in individual weight* ($<_w/2$) holds between two comparable reasonsets, if and only if from the reasons which the two sets *have in common* at least one reason of the first set weighs less than the corresponding reason from the second set, while the opposite is not the case.

Formally:

```
∀s1,s2((s1 <w s2) ≡

  Comparable_reasonsets(s1, s2) &

  ∃*r1,*r2,*c1,*c2(
     Cr(*r1, *c1) & (*r1 ∈ s1) &
     Cr(*r2, *c2) & (*r2 ∈ s2) &
     Similar_reasons(*r1, *r2) &
     (weight(*r1,*c1) < weight(*r2,*c2))) &

  ∀*r3,*r4,*c3,*c4(
     Cr(*r3, *c3) & (*r3 ∈ s1) &
     Cr(*r4, *c4) & (*r4 ∈ s2) &
     Similar_reasons(*r3, *r4) →
        ~(weight(*r4,*c4) < weight(*r3,*c3))))
```

$=_w/2$

The relation *equal in individual weight* ($=_w/2$) holds between two comparable reason sets, if and only if all the reasons which the two sets *have in common* pair wise have equal weights.

Formally:

```
∀s1,s2((s1 =w s2) ≡
  Comparable_reasonsets(s1,s2) &
    ∀*r3,*r4,*c3,*c4(
      Cr(*r3, *c3) & (*r3 ∈ s1) &
      Cr(*r4, *c4) &(*r4 ∈ s2) &
      Similar_reasons(*r3, *r4) →
        (weight(*r4,*c4) = weight(*r3,*c3))))
```

Notice that between two comparable reason sets not necessarily one of the relations 'stronger than', 'weaker than', or 'equal in individual weight' holds.

<u>Stronger</u>

There may be several ways in which one set of reasons is overall stronger than another set. One way is that a set of reasons is stronger than another set *on logical grounds*. In this connection there are (at least) two possibilities:

1. the first set is a similar superset of the second, while the second is equal or weaker in individual weight;
2. the first set is stronger in individual weight than the second, while the second is either a similar reason set of a similar subset of the first.

Formally:

```
∀s1,s2(
  (similar_superset(s1, s2) &
    (s2 <w s1) ∨ (s2 =w s1)) →
  Stronger(s1, s2))

∀s1,s2(
  ((s1 >w s2) &
    similar_reasonset(s2, s1) ∨
      similar_subset(s2, s1)) →
  Stronger(s1, s2))
```

<u>Weaker</u>

There are (at least) two logical grounds on which a set of reasons can overall be weaker than another set, namely:

1. the second set is a similar superset of the first, while the second is equal or stronger in individual weight;
2. the first set is weaker in individual weight than the second, while the first is not a similar superset of the second.

Formally:

```
∀s1,s2(
   (similar_superset(s2, s1) &
      (s2 >w s1) ∨ (s2 =w s1)) →
   Weaker(s1, s2))

∀s1,s2(
   ((s2 >w s1) &
      similar_reasonset(s1, s2) ∨
      similar_subset(s1, s2)) →
   Weaker(s1, s2))
```

Equal

A set of reasons is overall equal to another set on logical grounds if (but not necessarily only if):

1. they are similar sets, and
2. they are equal in individual weight.

Formally:

```
∀s1,s2(((s1 =w s2) & similar_reasonset(s1, s2)) →
   Equal(s1, s2))
```

9. COMPARATIVE REASONING ABOUT SETS OF CONTRIBUTIVE REASONS

The relations of strength between reason sets as defined in the previous section are quite tight, and will not hold very often. It may therefore seem that they are not very useful for practical reasoning purposes. However, it is thinkable that there are other logical grounds for the existence of one of the mentioned relations between reason sets than the ones discussed in section 8. Moreover, and more importantly, there may also be other than logical grounds on which a set is stronger than, weaker than, or equal to another set. In fact, the determination which of two sets is overall stronger or weaker than the other will most often be just a matter of decision making. But also then the following relations should hold:

```
∀s1,s2(Stronger(s1,s2) → ~Weaker(s1,s2))
∀s1,s2(Stronger(s1,s2) → ~Equal(s1,s2))
∀s1,s2(Weaker(s1,s2) → ~Stronger(s1,s2))
∀s1,s2(Weaker(s1,s2) → ~Equal(s1,s2))
∀s1,s2(Equal(s1,s2) → ~Stronger(s1,s2))
∀s1,s2(Equal(s1,s2) → ~Weaker(s1,s2))
```

These relations can be used to reason about the relative strength of reason sets, even when the tight logical relations of the previous section do not exist. And there are even more ways to reason about the relative strength of sets of contributive reasons, based on the transitivity of the stronger than. equal to, and weaker than relations.

If one set of reasons is *on the above mentioned logical grounds* stronger than another set, and this other set is, again *on the above mentioned logical grounds*, stronger than a third set, the first set is stronger than the third set. The same transitivity holds for the equal to and weaker than relations, *to the extent that they exist on the above mentioned logical grounds.*

Because the logical characterizations of these relations as given in the previous section are not definitions, a reason set may be stronger than, equal to, or weaker than another reason set for another reason, for instance just because it was decided to be so. As a consequence, the relations stronger/2, equal/2 and weaker/2 cannot be assumed to be transitive.

Nevertheless it is reasonable to assume that some weaker form of transitivity holds. If set 1 is stronger than set 2 and set 2 is stronger than set 3, then normally set 1 will be stronger than set 3. If set 1 is equal to set 2 and set 2 is equal to set 3, then normally set 1 will be equal to set 3. And, finally if set 1 is weaker than set 2 and set 2 is weaker than set 3, then normally set 1 will be weaker than set 3. This *weak transitivity* can be expressed in terms of abstract reasons as follows:

```
Ar((*stronger(a,b) & stronger(b,c)), *stronger(a,c))
Ar((*equal(a,b) & equal(b,c)), *equal(a,c))
Ar((*weaker(a,b) & weaker(b,c)), *weaker(a,c))
```

Moreover, if a set of contributive reasons *A* is stronger than set *B* and if set *B* is equal to set *C*, then *A* will normally be stronger than *C*:

```
Ar((*stronger(a,b) & equal(b,c)), *stronger(a,c))
```

If a set of contributive reasons *A* is equal to set *B* and if set *B* is stronger than set *C*, then *A* will normally be stronger than *C*:

```
Ar((*equal(a,b) & stronger(b,c)), *stronger(a,c))
```

If a set of contributive reasons *A* is weaker than set *B* and if set *B* is equal to set *C*, then *A* will normally be weaker than *C*:

```
Ar((*weaker(a,b) & equal(b,c)), *weaker(a,c))
```

If a set of contributive reasons *A* is equal to set *B* and if set *B* is weaker than set *C*, then *A* will normally be weaker than *C*:

```
Ar((*equal(a,b) & weaker(b,c)), *weaker(a,c))
```

The practical use of comparative reasoning by means of sets of reasons is greatly increased by:

- the fact that the relations stronger than, weaker than and equal can hold between sets of comparable reasons on other than logical grounds, e.g because of a decision, and
- the existence of (weak) transitivity between these relations, as discussed above.

10. COMPARING ALTERNATIVES

In the qualitative comparison of two alternatives, four sets of reasons are involved:

- the reasons pleading for the first alternative;
- the reasons pleading against the first alternative;
- the reasons pleading for the second alternative;
- the reasons pleading against the second alternative.

In principle, a first alternative is better than a second alternative, if either one of the following situations occurs:

1. The first alternative is stronger in pro-reasons than the second, while it is equal or weaker in the con-reasons.
2. The first alternative is weaker in con-reasons than the second, while it is equal in the pro-reasons.
3. The second alternative is weaker in pro-reasons than the first, while it is equal or stronger in the con-reasons.
4. The second alternative is stronger in con-reasons than the first, while it is equal in the pro-reasons.

Formally[25]:

```
Ar((*stronger(r+(a1), r+(a2)) &
    weaker(r-(a1), r-(a2)) ∨ equal(r-(a1), r-(a2))),
  *better(a1, a2))

Ar((*weaker(r-(a1), r-(a2)) & equal(r+(a1), r+(a2))),
  *better(a1, a2))
```

[25] That the indicated relation only holds in principle is formalized by specifying the connection in terms of an abstract *contributive* reason.

```
Ar((*weaker(r⁺(a2), r⁺(a1)) &
    stronger(r⁻(a2), r⁻(a1)) ∨ equal(r⁻(a2), r⁻(a1))),
  *better(a1, a2))

Ar((*stronger(r⁻(a2), r⁻(a1)) & equal(r⁺(a1), r⁺(a2))),
  *better(a1, a2))
```

Similarly, the first alternative is worse than the second alternative, if either one of the following situations occurs:

1. The first alternative is weaker in pro-reasons than the second, while it is equal or stronger in the con-reasons.
2. The first alternative is stronger in con-reasons than the second, while it is equal in the pro-reasons.
3. The second alternative is stronger in pro-reasons than the first, while it is equal or weaker in the con-reasons.
4. The second alternative is weaker in con-reasons than the first, while it is equal in the pro-reasons.

Formally:

```
Ar((*weaker(r⁺(a1), r⁺(a2)) &
    stronger(r⁻(a1), r⁻(a2)) ∨ equal(r⁻(a1), r⁻(a2))),
  *worse(a1, a2))

Ar((*stronger(r⁻(a1), r⁻(a2)) & equal(r⁺(a1), r⁺(a2))),
  *worse(a1, a2))

Ar((*stronger(r⁺(a2), r⁺(a1)) &
    weaker(r⁻(a2), r⁻(a1)) ∨ equal(r⁻(a2), r⁻(a1))),
  *worse(a1, a2))

Ar((*weaker(r⁻(a2), r⁻(a1)) & equal(r⁺(a1), r⁺(a2))),
   *worse(a1, a2))
```

Finally, the first alternative and the second alternative are equally good, if they are equal both in pro and con reasons:

```
Ar(*equal(r⁺(a1), r⁺(a2)) & equal(r⁻(a1), r⁻(a2)),
   *equally_good(a1,a2)
```

The relations `Better/2`, `Worse/2`, and `Equally_good/2` are mutually exclusive:

```
∀a1,a2(
   Better(a1, a2) →
      ~Worse(a1, a2) & ~Equally_good(a1, a2) &
   Worse(a1, a2) →
```

```
    ~Better(a1, a2) & ~Equally_good(a1, a2) &
  Equally_good(a1, a2) →
    ~Worse(a1, a2) & ~Better(a1, a2))
```

The relation `better/2` cannot be taken to be transitive. However, if alternative A is better than alternative B, while B is better than C, it is at least plausible that A is better than C. This weak transitivity can be expressed as follows:

```
Ar((*better(a,b) & better(b,c)), *better(a,c))
```

Moreover, if alternative A is better than alternative B, while B is just as good as C, it is plausible that A is better than C. The same counts if alternative A is just as good as B, while B is better than C :

```
Ar((*better(a,b) & equally_good(b,c)), *better(a,c))
Ar((*equally_good(a,b) & better(b,c)), *better(a,c))
```

The same holds for the relations `worse/2` and `equally_good/2`:

```
Ar((*worse(a,b) & worse(b,c)), *worse(a,c))
Ar((*worse(a,b) & equally_good(b,c)), *worse(a,c))
Ar((*equally_good(a,b) & worse(b,c)), *worse(a,c))

Ar((*equally_good(a,b) & equally_good(b,c)),
  *equally_good(a,c))
```

The practical use of comparative reasoning by means of sets of reasons is greatly increased by:

- the fact that the relations better, worse and equally_good can hold between alternatives on other than logical grounds, e.g because of a decision, and
- the existence of (weak) transitivity between these relations, as discussed above.

11. APPLICATION OF THE FORMALIZATION

To illustrate the formalization described above, I will formalize the example about the caustic soda case and the yew case where QCR is applied to case based reasoning. I will use the follow abbreviations:

`Ds`: defendant created a dangerous situation to which plaintiff fell victim
`Ec`: it was easy and cheap to avoid the danger
`Dh`: potential damages were high
`Na`: defendant was not aware that he created a danger

N: defendant was negligent

Csds: defendant created a dangerous situation to which plaintiff fell victim in the caustic soda case
Csec: it was easy and cheap to avoid the danger in the caustic soda case
Csdh: potential damages were high in the caustic soda case
Csna: defendant was not aware that he created a danger in the caustic soda case
Csn: defendant was negligent in the caustic soda case

Yds: defendant created a dangerous situation to which plaintiff fell victim in the yew case
Yec: it was easy and cheap to avoid the danger in the yew case
Ydh: the potential damages were high in the yew case
Yna: defendant was not aware that he created a danger in the yew case
Yn: defendant was negligent in the yew case

The following premises are assumed:

```
Csds & Csec & Csdh & Csna & Csn

Yds & Yec & Ydh & Yna

Ar(*ds, *n) & Ar(*ec, *n) & Ar(*dh, *n) & Ar(*na, *~n)

∃i(*csds = instantiation(*ds, i))
∃i(*yds= instantiation(*ds, i))
∃i(*csec = instantiation(*ec, i))
∃i(*yec= instantiation(*ec, i))
∃i(*csdh = instantiation(*dh, i))
∃i(*ydh= instantiation(*dh, i))
∃i(*csna = instantiation(*na, i))
∃i(*yna = instantiation(*na, i))
∃i(*csn= instantiation(*n, i))
∃i(*yn = instantiation(*n, i))
```

Given these premises and the assumption that the derivable reasons are the only ones, it is possible to derive that:

```
r⁺(*csn) = {*csds, *csec, *csdh}
r⁻(*csn) = {*cna}

r⁺(*yn) = {*yds, *yec, *ydh}
r⁻(*yn) = {*yna}

similar_reasonsets(r⁺(*csn), r⁺(*yn))
```

```
similar_reasonsets(r⁻(*csn), r⁻(*yn))
```

$r^+(*csn) =_w r^+(*yn)$
$r^-(*csn) =_w r^-(*yn)$

From these last four sentences it follows that:

```
equal(r⁺(*csn), r⁺(*yn))
equal(r⁻(*csn), r⁻(*yn))
```

and

```
equally_good(*csn, *yn)
```

To draw the additional conclusion that the defendant in the yew case acted negligently, an additional premise is necessary. If in one case a particular decision was taken, and a similar decision in another case would be at least as good (equally good, or even better), this is a reason why this similar decision should be taken in the other case[26]:

```
Ar(
   *decision(c1,*d1) & similar(*d1,*d2) &
    (equally_good(*d1,*d2) v better(*d2,*d1)),
   *sb(decision(c2,*d2))
```

In the caustic soda case the decision was that defendant acted negligently:

```
Decision(caustic_soda_case, *csn)
```

Moreover, the (possible) decisions `*csn` and `*yn` both instantiate `*n` and are therefore similar.

As a consequence it follows that:

```
Cr(*decision(caustic_soda_case, *csn)&
    similar(*csn,*yn) &
      (equally_good(*csn,*yn) v better(*csn,*yn)),
  *sb(decision(yew_case,*yn))
```

There are no contributive reasons why the decision in the yew case should not be `*yn`[27] :

[26] In the formula below, the function expression `sb/1` is used to express that the decision in the second case *should be* `*d2`.

[27] The reason that defendant was not aware that he created a danger was already taken into account in the case comparison and is therefore not taken into consideration anymore (excluded; see chapter 3, section 3.5).

```
r⁻(*sb(decision(yew_case,*yn))= ∅
```

Therefore the reasons why the decision in the yew case should be to assume negligence outweigh the reasons against this conclusion:

```
r⁺(*sb(decision(yew_case,*yn))>
  r⁻(*sb(decision(yew_case,*yn))
```

It therefore follows that in the yew-case negligence should be assumed:

```
Sb(decision(yew_case,*n))
```

12. RELATED RESEARCH

The topics discussed in the previous sections have been dealt with before in the literature on AI and/or law. QCR is the topic of Brewka and Gordon 1994. Presently I am not aware of similar work. Quantitative comparative reasoning is dealt with in Keeney and Raiffa 1993.

Legal theory construction, although not always under that name, is the topic of an enormous amount of literature. Most relevant in connection with the present research is the work of MacCormick 1978, Dworkin 1978 and 1986, McCarty 1997, Bench-Capon and Sartor 2001 and 2003, Hage 2000 (GTE) and 2001 (FLC), Peczenik and Hage 2000 and Hage and Sartor 2003. Concerning the logic of goals (legal principles, human rights), the work of Alexy 1979, 1996, 2000 and 2003 is particularly relevant.

The core texts with regard to case based reasoning in connection with AI and Law are still Ashley 1990, 1991 and 1992. Relevant other work is Rissland and Skalak 1991, Aleven 1997 and 2003, Hage 1997 (RwR), section V,9, and Roth 2003. Prakken and Sartor 1998 do not deal so much with case-based reasoning in the sense used here, but rather with the justification of rules on the basis of cases

Legal proof is also the subject of a tremendous amount of literature, e.g. Twining 1985 and 1991; Edwards 1988; Prakken e.a. 2003. To my knowledge (supported by the expert advice of H. Crombag), comparative reasoning as a tool for reasoning about proof has not been the subject of much discussion yet.

Finally, this chapter, and in particular the second part of it, elaborates the theory of defeasible reasoning in the law, and in particular reason-based logic as a logical tool to deal with it. Relevant related research has been published in, amongst others, Verheij 1996, Prakken and Sartor (eds.) 1997, Hage 1997 (RwR), Prakken 1997, Brozek 2003 and Sartor 2005.

Chapter 5

RULE CONSISTENCY

1. INTRODUCTION

The purpose of this chapter is to introduce and develop a theory about the consistency of rules. There are at least three reasons why the consistency of rules differs from the consistency of descriptive sentences. First, many rules have a conditional structure, but their consistency cannot be treated as the consistency of conditional sentences. Second, consistency of both sentences and rules is relative to a set of constraints that determine which states of affairs can go together. Part of the complications in connection with rule consistency is that rules themselves can function as constraints relative to which consistency has to be judged. And, finally, there can be exceptions to rules that block the application of applicable rules.[1] Such exceptions can prevent threatening rule conflicts, thereby making seemingly inconsistent rules consistent. I will try to develop a theory of rule consistency that takes all these three aspects into account.

To my knowledge, the consistency of rules has not received much attention yet in the literature about legal logic. A topic that may seem related and that has received attention is that of *deontic consistency*, also called normative consistency.[2] This concerns questions as whether there *can* be logical relations between deontic sentences, prescriptions, or norms such as

1 A rule is applicable if its conditions are satisfied. See chapter 3, section 5.3.

2 An overview can be found in Den Haan 1996. See also Hamner Hill 1987 and Lindahl 1992.

that it is forbidden to steal and that it is permitted to steal.[3] Deontic consistency is only to a limited extent related to rule consistency, however, because the rules that can be (in)consistent need not be deontic at all. The question whether the conceptual rules (legal definitions) that surf boards count as vehicles and that nothing without wheels counts as a vehicle, are consistent falls, for instance, under the topic of this paper, but has nothing to do with deontic consistency.

Before continuing the discussion of rule consistency, I want to point out that consistency in connection with rules is not exactly the same phenomenon as consistency in connection with descriptive sentences. The use of the term 'consistency' in connection with rules may therefore give rise to some confusion. However, the phenomenon with which I will deal in this chapter has enough in common with 'ordinary' consistency, to justify the use of the same term. Moreover, an alternative term, such as 'compatibility', may give rise to other misunderstandings. Therefore I will continue to write about rule consistency, under the acknowledgment that the phenomenon for which the term stands is in some respects different than the consistency of descriptive sentences.

2. RULES AS CONDITIONALS

At first sight, it seems attractive to treat rule consistency as a special form of the consistency of conditional sentences. At second sight, this approach turns out to be less attractive, because if the consistency of rules were the same as that of conditional sentences, the following two rules would be consistent:

Thieves are punishable.
Thieves are not punishable.

[3] Deontic consistency is the issue at stake in the discussion of norm conflicts in the sense of Kelsen 1979, of norm contradictions and norm collisions in the sense of Hamner Hill 1987, of norm consistency in the sense of Von Wright 1991, of disaffirmation conflicts and compliance conflicts in the sense of Lindahl 1992, and of norm conflicts in the sense of Ruiter 1997.

Their consistency would follow from the fact that the following sentences are *not* inconsistent[4]:

```
∀x(Thief(x) → Punishable(x))
∀x(Thief(x) → ~Punishable(x))
```

Instead of being inconsistent, these sentences allow the derivation of

```
~∃x(Thief(x))
```

Intuitively, however, a legislator should not be able to remove thieves from the world, merely by issuing both the rules that thieves are punishable and that they are not punishable.

The first conclusion to draw, therefore, is that a theory in which rules are treated like conditional sentences and that considers rule consistency as similar to the consistency of conditional sentences, is unsatisfactory. There is reason to search for a notion of consistency that is especially suited to rules.[5] A relevant intuition in this connection is that the consistency of rules should not depend on whether certain states of affairs obtain. We want, for instance, the rules that thieves are punishable and that they are not punishable to be inconsistent, independent of whether there are thieves. If there are thieves, the two rules can, barring exceptions, be used to derive an inconsistency in the traditional sense, because then it can be derived that these thieves are both punishable and not. However, we want the inconsistency of the rules to be independent of whether there are facts that satisfy their conditions.

Yet, it is important for the consistency of rules whether the rules *can* be applied to the same case. For instance, the rules that thieves are punishable and that non-thieves are not punishable are intuitively consistent. In this connection, three kinds of situations can be distinguished. The first situation, exemplified by the rules that thieves are both punishable and not punishable, is that two rules attach incompatible consequences to the same category of cases. If the one rule is applicable, the other rule is applicable too. The

4 Arguably this formalization in the form of conditional sentences is incorrect. Saying that thieves are punishable is not the same as saying that if somebody is a thief, he is punishable. The rules that thieves are punishable and that they are not punishable are inconsistent because they attach incompatible consequences to the same category of cases. It is well defendable that they are therefore more similar to the statements that John is punishable and that John is not punishable, than to conditional sentences. In the rest of this paper, I will ignore this line of thought, if only because the following treatment of rule consistency is compatible with it.

5 Obviously, the reasons given here why rule consistency is different from the consistency of descriptive sentences are not decisive. It is well possible to treat rule consistency in the same way as consistency of descriptive sentences and take the phenomenon that rules are only inconsistent if certain facts are present, into the bargain.

second situation is when one rule deals with a subset of the cases with which the second rule deals. An example would be the rules:

Thieves are punishable.
Thieves below the age of twelve are not punishable.

The third situation is when two rules deal with sets of cases that are logically unrelated, but which may have members in common. An example would be the rules:

Thieves are punishable.
Minors are not punishable.

In general, the inconsistency of rules depends both on the incompatibility of the conclusions of the rules and on the compatibility of the rule conditions. The basic idea is that a set of rules is inconsistent if it is possible that there is a case in which the conditions of all the rules are satisfied, while the consequences that are attached to this case by these rules are incompatible. This basic idea needs to be refined, however. For instance, the rules that thieves are punishable and that minors are not, are inconsistent, because there is a possible case (a minor thief) to which the rules attach incompatible consequences. If the rule that non-thieves are not punishable is added to these two rules, there cannot be a case anymore that satisfies the conditions of all the three rules, because it is not possible that somebody is both a thief and a non-thief. According to the basic idea about rule consistency, the resulting set of three rules would be consistent, because there cannot be a case anymore in which all three rules are applicable. It should not be possible, however, to make an inconsistent set of rules consistent by adding a rule with conditions that are incompatible with those of one of the rules in the inconsistent set. To avoid this complication, we can require that a set of consistent rules does not contain an inconsistent subset. In other words, a set of rules would be inconsistent if it contains an inconsistent subset.[6] This leads me to the following provisional theory about rule consistency[7]:

The rules in a set s are consistent if and only if it is not so that there are a subset s' of s and a possible case f such that

a. *the facts in f satisfy the conditions of all the rules in s', and*
b. *the rules in s' attach incompatible consequences to f.*

[6] Obviously, the subset need not be a proper one.

[7] For the purpose of this theory, and the improvements upon it that will be proposed, a case is taken to be a set of facts, and a possible case is therefore a set of states of affairs. More about facts, states of affairs and their mutual relations in chapter 3, section 2.

This provisional theory will be developed in the rest of this paper.

3. CONSISTENCY, COMPATIBILITY AND CONSTRAINTS

Descriptive sentences are called *consistent* if it is possible that they are all true. For instance, the sentences 'John is a thief' and 'John is a minor' are consistent, because it is possible that John is both a thief and a minor. In other words, because the *states of affairs* that John is a thief and that he is a minor are *compatible*, the *sentences* that express these states of affairs are *consistent*. The sentences 'John is a thief' and 'John is not a thief' are inconsistent, because it is not possible that John both is and is not a thief. It is the *incompatibility* of the *states of affairs* that John is a thief and that he is not a thief that makes the corresponding *sentences inconsistent*.

Compatibility of states of affairs is always relative to some background of *constraints*.[8] The states of affairs that John is a thief and that he is not a thief are incompatible because of the constraint that a state of affairs cannot both obtain and not obtain. A similar constraint is that the compound state of affairs that John is both a thief *and* a minor can only obtain if *both* the states of affairs that John is a thief and that he is a minor obtain. Such constraints are usually called *logical* constraints. Besides logical constraints, there are also other constraints. There are *physical* constraints that prevent somebody from being in two non-adjacent countries at the same time. It is, for instance, physically impossible that John is both in France and in Austria. *Conceptual* constraints make it impossible that something is both a square and a circle.

This is the occasion to introduce a terminological convention. The expressions 'compatible' and 'incompatible' will be used for *states of affairs* which can, or cannot, go together relative to a set of constraints. The expressions 'consistent' and 'inconsistent' are used for both *descriptive sentences* and for *rules*, with different criteria for sentence and rule consistency.

What is possible depends on the constraints that are taken into account. I will develop this idea by means of the notion of a possible world. A world is a set of states of affairs that is possible relative to some set of constraints c, in the sense that the facts of that world satisfy the constraints in c. This set should be maximal in the sense that it is not possible to add a state of affairs

[8] This point has, in a different context, also been made by Prakken and Sartor 1996, 184/5.

to it without violating a constraint. A state of affairs is possible (can obtain), if there is at least one possible world in which this state of affairs obtains.

Next to the familiar logical and physical constraints, there can also be legal constraints on possible worlds. For instance, it might be the case that in a legally possible world somebody cannot both be a thief and not punishable.[9] As this example shows, the constraints on possible worlds can be the result of human culture. By adopting rules, humans can impose additional constraints on the world in which they live. Rule-based constraints are contingent in the sense that they are absent in a world in which these rules do not exist. But when they exist, they rule out certain combinations of states of affairs as impossible, and necessitate other states of affairs.

It might be objected that rules should not be treated as constraints on possible worlds, but rather as entities that obtain in some possible worlds and are absent from other possible worlds. Only the 'logical' consequences of the existence of rules should be treated as constraints on possible worlds. For instance, it would be a constraint on possible worlds that if the rule that thieves are punishable exists in some of them, in those worlds thieves are punishable. But it would not be a constraint on possible worlds in general that thieves are punishable. This objection presupposes that there is a sharp demarcation between facts that happen to obtain in a world (such as the existence of a rule), and constraints on possible world that hold non-contingently, such as the logical consequences of the existence (validity) of rules. In my opinion there is no such sharp demarcation, however. It is a matter of choice, or at least something that is mind-dependent, what counts as a constraint and what as merely contingent.

Moreover, sometimes the legislator explicitly wants some rules to count as background in order to prevent other rules from being inconsistent. Take for instance the Dutch rules about theft and embezzlement.[10] The Dutch legislator threatens embezzlement with a lesser penalty than theft. If some concrete act would count both as embezzlement and as theft, this would lead to an inconsistency. However, by defining theft and embezzlement such that an act cannot fall under both classifications, the potential inconsistency is avoided. The purpose of these definitions is precisely that they function as constraints on legally possible worlds that make it impossible that an act is both a case of theft and of embezzlement.

Apparently it is possible to treat the existence of a rule as a merely contingent fact in a possible world, but also to consider the effects of a rule

9 Exceptions to rules are disregarded at this stage of the presentation.

10 For the purpose of this example, I ignore some complications in the Dutch law.

as constraints on worlds that one counts as possible. This double role of rules, both as part of a contingent set of rules that is judged on its consistency, and as a constraint on possible worlds that determines what counts as consistent, is explored in the rest of this paper.

If the compatibility of states of affairs is relative to a set of constraints, this has implications for our provisional definition of rule consistency:

The rules in a set s are consistent relative to a set of constraints c if and only if it is not so that there are a subset s' of s and a possible case f such that

- *the states of affairs in f are compatible relative to c,*
- *the states of affairs in f satisfy the conditions of all the rules in s', and*
- *the rules in s' attach consequences to f that are incompatible relative to c.*

Let me illustrate the implications of the above theory of rule consistency by means of some examples.[11]

EXAMPLE 1

```
1: *thief(x) ⇒ *punishable(x)
2: *thief(x) ⇒ *~punishable(x)
```

The rules 1 and 2 are logically inconsistent, because if John is a thief, this fact satisfies the conditions of both rules, while the conclusions of the two are logically incompatible.[12] Notice that the inconsistency of the rules does not depend on the presence of the fact that John is a thief. This fact merely illustrates the inconsistency.

EXAMPLE 2

```
1: *thief(x) ⇒ *punishable(x)
3: *minor(x) ⇒ *~punishable(x)
```

The rules 1 and 3 are logically inconsistent, for the same reasons as in example 1. The inconsistency is illustrated by the case of John who is both a thief and a minor.

[11] In these examples I use the formalism of RBL as exposed in chapter 3.

[12] I assume that it is clear what is logically incompatible. In section 7 the notion of logical compatibility is made more precise. Moreover, in this, and some of the following examples I do not make the logical constraints relative to which the rules are inconsistent explicit. In general, logical constraints are left implicit, while other constraints are explicitly indicated by specifying the set of constraints that, together with the unspecified logical constraints, determine what counts as possible.

EXAMPLE 3

```
1: *thief(x) ⇒ *punishable(x)
4: *minor(x) ⇒ *protected(x)
5: *protected(x) ⇒ *~punishable(x)
```

The rules 1, 4 and 5 are logically inconsistent, because the rules 1 and 5 are logically inconsistent. Rule 4 plays no role in this connection. In example 4 in the next section, we will encounter a related situation in which rule 4 does have a role to play.

4. RULES AS CONSTRAINTS

Rules function as constraints on the worlds in which they exist. In the Netherlands the rule exists that thieves are punishable. As a consequence the states of affairs that somebody is a thief and that he is not punishable are, barring exceptions to the rule, legally incompatible. In a legal system where this rule does not exist, these states of affairs might be compatible. The phenomenon that rules can function as constraints on possible worlds has implications for the above theory of rule consistency. To illustrate this, I will adapt example 3:

EXAMPLE 4

```
1: *thief(x) ⇒ *punishable(x)
4: *minor(x) ⇒ *protected(x)
________________________________________
c = {L; 5: *protected(x) ⇒ *~punishable(x)}
```

The third rule of example 3 is removed from the set of rules that is evaluated with regard to its consistency, and added to the set c of constraints that govern the world in which the rules 1 and 4 are evaluated.[13] The first thing to notice is that the remaining rules 1 and 4 are *logically* consistent. This is not surprising, because the inconsistency of the rules 1, 4 and 5 in example 3 depended on the presence of rule 5. If this rule is removed from the set, the logical consistency is restored.

However, if the removed rule is added to the constraints relative to which consistency is evaluated, the rules 1 and 4 become inconsistent relative to the constraints in c, since these constraints make the states of affairs that

[13] The L in the set of constraints is shorthand for the set of logical constraints that is not mentioned explicitly if the only constraints are those of logic.

somebody is punishable and that he is protected incompatible. So the rules 1 and 4 are logically consistent, but they are inconsistent relative to the set c of constraints which includes rule 5. It makes no difference whether the rules 1, 4 and 5 are evaluated on logical consistency, or that the consistency of the rules 1 and 4 is evaluated relative to constraints including rule 5. Nevertheless there is a difference if only the consistency of the rules 1 and 4 is considered. They are logically consistent, but relative to rule 5 they are inconsistent.
The following two examples aim to illustrate that it makes a difference whether a rule is part of a set that is evaluated on logical consistency, or whether this rule is taken as part of the constraints:

EXAMPLE 5

```
1: *thief(x) ⇒ *punishable(x)
3: *minor(x) ⇒ *~punishable(x)
6: *minor(x) ⇒ *~thief(x)
```

EXAMPLE 6

```
1: *thief(x) ⇒ *punishable(x)
3: *minor(x) ⇒ *~punishable(x)
-----------------------------------
c = {L; 6: *minor(x) ⇒ *~thief(x)}
```

We have seen in example 3 that the rules 1 and 3 are *logically* inconsistent. This logical inconsistency is maintained if rule 6 is added to the rules 1 and 3, because the resulting set still has an inconsistent subset and is therefore inconsistent. However, the situation changes if rule 6 is taken *as one of the constraints* relative to which the consistency of the rules 1 and 3 is evaluated, as in example 6. The conditions of the rules 1 and 3 are not compatible relative to a background that contains rule 6. As a consequence the rules 1 and 3 are consistent *relative to this set of constraints*, even thought the rules 1, 3 and 6 are logically inconsistent. Apparently it makes a difference whether a rule is considered as part of the set that is evaluated with regard to its logical consistency, or as part of the constraints for the consistency of the other rules.

In the examples 3 and 4 it did not matter for the consistency of the set whether rule 5 was part of the set, or part of the background, while in the examples 5 and 6 it makes a difference whether rule 6 is part of the set of evaluated rules, or part of the constraints. This difference can be explained by pointing out that in the examples 5 and 6, rule 6 made the *conditions* of the rules 1 and 2 incompatible, while in the examples 3 and 4, rule 5 made the *conclusions* of the rules 1 and 2 incompatible.

This is an important observation regarding the influence of the constraints on the consistency of a set of rules. The more demanding the background, the more strict are the constraints on the states of affairs that are compatible. If a set of states of affairs is incompatible relative to a certain background c, it will be incompatible relative to any background c' which imposes more constraints than c.[14] The consistency of a set of rules varies positively with the compatibility of the conclusions of these rules and negatively with the compatibility of the rule conditions. As a consequence, the addition of constraints to the background contributes to the consistency of rules by making the rule conditions incompatible. Addition of constraints detracts from the consistency of rules by making the rule conclusions incompatible. The overall effect of adding to the background of constraints on the consistency of a set of rules depends on the conditions and conclusions of the rules that are evaluated with regard to their consistency and the contents of the constraints that are added to the background.

5. CONDITIONLESS RULES

Until now we have only considered conditional rules. There are also rules without conditions, such as the rule that it is forbidden to steal. Such rules share some characteristics with rules that have conditions, in particular that they can have exceptions. For the evaluation of their consistency they seem a little different, however. The first part of the definition of rule consistency, that there is a set of compatible states of affairs that satisfies the conditions of all the rules, seems not to apply to conditionless rules.

This seeming complication can be remedied by treating conditionless rules as rules with conditions that are always satisfied. If conditions that are always satisfied are denoted by the term `*true`, conditionless rules are represented as rules with `*true` as their condition part. For instance[15]:

`*true` $\Rightarrow$ `*od(`x`, ¬steal)`

The rules that it is forbidden to steal (all actors ought to refrain from stealing) and that it is permitted to steal are then easily shown to be

[14] This observation does not hold without restrictions if exception-introducing constraints are added to the background.

[15] In this example, the two place predicates `Od` and `Pd` stand for ought-to-do and permitted-to-do respectively. Their first parameter is a set of actors (all actors if it is a variable), and the second parameter stands for an action type. The operator ¬ maps action types onto action types. The intended interpretation is that `¬action` stands for refraining from `action`.

inconsistent with regard to the constraint that an action is not both forbidden and permitted for the same actors[16]:

EXAMPLE 7

```
7: *true ⇒ *od(x, ¬steal)
8: *true ⇒ *pd(x, steal)
───────────────────────────────────────────
c = {L; ∀x,action(Od(x, ¬action) ≡ ~Pd(x, action))}
```

The inconsistency of the rules 7 and 8 against the background c is illustrated by any case, since any case satisfies the conditions of these two rules.

6. EXCEPTIONS TO RULES

It is not uncommon that two rules in a legal system attach incompatible consequences to a case. For instance, the rule that an owner is allowed to do anything he likes with his property collides with many rules that limit his property right. In such cases, the law contains a *prima facie* rule conflict. Many prima facie rule conflicts turn out not to be *actual* conflicts, because one of the prima facie conflicting rules is left out of application by making an exception to it. Two or more rules are in actual conflict when they *actually* apply to one and the same case, and attach incompatible consequences to this case.

I will again use an example to sharpen our intuitions concerning the effect of exceptions to the consistency of rules. Take the following three rules:

1: Thieves are punishable.
3: Minors are not punishable.
9: In case of minors the rule that thieves are punishable does not apply (there is an exception to it).

These rules interact in case of a minor who is a thief. If rule 9 is left out of consideration, the rules 1 and 3 are inconsistent, because they lead to incompatible results in case of a minor thief. Rule 9 prevents that rule 1 is applied, however, so that the prima facie rule conflict is not actualized.[17]

[16] Some would want to include this constraint into the set of logical constraints. In general the example leaves a lot to be said concerning deontic logic. This is beyond the scope of this paper, however.

[17] A logical account of the operation of exceptions to rules can be found in chapter 3.

Therefore the rules 1 and 3 are in my view consistent with regard to a set of constraints that includes rule 9, although they are logically inconsistent.

The observation that rules can have exceptions which prevent them to come into an actual conflict leads to the following adapted version of the above theory of rule consistency:

> *The rules in a set s are consistent relative to a set of constraints c if and only if it is not so that there are a subset s' of s and a possible case f such that*
>
> a. *the states of affairs in f are compatible relative to c,*
> b. *the states of affairs in f satisfy the conditions of all the rules in s',*
> c. *there is no exception to either one of the rules in s', and*
> d. *the rules in s' attach consequences to f that are incompatible relative to c.*

Exceptions ought to be exceptional. I take this to mean that there are no exceptions to rules unless there are special reasons to make them. Such reasons exist if there are rules that attach the presence of an exception to a rule to the presence of some facts. For instance, if somebody is a minor, the rule that thieves are punishable should not be applied to him. Since this exception holds, in principle, for all minors, there is a rule[18] to the effect that in case of minors there is an exception to (amongst others) the rule that thieves are punishable. In general I propose the theory that there can only be an exception to a rule if there is another rule, the conditions of which are satisfied, and which is not subject to an exception itself, that has as its conclusion that there is an exception to the first mentioned rule.[19] I will call exceptions that do not satisfy the above mentioned constraint *free-floating exceptions*. A good theory about rule exceptions should, in my opinion, make such free-floating exceptions impossible.

The implications of the amendment to the theory of rule consistency which takes exceptions into account are illustrated by the following examples:

[18] Logically the presence of an exception to a rule can be based on any reason against applying this rule that outweighs the rule's applicability and possible other reasons for applying it. (See chapter 3, section 5.4.) From the perspective of a legislator, however, the obvious way to create exceptions to rules is to make rules to this effect.

[19] This theory will be formalized in section 11.

EXAMPLE 8

```
   1: *thief(x) ⇒ *punishable(x)
   3: *minor(x) ⇒ *~punishable(x)
---------------------------------------------
   c = {L; 9: *minor(x) ⇒
      *exception(*thief(x) ⇒ punishable(x))}
```

Rule 9 holds that if somebody is a minor, the rule that thieves are punishable does not apply to him.

The rules 1 and 3 by themselves are logically inconsistent. Inclusion of rule 9 in the background makes that if the conditions of rule 3 are satisfied, there is an exception to rule 1, which takes the rule conflict away. As a consequence, the rules 1 and 3 are consistent relative to a background that contains rule 9.

Exceptions can also make a consistent set of rules inconsistent[20]:

EXAMPLE 9

```
   1: *thief(x) ⇒ *punishable(x)
   3: *minor(x) ⇒ *~punishable(x)
   c = {9: *minor(x) ⇒
          *exception(thief(x) ⇒ *punishable(x));
   10: *second_offender(x) ⇒ *exception(rule-9)}
```

We have seen in example 8 that the rules 1 and 3 are consistent with respect to a set of constraints that includes rule 9. The addition of rule 10 to the background makes that there is no guarantee anymore that, in case of a minor, there is an exception to rule 1. This is illustrated by the case that John is not only a thief and a minor, but also a second offender. In that case there is an exception to rule 9, and presumably no exception to rule 1. This illustrates that if rule 10 is added to the background, there are possible cases in which the conditions of both the rules 1 and 3 are satisfied, and in which these two rules are in actual conflict.

7. MODEL THEORY FOR RULES

Model-theoretic semantics for logic specifies the meanings of logical operators by means of the truth conditions of sentences in which these

[20] In the formalization of rule 10, rule 9 is referred to by 'rule-9'.

operators occur. Since rules are assumed[21] to have no truth values, and therefore also no truth conditions, this kind of semantics does not work for rules. It can, however, be adapted to rules by specifying what must be true if a particular rule exists, or is valid. Because the formalism that I develop for this purpose is strongly inspired by the usual model-theoretic semantics for predicate logic, I call it a model theory for rules.

Model-theoretic semantics traditionally focuses on the truth values of sentences. I will present the model theory in such a way that the emphasis is on the states of affairs that obtain. For instance, a world only counts as logically possible if it satisfies the constraint that if a state of affairs of the form `*a & b` obtains, the states of affairs of the forms `*a` and `*b` must also obtain, and vice versa. There is a close connection between this approach and traditional model-theoretic semantics, because a sentence that expresses a state of affairs is true if and only if this state of affairs obtains. I prefer the emphasis on states of affairs, because the effects of rules are in the first place that states of affairs obtain and only in the second place that particular sentences are true.

A second difference in presentation, in line with the first, is that I do not take the notion of a possible world for granted. Traditionally model-theoretic semantics specifies which relations exist between the truth values of sentences in a possible world. I turn this around and specify which relations between states of affairs must hold for a world to be a possible one. In this way the function of rules as constraints on possible worlds is highlighted. This makes it also easier to distinguish different notions of possibility as defined by different sets of constraints that are taken into account. We have seen in section 4 how variants of rule consistency depend on various notions of possibility and compatibility. These distinctions can be treated more naturally in a theory that focuses on possibility rather than on relations between truth values.

Central in the model theory for rules is the notion of a constraint. Logical constraints hold in general for all *logically possible worlds*. These are, in the present context, the constraints of predicate logic, augmented with one additional constraint that characterizes the logic of rules. Together, these constraints on all logically possible worlds are called the constraints of *Rule Logic*.

I will present the model-theoretic characterization of Rule Logic in two stages. First I disregard that exceptions should be minimized. This leads to a

[21] In the present paper I will not argue for this assumption, except for pointing out that the lack of a truth value immediately follows from the treatment of rules as logical individuals.

relatively simple characterization that has the drawback that exceptions to rules are possible, even if there are no reasons for their presence. Then, in section 11, I will formulate an additional constraint that takes the minimization of exceptions into account.

8. CONSTRAINTS

The notion of rule consistency will be formalized by model-theoretic means, namely in terms of possible worlds. Intuitively, a set of rules is inconsistent if there is a possible world in which the conditions of all the rules are satisfied and in which there is no exception to either one of the rules, while there is no possible world in which the conclusions of all the rules obtain. Variations on the notion of consistency are realized by different characterizations of possible worlds.

Some kinds of states of affairs tend to go together, while other ones exclude each other. For instance, the states of affairs that *x* kisses *y* tends to go together with the state of affairs that *x* touches *y*[22], and the state of affairs that *x* is a circle tends (very strongly) to exclude the state of affairs that *x* is a square. These relations between (usually generic) states of affairs are called *constraints* on possible worlds.

Rules, including legal rules, are a special kind of constraints. The rule that thieves are punishable makes that the state of affairs that somebody is a thief goes together with the state of affairs that this person is punishable. The unconditional rule that it is forbidden to steal, makes that every state of affairs goes together with the state of affairs that it is forbidden to steal. The power-conferring rule that the government and the parliament together are competent to make laws, makes that the states of affairs that these bodies are the government and parliament go together with the state of affairs that these bodies are competent to make laws.

The symbol ⇒ is used to denote constraints in general and rules in particular. The predicate `Valid` serves to express that a rule exists, or – what boils down to the same thing – is valid. It is defined by the following sentence:

`Valid(`*rule*`) ≡def. ∃`*x*`(`*x* `=` *rule*`)`

[22] This example stems from Barwise and Perry 1983, 12.

Finally, there is an one-place predicate `Exception` that ranges over instantiated rules and expresses that there is an exception to the rule in question for the case to which the rule is instantiated.[23] For instance:

`Exception(*thief(john) ⇒ *punishable(john))`

The first model-theoretic characterization of worlds that are possible according to Rule Logic runs as follows:

CONSTRAINTS ON WORLDS THAT ARE LOGICALLY POSSIBLE ACCORDING TO L_{RL}

Let L_{RL} be the language of Rule Logic. L_{RL} = {`S1, S2, ..., Sn`}, where `S1 ... Sn` are all the well-formed closed sentences of L_{RL}.

Let `Si` be a sentence in L_{RL}, and let `*sa`$_i$ denote the state of affairs that is expressed by `S`$_i$. `*sa`$_i$ is then a state of affairs that is *possible relative to* L_{RL}.[24]

Let the set SA be the set of all states of affairs that are possible relative to L_{RL}, and let W be the power set (the set of all subsets) of SA. Intuitively, W stands for the set of all worlds, the content of which is expressible in L_{RL}. Every w ∈ W is a subset of SA.

There are no other constraints on the states of affairs that are elements of the worlds in W. There are, for instance, worlds in W in which the state of affairs `*p & q` obtains, but in which the state of affairs `*q` does not obtain. Such worlds are possible relative to L_{RL}, but they are not logically possible according to Rule Logic.[25] Worlds that are logically possible are subject to a number of additional constraints. The set of these logically possible worlds is denoted by W_{RL}.

[23] More about this predicate and its relations to the predicates `Applicable` and `Applies` in chapter 3, section 5.4.

[24] L_{RL} may be thought of as the conceptual scheme by means of which worlds are 'captured'.

[25] One may argue for the position that only logically possible worlds are really possible, thereby excluding possible worlds in which both the states of affairs *a & b and *~a obtain. My reason for taking the worlds that are expressible by means of some language as basic is that I want to emphasize that logical constraints do not take a special position, but are ‘ordinary’ constraints, just like the physical ones, the mathematical ones, and the legal ones.

CONSTRAINTS ON WORLDS THAT ARE LOGICALLY POSSIBLE ACCORDING TO RULE LOGIC

1. if $*p \in w$ then $*{\sim}p \notin w$, if $*{\sim}p \in w$, then $*p \notin w$, if $*p \notin w$, then $*{\sim}p \in w$, and if $*{\sim}p \notin w$, then $*p \in w$.
2. $*p \;\&\; q \in w$ if and only if both $*p \in w$ and $*q \in w$.
3. $*p \vee q \in w$ if and only if either $*p \in w$, or $*q \in w$, or both.
4. $*p \rightarrow q \in w$ if and only if either $*p \notin w$, or $*q \in w$, or both.
5. $*p \equiv q \in w$ if and only if either both $*p \in w$ and $*q \in w$, or both $*p \notin w$ and $*q \notin w$.

These constraints correspond to the traditional constraints of propositional logic stated in terms of relations between states of affairs.

6. $*\exists x(r(x)) \in w$ if and only if there is an individual a in w, such that $*r(a) \in w$.
7. $*\forall x(r(x)) \in w$ if and only if there is no individual a in w, such that $*r(a) \notin w$.

These constraints give the traditional meaning of the quantifiers, again stated in terms of states of affairs.[26]

A constraint that is characteristic for Rule Logic is that if the conditions of an existing rule are satisfied and there is no exception to this rule, the conclusion of this rule obtains. Let `*conditions/σ` and `*conclusion/σ` denote the states of affairs expressed by respectively the conditions and the conclusion of a rule with their variables instantiated according to instantiation σ. Then the above mentioned constraint becomes:

8. If `*Valid(*conditions ⇒ *conclusion)` ∈ w, and
   `*conditions/σ` ∈ w, and
   `*exception(*conditions/σ ⇒ conclusion/σ)`
   ∉ w, then
   `*conclusion/σ` ∈ w.

Finally there is a constraint to guarantee that terms that denote states of affairs expressed by logically equivalent sentences are co-referential:

[26] To gain simplicity at the cost of precision, the formulations of the constraints 6 and 7 do not deal with compound formulas, or the use of quantifiers or function expressions within the scope of the quantifiers.

9. If and only if for all worlds $w \in W_{RL}$ it holds that `*p ≡ q` $\in$ w, then `*p = *q`.

The constraints of Rule Logic are abbreviated as c(RL).

9. COMPATIBILITY OF STATES OF AFFAIRS

Given the model theory for Rule Logic, it is possible to give a formal characterization of rule consistency. The starting point is the characterization of compatible states of affairs:

RELATIVE COMPATIBILITY OF STATES OF AFFAIRS

Let c be a set of constraints, and let W_c be the set of worlds $w \in W_{RL}$, such that for every constraint $c_i \in c \cup c(RL)$, it holds that `*Valid(ci)` $\in$ w. The states of affairs in a set s are then said to be compatible relative to the set of constraints c if and only if there is some set of states of affairs $s' \in W_c$ such that $s \subseteq s'$.

LOGICAL COMPATIBILITY OF STATES OF AFFAIRS

The states of affairs in a set s are logically compatible if and only if they are compatible relative to the set of constraints c(RL): $s \subseteq s'$, where $s' \in W_c^{(RL)}$.

Let me illustrate this by means of the following examples:

EXAMPLE 10

s = {`*punishable(john), *~punishable(john)`}

The states of affairs in this set are logically incompatible, because of the first constraint on logically possible worlds.

EXAMPLE 11

s = {`*thief(john), *~punishable(john)`}

The states of affairs in this set are logically compatible, because there is no constraint on logically possible worlds that prevents the co-occurrence of these states of affairs.

We have seen that it is also possible to define a notion of compatibility that treats constraints, including rules, as a kind of background relative to which compatibilities are judged. If such a background contains the rule that thieves are punishable, the states of affairs that somebody is a thief and that he is not punishable, are incompatible relative to this background. The compatibility can then be restored by adding the presence of an exception to the rule that thieves are punishable to the set of states of affairs that is evaluated with regard to its compatibility, or to the background of constraints. This is illustrated by the following two examples:

EXAMPLE 12

```
s = {*thief(john), *~punishable(john)}
c = {*thief(x) ⇒ *punishable(x)}
```

The states of affairs in s are logically compatible, but incompatible relative to c because, barring exceptions, there is no world possible relative to c, in which a thief is not punishable.

If the set s is to be compatible relative to c, c should contain an exception to the rule that thieves are punishable. The following set s is compatible relative to c, because c contains the necessary exception:

EXAMPLE 13

```
s = {*thief(john), *~punishable(john), *minor(john)}
c = {*thief(x) ⇒ *punishable(x),
    *minor(x) ⇒ *exception(thief(x)⇒ punishable(x))}
```

10. THE CONSISTENCY OF RULES

By means of the notions of logical compatibility of states of affairs and compatibility of states of affairs relative to a set of constraints, it is possible to give a formal characterization of rule consistency.

Let r = $\{r_1 \ldots r_n\}$ be a finite set of n rules,
where r_i = $*\text{conditions}_i \Rightarrow *\text{conclusion}_i$, for i = 1 to n.

Let s = $\{\sigma_1 \ldots \sigma_n\}$ be a set of n instantiations for the variables that occur in r, where σ_i is applied to the variables in r_i. For instance, let r_3 be `*thief(x) ⇒ *punishable(x)`, and let σ_3 be {x -> john}. Then the instantiation of r3 by means of σ3, r_3/σ_3), is

```
*thief(john) ⇒ *punishable(john)
```

Let $I_{\text{conditions}}(r, \sigma)$ be the set of the instantiations by means of σ of the conditions of all rules in r. That is:

$$I_{\text{conditions}}(r, \sigma) = \{*\text{conditions}_1/\sigma_1), \ldots \text{conditions}_n/\sigma_n\}.$$

Let $\texttt{I}_{\texttt{conclusion}}\texttt{(r, }\sigma\texttt{)}$ be
$\{\texttt{*conclusion}_1/\sigma_1\texttt{), ... *conclusion}_n/\sigma_n\}$.

Let $\texttt{I}_{\texttt{\sim exception}}\texttt{(r, }\sigma\texttt{)}$ be
$\{\texttt{*\sim exception(conditions}_1/\sigma_1\texttt{)} \Rightarrow \texttt{conclusion}_1/\sigma_1\texttt{) ...}$
$\texttt{*\sim exception(conditions}_n/\sigma_n\texttt{)} \Rightarrow \texttt{conclusion}_n/\sigma_n\texttt{)}\}$.

Then the following definition captures the notion of rule consistency relative to a set of constraints:

RELATIVIZED RULE CONSISTENCY:

The rules in the set s are consistent relative to a set of constraints c, if and only if it is not so that there is a set s' ⊆ s and a set of instantiations σ, such that

a. the states of affairs in the set $\texttt{I}_{\texttt{conditions}}\texttt{(s', }\sigma\texttt{)} \cup \texttt{I}_{\texttt{\sim exception}}\texttt{(r, }\sigma\texttt{)}$ are compatible relative to $\texttt{c} \cup \texttt{s} \cup \texttt{c(RL)}$,
b. the states of affairs in the set $\texttt{I}_{\texttt{conclusion}}\texttt{(r, }\sigma\texttt{)}$ are incompatible relative to $\texttt{c} \cup \texttt{s} \cup \texttt{c(RL)}$.

The compatibility of the joint rule conditions and conclusions and the absence of exceptions to the rules is judged against the background of both the set of constraints and the rules themselves, because the rules that are evaluated with regard to their consistency also are constraints on the world in which they exist.

LOGICAL CONSISTENCY OF RULES

The rules in the set s are logically consistent, if and only if it is not so that there is a set s' ⊆ s and a set of instantiations σ, such that

a. the set $\texttt{I}_{\texttt{conditions}}\texttt{(s', }\sigma\texttt{)} \cup \texttt{I}_{\texttt{exception}}\texttt{(r, }\sigma\texttt{)}$ is compatible relative to $\texttt{s} \cup \texttt{c(RL)}$,
b. the set $\texttt{I}_{\texttt{conclusion}}\texttt{(r, }\sigma\texttt{)}$ is incompatible relative to $\texttt{s} \cup \texttt{c(RL)}$.

Let me re-use some examples of the sections 3 and 4 to illustrate these definitions:

EXAMPLE 1

```
1: *thief(x) ⇒ *punishable(x)
2: *thief(x) ⇒ *~punishable(x)
```

The rules 1 and 2 are logically inconsistent, as is illustrated by the set of instantiations $\{\sigma\texttt{1, }\sigma\texttt{2}\}$, where $\sigma\texttt{1} = \sigma\texttt{2} = \{x \rightarrow \texttt{john}\}$.

EXAMPLE 3

```
1: *thief(x) ⇒ *punishable(x)
4: *minor(x) ⇒ *protected(x)
5: *protected(x) ⇒ *~punishable(x)
```

That the rules 1, 4 and 5 are logically inconsistent is illustrated by the set of instantiations {σ1, σ4, σ5}, where
σ1 = σ4 = σ5 = {x → john}.

EXAMPLE 4

```
1: *thief(x) ⇒ *punishable(x)
4: *minor(x) ⇒ *protected(x)
--------------------------------------------
c = {5: *protected(x) ⇒ *~punishable(x)}
```

The rules 1 and 4 are also inconsistent relative to c because there can be no instantiation σ that makes the states of affairs `*punishable(x)/σ` and `*protected(x)/σ` co-obtain in a world in which the constraint in c exists.

EXAMPLE 5

```
1: *thief(x) ⇒ *punishable(x)
3: *minor(x) ⇒ *~punishable(x)
6: *minor(x) ⇒ *~thief(x)}
```

The rules 1, 3 and 6 are logically inconsistent, because it is logically possible that somebody is both a thief and a minor, while it is logically impossible that somebody both is and is not punishable. Notice that rule 6 has no influence on the consistency of the set as a whole. The inconsistency is caused by the rules 1 and 3, and cannot be removed by rule 6.

EXAMPLE 6

```
1: *thief(x) ⇒ *punishable(x)
3: *minor(x) ⇒ *~punishable(x)
--------------------------------------------
c = {6: *minor(x) ⇒ *~thief(x)}
```

We have seen that the three rules taken together are *logically* inconsistent. However, the conditions of the rules 1 and 3 are not compatible relative to c, because there can be no instantiation σ that makes the states of affairs `*thief(x)/σ` and `*minor(x)/σ` co-obtain in a world in which the constraint in c exists. Therefore the rules 1 and 3 are consistent against the background of c.

EXAMPLE 8

```
1: *thief(x) ⇒ *punishable(x)
3: *minor(x) ⇒ *~punishable(x)
--------------------------------------------------
c = {*minor(x) ⇒
        *exception(thief(x) ⇒ punishable(x))}
```

The rules 1 and 3 are consistent relative to c, because there can be no instantiation σ of *x* that makes the state of affairs `*minor(x)/σ` obtain in a world in which the constraint in c holds, and in which the state of affairs `*exception(thief(x)/σ ⇒ punishable(x)/σ)` does not obtain.

11. MINIMIZING EXCEPTIONS

Arguably there are no exceptions to rules whose conditions are satisfied, unless there is a special reason for it. Such a reason consists of facts that are made into an exception by some other rule. It is possible to modify the constraints on worlds that are possible according to Rule Logic to take this into account. The result of such a modification is that the number of exceptions is minimized to those that are necessary because of the other facts and rules that obtain in the world, namely to the so-called 'grounded' exceptions. Minimization of exceptions is a logical technique that is widely employed in the study of so-called non-monotonic logics.[27] In this chapter I will present a technique for minimizing exceptions that is based on the observation that exceptions to rules are reason-based in the sense that there cannot be an exception without a reason for its existence. To this purpose I will built on the way exceptions have been dealt with in chapter 3, sections 5.4 and 7.

According to the analysis presented there, there is an exception to a rule when the rule is applicable and nevertheless not applied. Since applicability is a contributive reason to apply a rule, non-application must either be based on contributive reasons against application that outweigh the reasons for application (including the rule's applicability), or on a decisive reason against application. In other words, RBL requires that exceptions are based on reasons. Moreover, RBL requires that contributive reasons are based on abstract reasons, thereby preventing that there are free floating contributive reasons. By making the additional demand that decisive reasons against the application of a rule are based on rules that apply:

[27] Cf. Lukaszewicz 1990, chapter 6.

$$\forall{*}r, rule(\mathrm{Dr}({*}r, {*}\mathrm{exception}(rule)) \equiv \exists{*}c(\mathrm{Applies}({*}c \Rightarrow {*}\mathrm{exception}(rule))))$$

it is safeguarded that there are no free floating exceptions. If the counterparts of this sentence and the axioms of RBL are added to the constraints on possible worlds according to Rule Logic, the occurrence of free floating exceptions in these worlds is prevented.

Chapter 6

WHAT IS A NORM?

1. INTRODUCTION

One of the central notions in legal theory and in legal logic is that of a *norm*. There are several kinds of entities that might be called norms. The following list contains some examples:

- *General norms*, such as 'Everybody with an income ought to submit a tax declaration', or 'It is forbidden to kill human beings'.
- *Specific norms* such as 'Margaret must pay Jane €100,-'.
- *Permissive norms* such as 'It is permitted to smoke in the canteen'.
- *Assignments of rights*, such as 'Everybody has the right to petition the government'.
- *Procedural rules*, such as 'A contract is made through offer and acceptance'.
- *Commands* such as 'Shut the door'.
- *Technical directives*, e.g. in recipe's such as 'Take three spoons of sugar'.
- *Power conferring norms*, such as 'The mayor has the power to make emergency regulations'.
- *Descriptions of normative situations* such as 'In Belgium one ought to drive on the right hand side of the road'.

Because of its central role, it would be desirable if the notion of a norm were clear. Regrettably, however, it is not. There circulate several theories about, and conceptions of norms.

According to Kelsen, a norm is *the meaning of an act of will* (Sinn eines Willensaktes), that is expressed in language by means of an 'imperative' (Imperativ), or an ought sentence (Soll-Satz).[1]

Von Wright distinguishes three main types of norms. First there are norms in the sense of *rules*. These include the rules of games, which determine which moves are correct, permitted, prohibited, or obligatory. The rules of languages also belong to this main type. The second main type distinguished by Von Wright consists of *prescriptions*, or regulations. The laws of the state provide an example of this main norm type, just as military commands and orders and permissions given by parents to children. In general, prescriptions are commands or permissions, given by someone in a position of authority to someone in a position of subject. The third main type consists of norms in the sense of *directives* or technical norms. They specify the means to be used for the sake of attaining a certain end.[2]

Alchourrón and Bulygin distinguish two conceptions of norms, the *hyletic* conception and the *expressive* conception.[3] They write that according to the hyletic conception, norms are proposition-like entities, the meanings of normative sentences. In contrast to descriptive sentences, which have descriptive meaning, normative sentences have prescriptive meaning. For instance, where the sentence *John walks* describes that John walks, the sentence *John ought to walk* prescribes John to walk. *Expressive norms* are the result of prescriptive use of language. They are expressions in a certain pragmatic mood (commands), and should not be identified with what is commanded. The expression cannot be identified with its content. Expressive norms are not meanings, while hyletic norms are.

There are not only different theories about the nature of norms, there are also entities that are related to, but allegedly not identical to norms. For instance, in *Norm and Action*, Von Wright distinguished between norm-formulations (linguistic entities), norms, normative statements (e.g. In Belgium it is forbidden to steal), and norm-propositions (e.g. In Belgium a norm exists to the effect that it is forbidden to steal).[4] Bulygin has contested the view that there is a difference between normative statements and normative propositions, because the former are merely shorthand for the latter.[5] Mazzarese, then, has argued that the notion of norm(ative) propositions does not make sense.[6]

[1] Kelsen 1979, 2.
[2] Von Wright 1963, 6f.
[3] Alchourrón and Bulygin 1981.
[4] Von Wright 1963, 93f and 105f.
[5] Bulygin 1999.
[6] Mazzarese 1991 and 1999.

Apparently our conceptual machinery around the notion of a norm can benefit from some cleaning up. In this chapter I will attempt to make a beginning with this cleaning operation. The result will be some conceptual distinctions and the suggestion that next to these distinguished concepts, the notion of a norm is superfluous.

2. THE COMMAND THEORY OF NORMS

The first part of my argument concerns the so-called expressive conception of norms. According to Alchourrón and Bulygin, *expressive norms* are the result of prescriptive use of language.[7] This characterization of norms is ambiguous. On the one hand it may mean that (at least some cases of) prescriptive uses of language *are* norms, and that the single prescriptive use of language therefore constitutes a norm, just as saying 'I agree' under suitable circumstances constitutes the acceptance of an offer. On the other hand it may mean that using language in a prescriptive way has as its consequence that a norm comes about, just as acceptance of an offer to sell leads to the obligation to do what was agreed. In this latter case, the norm is not identical with the prescriptive language use, but is an immediate consequence.

Alchourrón and Bulygin continue their description of expressive norms by pointing out that sentences expressing the same proposition can be used on different occasions to do different things. For instance, the proposition expressed by 'Peter puts the book on the table' can be used to make an assertion (Peter puts the book on the table), a question (Does Peter put the book on the table?), or a command[8] (Peter, put the book on the table!). Next they introduce the symbol $\vdash$ to indicate that a proposition is asserted, and the symbol ! to indicate that a proposition is commanded. So $\vdash$p indicates that p is asserted, and !p indicates that p is commanded. The combinations $\vdash$p and !p do not express propositions, although they make use of propositions, but they express what a speaker *does* on a certain occasion. In other words, these combinations stand for speech acts. As if to tell us that they intend the expressive conception of norms to be the speech act theory, Alchourrón and Bulygin write that !p symbolizes a norm in the expressive conception and that norms in the expressive conception are essentially commands. Let us

7 Alchourrón and Bulygin 1981, 96. A similar view was exposed in Wolenski 1982 (DS).

8 Later in this chapter I will use the expression 'order' for this type of situation, and reserve the expression 'command' for a somewhat different situation.

therefore call the expressive conception of norms in its first interpretation the *command theory of norms*.[9]

The command theory of norms has much in common with the theory about moral ought judgments as exposed by Hare in *The Language of Morals*.[10] According to Hare, the word 'ought' is used for prescribing and this means in turn that an ought judgment (in the proper context) implies an imperative. This so-called 'prescriptive meaning' would be characteristic of the word 'ought'. So, where Alchourrón and Bulygin use speech acts to analyze the nature of norms, Hare uses speech acts to analyze the meaning of the word 'ought'.

Hare's theory of prescriptive meaning has been criticized by Searle for committing the *speech act fallacy*.[11] Because I think that this criticism also applies to the command theory of norms, I will go into some detail in describing it.

The general form of the speech act fallacy is that from 'Word W is used to perform speech act A' it is inferred that 'It is (part of) the meaning of W that it is used to perform speech act A'. Applied to ought judgments, the fallacy would be that from the fact that 'ought' is used to prescribe, it is inferred that (part of) the meaning of 'ought' is that it is used to prescribe, or its prescriptive meaning. To rebut the speech act fallacy, Searle points out that words like 'ought' are often used in other speech acts than prescribing and that in those cases 'ought' has the same meaning as in prescriptive speech acts. For instance, the word 'ought' means the same in 'Ought he to repay his debts?' as in 'He ought to repay his debts.' The more general point behind the speech act fallacy is that speech acts that can be performed by means of a particular word and that maybe even are typically performed by the use of this word, do not determine the meaning of the word.

Let me elaborate this point by delving a little deeper into speech act theory. According to Austin, the act of saying something, e.g. 'The cat is on the mat' is the performance of an *illocutionary act*.[12] Austin expresses this by saying that *in* saying something, one performs an illocutionary act. Examples of such illocutionary acts, speech acts to use the terminology made popular by Searle, are asking or answering a question, giving

9 This 'strong' version of the command theory should be distinguished from the weak variant, according to which norms do not merely describe, but have behavior guiding force. This weak version is implicitly discussed and rejected as based on a wrong opposition in section 7.

10 Hare 1952, 155f.

11 Searle 1969, 136f. See also the discussion of the related 'Frege-Geach problem' in Miller 2003, 40f.

12 Austin 1975, 94f.

information, pronouncing a sentence, making an appointment, and – not mentioned by Austin, but certainly an example – prescribing behavior.

Following Searle we can distinguish two elements within an illocutionary act.[13] Speech acts have an illocutionary force, which determines what kind of speech act it is. They also have a propositional content, which indicates what the speech act is about. Different speech acts can have the same propositional content. For instance, the sentence 'My daughter puts her coat on' expresses an assertion with the propositional content that my daughter puts her coat on. The sentence 'Please, put your coat on', directed to my daughter, is a request with the same propositional content. And 'Put your coat on!', directed to my daughter, is an order, again with the same propositional content. Speech acts with the same illocutionary force can have different propositional contents. E.g. the orders 'Put your coat on!' and 'Give me the money!' are different speech acts because of their different propositional content. The propositional content exists of references to one or more entities, normally extra-linguistic, and predication applied to the referents of the referring expressions. Because illocutionary acts have a propositional content, the performance of an illocutionary act includes the performance of a propositional act, namely expressing the propositional content of the illocutionary act. Searle's point about the speech act fallacy can now be rephrased by stating that the contents of a propositional act are not determined by the illocutionary acts in which these propositional acts tend to occur. In the sentence 'You ought to repay her the money you borrowed from her' all the words contribute to the propositional content. These words include the word 'ought'.[14] Since the meaning of the propositional content is independent of the kind of speech act performed by uttering the sentence, the meaning of the word 'ought' in it should also be independent of the kind of speech act. Therefore this meaning cannot be 'prescriptive' merely for the reason that such sentences can well be used for prescribing.

What does this mean for the command theory of norms? If the command theory is taken literally, norms would be a kind of illocutionary acts. Since

[13] Searle 1969, 22f.

[14] It might be objected that the word 'ought' typically does not belong to the propositional content, because it indicates that the propositional content, formed by the rest, is prescribed rather than described. This objection would rest on a mistake. A similar argument would be that the word 'is' in 'The cat is on the mat' does not belong to the propositional content, because it indicates that the position of the cat relative to the mat is described, rather than prescribed. But that is hard to reconcile with the meaning of 'is' in the question 'Is the cat on the mat?'. The word 'is' belongs to the propositional content, and so does the word 'ought'.

acts are events that have a particular location in space and time, norms would also have such a particular location. This space-time location would not be that the norm is valid during a certain period in a particular territory, but rather that the norm (being an act) occurred at a certain time in a certain place. This is plain nonsense. Therefore, the command theory, interpreted as the theory that norms are a kind of speech acts, is obviously incorrect, if it is meant to be a theory about norms in the (or some) ordinary sense of the word.

If the command theory is given a different interpretation, namely that the illocutionary force of prescriptions somehow is part of the nature of norms, the command theory would involve a variant on the speech act fallacy. If norms such as 'It is forbidden to steal' are often used to command ('Refrain from stealing'), this does not imply that it is the nature of the norm 'It is forbidden to steal' that it is *used for* commanding. The use made of norms in performing speech acts does not determine the nature of norms, just like the use of words in performing speech acts does not determine the meanings of these words.

An entirely different issue is whether it is part of the nature of a norm *that it prescribes*. When prescribing is seen as a speech act, it seems obvious that norms do not prescribe, because norms do not perform speech acts. However, norms might have something like 'prescriptive force', and maybe this is meant by the expressive notion of norms. Having prescriptive force, or – presumably more accurately – behavior guiding force, is quite different from performing, or being instances of, the speech act of prescribing however. Acceptance of the view that norms have prescriptive force in this sense is therefore not adoption of the strong version of the command theory of norms.

3. NORMS AS EFFECTS OF COMMANDS

The second interpretation of the expressive conception of norms is that norms are not commands themselves, but that they are brought about by commands. On this interpretation, the distinction between the expressive and the hyletic conception of norms becomes less than clear. Hyletic norms are defined as the meanings of normative sentences, and it seems very well possible that the validity of norms in this sense is brought about by commands. For instance, if an army officer commands a soldier to present his arm, this has the consequence that the soldier ought to present his arm. This ought may very well be interpreted as the meaning of the sentence 'the soldier ought to present his arm'. To assess this theory that norms are the effects of commands, we must delve even deeper into speech act theory.

3.1 Searle's distinctions

Searle uses a distinction between directions of fit to analyze different kinds of speech acts.[15] I borrow an example of Searle (which Searle in turn borrowed from Anscombe[16]) to clarify this distinction. Suppose I make a shopping list, which I use in the supermarket to put items in my trolley. A detective follows me and makes a list of everything that I put in my trolley. After I am finished, the list of the detective will be identical to my shopping list. However, the lists had different functions. If I use the list correctly, I place exactly those items in my trolley that are indicated on the list. My behavior is to be adapted to what is on my list. In the case of the detective it is just the other way round; the list should reflect my shopping behavior.

If we consider my behavior as (part of) the world, we can say that my shopping list has the world-to-word direction of fit, because my behavior must fit the words on the list. The detective's list, on the contrary, has the word-to-world direction of fit, because his list must fit the world (my behavior).

The fit holds between the propositional content of a speech act and the world. The illocutionary force of a speech act determines which direction of fit is involved. Searle distinguishes five main kinds of speech acts[17]:

- *Assertives* commit the speaker to something's being the case. They have the word-to-world direction of fit. For instance, the sentence 'It's raining' can be used for an assertive speech act.
- *Directives* are attempts of the speaker to get the hearer to do something. They have the world-to-word direction of fit. For instance, the sentence 'Give me your money' can be used for a directive speech act.
- *Commissives* commit the speaker to some future course of action. They have, according to Searle, also the world-to-word direction of fit. For instance, the sentence 'I promise to lend you my car' can be used for a commissive speech act. The difference between commissives and directives is, according to Searle, that directives direct the *hearer*, while commissives commit the *speaker*.
- *Declarations* bring about a correspondence between the speech act's propositional content and the world. They have, what Searle calls, a double direction of fit, because the world is made to fit the propositional content of the speech act, while that content comes to fit

[15] Searle 1979, 3/4.
[16] Anscombe 1957.
[17] Searle 1979, 12f.

the world. For instance, the sentence 'I hereby give you my car' can be used for a declaration.
- *Expressives*, finally, express the speaker's psychological state. For instance, the sentence 'I thank you for lending me your car' expresses the speaker's gratitude. Expressives have no direction of fit at all, because they express, rather than describe the speaker's psychological state.

3.2 Constitutives, commissives, orders and obligations

Searle's analysis of different kinds of speech acts by means of the difference in directions of fit provides a suitable starting point for the analysis of a number of legal phenomena, including the nature of norms. However, it is no more than a starting point. In particular Searle's theory about declarations seems to be not fully satisfactory. Therefore I will propose a number of amendments.

My first amendment is merely terminological. Declarations in Searle's sense are speech acts by means of which facts are created. Searle's own examples include that somebody gets appointed as chairman and that somebody's position is terminated. Since these acts are constitutive (in the case of the termination in a negative sense), I propose to call these speech acts by means of which the world is changed *constitutive acts*, or *constitutives*.

The second amendment concerns the direction of fit of constitutives. According to Searle they have a double direction of fit, because the world is altered to fit the propositional content of the speech act by representing the world as being so altered.[18] This expression 'double direction of fit' is somewhat misleading, because it suggests that both directions are equally important. If somebody copies my computer program, his program comes to be identical to mine and mine comes to be identical to his. However, his copy of the program comes to be identical to my copy in a more basic sense than the other way round, because his copy of the program is adapted to my copy and not the other way round. Approximately the same holds for the double direction of fit: the words come to fit the world only because the world has been adapted to the words. Therefore I propose to speak, in the case of constitutives, of a world-to-word direction of fit.

However, the world-to-word fit of constitutives is not the same as the world-to-word fit of directives. An order is a typical example of a directive in Searle's sense. In the present context I use the notion of an order in a

[18] Searle and Vanderveken 1985, 53.

technical sense that makes an order different from a command. Where a command requires a setting in which the commanding person has some authority over the person that is commanded, such a setting is lacking (or irrelevant) in the case of orders. Everybody can order anybody. The issuing of an order will normally exercise some psychological pressure on the hearer to do what (s)he is being directed to do. However, there is no guarantee that the order will be obeyed and that the world will actually come to correspond to the directive's propositional content. That is why Searle writes about the fit of *successful* directives, and 'successful' means in this context *effective*.

Constitutives also need to be successful to create the world-to-word fit, but their success is not the effectiveness but rather the *validity* of the speech act. Searle correctly remarks that declarations (my constitutives) normally require an extra-linguistic institution, a system of constitutive rules, in order that the declaration may successfully be performed.[19] To take a legal example, the law contains constitutive rules that determine how a juridical act is to be performed. If these rules are followed in a concrete case, the act in question is valid. The institution not only defines when constitutive acts are valid, but also connects consequences to valid constitutives, for instance that a contract comes into being. These consequences are *changes* in the world (of law), that account for the world-to-word fit of constitutives.[20]

To distinguish between the world-to-word fit of constitutives and of directives, I call the world-to-word fit of constitutives *direct*, because these effects are the immediate consequence of the performance of the speech act. I call the world-to-word fit of directives *indirect*, because this fit only obtains if the speech act is followed by the behavior that it directs the hearer to perform.

The third amendment concerns the analysis of commissives. According to Searle, commissives have the world-to-word direction of fit, which would - in my terminology - be the indirect world-to-word fit. This means that a commissive would only be successful if the behavior to which the speaker committed himself was actually performed. However, if I make a promise, and nothing extraordinary is the case, I immediately come under the obligation to do what I promised to do. In other words, making a promise has a direct world-to-word fit. Therefore I prefer to treat promises as a species of constitutives, rather than as a separate category of commissives. In general it seems to me that commissives are a kind of constitutives and therefore need not be a special category.[21]

19 Searle 1979, 18.
20 More about this kind of analysis of juridical acts in chapter 7, section 10.
21 Essentially the same point was made by Ruiter 1993, 67f.

Commissives have a counterpart in constitutives that impose obligations on others than the speaker. For instance, an officer in the army gives a command to a subordinate soldier. In that way he imposes on the soldier the obligation to do what was commanded. Let us call these constitutives, which require a setting of rules, *commands*. Commands can then be opposed to orders that do not require such a setting. Everybody can order anybody and the success of the order only depends on whether it is obeyed. Orders have an indirect world-to-word direction of fit. In opposition to orders, valid commands have the direct world-to-word fit. Their success lies in bringing about an obligation and only in a derived sense in bringing about behavior.[22] Where orders are directives, commands are constitutives.

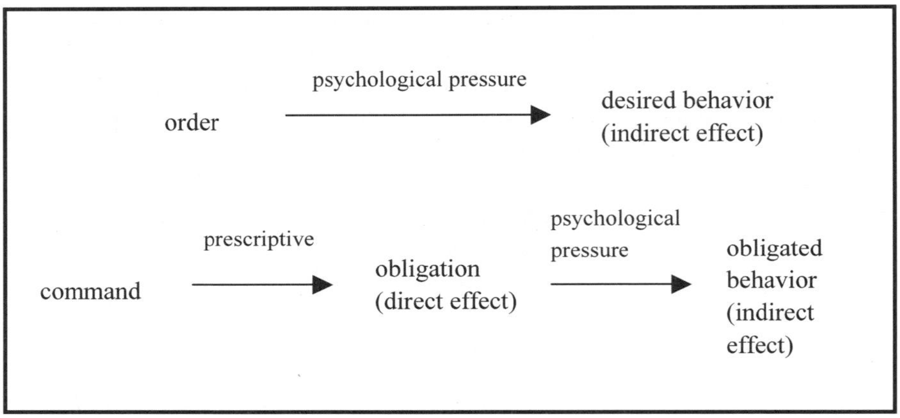

3.3 Conventional acts

According to Searle, a successful declaration makes the world fit the declaration's propositional content. This may be correct, but the correctness depends more on a particular definition of declarations than on insight in the way in which successful declarations bring about changes in the world.[23] Let me explain this by means of an example. Suppose that an officer in the army commands a soldier to present his arm. The officer has the power to give this command and there are no invalidating circumstances. Therefore the

[22] Ruiter 1993, 70f. makes the same distinction.

[23] This criticism of Searle depends on treating commands as constitutives, that is as declarations in the terminology of Searle. However, Searle himself proposes to treat commands as directives and thus avoids this criticism, only to be liable to the criticism of overlooking that commands and orders are different and that commands have much in common with speech acts which Searle does call declarations.

command has the direct effect that the soldier ought to present his arm. According to Searle's analysis, the world should fit the propositional content of the command. This content is that the soldier presents his arm. However, the *direct* result of the command is not that the soldier presents his arm, but that the soldier *ought* to present his arm. Although the command's effect in the world is related to the command's propositional content, it is not identical. How can this be explained?

The answer can be found in the setting of rules that defines when a command is validly given and what are the consequences of a validly given command. In the present case, these rules state that the addressee of the command *ought* to perform the action that he is commanded to perform. The ought, which belongs to the consequences of the command, derives from the rule that attaches consequences to commands, rather than from the command itself. It is the ought of owing to do what is commanded and not the ought contained in the command. In fact, there is in general not even an ought contained in a command.[24]

Schematized, the issue can be stated as follows:

rule:	If an officer commands to do X, then soldiers **ought to** do X.
fact:	An officer commands: *Present arm*!
result:	A soldier **ought to** *present arm.*

In this schema, the obligation is in boldface, while the content of the obligation is italicized. In this way it becomes clear that the *obligation* derives from the rule, while the *content* of the obligation is provided by the command.[25]

The world does not automatically come to fit the propositional content of a successful constitutive. The effects of successful constitutives depend on the rules that attach consequences to the constitutives. A rule about the appointment of chairpersons may make the world precisely fit the

[24] MacCormick 1972.

[25] This view of the operation of commands is similar to Kelsen's view of competence conferring norms. According to Kelsen (1979, 83), a competence conferring norm includes the prescription to do what the competent norm-giver prescribes. See also Patarro 2001, who characterizes competence norms as 'remitting norms'. In this view, the obligation to do what was prescribed by the norm-giver does not derive from the contents of the given norm, but from the competence conferring norm. The given norm merely determines the content of what ought to be done. On my analysis of commands, the command merely determines the content of what ought to be done, while the obligation to do what is commanded derives from the setting of rules that surrounds the command. In section 8.4 I will argue, contra Kelsen and Patarro, that this analysis, which seems to be correct for commands, is not correct for rules.

propositional content of the appointment. Such a rule might be that if X appoints Y as chairperson by saying that Y is chairperson, Y *is* chairperson. However, as the example above illustrated, a rule about army commands may make that a deontic version of the propositional content comes to hold: the command does not bring about that the soldier presents his arm, but that he ought to present his arm.

This observation can be generalized from speech acts to acts in general. Many acts derive their meaning from a setting of rules that define who is competent to perform acts of a particular type, what count as valid acts of this type and what are the consequences of this type of act. Examples are raising one's hand at an auction, baptizing ships, officially raising a flag and laying down one's king in chess. These acts may be called *conventional* acts. Conventional acts which are not speech acts, have no propositional content and their effects can therefore not be that the world comes to fit their propositional content. Their effects are completely determined by the rules that define them. In the examples mentioned above, these effects are respectively that one makes a bid, that a ship receives a name, that honor is paid to the country of the flag and that one gives in.

Constitutive speech acts are in my opinion best considered as a subcategory of this general category of conventional acts. Their effects are also completely determined by their defining rules. However, in the case of speech acts it will normally be fruitful to have rules that make the effects of the speech acts somehow dependent on their propositional contents. Precisely in which way the effects of constitutive speech acts depend on their content is determined by the kind of speech act. This is demonstrated by the examples about the appointment to chairperson and the command in the army. In the appointment example, the effect of the speech act corresponds precisely to the propositional content of the speech act. In the example of the army command, the effect is a deontic version of the propositional content.

It seems therefore that the world-to-word direction of fit of constitutive speech acts is not something that is special for these speech acts. It is not even the case that all constitutive speech acts have this direction of fit exactly. Whether, and to which extent, the world fits the content of successful constitutive speech acts depends fully on the conventions that govern these acts. The theory of constitutive speech acts is not something independent, but rather part of a general theory of conventional action.

3.4 Conclusions concerning the command theory

If the above analysis of commands is approximately correct, the relation between commands and the obligations that arise from them is weaker than might seem at first sight. Commands are no more than conventional acts to which the conventions assign the quality that they lead to obligations. The obligation to do what was commanded stems primarily from the conventions; the command gives the content to this obligation. It seems therefore somewhat misleading to state that norms are the effects of commands. Maybe some norms are brought about by commands, but there is no inherent connection between commands and norms.

That such an inherent connection is absent becomes also clear from the fact that some norms exist for which there is no corresponding command. Arguably the norm that one ought not to kill other human beings existed without ever having been commanded.[26]

A third argument against the command theory is based on the existence of permissive norms. It is not clear how a permission to do something could be the result of a command. Of course it is possible to broaden the notion of a command to make it include the sources of permissions, but this would make the command theory true by trivializing it. It would become the theory that norms are the results of the causes of norms.

The conclusion of all these considerations must therefore be that command theory of norms is incorrect, both in the version that norms are commands and in the version that norms are (rather than can be) the effects of commands. It has become time to look at alternatives for the command theory.

4. DEONTIC FACTS

As an alternative for the command theory of norms, I want to investigate the theory that norms are a special kind of facts, namely deontic facts. Before giving substantial reasons for this view, I want to present some linguistic evidence for it.

4.1 Linguistic evidence for the view that norms are deontic facts

The natural way to say that a certain fact is the case is to utter a declarative sentence that expresses this fact. For instance, the natural way to say that it is a fact that Bush was the president of the United States in 2001, is to say

[26] One might argue that there are commands without a commander, or that norms without a clearly identifiable commander are commands of God, but such manoeuvres seem to me attempts to save what cannot be saved.

'Bush was the president of the United States in 2001'. And the normal way to say that it is a fact that Mount Everest is the highest mountain is to say 'Mount Everest is the highest mountain'. Similarly, one can say that it is forbidden to steal, and this sentence is naturally interpreted as expressing that (it is a fact that) it is forbidden to steal. Even more, one can very well say 'it is a fact that it is forbidden to steal'. The same counts for sentences such as

> Everybody with an income ought to submit a tax declaration.
> It is forbidden to kill human beings.
> Margaret must pay Jane €100,-.
> It is permitted to smoke in the canteen.
> In Belgium one should drive on the right hand side of the road.

It might be objected against these examples that they have a misleading form: Because they have the same surface structure as declarative sentences, it seems that they just *are* declarative sentences. Appearances are deceptive, the objection continues, because the example sentences really express norms and, as everybody knows, norms are not facts. This objection just might be true. But to reject these sentences as examples of norms that are facts, more is needed. This more should amount to substantial evidence that norms are not facts and that the example sentences have a deceptive surface structure. The burden of proof is on the person who claims that there is deception.

The usual 'proof' that norms are not facts runs that norms guide human behavior; somewhat unhappily formulated[27]: norms are 'prescriptive'. Facts on the other hand are not prescriptive and therefore facts are not norms. The crucial error in this proof is the assumption that facts as such do not guide behavior. That facts do not guide behavior is usually merely assumed. I have seldom seen an argument why facts cannot guide behavior. In the following sections I will provide the reader with an argument why facts themselves, without accompanying desires, can guide behavior. I will call these facts *deontic facts*.

My argument consists of three parts. I will start with brief discussions of the views of Searle and Weinberger, to show how the idea of deontic facts so to speak hovers in the air and to make the reader familiar with a style of thinking about reality that allows the existence of deontic facts. Then I present a more abstract account of the elements of the world. This account will lead to a moderate form of ontological idealism. The third step starts from this moderate idealism and goes on to show how it allows the existence

[27] Why this formulation is unhappy should be clear from the sections 2 and 3 of this chapter.

of facts which, without accompanying desires or rules, both guide and motivate behavior.

4.2 Searle on social and institutional facts

In his *The construction of social reality*, Searle addresses the question how social and institutional facts are possible. Both kinds of facts are according to Searle objective facts in the world, but nevertheless only facts by human agreement. Typical examples of these 'special' facts would be that Parliament decides on a proposal for a bill, that this piece of paper before me is money and that Gerald and Margaret are married.

Searle gives a hierarchical taxonomy of some types of facts, in order to indicate which place social and institutional facts take in the fabric of the world.[28] According to this hierarchy a particular kind of facts are *social facts*. Social facts are collective intentional facts, such as hyenas attacking a lion and people taking group decisions. What is special in social facts is firstly that they do not only depend on what goes on physically, but also on what the physical thing is meant to be. In other words, social facts have an *intentional component*. And, secondly, social facts are special because the intention involved in them is not merely personal intention, but the *collective intention* of the members of a group. This collective intention is not the same as merely a common personal intention. The members of Parliament do not merely decide for the bill as a personal matter, but they vote with the intention to participate in group decision making.

Some social facts consist of the assignment of a function to something. Searle gives as an example that a physical object (presumably of the right shape) is assigned the function of a screw driver. These social facts, which are based on function assignment, are called *functional facts*. Within this category of functional facts, there are facts with an agentive function. This means that their function is to be used for some purpose (functional facts). In this connection one might think of keys, which have the function of opening locks. A subcategory of the functional facts consists of those functional facts whose function only exists because of its social acceptance. A screw driver can be used to drive screws, even if this suitability is not socially accepted, but money can only be used as such because of its being accepted as money. The latter category of functional facts, where the function depends on social acceptance, consists, according to Searle, of *institutional facts*. This social acceptance takes the form of status assignment: certain pieces of paper or metal are assigned the status of money.

[28] Searle 1995, 121f.

The status assignment involved in institutional facts takes the general form of *X counts as Y in C*, where X is the entity to which status is assigned, Y is the assigned status, and C denotes the circumstances under which X has the status Y. In this connection it is important that status assignment can be reiterated. For instance, the pronunciation of certain words counts under circumstances as a promise and under additional circumstances, this promise may amount to a legally enforceable contract. In this way a recursive structure of institutional facts built on top of other institutional facts can result.[29] It is important for Searle that such a recursion always bottoms out on brute facts. In this connection, Searle writes about the logical priority of brute facts over institutional facts. 'Institutional facts, so to speak, exist on top of brute physical facts'.[30]

Independent of whether one agrees with all the details of Searle's account of institutional facts, Searle has made a strong case for the existence of facts that in part depend on their being recognized as such. Searle writes in this connection of the *self-referentiality* of social concepts.[31] This self-referentiality applies not to the tokens of social concepts, but only to the types. For instance, a particular contract would also be a contract if it were not socially recognized as such. However, contracts in general could not exist if the phenomenon of contracts were not socially recognized.

4.3 Weinberger on the dual nature of norms

In his paper *The norm as thought and reality*, Weinberger applies a line of thinking to norms that is in some respects similar to that of Searle.[32] On the one hand, norms are, according to Weinberger, ideal entities. With this he means that 'they are thoughts in an objective sense, derived by abstraction from the process of consciousness'. Norms can be expressed linguistically, but this is not crucial for their existence, as is shown by norms of customary law. Norms as ideal entities can stand in logical relation to other norms. Weinberger stresses in this connection the logical gap between is and ought:

1. normative sentences (presumably sentences expressing norms - JH) cannot be restated in a declarative sentence without change of meaning;
2. no normative sentence can be deduced from purely declarative premises;

[29] This is, although in different terminology, a central theme of chapter 7.
[30] Searle 1995, 34f.
[31] Searle 1995, 32f and 52f.
[32] MacCormick and Weinberger 1986, 31-48.

3. no declarative conclusion can be deduced from only normative sentences.

Despite the logical gap between normative sentences and declarative sentences, Weinberger also sees a factual aspect in norms. Norms are not only thoughts, but also reality. The existence of ideal entities (such as norms) is, according to Weinberger, not without connection with material existence. He mentions two points of contact between ideal existence and material reality. One is in 'acts', material proceedings with an ideal content, such as psychic acts, acts of understanding, acts of will. The other is that ideal entities exist in time, just like physical entities. An example that illustrates both points is that of (intentional) legislative acts by means of which norms are created and derogated. The norm exists from the time it was created and stops existing when it is derogated.

Although Weinberger emphasizes the factual aspect of norms, he remains rather vague about their precise ontological status. He states that norms are to be distinguished from the acts by means of which some of them are created, from their linguistic formulations and also from (the absence of) behavior that respects the norm. Nevertheless, norms function as a motivational element in human behavior, and the social reality of norms is indicated by the fact that behavior in conformity with norms or contrary to norms gives rise to positive or negative social consequences.

Searle was much clearer about the status of social and institutional facts. Social facts are facts involving collective intentions, while institutional facts are cases of collective assignment of non-causal functions. The problem with Searle's analysis, however, is that it does not fit norms. Norms are neither cases of collective intentionality, nor cases of function assignment. Admittedly, Searle's analysis was not meant to cover norms, but given the similarity in some respects to Weinberger's view of norms, it might be useful for understanding norms.

4.4 A moderate form of idealism

Both Weinberger and Searle recognize facts that somehow involve the human mind. Social facts, of which institutional facts are a special kind, are according to Searle based on collective intentionality. Weinberger recognizes the existence of what he calls 'humanly conditioned facts', such as the existence of the state, of established ways of live, and of more or less stabilized social or individual patterns of conduct.[33] For their portrayal we

[33] MacCormick and Weinberger 1986, 82f.

must, according to Weinberger, take recourse to the concept of intentional action and to practical sentences, as contrasted to declarative sentences.

Nevertheless both Weinberger and Searle emphasize that they are not committed to idealism. Weinberger points out that his conception of norms as both ideal and real does not lead to idealism, amongst others because material reality is distinguished from ideal entities and because it 'furthers understanding of the functional relation between material reality and ideal entities …'.[34]

Searle goes at some length in arguing for both what he calls external realism and the correspondence theory of truth. His main argument for realism is that realism is presupposed by a normal understanding of many speech acts, such as description. Moreover, the existence of social and institutional facts also presupposes the presence of brute facts, because social and institutional facts are 'created' by superimposing collective intentions upon other facts. This creates a recursive structure which in the end must bottom out on brute facts.[35]

Despite this emphasis of both Weinberger and Searle that the acceptance of institutional facts does not commit to ontological idealism, I believe that the opposite is the case. Idealism comes in different forms, however, and some forms are less attractive than others. It seems that the emphasis with which both authors write that they are not committed to idealism is inspired by extreme forms of idealism, such as the view that everything is only a mental phenomenon and that there exists nothing outside the mind. In the following sections I will propose a moderate form of idealism, which combines the possibility of assuming a mind-independent reality with a natural explanation of the existence of mind-dependent facts. My starting point will be some observations about the nature of truth.

5. THE CORRESPONDENCE THEORY OF TRUTH

The notion of a fact is closely related to that of truth. The correspondence theory of truth is the most natural theory of truth that exists, even to the extent that it is hardly imaginable to be wrong.[36] It might be described as the theory that 'for a judgment (or, say, a proposition) to be true is for it to

[34] MacCormick and Weinberger 1986, 38.

[35] Searle 1995, 149f.

[36] It may be argued that Tarski's semantic theory (The sentence 'S'is true if and only if s) is even more natural, but it is at least arguable that this theory and the correspondence theory coincide. They coincide if the phrase 's', by means of which the truth conditions of 'S' are given, is understood as stating that the state of affairs denoted by 's' obtains.

correspond with the facts'. Nevertheless history has shown that several alternatives are possible, including the coherence theory, the consensus theory, the pragmatist theory and the redundancy or deflationist theory.[37]

5.1 Criticisms of the correspondence theory

Part of the motivation behind the development of alternatives for the correspondence theory is that the correspondence theory of truth seems vulnerable to serious criticism that can take different forms, but which in the end boils down to it that the facts with which propositions should 'correspond' cannot be identified independent of the sentences that express them. Strawson, who formulated this line of criticism eloquently, wrote:

> 'The only plausible candidate for the position of what (in the world) makes the statement true is the fact it states; but the fact it states is not something in the world. ...
>
> Facts are what statements (when true) state; they are not what statements are about. They are not, like things or happenings on the face of the globe, witnessed or heard or seen, broken or overturned, interrupted or prolonged, kicked, destroyed, mended or noisy.'[38]

Briefly stated: unlike material objects or mental states, facts are not part of the 'furniture of the world'. They are language dependent in the sense that they cannot be characterized otherwise than as the correlates of true descriptive sentences (propositions). And consequently, the issue whether a sentence matches the facts, makes no sense.

A complementary line of criticism runs that the statement that a sentence is true does not add anything to the statement made by that sentence.[39] The statement '"The cat is on the mat" is true' says the same as the statement 'The cat is on the mat', although grammatically it is a statement of the meta-language saying that a statement of the object language has a particular characteristic, namely that it is true. As a means of giving information, the truth-predicate is redundant. Maybe it can be used for different purposes, such a emphasizing what was said (It is *true* that I repaid my debt) or endorsing things without specification (Everything stated in my book is true). To fulfill these functions, the word 'true' does not need to stand for a

[37] See for overviews of truth theories Puntel 1983, Kirkham 1992 and Blackburn and Simmons 1999.

[38] Strawson 1971, 195.

[39] This line of criticism has been advanced explicitly in Ramsey 1999.

characteristic, however. The notion of truth as a characteristic of sentences or propositions is redundant, at least thus runs the criticism.

5.2 Language-dependent entities

Strawson is right when he points out that facts are not independent of the language by means of which they are expressed. From this it does not follow, however, that the sentence 'The cat is on the mat' does not derive its truth value from corresponding or failing to correspond to the fact that the cat is on the mat. This fact may be language-dependent in the sense that it is the correlate in the world of a true sentence, but this does not mean that it is not part of the world.

Suppose that the world contains a number of entities, including cats and mats and that these entities have properties and stand in relations towards each other. Because of these properties and relations, some propositions are true and other ones are false. Why not assume that *because of these propositions being true or false*, the world contains a number of additional entities in the form of facts, such as the fact that the cat is on the mat? These entities are not independent of the other entities such as cats and mats, that stand in relations to each other and neither are they independent of the language in which their corresponding propositions are expressed. This dependence on other entities and on language does not mean that these entities do not exist; it only means that they exist in dependence on other entities. As the argument of Searle about institutional facts shows, this is not very special or exceptional.

Facts exist in the world, but their existence is based on other existing entities and on a language that makes declarative sentences possible which express propositions and which in turn are made true or false by the contents of the world. In at least this sense, part of the contents of the world is language-dependent. And since language is a phenomenon in which the mind is involved, part of the contents of the world is also mind-dependent. The mind-dependentness of the world goes further than that, however, because the entities in the world about which sentences make statements are themselves in a sense mind-dependent. Searle argued that some entities in the world may depend on other entities, but as he also pointed out, there must at least be some entities that do not depend on other entities, because the recursive structure of entities that depend on other entities must somewhere 'bottom out'. Searle saw this as a reason why some entities must exist in a mind-independent reality. However, from the fact that some entities are not dependent on other *entities*, it does not follow that they are independent of the *mind*.

To see how this might be the case without assuming that everything is merely mental, one can start with the Kantian distinction between a reality in itself, and a mind-dependent counterpart of it, which we might call the 'world'. Maybe Searle is right when he writes that the assumption of something that exists independent of the mind, of representation, and of our knowledge, is necessary to make sense of much of our acting. But this independent reality is by definition not categorized; it does not contain entities, let alone that there are relations between its entities, or that these entities have characteristics . In short, this reality in itself does not contain the 'furniture' that is necessary to make some propositions true and other ones false. Even more, we cannot say anything sensible about it, otherwise than that it underlies the world about which we can say sensible things that are true or false. We can, and - if Searle is right - even must, postulate that there is such a reality in itself, on which we superimpose structure in order to make the resulting world contain entities that have characteristics and that stand in relations to each other. However, this reality in itself is not the thing about which we talk in our non-philosophical life. We talk about the structured thing, which contains entities that have characteristics and that stand in relations to each other. What makes true sentences true and false sentences false, is the world, not the reality in itself.

The world (as opposed to reality) may contain basic entities, which do not depend on other entities. However, for an entity to exist, it must – at least in principle – be discernable from other entities: *no entity without identity* (Quine). There must be determinate identity conditions for entities and these conditions are obviously mind-dependent. This means that even the basic entities are in a sense mind-dependent. Not in the sense that their existence is a purely mental phenomenon, but in the sense that their individuality depends on conditions that are mind-dependent.

5.3 The correspondence theory rehabilitated

I have argued that the world (in opposition to reality) contains facts. These facts are not independent entities. They depend for their existence on the entities to which the sentences expressing these facts refer and on the characteristics and relations of these entities. These entities and their characteristics and relations make a number of sentences true and the truth of those sentences makes that the facts expressed by them obtain. Ontologically, the presence of facts depends on the truth of the sentences expressing them and not the other way round. Therefore a correspondence theory of truth that holds that sentences are true because they correctly represent independently existing facts[40], is incorrect. However, a correspondence theory may also hold that a sentence is true if the state of affairs that is expressed by it obtains. Such a correspondence theory would in my opinion be correct.

Strawson's criticism of the correspondence theory seems to be directed at the first, incorrect version and that gives his criticism its bite. But his criticism does not affect the second, correct version.

Ramsey's criticism, that the notion of truth is superfluous, refuses to take into account the ontological redundancy built into our conceptual apparatus. We speak about truth as a characteristic of sentences or propositions and by this we mean correspondence to the world. It is possible to make sense of such talk, even if it might be redundant in a number of cases. Ramsey's redundancy theory of truth is best seen as the theory that the ontology implied by our way of talking about facts and truth is redundant. Even if Ramsey's theory in this interpretation would be correct, it is incorrect as a theory about the nature of truth. If the notion of truth is redundant, this does not mean that the correspondence theory about this notion is wrong.

5.4 Ockam's razor?

The moderate form of idealism I have argued for above holds that:

1. There may be a mind independent reality but if there is one,
   a. it is not what makes declarative sentences true or false;
   b. it does not contain any entities.
2. Declarative sentences are true when they correspond to (facts in) the world (correspondence theory of truth).
3. Correspondence in this sense requires the presence in the world of the fact expressed by the sentence.
4. A number of entities in the world, including all facts, are dependent on other entities in the sense that they are mentally added to the contents of the world because of the presence or absence of these other entities.

Before continuing with a discussion of deontic facts, I want to point out one peculiarity of the view that facts are mentally superimposed upon other entities in the world. This peculiarity is a kind of multiplication of entities. The point was already implicitly made by Strawson when he wrote that statements are about entities in the world, not about facts. Take for instance 'The cat is on the mat'. This sentence, if true, is made true by the position of

[40] Such a theory is proposed in Devitt 1991, 29.

the cat relative to that of the mat. Moreover, the sentence is about the cat and about the mat, not about the fact that the cat is on the mat. Is not it a senseless operation to add a new entity to the world that reflects the relation between the cat and the mat, which were already part of the world? Does the addition of the fact that the cat is on the mat change anything in the world?

Well, there is a change, namely that there is an additional fact, but this change is trivial, because basically nothing has changed. All basic entities have remained the same and their characteristics and relations have remained the same too. The addition of the fact is in a sense merely a duplication of what was already there.

Does not the moderate idealism I proposed lead to unnecessary multiplication of entities? Maybe the multiplication is unnecessary in the case of some facts (but not all facts, as I will argue in the next section), but this is not an argument against the form of idealism I argued for. It might be an argument against our language and the conceptual scheme embedded in it, that allows the introduction of facts as new entities. However, given this peculiarity of our language and conceptual scheme, a good descriptive[41] ontological theory should take it into account. It is not an objection against a descriptive ontology if it accounts for peculiarities of our 'ways of world making' that seem unnecessary.

6. REASON-BASED FACTS

At first sight it might seem attractive to adopt a simple realistic ontology, according to which reality is independent of human conceptualization or cognition, but in the previous section I have argued that this reality cannot be the thing that gives propositions their truth values, because truth in the sense of correspondence requires a world that is to some extent mind- and language-dependent. Even if this concession is made, the world might still be so simple that at least atomic states of affairs[42] are independent of each other. For instance, the states of affairs that it is raining and that 3+2 equals 5 have nothing to do with each other, and if one of them obtains, this has no implications on whether the other one obtains.

[41] Cf. the distinction between descriptive and revisionary metaphysics in Strawson 1959, 9.

[42] Atomic states of affairs are states of affairs expressed by atomic sentences, sentences that do not contain a logical operator such as the conjunction or disjunction.

6.1 Dependent facts

The seeming independence of atomic states of affairs of each other is not realistic.[43] The states of affairs that it is raining and that the sun shines are both atomic, but clearly they are not independent of each other. Logically as well as physically and meteorologically it is possible that both obtain simultaneously, but nevertheless the presence of the one at least tends to prohibit the presence of the other one. The precise nature of their negative connection is well worth attention, but it falls outside the scope of this chapter. Instead I will focus on relations between atomic states of affairs that depend on the way in which people impose structure upon the world.

Many facts only obtain to the extent that other facts obtain. Sometimes one or more facts add up to some other, new fact. For instance, the atomic facts that it is raining and that it is cold together add up to the logically compound fact that it is both raining and cold. Apparently the same holds for the facts that in chess the black king is threatened by a white piece and that this threat cannot be taken away in one move, which together add up to the fact that black is check-mated. The latter fact is from one point of view nothing else than the combination of the former two. However, and this makes a difference with the example of the logically compound fact, from another point of view it is another fact, because if the rules of chess would have been different, the check-mate would not have obtained.[44] Moreover, it is not only a matter of the meaning of the expression 'check-mate' that procures the relation between the facts. The rules of chess concerning the issue of check-mating might have been different, without a change in the meaning of the word ‘check-mate’. This word might still stand for the situation check-mate, while under different rules it might be the single

[43] I have already argued that states of affairs are never completely independent, because they depend on the state of the world and the language to which the sentences expressing the states of affairs belong. The dependence discussed here is the dependence of states of affairs upon other states of affairs. Notice, however, that the dependence of facts upon each other is a special case of the dependence of entities upon each other as discussed in the previous section, because facts are a kind of entities.

[44] It may well be argued that this point about the rules of chess do not establish a difference with the logic example. Indeed, if the rules of logic would have been different, the atomic facts that it is raining and that it is cold would *not* have added up to the logically compound fact that it is both raining and cold. The difference between the two examples, if there is one, is based on the difference between the rules of logic and the rules of chess, where the former rules are somehow necessary (they are treated as constraints) and the latter as merely contingent.

consequence of being check-mated that the check-mated party can remove a piece at choice from the opponent's game, and continue the game.[45]

Other examples of situations in which one or more facts add up to some new fact are that the fact that a soldier runs away at the approach of the enemy implies that the soldier is a coward (or prudent) and that the composition and the use of colors in the picture make the picture into a beautiful one.

It is also possible that one or more facts do not add up to some new fact, but that in some sense they 'cause' this new fact to obtain. For instance, that I hit a winning service 'causes' the fact that I take advantage in the game of tennis we are playing. Or, that I contract to buy your house brings me under the obligation to pay you the price of the house.[46]

In soccer the rule exists that if the ball passes the goal line (and some other conditions are fulfilled) a goal has been scored. The scoring of the goal is in some sense the same fact as the ball's passing the goal line, only with a new label attached to it. In another sense it is a new fact that is brought about by the ball's passing the goal line and the status assigned to it. In situations like this we speak of *supervenience*. One fact supervenes on another fact when there could not be a difference in the first without there also being a difference in the second, but not the other way round.[47] There could not be a difference in the goal without there also being a difference in the ball's passing the goal line. However, not every difference in the way the ball passes the goal line needs to bring about a difference in the goal.

In all these cases there is some substrate of facts that thanks to some rules add up to, or cause, some other facts. These new facts cannot obtain without the basis provided by those other facts. I propose to call these new facts *reason-based facts*, because the facts on which they are based are the reasons why the new facts are present. Reason-based facts can in their turn underlie new reason-based facts. This is illustrated by the chess-example above: the facts that the black king is threatened, and that the threat cannot be removed in one move, are both reason-based themselves.

[45] It might be objected here that it is possible to change a little in the conditions under which a check-mate is achieved, and also a little in the consequences of being check-mated, but that if the changes are big enough, the word 'check-mate' has come to stand for something else than for the condition of check-mate. In other words, the word may function as a label for a state that can be given a different, but not any content. This seems to me a valid objection, the discussion of which falls outside the scope of this chapter, however.

[46] Obviously the causation at stake here is not physical causation, whatever that may be. Cf. in this connection the distinction between causation and constitution as made in chapter 7, section 2.

[47] Cf. Jones 1995.

6.2 Two kinds of reason-based facts

The notion of a reason-based fact is ambiguous. On the one hand it may mean a *concrete* fact that obtains because of its underlying reasons. Such a fact is reason-based in the broad sense. On the other hand it may also mean a *type of* fact, which can only obtain on the basis of underlying reasons. The existence of a rule is an example of a concrete fact that may be reason-based in this first, broad sense, but does not belong to a fact type that is reason-based in the second, narrow sense. For instance, the existence of a rule created by means of legislation is reason-based, but the existence of social rules is not reason-based. The validity of a contract, on the contrary, is reason-based in the second, narrow sense. A contract cannot be valid if there are no reasons for its being valid.

Reason-based facts supervene upon other facts, and the way in which they supervene upon them is defined by rules.[48] For instance, the fact that I told you that I would pay you a thousand dollars is made into the reason-based fact that I promised to pay you a thousand dollars. The connection between the former fact and the reason-based fact to which it amounts is created by the convention that saying that one promises counts, under suitable circumstances, as promising.[49] The reason-based fact that I promised to pay thousand dollars in turn underlies the reason-based fact that I owe you a thousand dollars. This connection is made by the rule that one ought to do what one has promised.

The principal difference between independent facts and reason-based facts in the narrow sense is that some of the former can obtain independent of other facts, while the latter always depend on the reasons for their existence.

7. DEONTIC FACTS

In my opinion the so-called *deontic facts* are a special kind of reason-based facts in the narrow sense. Their existence is based on other facts, which are the reasons for their existence and the connection between these reasons and the deontic facts based upon them is created by rules that attach the deontic facts as consequences to the reasons for their presence. For instance, the fact that it is forbidden to enter the building is a consequence of the prohibition

48 In this chapter I use the word 'rule' in a broad sense, broader than the sense in which it is for instance used in chapter 3.

49 Searle 1969, 57f.

issued by the building's owner and the connection between the prohibition and the deontic fact is created by the rule that says that if the owner of a building prohibits entrance, entrance of the building is forbidden.

7.1 The gap between 'is' and 'ought'

The idea that there are deontic facts might meet some objections, based on the distinction between is and ought. Spelled out, the argument against the existence of deontic facts might run along the following line:

> Facts belong to the realm of the 'is' and as a consequence not to the realm of the 'ought'. What is deontic belongs to the realm of the 'ought', and not to that of the 'is'. Deontic facts are therefore a contradictio in terminis.

The basic error behind this line of thinking is the assumption that the realms of 'is' and 'ought' are separated. Obviously, on the level of speech acts, there is a difference between describing and prescribing. But this difference does not show that there are two separate realms, that of 'is' and that of 'ought', just as the difference between the speech acts promising and baptizing does not show that there are two separate realms of promise and of baptism. Just as obviously, there is a difference between the facts (!) that John pays a visit to the dentist and that John ought to pay a visit to the dentist, but this difference between facts does not show that the fact that John ought to pay a visit to the dentist is actually not a fact at all.

The temptation to make a sharp distinction between 'is' and 'ought' might stem from a Humean picture of the world, according to which the world is inert and desires are the motivating forces behind human behavior. In itself this Humean picture does not lead to the gap between is and ought, but when the concept of 'ought' is inherently tied to motivation, the gap is seemingly accomplished. Theories that assume such an inherent tie between ought and motivation are called 'internalist' and these internalist theories are opposed to externalist theories, according to which there is no inherent tie between what one holds to be obligatory and between what one is motivated to do.[50]

The theory of Hare about the acceptance of ought-judgments as exposed in *The Language of Morals* provides a good illustration of an internalist view of the ought. According to Hare, ought-judgments entail commands in the sense that acceptance of an ought judgment leads, barring weakness of the

[50] See for a more extensive account of the distinction between internalism and externalism Smith 1994, 60f and the literature mentioned there.

will, to the motivation to act in accordance with what ought to be done. There is a seeming counter example, for instance when somebody agrees that legally he ought to refrain from stealing, but is not motivated to act in accordance with the law. In Hartian terminology, such a person would not take the internal point of view towards the law.[51] Hare would say that the 'ought' in the legal ought-judgment is an 'inverted commas ought'. The person in question does not really accept the ought-judgment, but only accepts that according to the law he ought to perform some kind of behavior. Since he is not committed to the law, he is not committed to the ought-judgment either. This acceptance of an 'ought'-judgment is not a 'real' acceptance, and therefore it does not commit to acting in accordance with it.[52]

The combination of the views that the world is inherently inert and that ought is inherently connected to motivation, leads to the view that the world cannot contain an ought. If the world consists of all the facts and does not contain an ought, the facts cannot involve an ought and therefore there cannot be deontic facts.

There are at least two ways to escape the conclusion of this line of argument and they are compatible with each other. One way is to argue that there is no distinction between real oughts and inverted commas oughts. The other way is to argue that, otherwise than Hume thought, the world need not be inert.

7.2 The social existence of rules

As Hare stressed, oughts are supervenient upon (other) facts.[53] It is not well possible to say that under circumstances C you ought to have done A, but that under the same circumstances it might have been the case that you had no obligation concerning A. If all the brute facts in the world are the same, the oughts must be the same too. The connections between the brute facts and the oughts that supervene upon them[54] can be expressed by means of principles (Hare's term) or rules. For every ought it is in principle possible to specify both the brute facts upon which it supervenes and the rule that connects the ought to its underlying facts. On the Humean world picture the world contains the brute facts, but not the rules which attaches oughts to

[51] Hart 1961, 55f.

[52] Hare 1952, 18f.

[53] E.g. Hare 1952, 153f.

[54] It is well possible that oughts supervene on non-brute facts, but then these non-brute facts supervene on other facts which are either brute or supervene on other facts, which … etc. In the end this recursion must bottom out on brute facts, as Searle (1995, 34) pointed out.

them. As far as the world is concerned, there may be different sets of rules, with different sets of oughts connected to the contents of the world. Given the world, every ought is relative to a set of rules that connects this ought to the contents of the world.

This relativity is the basis for Hare's theory of inverted commas oughts, and it is also the basis for Raz's theory of detached legal judgments. According to Raz[55]

> 'a detached legal statement is a statement of law, of what legal rights or duties people have, not a statement about their beliefs, attitudes, or actions, about the law. Yet a detached normative statement does not carry the full normative force of an ordinary normative statement. Its utterance does not commit the speaker to the normative view it expresses. ...'

In case of legal ought judgments[56], Raz's theory is essentially a special variant of Hare's theory about inverted commas oughts. These judgments are characterized by the fact that they rest on the application of a rule without endorsing that rule. In this way it is possible to give a moral judgment based on the rules of conventional morality without subscribing to conventional morality, or on the rules of a particular legal system without taking the internal point of view towards that system.[57]

As said, the alleged impossibility of deontic facts stems from the view that the rules on which these facts are based are not part of the world and that the oughts are therefore not part of the world either. But the impossibility of deontic facts does not follow from this view. Firstly because from the fact that oughts are based upon rules that are not part of the world it does not follow that these oughts are not part of the world too. This would only follow on the additional and controversial assumption that something can only be part of the world if everything on which it is based is part of the world too. I will return to this point in the following subsection.

Second, it does not follow because it is far from obvious that the rules on which deontic facts are based are not part of the world themselves. In fact, the examples I gave about the rules of conventional morality and the rules of a particular legal system illustrate the opposite. The contents of conventional morality and of a legal system is, at least to a large extent, a matter of social fact and Searle has argued extensively - and in my opinion convincingly - that such social facts are facts in the world.

55 Raz 1979, 153/4.

56 Raz's notion of detached legal judgments need not be confined to ought judgments, although his allusion to the normative view they express suggests otherwise.

57 In Hage and Peczenik 2001 it is argued that such detached legal ought judgments are only possible to a limited extent.

Summarizing we can say that deontic facts are possible to the extent that they are based upon fact in the world and rules that exist in the world. Whether the belief in the presence of these facts (acceptance of ought judgments that express these facts) is inherently tied to motivation is another matter, which I will address in the following subsection.

7.3 Why the world is not inert

The idea that the world must be inert, because the motivation for behavior stems from the human mind (desires), presupposes a form of ontological realism that allows only mind-independent entities in the world. In section 5 I have argued for a moderate form of idealism, according to which the world contains a number of mind-dependent entities, without necessarily being completely mind-dependent. The idea was that a number of entities in the world, including all facts, are the result of a mental operation performed on already existing entities in the world. This mental operation may be limited to mere conceptualization (e.g. calling a horse an animal), but it may also involve the creation of new facts, such as the presence of goals in soccer, that are built upon other facts such as that the ball passed the goal line. Now I will elaborate this account of mind-dependent facts by arguing how these facts may have a built-in disposition to motivate behavior.

We have seen how it is possible to add new facts to the existing ones, purely by assigning status to what already exists. The utterance of particular words can receive the status of making a promise, and making a promise can receive the status of entering into a contract. From a physical perspective there is only one event, from a social perspective there is the additional event of a promise made, and from a legal perspective there is yet another event, the coming into existence of a contract. One might wonder whether it makes sense to have such a multiplication of facts, without any change in the layer of physics.

Those new facts that are superimposed on already existing ones are not identical to the facts on which they are superimposed. Making a promise is not the same as uttering particular words on a particular occasion. The utterance of those words has, using the terminology of Searle, a particular status, but this status is not inherent to the utterance. It might have had no social status at all, or a quite different status. For instance, saying 'I will repair your bike this afternoon' under the suitable circumstances counts as making a promise. That it counts as such is a result of social conventions, including the existence of the institution of promising and the ways in which they can be made. Had the institution of promising not existed, or should promises be made quite differently, the utterance of these same words would not have constituted a promise, that is, they would not have had the status they actually have.

Before continuing, I would like to propose a change in terminology. Searle analyzed institutional facts in terms of status assigned to underlying entities. It seems to me that the word 'status' functions well in the case of institutional facts, but that it is a bit narrow for everything that is mentally added to the world. Therefore I would like to introduce the word 'meaning' in a broad sense that includes word meaning and sentence meaning, but that also includes the meaning that her children have for a mother, or the meaning of a bombing attack in international politics. Status in Searle's sense would be a special case of meaning too.

Meanings in this broad sense can be personal. The meaning of her children for a mother is a fair example of such personal meaning. Meanings can also be shared in a group. Word meaning is an example of this 'social meaning'.[58] And, finally, meaning can also be institutional. A good example of institutional meaning would be the meaning of the signature of the King under a recently passed bill.

Back to promises. If some event is described as making a promise, the event classified as a promise necessarily or inherently has the social meaning that promises have. In other words, the fact of the promise inherently has the meaning that the fact that the promising words were uttered merely has contingently. In this sense, the fact that a promise was made is different from the fact that these words were uttered and for this reason it makes sense to have promises next to the utterances of promising words.

The fact that a promise was made has the social meaning of a promise, but in a sense masks the way this social meaning has come about. If you know that a promise was made and you know the social conventions concerning how promises are made, you have some vague idea of what might have happened. For instance, if you know that John promised to marry Jane, you can guess what happened during a Saturday night after a romantic dinner. But the knowledge that a promise was made is very clear about the social meaning of what happened: it counts as making a promise with all the consequences attached by social rules to the existence of a promise. In the fact that a promise was made, the social meaning dominates and the physical substrate of the promise making event is at best hinted at. The fact that a promise was made is mostly a fact about social meaning. Similarly the fact that a contract was made is mostly a fact with legal meaning. Again the

[58] That word meaning is also conventional does not detract from the fact that it is a kind of meaning shared within a group. The group is in this case the group of speakers of the language in question.

physical substrate, although necessarily present in the background, is hardly reflected in the fact.

The point I wanted to make with these examples is that there are facts that almost exclusively consist of the meaning, e.g. social or legal meaning, assigned to other events. These other events have this meaning contingently, while the facts that are superimposed upon them have this same meaning inherently, and sometimes these facts are hardly anything more than that this meaning exists. The underlying facts to which the meaning is attached must be there, for otherwise there would be nothing to attach the meaning to. But the superimposed facts, although necessarily based on other facts, abstract from their basis and consist (almost) completely of the meanings assigned to this basis.[59]

The point of having promises and contracts is that they create justified expectancies concerning future conduct. Crucial in the meaning of a promise is that the promisor has, at least pro tanto, the obligation to do what he promised to do. This obligation is inherent to the presence of a promise. Without it, the promise would not have been a promise but merely the utterance of the promising words. Of course, it is possible to attach other consequences to the utterance of the words 'I promise to do X', but when this happens, the institution of promising is abandoned and possibly replaced by some other institution.

The fact *that a promise was made* indicates the source of the resulting obligation, namely that it stems from the promise. The fact that the person P, who promised to do X, *ought to do* X, abstracts from this source. Duties to do things are all based on some source, but the fact that somebody has the duty, or ought, to do X abstracts from these sources, just like the fact that a promise was made abstracts from the precise way in which the promise was made. The fact that a promise was made consists almost completely of the social meaning of the underlying event, and in a similar way the fact that A ought to do X consists completely of the meaning of the underlying source of the duty. The best way to express this meaning is precisely to say that A ought to do X, and all other explanations of it, such as that A has a good reason to do X, that people can expect that A will do X, that they are justified in this expectation, etc. are at best approximations of what is best *described* by means of the word 'ought'. In this sense, 'ought' cannot be defined; it just stands for 'facts of the ought-type', such as that A ought to do X, or that B ought to refrain from Y.

Facts of the ought-type may be called *deontic facts*. Deontic facts are the (presence of the) meaning of their underlying facts. For instance, the fact

[59] This account of the role of meaning in facts is one of the central themes of Hage 1987.

that A ought to do X is the meaning of, what is attached to, the fact that some authority commanded A to do X. The fact that he was commanded to do X has contingently some meaning. This same meaning is inherent to the fact that A ought to do X, and it is expressed by the sentence 'A ought to do X'.

Because the fact that A ought to do X has behavior guiding meaning for A, the utterance towards A of the sentence 'You ought to do X' reminds A of the presence of this behavior guiding meaning, and therefore is suitable to exhort A to do X. But the behavior guiding meaning is not the outflow of the utterance, but is inherent to the deontic fact expressed by the utterance.

Because deontic fact, like all facts, are part of the world, and because deontic facts, a least those of the ought-type, inherently have behavior guiding meaning, the world has behavior guiding meaning. It is not, as the Humeans would have it, inert. Maybe there is not a serious disagreement with the Humeans here, because the behavior guiding force does not stem from reality in itself, independent of human assignment, and in this respect the picture sketched here is Humean. The main point of my argument above is that the world, as opposed to reality, is partly the result of human assignment of meaning, and that, as a consequence, the world contains the meanings that humans have added to it. Maybe the difference with the Humeans is that I think that it is this partly human made world that is the object of our knowledge, the place we live in and the thing that contains the facts that provide the reasons for our behavior. Reality in itself may be a theoretical construct needed to make sense of our behavior, as Searle would have it, but it is not the thing that should take a major place in our practical or theoretical life. The world is what matters to us, and this world is not inert.

7.4 Types of deontic facts

Deontic facts are facts that inherently have behavior guiding meaning. Acceptance of such facts, that is the belief that such a fact is present, tends to motivate behavior.[60] Traditionally three kinds of deontic facts (norms) are distinguished, namely obligations (oughts), prohibitions (ought nots) and permissions.

Since the purpose of deontic facts is to guide behavior, deontic facts are about actions. Moreover, since only future behavior can be guided and since

[60] This is perhaps a too simple statement about the nature of deontic facts, given the possibility of 'inverted commas' or 'detached' versions of deontic beliefs. I will ignore this complication here.

acts that have actually been performed cannot be guided anymore, deontic facts concern future acts. These future acts can only be specified by means of the type of action to which they belong. Therefore deontic facts require, prohibit or (strongly) permit action types. Often, but not always, the actors for which the requirement, prohibition or permission holds are specified. Sometimes the actors are referred to by means of a general category, sometimes they are individually specified. Examples of deontic facts would therefore be:

- It is obligatory to drive on the right hand side of the road.
- Men are not allowed to enter the ladies dressing rooms.
- Everybody is permitted to express his opinion about political issues.
- Jane ought to repay the money she borrowed from Margaret.

Because of their inherent behavior guiding force, deontic facts seem to be suitable candidates for being norms. But there are other attractive candidates in the form of deontic rules. Rules like 'It is forbidden to steal', and 'When it is dark, car drivers are obligated to turn on the car lights' are also suitable candidates for counting as norms. To add to the complexity in this connection, the sentences expressing these rules would also qualify as sentences that express deontic states of affairs. To be able to say more about the nature of norms, we need an analysis of rules that pays attention to the relation between rules, deontic facts, commands, and legislative acts. In the following section I will try to provide such an analysis.

8. OF RULES

In the previous section, rules were mentioned as connections between reasons and reason-based facts. Such rules are to be distinguished from both propositions and states of affairs. Rules in the sense of the word relevant here[61], are in my opinion entities used by humans to impose structure upon the world. I will try to clarify this view of rules.

[61] The intended sense is the broad one of rules as constraints on possible worlds, and not the narrow one of rules that lead to decisive reasons in contrast to principles or abstract reasons that merely lead to contributive reasons. See chapter 3 section 3 for this distinction.

8.1 The ontological effects of rules

Maybe the first thing to notice is that not all rules have as their primary aim to guide action. Obviously many rules such as traffic rules, or rules of a game aim to guide human behavior. But just as obviously, rules defining when a chess player is check mated, rules stating the number of members of Parliament and rules spelling out the organs of the United Nations do not have as their primary aim to guide behavior. They may be seen as supporting other rules that do guide behavior, but even from this perspective they do not guide behavior themselves. The same counts for power conferring rules, which give persons the power to perform some kinds of actions. Knowing that rules do not necessarily guide behavior is the first step on the road to a better insight in what rules are.

One type of rules are rules of meaning. We have rules for the use of the words 'square' and 'rectangle' which make that everything that falls under the concept of a square also falls under the concept of a rectangle. These meaning rules not only govern the use of these words, but by means of them, the users of these rules also impose structure on the world: Given these rules, all squares must be rectangles. Similarly, given the conventions governing the use of the word 'bachelor', all bachelors must be unmarried. There is nothing spectacular about these structures we impose on the world by meaning conventions. All we do is use words in a particular way and, given this use, some relations between types of states of affairs come to hold, as by definition. The rules that govern our linguistic behavior indirectly have also effects upon the world. We may call this phenomenon the *ontological effect* of rules.

Rules governing the meanings of logical operators illustrate the same phenomenon. Given the meaning of the operator `&`, the sentence `P & Q` must be true if both the sentences `P` and `Q` are true. In an ontological fashion, the same can be expressed by saying that the state of affairs `*p & q` must obtain if both the states of affairs `*p` and `*q` obtain. The relation that on the language level exists between the truth values of sentences is reflected on the ontological level in the relation between states of affairs. This relation is brought about by a rule of language.

The relation between one fact that is a reason for the presence of some other fact and the reason-based fact supervening upon the reason, is brought about by a rule. In the example given in the previous section about scoring a goal, this is a rule of soccer, but there are many examples with other rules. For instance, the rule that thieves ought to be punished makes that the fact that X ought to be punished supervenes on the fact that X is a thief.

If a rule exists, not all combinations of facts are equally possible anymore. For instance, without the meaning rule that squares are a kind of rectangles, there might have been squares that are not rectangles. Without the rule that if the ball passes the goal line a goal is scored, it would be possible that the ball passes the goal line without a goal being scored. However, if this last rule exists, a special explanation is needed if the ball passes the goal line without a goal being scored. The two types of facts, the ball passing the goal line and a goal being scored, normally go together.

By having rules, humans make that facts supervene upon each other. By using the rule of soccer, they make that scoring a goal supervenes on the ball's passing the goal line. By using the rule that thieves ought to be punished they make that the fact that X ought to be punished supervenes on X's being a thief. There is a structural connection between facts that are based upon each other. By using rules, humans create that structure. Supervenience based on rules is an example of the ontological effect of rules.

8.2 Legal rules

Legal rules also have ontological effects. To make the transition to legal rules as small as possible, we can start with legal meaning conventions. The Dutch Penal Code defines a number of crimes and thereby gives meaning conventions for, e.g., the notion of 'thief'. Given the convention for 'thief', somebody who takes away somebody else's good with the intention to appropriate this good illegally, is necessarily a thief.[62] This meaning convention structures the legal world by creating a connection between (compound) states of affairs of the types 'being a thief' and 'taking away somebody else's good with the intention to appropriate this good illegally'.

It is not only meaning conventions that have ontological effects in the law. There is also a legal rule that creates a connection between being a thief and being punishable. This rule *imposes* punishability. Another rule creates a connection between being the municipality council and being empowered to make by-laws. This is a *competence conferring* rule. Yet another rule creates a connection between having a driver's license and being permitted to drive a car. Finally, there is also a rule that connects the facts of having enjoyed an income and being obligated to make a statement to the tax officials. The last two rules, which have deontic states of affairs in their conclusion parts (being *permitted* to drive and *being obligated* to make a statement), are deontic rules.

Deontic rules have ontological effects by attaching deontic facts to the facts that satisfy their conditions. Enjoying an income and being obligated to

[62] Cf. art. 310 of the Dutch Penal Code.

make a statement to the tax officials go together in a way which is not identical, but nevertheless quite similar to the way in which being a square and being a rectangle go together.

Deontic rules are a kind of rules and derive many of their characteristics from being rules. Nevertheless they have also some peculiarities of their own. A characteristic that holds especially for deontic rules is that they often lack conditions. For instance, the deontic rule that it is forbidden to drive more than 35 miles an hour has no condition part. The same counts for the deontic rule that everybody is permitted to hold political speeches. Deontic rules without conditions do not impose structure upon the world, but rather create deontic facts. The deontic rule that it is forbidden to drive more than 35 miles an hour calls the deontic fact into life that it is forbidden to drive more than 35 miles an hour. The presence of this deontic fact is based on the existence of the deontic rule that caused its existence. Such deontic rules without conditions are difficult to distinguish from the deontic facts that are based on them and that sometimes have the same formulation.[63]

8.3 The world-to-word fit of rules

If a rule exists, the world is adapted to the contents of the rule. Rules can therefore be said to have the direct world-to-word direction of fit.[64] Nevertheless the way in which this fit comes about is different for rules than it is for constitutive acts. Constitutives cause *changes* in the world; rules influence the world, but not by causing changes. Their effects are more like constraints on the possible content of the world.[65]

For instance, if the rule that thieves are punishable exists, it is not possible that somebody is a thief without being also punishable.[66] If the rule exists that thieves are punishable and if I know that X is a thief, I can refrain from drawing the conclusion that X is punishable, but that does not prevent that X *is* punishable. It would be the same as if I would refuse to apply the rule that squares are rectangles. Such a refusal would not make some square into a non-rectangle; it would only mean that I make a mistake in my use of language. Similarly, my refusal to apply an applicable rule only means that I make a mistake in not applying the rule.[67] As long as the rule exists, thieves

63 I will say some more on the relation between deontic rules and the deontic facts based on them in section 8.5.

64 Directions of fit are explained in section 3

65 Cf. the distinction between constitution and causation in chapter 7, section 2.

66 This would be different if an exception to the rule can be pointed out.

67 For the present purposes I ignore the possibility that there are good reasons against applying the rule, and its consequences for whether the rule should be applied.

are punishable. Only if the rule is abandoned (e.g. derogated), the relation between being a thief and being punishable disappears.

8.4 Deontic rules and commands

This contrast between the way in which constitutive acts and rules have the world-to-word direction of fit can be sharpened by paying attention to legislation. Legislation is a constitutive act by means of which (amongst others) deontic rules are created. A legislative act brings about a change in the world, because a deontic rule that did not exist before has come into existence. Moreover, if a deontic rule comes to exist, the structure that the deontic rule imposes upon the world also comes to hold. So if the legislator makes the deontic rule that thieves ought to be punished, the direct effect of this constitutive is that the deontic rule that thieves ought to be punished comes into existence. The indirect effect is that the state of affairs that thieves ought to be punished comes into existence too. (This assumes that before the deontic rule was created it was not yet the case that thieves ought to be punished.) An even more indirect effect obtains if the deontic rule is acted upon, and thieves are actually punished.

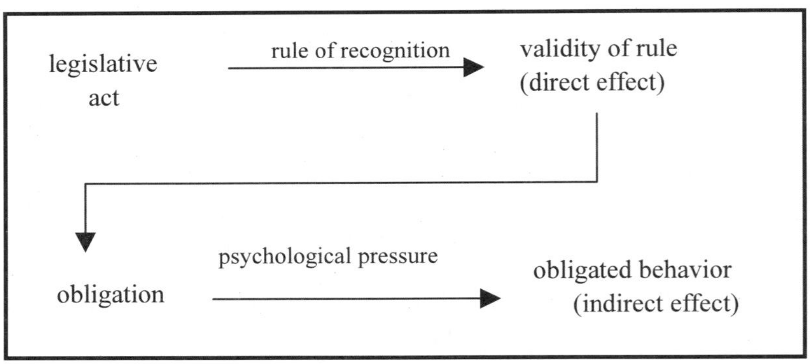

It may be useful to contrast this with issuing a command. The direct effect of a valid command is that an obligation is called into existence. This obligation can, but need not, lead to the obligated behavior.

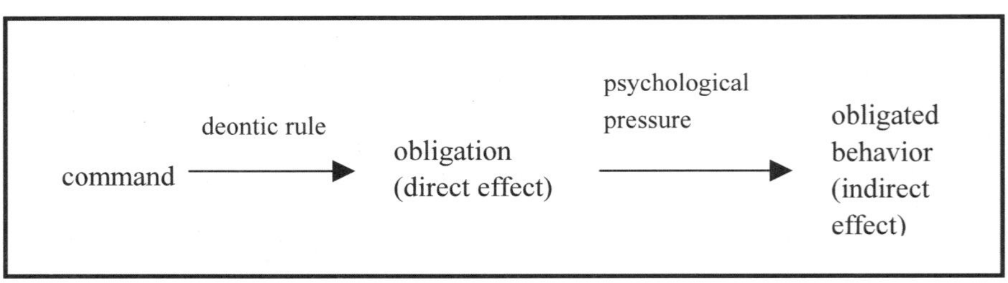

Notice that the rule that attaches the existence of a deontic rule to the validity of a legislative act is not a deontic rule. It does not prescribe to obey validly made deontic rules. The obligation that results from a valid deontic rule derives from the deontic rule itself and not from the power-conferring rule. In this respect the ought derived from a deontic rule differs from the ought brought about by a command. The latter ought derives from the deontic rule that prescribes to obey particular commands.[68]

The structure that a (deontic) rule imposes upon the world is a case of the direct world-to-word direction of fit. The immediate effect of the existence of a deontic rule is that some deontic fact obtains. A deontic rule does not have the indirect world-to-word fit. This indirect fit belongs to the deontic fact that exists because of the deontic rule.[69]

The mirror of a legislative act that calls a (deontic) rule into existence is a derogative act. By means of a derogative act, a rule is taken away from the institution, and indirectly also the consequences that the rule had for the structure of the world. Notice, by the way, that derogation is an act and not a rule.[70]

8.5 The descriptive counterpart of deontic rules

Rules, including deontic rules, have the world-to-word direction of fit. As a consequence, they have no truth values. A truth value depends on the success of the word-to-world fit between a sentence or proposition and the world. Only entities with the word-to-world direction of fit can have a truth value and this truth value is 'true' if the states of affairs represented by them obtain in the world. Entities with the world-to-word direction of fit, such as rules, can therefore not have truth values.

[68] Cf. the discussion of Kelsen's differing view on this subject in section 3.3.

[69] Weinberger 1989, 226 also distinguishes between the word-to-world and world-to-word direction of fit. He ascribes the (indirect) world-to-word direction of fit to norms. Since Weinberger does not distinguish between norms and the deontic facts which are based on them, his views seem partly correct to me, namely to the extent that they deal with deontic facts.

[70] Kelsen 1979, 84f. offers the view that derogation takes place by means of norms. This imposes the difficult task to explain why derogating norms cannot be derogated themselves. If derogation is considered as an act, derogations cannot be derogated themselves, because it is impossible to undo acts by 'derogating' them.

Conventional acts can, however, be nullified and this holds also for derogations. Nullification is not taking the act away, but taking away the consequences that are (normally) attached to this fact.

Nevertheless, sentences such as ‘Thieves ought to be punished’ seem to be true or false, and yet they also seem to express deontic rules. Do not sentences like this illustrate that deontic rules can have truth values? My answer to this argument is that it mixes up rule formulations and the descriptive counterparts of rules. Descriptive counterparts of rules are sentences expressing states of affairs that obtain thanks to the application of a rule. To clarify the difference between rules and their descriptive counterparts and to distinguish between the descriptive counterparts of deontic rules and other assertive deontic sentences, I will say a little about the meaning of referring expressions.

We use referring expressions to identify a subject we want to say something about.[71] The simplest case of a referring expression is a proper name that rigidly denotes the object of reference. The proper name needs not have any meaning, otherwise than standing for what it names.[72]

The use of definite descriptions is somewhat more complex, because their linguistic meaning plays a role in identifying their object of reference. Definite descriptions can be used in a referential and in an attributive way.[73] If a definite description is used in a referential way, its descriptive component is used - in combination with the context of its utterance, including the beliefs of the audience - to identify the object of reference for the audience. Any descriptive expression that succeeds in making this identification suffices. For instance, if I want to refer to a long-haired *man* with a glass of *white wine* in his hands, I may succeed in identifying him by referring to the *lady* with a glass of *sherry* in her hand. The linguistic meaning of a definite description that is used referentially is not essential. This meaning is only an additional means, in combination with the circumstances of utterance, to identify the referent for the audience. As the example shows, there is no need for the definite description to be true of the referent.

The opposite is the case when a definite description is used in an attributive way. In that case the description is used to refer to those persons of objects that satisfy the description. For instance, the description ‘the murderer of Jones’ is used attributively if I say ‘The murderer of Jones must be insane’, when I am not acquainted with the murderer, but infer his insanity from the terrible way in which he mutilated Jones' corpse.

Often when an attributive use is made of a referring expression, what we want to say about the thing(s) to which we refer depends on the

71 Searle 1969, Ch. 4.
72 Cf. Kripke 1972.
73 Cf. Grayling 1997, 114f. and Donnellan 1966.

characteristic used in the referring expression. We ascribe insanity to Jones' murderer at least partly because of his being the murderer. In general (and by definition) it holds that if a descriptive phrase is used for attributive reference, the objects of reference posses the quality expressed in the descriptive phrase.

The distinction between referential and attributive use also holds for referring expressions that are not definite descriptions. In fact, it is rather common to use terms attributively if one wants to say something about all members of a class *as such*. For instance, the sentence 'Birds can fly' is about birds as such and not about all things that happen to be birds.[74]

Attributively used terms play a crucial role in the formulations of rules. Consider the following examples of rule formulations:

- *Thieves* are punishable.
- *Murderers* ought to be punished.
- *Stealing* is forbidden.
- *The municipality council* can levy taxes on real estate.
- *Cars* are four-wheeled vehicles propelled by a combustion engine.

In each case, the italicized phrase consists of an attributively used expression.

Rule formulations must refer to the subject of their regulation attributively, because rules attach legal consequences to the subject *because of* these characteristics . Thieves are punishable, precisely because they are thieves. Acts of stealing are forbidden, because they are acts of stealing. And four-wheeled vehicles propelled by a combustion engine are cars, just because they are four-wheeled vehicles propelled by a combustion engine. One reason why rule formulations refer attributively to their subjects is that rules impose structure upon the world by creating connections between *types* of facts. Another reason why rule formulations must refer to their subjects attributively is that referential use of referring expressions presupposes a context of utterance. Such a context is absent in the case of rule formulations, which - in contrast to rule-creating speech acts - are not uttered at all.

The relations between facts that are constituted by rules can be described by assertive sentences. Since these relations exist between *types* of facts, the facts are referred to by terms that are used attributively. For instance, the

[74] If all birds happen to be painted red, one cannot express this by saying 'Birds are painted red', but one should use the sentence 'All birds are painted red''. It is, however, possible to express that birds can fly by using the sentence 'All birds can fly'. This last sentence is ambiguous between using the expression 'all birds'' referentially and attributively. The subject-term 'birds' without prefix can only be used attributively.

connection created between being a thief and being punishable is described by the sentence 'Thieves are punishable'. The referring expression in this sentence, 'Thieves', is used attributively. The sentence does not deal with everybody who happens to be a thief, but with thieves because they are thieves. The description describes the relation between being a thief and being punishable and this description of relations between classes can be carried out by referring attributively to the members of the class. Notice that the sentence that describes the relation between being a thief and being punishable has the same formulation as the rule that makes thieves punishable. Without context, it is impossible to determine whether sentences such as 'Thieves are punishable' are formulations of rules which have the world-to-word direction of fit, or sentences that describe the effects of rules and which have the word-to-world direction of fit.

Sentences that describe the relation between class members by referring attributively may be called universal attributions[75], and - if they correspond to a similarly formulated rule - *descriptive counterparts of rules*. Often, when a universal attribution is true, this is because the corresponding rule exists. For instance, thieves are punishable, because of the rule that thieves are punishable. This is not necessary, however. Sometimes relations between class members as such hold[76] without a corresponding rule. In that case there will be other rules, or – more generally and more accurately, constraints - that cause this relation to obtain. For instance, suppose that in some country owners of a crowbar are punishable. It seems that in that country a rule must exist to the effect that owning a crowbar is punishable. However, the same effect can also be obtained by the existence of the rules that (amongst others) owners of a crowbar are considered to be a threat to the public order and that it is punishable to be a threat to the public order.

The descriptive counterparts of rules do *not* describe rules. For instance, the descriptive counterpart 'Thieves are punishable' does not mean that the rule that thieves are punishable exists. Descriptive counterparts describe the *effects* of rules.

[75] Some of these universal attributions are case – legal consequence pairs (CLCPs) in the sense of chapter 1, section 3.3.

[76] There are also relations between class members which happen to exist, such as the relation between being a Belgian citizen and being shorter than four meters. These relations are not relations between class members *as such*.

9. WHAT IS A NORM?

It becomes time to return to the question with which I began this chapter: What is a norm? In the course of my argument I have distinguished several kinds of entities that more or less qualify for the status of a norm. I will briefly repeat what I had to say about them.

In connection with the command theory of norms, I distinguished two kinds of 'normative' speech acts, that is orders and commands. An *order* in the sense in which I used this term, is a speech act intended to move somebody else to perform, or to refrain from performing, some kind of behavior. If the order is successful, the intended behavior takes place. There are no other consequences of an order.

Commands, again in the technical sense in which I used the term, are speech acts by means of which an obligation is imposed on somebody else. Commands require a setting of rules that empower the commander to issue commands with this effect, and make the commanded persons liable to have obligations imposed on them in this way. Commands that satisfy the conditions of such a framework are said to be valid, and the normal consequence of a valid command is that the corresponding obligation comes into existence. A command is successful if the intended obligation arises; it is not necessary for a successful command that the resulting obligation is fulfilled, although such a fulfillment will normally be intended by the commander.

Commands are an example of what I called 'constitutives', speech acts by means of which states of affairs are brought about. Other examples are juridical acts, and among these, *legislative acts* take a special place. Legislative acts that satisfy the conditions of the rule framework within which they take place are said to be valid. Valid legislation has as its consequence that some piece of legislation is made and thereby that one or more rules are created, modified, or abrogated. If new rules are validly created, or existing ones validly modified, the resulting rules will normally be valid too.

Rules are constraints on possible worlds; they create through their existence (validity) necessary connections between states of affairs, or – if they are conditionless rules – they call states of affairs into being. *Deontic rules* are rules that have deontic consequences; they bring deontic states of affairs about, or they create exceptions to other deontic rules (permissive rules).

Deontic states of affairs are states of affairs that have prescriptive or prohibitive meaning. Recognition of such states of affairs will normally motivate the person in question to act in accordance with them.

Deontic states of affairs are expressed by *deontic descriptive sentences*. These sentences are true or false, dependent on whether the deontic states of affair expressed by them obtains or not. Some of these sentences are the *descriptive counterparts of deontic rules*. Their formulation corresponds to the formulations of deontic rules and they are often true because their corresponding rules exist (are valid).

Does it make sense to distinguish norms next to these categories, or to identify norms with one or some of them? Terminological conservatism pleads for maintenance of this popular term. However, the popularity might well be explained by its vagueness and its ensuing usefulness in divergent situations. My fear that this is the case makes me propose to ban the term 'norm' from theories about normative systems and practical reasoning.

Chapter 7

LEGAL STATICS AND LEGAL DYNAMICS

1. MODELING THE LAW

In this chapter I will present an abstract model of the law to account for two crucial characteristics of the law. The first characteristic is that the law is dynamic; regulations change, contracts are signed, property rights are acquired, etc. The second characteristic is that the elements of the law are not independent of each other, but hang together in a rule-like way: Legislation leads to valid regulations; the signing of a contract gives rise to obligations.[1] The model of the law as presented in this chapter can be summarized as follows:

- The law is a *system* of *states of affairs*.
- The law is *dynamic*: the states of affairs that obtain are subject to change due to the occurrence of events.
- The law is *interconnected*: there are (directed) connections between the states of affairs that obtain, based on what I will call *rules*.

The model uses three primitives:

- *States of affairs*. A state of affairs can be circumscribed as a possible part of the world as expressed by a (descriptive) sentence. An example

[1] These phenomena are analyzed from a jurisprudential point of view in chapter 6.

is the state of affairs that the contract has been signed as expressed by the sentence 'The contract has been signed'.[2]

- *Events*. An event causes a change of the obtaining states of affairs. An example is the event of signing some contract by which the state of affairs that the contract has been signed starts to obtain.[3]
- *Rules*. A rule is a directed connection between states of affairs. An example is the rule that, if a contract is signed, obligations of the contractors towards each other emerge.

I start with a description of the abstract model in the sections 2 to 5. The core of this chapter consists of the sections 6 to 12 in which I illustrate the uses of the model by analyzing some basic legal concepts.

2. TWO TYPES OF CONNECTIONS BETWEEN STATES OF AFFAIRS

The model presented here distinguishes between two types of connections between states of affairs: *causation* and *constitution*. Both terms, 'causation' and 'constitution', are used here in a technical sense. Causation occurs when a state of affairs comes about, or is changed as a consequence of an event.[4] Causation involves the lapse of time, while constitution is timeless. Suppose that A sells his car to B by signing a sales contract. The signing of the contract is an event which creates a contractual bond between A and B. The relation between the signing of the contract and the existence of the contractual bond between A and B is one of *causation*, because the contractual bond comes into existence because of an event, namely that the contract is signed.

The existence of the contractual bond brings with it that A is obligated to transfer the ownership of his car to B and that B is obligated to pay A the price of the car. The relation between the existence of the contractual bond and the obligations of A and B towards each other is one of *constitution*, because the existence of the contractual bond is a state of affairs, not an event, and the relation between it and the obligations of A and B is timeless.[5]

[2] More about states of affairs in chapter 3, section 2.1 and in section 3 of this chapter.

[3] The notions of states of affairs and events as I use them are related to, but not fully identical to those used by Von Wright (1963, 25f.).

[4] Notice that this use of the notion of causation is broader than pure physical causation. It also includes what Kelsen called imputation (Zurechnung). Cf. Kelsen 1960, 79f.

[5] That the relation between the existence of a contractual bond and the obligations is timeless does obviously not imply that the contractual bond and the obligations themselves

In the case of causation, an event changes which states of affairs obtain. States of affairs appear or disappear. Graphically, causation is depicted as a horizontal connection between states of affairs (figure 1).

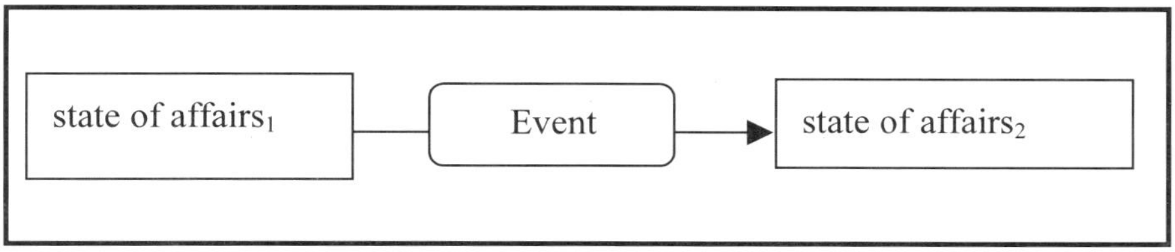

Figure 1: Causation

In the case of constitution, a state of affairs obtains thanks to another state of affairs that obtains. There is a rule that connects the states of affairs. Graphically, constitution is depicted as a vertical connection between states of affairs (figure 2).

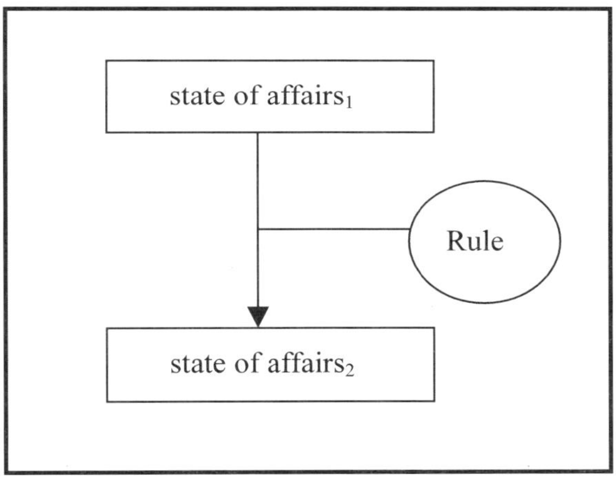

Figure 2: Constitution

In section 5 I show that there are not only rules of constitution, but also rules of causation. In the rest of this chapter, I elaborate the abstract model of the law based on the distinction between constitution and causation and show it to be helpful for understanding the law.

---

are timeless too. Neither does it mean that this relation will always exist. In theory the law might change in a way that the existence of a contractual bond does not involve obligations anymore. This topic is discussed, in different terminology, in chapter 6, section 8.

3. STATES OF AFFAIRS

It is possible to see the law (and the rest of the world) as a system of states of affairs. A *state of affairs* can be characterized as a possible part of the world expressed by a (descriptive) sentence. I take the notion of a state of affairs rather broadly. Examples of states of affairs are that:

1. It is raining.
2. George Washington was the first president of the USA.
3. The sun will rise tomorrow.
4. John has taken away Gerald's car.
5. John is a thief.
6. Meryl is under a contractual bond toward Jane to pay her $100.
7. Meryl ought to pay Jane $100.
8. A minor cannot make a valid will.
9. It is uncertain whether O.J. Simpson killed his wife.

As the examples illustrate, states of affairs can be in different tenses (examples 1-3), can supervene on each other (examples 4/5, 6/7), and can have different modalities (examples 7-9).

Obviously, some states of affairs obtain, while other ones do not obtain. E.g., the states of affairs that 3 + 4 equals 7 obtains, while the state of affairs that George Washington is the president of the USA does not obtain (anymore). States of affairs that obtain are called *facts* and are expressed by true sentences. States of affairs that do not obtain are called *non-facts* and are expressed by false sentences.

3.1 Temporary and durable states of affairs

The examples of states of affairs 1-3 above are in different tenses. The law is a *dynamic* system of states of affairs: it changes over time. For instance, the state of affairs that George Bush is president of the USA obtains today (January 2005), but did not obtain in 1967. Some states of affairs can stop or start obtaining, others cannot. For instance, the state of affairs that George Washington was the first president of the USA obtains and will always obtain, since it is a state of affairs about the past.

States of affairs that can stop or start obtaining are said to be *temporary*, the other ones are *durable*. An example of a temporary state of affairs is that it is raining; an example of a durable state of affairs is that the French Revolution took place in the 18th century. States of affairs that deal with the past are always durable, because the past does not change (although history does). Temporary states of affairs that only obtain for a moment are *momentary*. A momentary state of affairs is for instance that John hits Gerald.

Temporary states of affairs which deal with the present, such as the state of affairs that it is raining, are called *states*. In section 8, I show that having a rights can be though of as a state.

3.2 Supervenience

In the examples above, state of affairs 5 depends on state of affairs 4. The state of affairs that John is a thief obtains *due to* the state of affairs that John has taken away Gerald's car. It is said that the state of affairs that John is a thief *supervenes* on the state of affairs that he has taken away Gerald's car.[6]

Supervenience of a state of affairs on another state of affairs is a rather common phenomenon. It can, amongst others, be based on definitions. For instance, something counts as a motor vehicle in the sense of the Dutch Traffic Law (Wegenverkeerswet) if and only if it satisfies a number of conditions.

In general, modal states of affairs, discussed in the next subsection, always supervene on other states of affairs. For instance the state of affairs that Meryl *ought* to pay Jane $100 (example 7 above) supervenes on the state of affairs that Meryl is under a contractual bond toward Jane to pay her $100 (example 6 above).

3.3 Modalities

The examples 7-9 illustrate different modalities. I distinguish three categories of modal states of affairs: anankastic, deontic and probabilistic states of affairs. (Here I do not regard tense as a modality.)

Anankastic states of affairs[7] have to do with the necessary, the possible and the impossible. For instance, the state of affairs that the released stone *must* fall, is anankastic. Other examples are the states of affairs that hydrogen and oxygen *can* react, that the Democrats *cannot* win the elections, and that the conclusion of a deductively valid argument with true premises is *necessarily* true. A specific anankastic state of affairs in the law has to do with competence. To perform particular acts in the law, such as to engage into a contract, to issue a governmental order, or to legislate, the person who performs the act must have the competence to do so. If the competence is lacking, the particular juridical act cannot exist at all, or is void and has no

6 Jones 1995.

7 Cf. Von Wright 1963, 10.

legal consequences. In other words, competence has to do with what an actor can or cannot do.[8] I return to juridical acts in section 9.

Deontic states of affairs have to do with the obligated, the forbidden and the permitted. Examples are that Meryl ought to pay Jane $100, that smoking is prohibited in public buildings and that John is allowed to take a day off.[9] Two basic categories of deontic states of affairs are usually distinguished: deontic states of affairs of the *ought-to-do* type and of the *ought-to-be* type. Examples of the first category are that car drivers ought to drive on the right hand side of the road, that public officers are prohibited to accept bribes and that John is permitted to walk in the park. Examples of the second category are that car drivers ought to be sober and that it is forbidden that high public officers are members of Parliament. Deontic states of affairs should be distinguished from the non-modal states of affairs on which they supervene. An example is the state of affairs that there is a contractual bond between two parties, which underlies the state of affairs that one party ought to pay the other.

Probabilistic states of affairs have to do with the probable, the certain and the uncertain. Examples of probabilistic states of affairs are that it will probably rain, that the train definitely will be late, and that Jane might pay her bill. Probabilistic states of affairs should be distinguished from anankastic states of affairs: the reasons why something is necessary are not those which make something probable or certain. The announcement that the train will be late makes it highly probable that the train will be late, but does not make it necessary, because the announcement has only impact on our beliefs about the train, not on the train itself.

4. EVENTS

Events cause changes in the total set of obtaining states of affairs. For instance, if it starts to rain, the state of affairs that it is raining starts to obtain. Other examples of events are

[8] In the law, competence is sometimes assumed to be a state of affairs of the deontic modality. On that assumption, competence is considered to imply primarily the *permission* to perform an act in the law. However, it is better to consider the *capability* to perform the act as the primary modal state of affairs implied by competence. Since such capabilities are useless if their holders are not permitted to exercise them, the permissions to do what one is capable to do may be seen as the secondary modal state of affairs implied by competence.

[9] Deontic states of affairs are discussed more extensively in chapter 6.

1. The starting of the European Economic and Monetary Union.
2. The apple's falling on the ground.
3. Jane's dying.
4. John taking away the car of Gerald.
5. The Supreme Court annulling the judgment of the Court of Justice.
6. An international treaty being ratified.
7. The transfer of the ownership of a house.

Notice that the *occurrence* of an event is itself a (momentary) state of affairs, for instance the state of affairs that John takes away Gerald's car.

A special kind of events are *acts*: events that consist of the intentional behavior of an individual (examples 4-7). A special category of acts are the so-called *juridical acts* (examples 5-7). Juridical acts are discussed in section 9.

4.1 The effects of an event

By an event, one or more states of affairs *State of affairs*$_1$ stop obtaining and other states of affairs *State of affairs*$_2$ start to obtain (cf. figure 1). For instance, if the event that it starts to rain occurs, the state of affairs that it is not raining stops obtaining and the state of affairs that it is raining starts to obtain.

I will use rectangular boxes to denote states of affairs, and rounded boxes to represent events. Arrows indicate the directed connection between states of affairs. If the state of affairs that stops to obtain by an event is trivial or irrelevant, it is not shown (cf. figure 3).

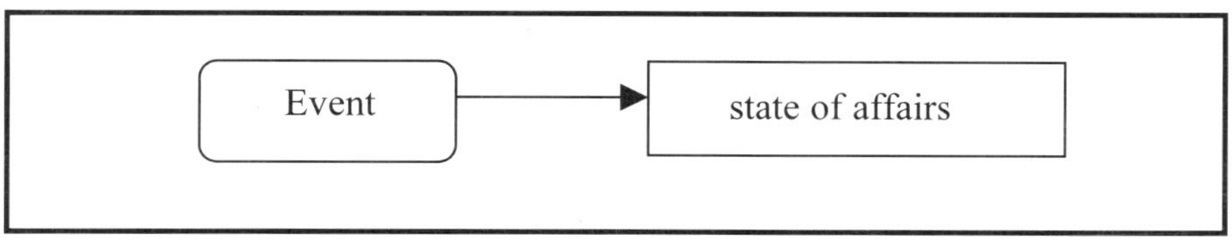

Figure 3: The initial state of affairs is sometimes not shown

Since the occurrence of an event is itself a state of affairs (it is a fact that it starts to rain), there is another way to depict the event of Figure 1:

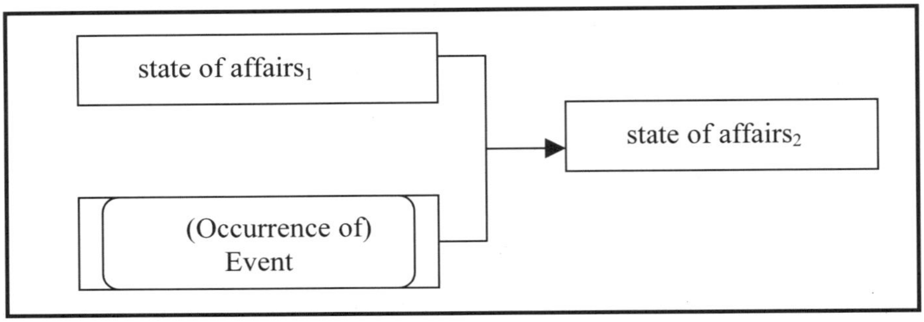

Figure 4: The occurrence of an event as a state of affairs.

To indicate that the occurrence of an event is a special state of affairs related to an event, it is shown as a rectangular box containing a rounded box.

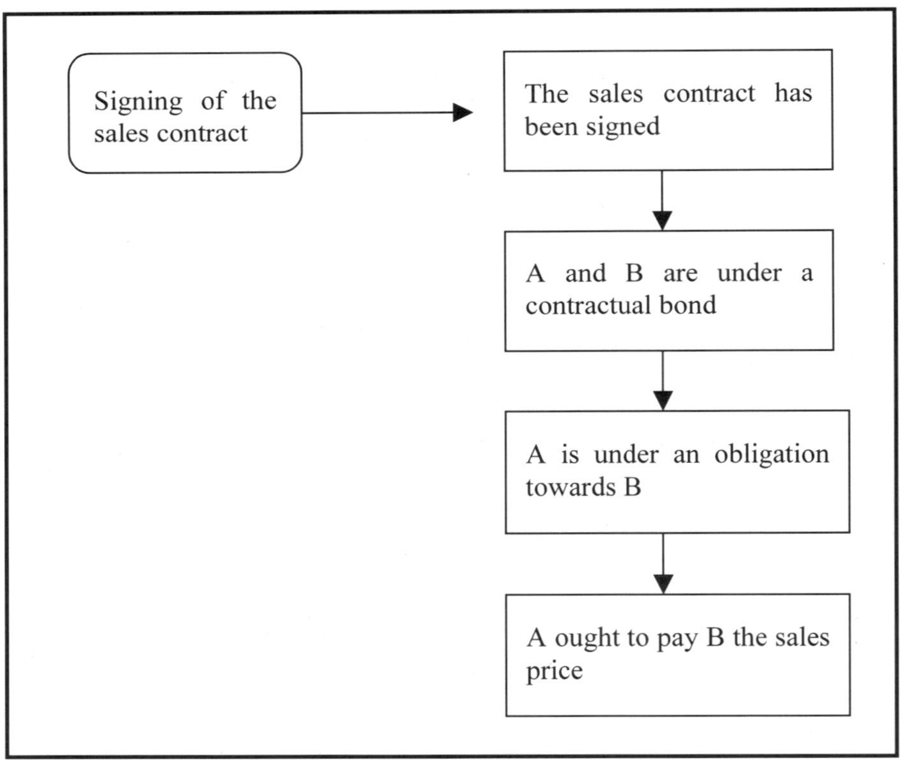

Figure 5: An event can have derived effects

An event can have effects on more than one level. For instance, the event of signing a sales contract trivially results in the state of affairs that the sales contract has been signed. The same event also has the (derived) effect that the signing parties have a contractual bond. Moreover, the contractual bond between the parties involves that the one party has an obligation toward the other party, which in turn involves that the party under the obligation has a duty to perform some action. The relations are depicted in figure 5. The vertical arrows stand for constitution.

4.2 Supervenience of events

Events can supervene on other events, just as states of affairs can supervene on other states of affairs. This is illustrated by the example of the signing of a contract that indirectly leads to the existence of a contractual bond (cf. figure 5). The event of signing of the sales contract is in a sense also the event of engaging into a contractual bond. Engaging into a contractual bond *supervenes* on the signing of the contract.

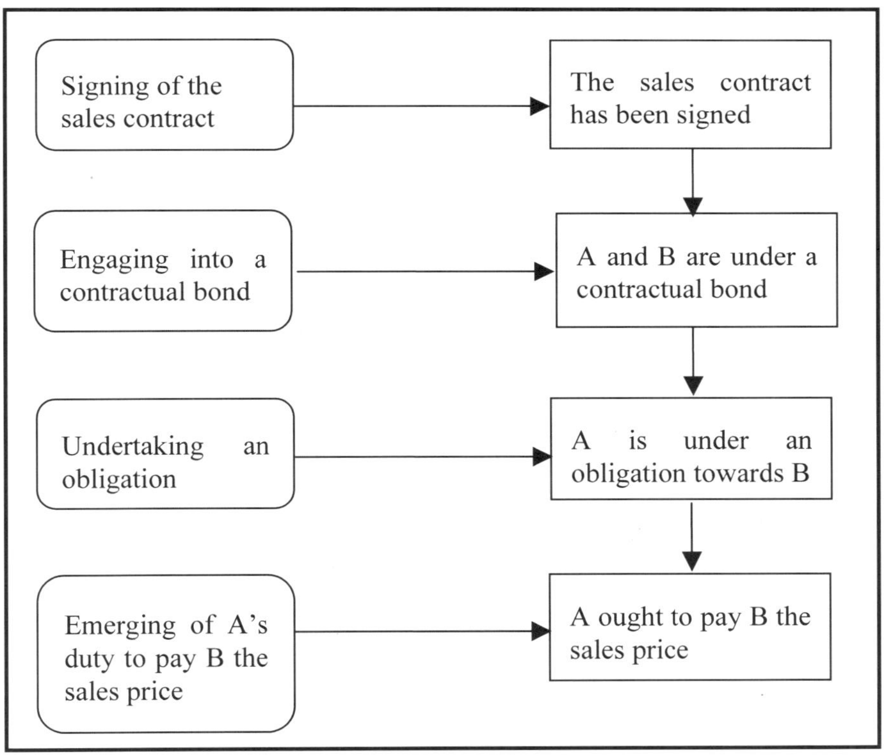

Figure 6: An event can supervene on another event

Each of the derived effects of the signing of the sales contract in figure 5 can be regarded as the result of an event that supervenes on the signing of the contract, as shown in figure 6.

In figure 6 arrows seem to be used in a new way, namely between supervening events. However, if the alternative way of depicting events (as in figure 4) is used, it turns out that the supervenience of events can be regarded as a special case of the supervenience of states of affairs. Cf. figure 7.

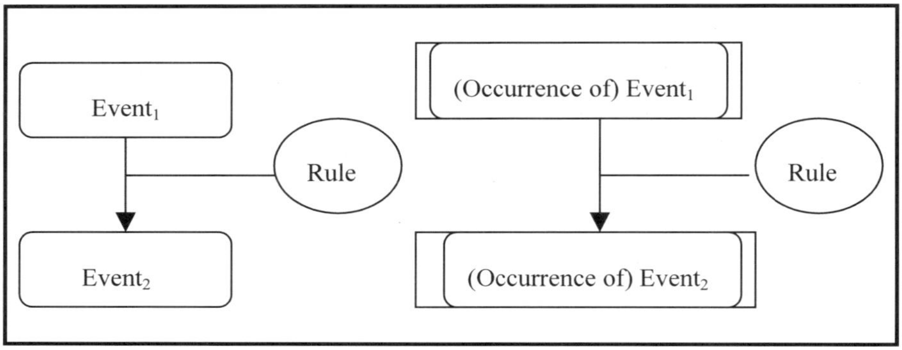

Figure 7: Two ways of depicting the supervenience of events

5. RULES

A connection between states of affairs which makes that one state of affairs 'brings about' another one, either in the sense of constitution and causation, is called a *rule*. It is, for instance, a rule that if a contract is signed, a contractual bond between the contracting parties comes into existence. The formulation of a rule should be distinguished from the state of affairs that this rule exists. It is possible to formulate all kinds of rules, but obviously not all of these possible rules exist. The existence of a rule is a particular state of affairs, which may obtain or not. Connections between states of affairs can only be based on rules that actually exist.

The reader should be aware of other philosophical and legal connotations of the term 'rule' that might be confusing. Rules in the sense of this chapter include many divergent phenomena, such as physical laws, rules of evidence, power conferring rules, and (other) legal rules.[10] For instance, Newton's law of gravitation is in my terminology a rule, because it connects the states of affairs that two bodies have masses m_1 and m_2, and the state of affairs that these bodies attract each other with a force equal to Gm_1m_2/r^2 (where G is the gravitational constant and r is the distance between the gravitational centers of the bodies).

It might be a rule of evidence that if three independent witnesses saw someone commit the crime, this person counts as having committed the crime. This hypothetical rule connects the states of affairs that Peter, Paul and Mary saw Snoopy kill Ice T, and that Snoopy counts as having killed Ice T.

It is a power conferring rule that if the legislator attributes some legal body with the competence to perform a particular juridical act, this body can perform that act. This rule connects for instance the states of affairs that the legislator gave the community council the power to make by-laws and that the community council can make by-laws.

In section 2 I mentioned two fundamental types of connections between states of affairs, namely constitution and causation. This distinction corresponds to a similar distinction between types of rules. If one state of affairs constitutes another one, there is a *constitutive rule* underlying the connection.[11] An example is the rule that someone is checkmated if the King is threatened and the threat cannot be taken away in one move. The state of affairs that the King is threatened and the threat cannot be taken away in one move is the *reason* that someone is checkmated.

A state of affairs can be brought about by an *event*. Rules that govern the relation between an event and the effects that result from it are called *causal rules*. An example is the rule that heating an object (an event) makes that the heated object is warmer than before. The event does not have to be a purely physical event. For instance, signing a sales contract is the (legal) cause for the existence of a contractual bond.

Since the condition part of rules can only contain states of affairs, there is no place for events in the rule conditions. Therefore causal rules must attach consequences to *the occurrence* of an event, which is a state of affairs, possibly in combination with other states of affairs. For instance, there might be a causal rule that if somebody has the competence to make regulations (a

[10] Rules in this sense are comparable to constraints in the sense of situation semantics. Cf. Barwise and Perry 1983, 94f. In chapter 5 the function of rules as constraints plays a central role.

[11] Notice that my use of the term 'constitutive rule', which is opposed to a causal rule, deviates from Searle's use, which distinguishes between constitutive and regulative rules. Cf. Searle 1969, 33f.

state of affairs) and exercises this competence (the occurrence of an event), the regulation that was made is valid (state of affairs of the conclusion). This construction is depicted in figure 8, in which the causal rule connecting the states of affairs that L is competent and that L makes regulation XYZ to the state of affairs that regulation XYZ is valid, is represented as a circle.

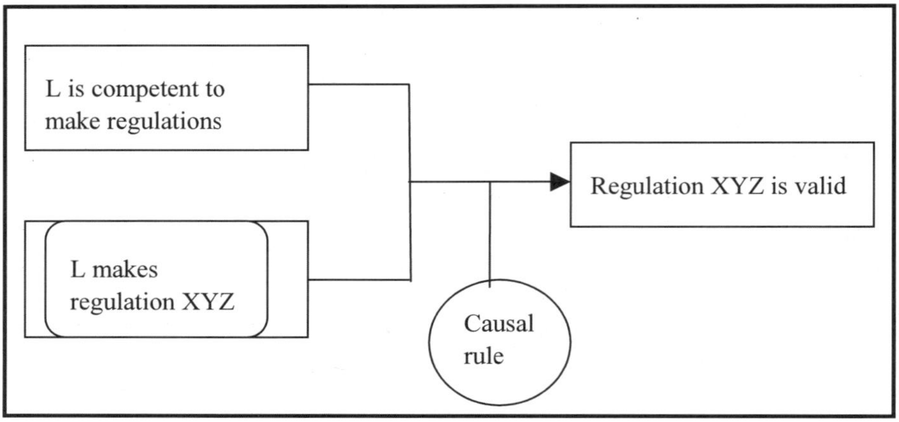

Figure 8: The occurrence of an event as a state of affairs

6. SIGNING A SALES CONTRACT

In the sections 6 to 11, I illustrate the uses of the abstract model of the law by analyzing some central legal topics. As a first example of the application of the abstract model, I elaborate the example of signing a sales contract that was used throughout the discussions above. The following figure extends figure 6.

The figure counts eight states of affairs, four events, and three rules. Four of the states of affairs form the initial state, where:

- the sales contract has not been signed by A and B,
- A and B are not under a contractual bond,
- A is not under an obligation towards B, and
- it is not the case that A ought to pay B the sales price.

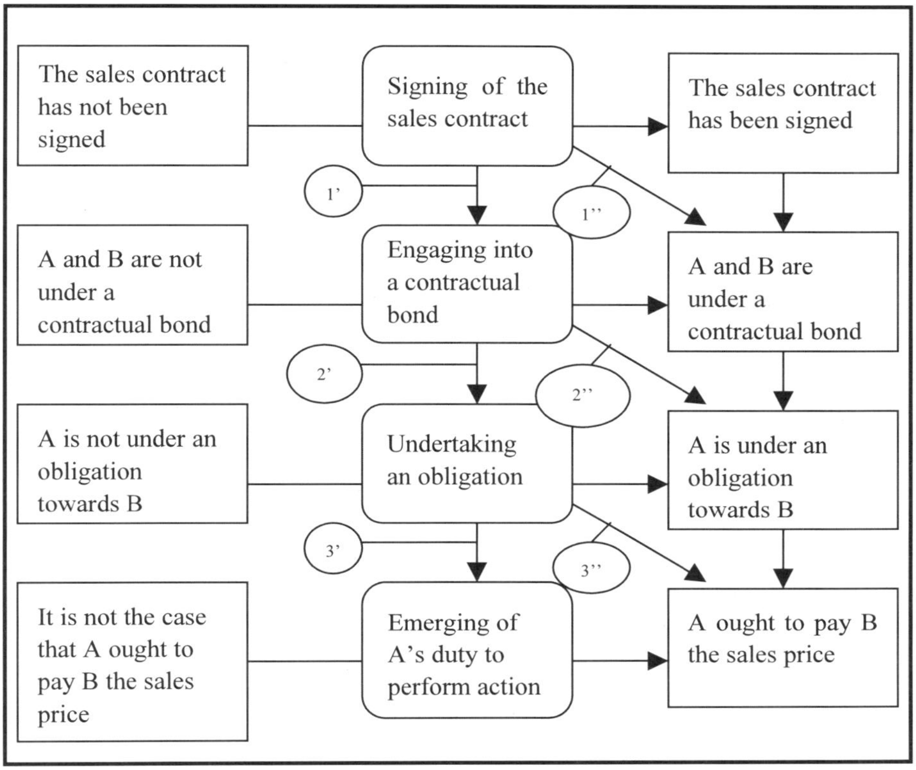

Figure 9: Signing a sales contract

In this initial state, four events take place:

- A and B sign the sales contract,
- A and B engage into a contractual bond,
- A undertakes the obligation towards B to pay him the sales price,
- the emergence of A's duty to pay B the sales price.

These events lead to the four states of affairs that form the final state:

- the sales contract has been signed by A and B,
- A and B are under a contractual bond,
- A is under an obligation towards B, and
- A ought to pay B the sales price.

The states of affairs in the final state supervene on each other: the state of affairs that A ought to pay B the sales price supervenes on the state of affairs that A is under an obligation towards B, which in its turn supervenes on the state of affairs that A and B are under a contractual bond, which supervenes on the state of affairs that the sales contract has been signed by A and B. The connections between these states of affairs result from three rules:

1. Signing a sales contract leads to a contractual bond.
2. A contractual bond implies obligations of the contracting parties towards each other.
3. An obligation implies the duty to perform the contents of the obligation.

The events also supervene on each other, just as the final states of affairs. The emergence of A's duty to pay B the sales price supervenes on A's undertaking the obligation towards B to pay him the sales price. A's undertaking of this obligation supervenes on A and B's engaging into a contractual bond, which in its turn supervenes on the signing of the sales contract. The connections between these events result from three rules, closely related to the three rules above:

1'. Signing a sales contract is a form of engaging into a contractual bond.
2'. Engaging into a contractual bond implies the undertaking of obligations of the contracting parties towards each other.
3'. Undertaking an obligation implies the emergence of the duty to perform the contents of the obligation.

In figure 9, three more rules are marked, which non-trivially connect the events and the final states of affairs:

1''. Signing a sales contract leads to a contractual bond.
2''. Engaging into a contractual bond implies obligations of the contracting parties towards each other.
3''. Undertaking an obligation implies the duty to perform the contents of the obligation.

There are also the trivial connections between the events and the states of affairs that start to obtain by them, e.g., the event of signing the contract that leads to the state of affairs that the contract has been signed. Notice that the non-trivial effect of an event (as results from the rules 1'', 2'' and 3'') is the trivial effect of its supervening event. The rules in a triplet such as 1/1'/1'' are closely related and are in practice not distinguished.

7. CLASSIFICATION

An important topic in law is classification. To make a legal rule applicable, a factual situation must be classified, to make it fall under the rule's conditions. It is important to note that classification in the law is not just determining whether something falls under the meaning of a word, but also assignment of a particular status. The possible outcomes of classification encompass diverse states of affairs. Something or somebody may be classified as, for instance, a vehicle, tortuous, force majeure, the cause of particular damages, mens rea, competent to issue licenses and liable to be punished. In the present model of the law, classification is treated as a special case of constitution. This means that classification is taken to be based on constitutive rules.

One type of classification is subsumption of a concrete object under an abstract category. The determination of whether some object classifies as a vehicle is an example that has become traditional.[12]

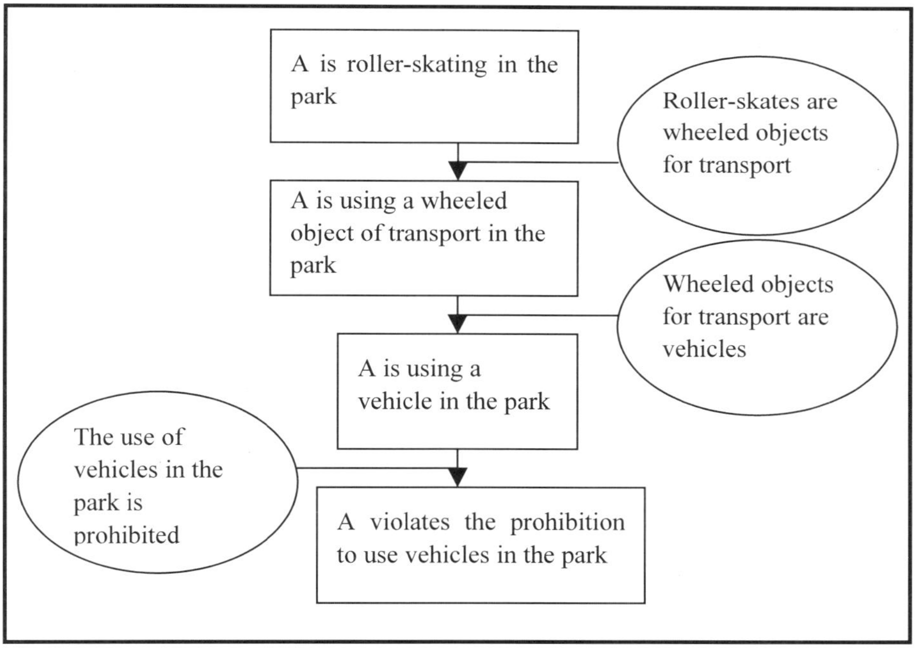

Figure 10: Classification as subsumption

Assume that there is a rule that the use of vehicles in the park is prohibited, and also a rule that defines vehicles as objects on wheels which are meant for transportation. Can roller-skates be classified as vehicles in the sense of

[12] Cf. Hart 1961, 123f.

the first rule?[13] Since roller-skates are objects on wheels meant for transportation and therefore vehicles, somebody roller-skating in the park is violating the prohibition to use vehicles in the park:

As a second example of classification, I discuss the classification of a tort as the cause of damages. In the Netherlands, a tort is classified as the cause of damages if the tort was a necessary condition (conditio sine qua non) for the damages and the damages can reasonably by imputed to the tort. In the present model, imputation is depicted as follows:

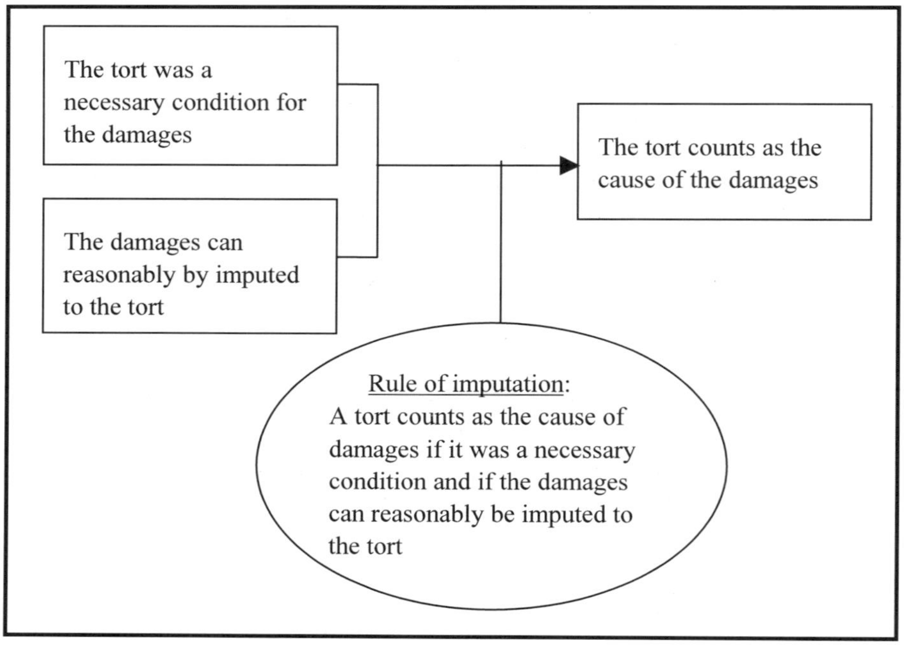

Figure 11: Classification as imputation

8. RIGHTS

I discuss three kinds of rights in terms of my model: claims against some concrete person (iura in personam), property rights (iura in re), and human

[13] In this example I assume that there is no special rule that governs the issue whether roller skates are vehicles.

rights. It turns out that the three kinds of rights can all be considered as *states*, i.e., momentary states of affairs (cf. section 3.1).

8.1 Claims

In his paper Tû-tû, Ross writes:[14]

> 'We find the following phrases, for example, in legal language as used in statutes and the administration of justice:
>
> 1. *If a loan is granted, there comes into being a claim;*
> 2. *If a claim exists, then payment shall be made on the day it falls due;*
>
> which is only a roundabout way of saying:
>
> 3. *If a loan is granted, then payment shall be made on the day it falls due.*
>
> That 'claim' mentioned in (1) and (2), but not in (3), is obviously (...) not a real thing; is nothing at all, merely a word, an empty word devoid of all semantic reference.'

Here Ross provides an account of phenomena like claims as mere intermediaries between facts: the intermediary is only a manner of speaking and does not really exist. While rejecting this reductionist consequence, MacCormick and Weinberger adopt the idea that certain legal states of affairs function as an intermediary between other (legal) states of affairs. They describe a particular category of legal concepts, called *institutional legal facts*, which are in my terminology related to states of affairs that supervene on other states of affairs.[15]

Institutional legal facts have certain features in common. For each of them, the law contains rules which lay down when, e.g., a contract, a corporation, or an obligation of reparation, comes into existence. These rules are called *institutive rules*. The law also contains rules that attach further legal consequences in case these concepts apply (if the concerning institutional legal facts obtain). These rules are called *consequential rules*. And, finally, the law has rules which determine when the phenomena at stake disappear again. These rules are called *terminative rules*. See figure 12.

[14] Ross 1957. Quotation after Lloyd 1979, 625.

[15] MacCormick and Weinberger 1986, 52/3. See also the discussion of reason-based facts in chapter 6, section 6.

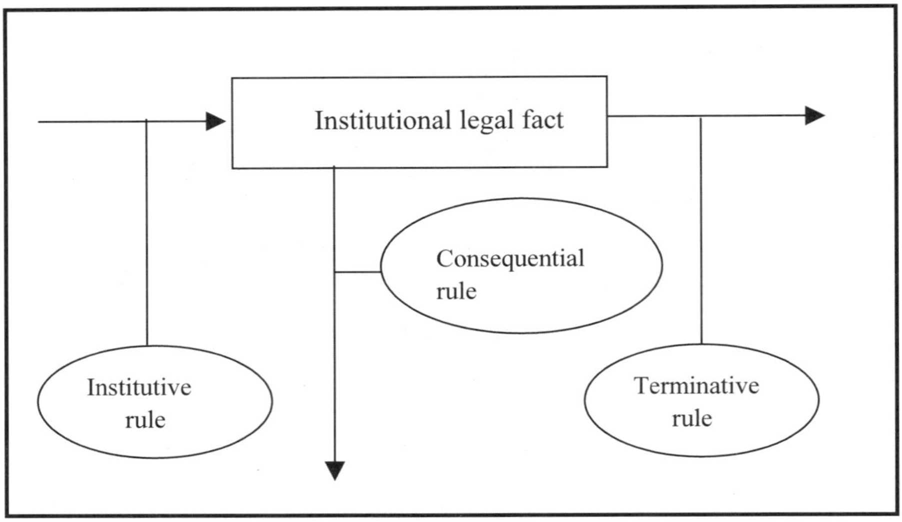

Figure 12: Institutional legal facts

The figure agrees with my model. Institutional legal facts are then states the coming into existence and disappearing of which is regulated by causal rules (institutive and terminative rules). Constitutive rules (consequential rules) deal with the states of affairs which are constituted by states. As Ross' discussion shows, claims fit nicely in this picture. [16]

8.2 Property rights

The next example deals with property rights, such as the ownership of a house. If A owns the house H, A is entitled, with the exclusion of everybody else, to use the house. Moreover, A has the power to transfer the ownership. The law may also attach other legal consequences to the ownership of a house. For instance, in the Netherlands and in Belgium, owners of houses are subject to special taxes. These consequences of ownership are attached to the state of ownership by legal rules. The rules might have been different, which goes to show that the legal consequences of ownership are not part of

[16] This way of looking at the structure of legal systems is also a central theme in Odelstad and Lindahl 2002 and Lindahl and Odelstad 2004.

the ownership itself, but rather states of affairs which are non-causally connected to ownership.[17]

The ownership of a house can be acquired in different ways. A common one is that somebody else was the owner and transferred his ownership to the new owner. Such a transfer is an event which has the direct effects that the original owner loses his property right and that the new owner acquires it. The transfer has also indirect effects, because all legal consequences which are attached to ownership disappear for the original owner and come into existence for the new owner.

Another way to acquire the ownership of a house is to build the house on ground which one owns. This event only causes a new ownership to come into existence, not the disappearance of a previous ownership. The passing away of the original owner is a way for an inheritor to acquire ownership. All these different ways of becoming the owner of a house indirectly lead to the legal consequences attached to ownership.

There are also several ways to lose ownership. Transfer is again the most prominent one, but passing away of the owner, devastation of the property, prescription, and expropriation are other ways to lose ownership.

As this example about the ownership of a house illustrates, property rights can be treated as 'empty' states, the coming into existence, the (legal) consequences, and the disappearance of which is governed by rules. Cf. figure 13.

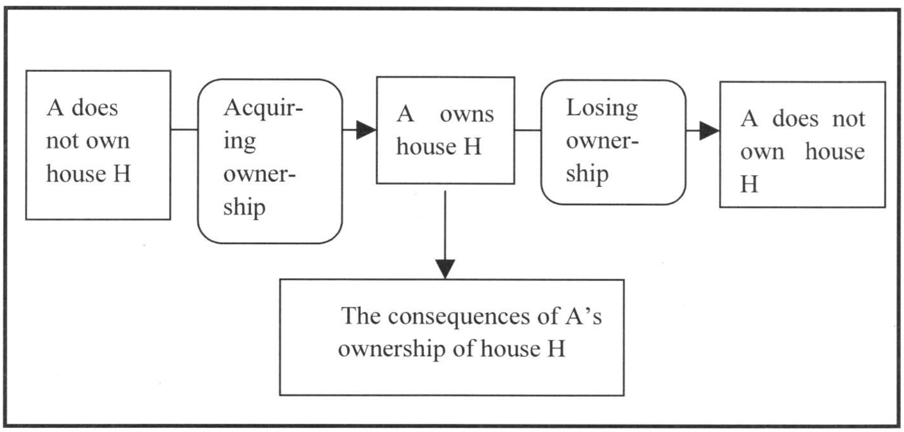

Figure 13: Acquisition, consequences, and loss of ownership

[17] It may plausibly be argued that some consequences of ownership are so essential that if they would not exist, the underlying state would not be ownership anymore, but rather some other state. The discussion of this view falls outside the scope of this paper.

8.3 Human rights

Human rights, such as the right of freedom of expression, differ in nature from property rights. Nevertheless, having a human right is also a state, and is in that respect very similar to having a property right. We take a closer look at the freedom of expression.

If P has the freedom of expression, this has several consequences. The first and foremost consequence is that P is in principle permitted to express his opinion about any issue. If we follow Dworkin, having a human right also involves that regulations that infringe these rights are invalid.[18] In other words, for regulations that infringe these rights, the rule that regulations which were validly made contain valid law, is not applicable.[19]

Legal systems usually attribute human rights to all persons on the basis of their being humans. This means that (instances of) human rights come into existence as soon as a human being comes into existence, and end when human beings pass away.

The important thing to the note about rights is that, in spite of the different nature of claims, property rights and human rights, the same scheme applies: there are events by which these rights come into existence and other events by which they disappear again and there are rules of law which determine the legal consequences of having these rights. In other words, rights are legal states on which legal consequences supervene (in the sense of the sections 3.1 and 3.2).

9. JURIDICAL ACTS

Juridical acts are acts to which the law assigns consequences because of the intention to invoke these consequences by means of the act. For instance, engaging into a contract is a juridical act, to which the law assigns the consequence that a contract exists.

A juridical act supervenes on another act which legally counts as a juridical act. To count as a juridical act, the underlying act must satisfy a number of conditions, such as the condition that the actor is competent to perform the juridical act in question. For instance, to be able to engage into a

[18] Cf. Dworkin 1978, 184f.
[19] Cf. Hage 1997, 173.

contract, both parties must have the competence to do so. To make legislation, the actor must have the competence to legislate.

Being competent is a kind of anankastic state of affairs (cf. section 3.3), which must supervene on another states of affairs. For instance, one must be of age to be competent to engage into a contract.

The following figure (from which the rules are left out) depicts a typical juridical act with its preconditions and its consequences. It is an adaptation of a part of figure 9.

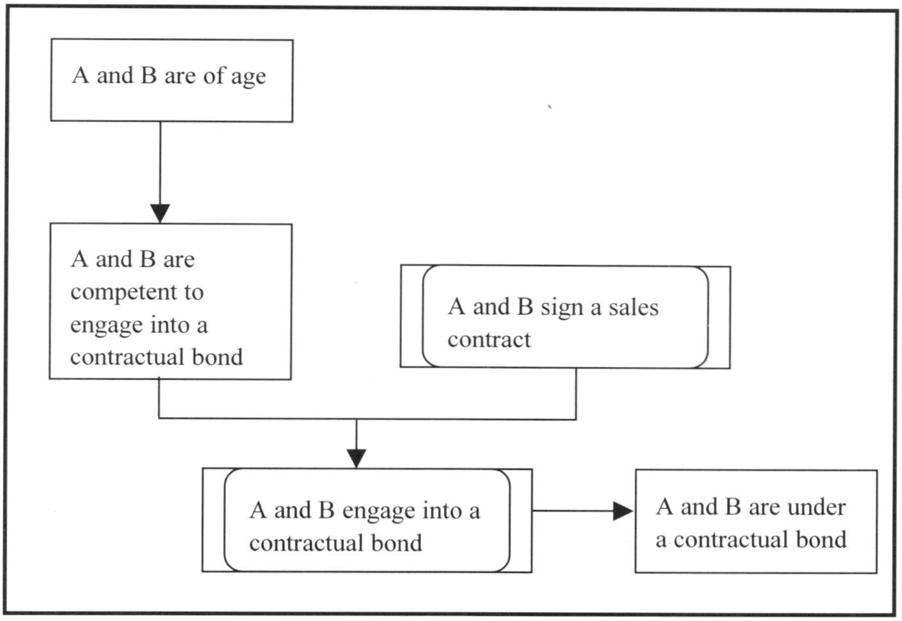

Figure 14: A juridical act and its consequences

Notice that this figure contains two actions, namely signing the sales contract and engaging into a contractual bond. The former counts as a juridical act, because the actor was competent to perform that juridical act. Notice moreover that the competence to engage into contracts is itself a state of affairs that supervenes on another state of affairs, namely being of age.

10. VALIDITY

In the law, the notion of validity is used for acts, for products, and for rules. If an act satisfies all the conditions that hold for a juridical act, the act is valid as a juridical act. Juridical acts can aim at the creation of a particular product, such as a contract, a license, or legislation. If the juridical act is valid, its product is also said to be valid: contracts, licenses and legislation are valid if the acts from which they result are valid as juridical acts.

In the case of legislation, there is still another form of validity. The rules which are created through valid legislation are said to be valid too. This validity is nothing else than the rule's mode of existence.[20] So, in the case of rules based on legislation, we can distinguish three kinds of validity which supervene on each other:

- validity of the legislative act as a juridical act;
- validity of the legislative product (e.g. the statute);
- validity of the rules created by means of the legislative product.

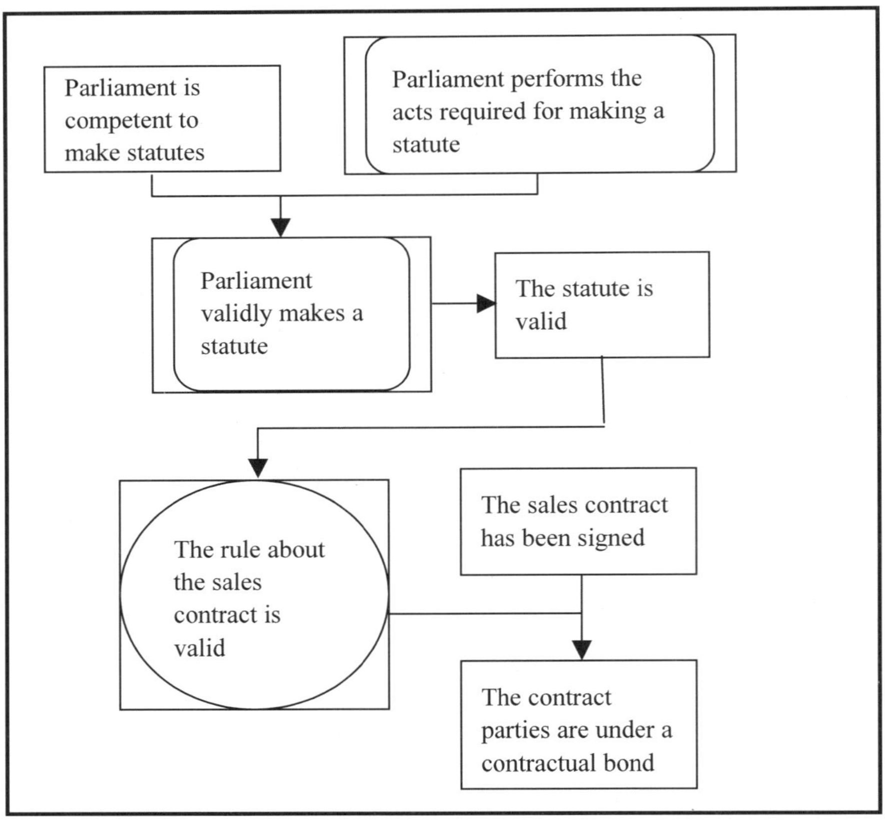

Figure 15: The validity of acts, products and rules

[20] Cf. Kelsen 1979, 136.

For instance, since Parliament is competent to make statutes, the acts Parliament performs to make a statute lead to the valid making of a statute. The resulting valid statute leads to the validity of some rule, say about sale contracts. The validity of the rule gives rise to a connection between states of affairs by constitution. Figure 15 gives an example containing the three kinds of validity. Notice that the rule and its validity (i.e., the state of affairs that the rule is valid) are shown in the figure in a dual way similar to the way in which an event and its occurrence are shown.

11. JURISTIC FACTS

Traditionally, continental jurisprudence distinguishes the notions of 'juristic fact', 'act', 'bare juristic fact', 'juridical act', and 'factual act', which seem to be closely connected to the primitives of my abstract model.

Juristic facts are facts to which the law attaches consequences. Examples of juristic facts are sale, theft, death and lapse of time. Possible legal consequences of these examples include the coming into existence of the vendor's right to be paid, the liability of the thief to be punished, inheritance and the preclusion of criminal proceedings, respectively. Juristic facts are divided into *acts* (that in the law cannot only be performed by humans, but also, more generally, by juristic persons), such as sale and theft and *bare juristic facts*, such as death and the passing of time.

Acts are divided in *juridical acts* and *factual acts*. Juridical acts require an intention aimed at legal consequences as manifested by a declaration and the competence to perform them. Examples of juridical acts are buying a house and recognizing a child. Factual acts are those acts that have legal consequences, but are not meant as such. Examples of factual acts are torts and undue payment.

The traditional categories and their relations are summarized in the following figure:

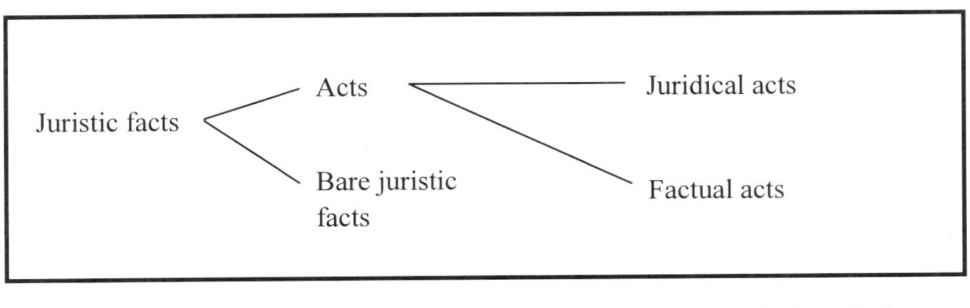

Figure 16: Traditional categories of juristic facts and their relations

How do these traditional categories fit in the model? The first thing to notice is that the notion of a state of affairs is preferable as element of the model to the notion of a fact. The choice for states of affairs has the advantage that it becomes possible to distinguish between obtaining and non-obtaining states of affairs. This is useful if one wants to deal with connections between hypothetical states of affairs, as in 'If the state of affairs that John has stolen obtains, then the state of affairs that John is punishable obtains', or - in more normal terminology - 'If John has stolen, then John is punishable'.

Second, it should be noticed that the model distinguishes acts (as a kind of events) from the occurrence of acts (as states of affairs). This has the advantages that the changes in the obtaining states of affairs which are caused by acts are appreciated and that the difference between causation and constitution can be made explicit. In the traditional model sketched above, acts are treated as a subcategory of facts, which seems to be a category mistake. It is therefore better to read 'act' in the traditional model as 'the fact that some act took place'.

Just like the traditional view, the model treats juridical acts as a kind of acts. It is interesting that (intended or unintended) legal consequences of juristic facts are central in the traditional categories. In the model, these correspond to the consequences that supervene on a state of affairs because of legal rules.

From this brief comparison, it will be clear that the model of the law presented in this chapter is richer than the traditional model, while remaining on a similar level of abstraction.

Chapter 8

DIALECTICAL MODELS IN ARTIFICIAL INTELLIGENCE AND LAW

1. INTRODUCTION

Dialectics and dialogues[1] play an important role in the field of Artificial Intelligence and Law.[2] There seem to be two major grounds for this popularity of dialectics and dialogues, corresponding to both form and content of legal reasoning. Legal reasoning is centered round the application of rules and principles and this kind of reasoning is defeasible. Dialectics provides a suitable tool to analyze and model this defeasibility.

Moreover, the law is an open system. As a consequence, there may be disagreement about the starting points of legal arguments, which in turn makes uncertain which legal conclusions are justified. Dialogues provide a

[1] The difference between dialectics and dialogues, as I use these terms, is explained in section 5. Ahead of this explanation, dialogues can be taken to be real dialogues governed by a dialogue protocol. Dialectics is the more general category, which also includes dialog-like presentations of logical systems.

[2] The three-ply arguments in the HYPO-system (Ashley 1991) can be seen as a kind of dialogues between hypothetical adversaries. This line is continued in later work building on the HYPO-foundations (e.g. Skalak and Rissland 1991 and 1992; Rissland, Skalak and Friedman 1996; Aleven 1997. More explicitly dialectical is the work of Gordon (1994 and 1995; Gordon and Karacapilidis 1997), Nitta et al. (1993 and 1995), Prakken and Sartor (e.g. Prakken 1995; Prakken and Sartor 1996), Loui et al. (1995 and 1997), Freeman and Farley (1996) and the former research group at Maastricht University and the University of Twente (Hage et al. 1992 and 1994; Leenes et al. 1994; Lodder and Herczog 1995; Verheij 1996, 2003 (both DL and AAA) and 2004; Lodder 1997, 1998 and 1999).

means to overcome the foundational difficulties that plague (legal) justification.[3] The open nature of the law makes the outcomes of legal procedures indeterminate. I will argue in section 7 that, as a consequence, the law in concrete cases depends on the decision making procedure, without an independent standard for the correctness of this outcome. In other words, the law is the result of a procedure and dialogues are a promising way to model such a procedure.

My purpose in this chapter is to give an overview of dialectical models as they are used in the field of Artificial Intelligence and Law and the closely related fields of logic and legal theory and to distinguish between the different functions that these systems fulfill.[4] I will distinguish between three main functions, which will be discussed in turn. In the sections 2 to 4 I discuss dialectical garbs for what is essentially a definition of logical validity. In the sections 5 and 6 the topic is dialogical approaches to the establishment of the premises of arguments. The sections 7 to 11 deal with the dialogical, or, more generally, procedural, determination of the law in concrete cases. This chapter is summarized in section 12.

2. THE PIONEERING WORK OF LORENZEN AND LORENZ

In their *From Axiom to Dialogue*, Barth and Krabbe distinguish three dimensions of logic systems.[5] One is the dimension of *syntax*. Important characteristics of a logic are the number and nature of the logical constants, the way in which the lexicon is divided into categories, such as terms and relations and the ways in which sentences are constructed from elements of the lexicon.

The second dimension is the dimension of logical strength. Even given a fixed syntax, a logic may have more or less derivational power. Barth and Krabbe distinguish between (in increasing power) minimal, constructive (intuitionistic) and classical (propositional) logic, but for the purpose of Law and AI, non-monotonic logics are relevant too, as even stronger than classical logic.[6]

3 Alexy 1978, 221f.

4 Dialectical approaches are also important in other fields. See e.g. Hamblin 1970, 253f. and Bench-Capon et al. 1992.

5 Barth and Krabbe 1982, 3-13.

6 Non-monotonic logics will usually have a different syntax than propositional logic and in this respect, the comparison is not fully correct.

The third dimension, which is the most important for this chapter, is the dimension of garb. The 'same' logic can be presented in different forms. Barth and Krabbe distinguish between, amongst others, axiomatic, model-theoretic and dialectical presentation of a logic. In my discussion of dialectical garbs for logical theories, I will deal with two ways in which a dialectical presentation of a logic can be fruitful. First comes the seminal work of Lorenzen and Lorenz, to illustrate some of the basic ideas behind the dialectical approach. Second, I will show how the dialectical garb can be used to model the defeasible nature of reasoning with rules and principles.

2.1 Validity as the outcome of a winning strategy

In their *Dialogische Logik*, Lorenzen and Lorenz show how it is possible to characterize logical validity in terms of critical dialogues, rather than by means of axioms or truth tables.[7] Let me illustrate their approach by means of two examples. The setting of the examples is that there are two dialogue parties, called P (proponent) and O (opponent). Both parties have an associated set of sentences (possibly empty) to which they are committed. Commitment means that parties are not allowed to attack sentences to which they are committed. P makes a claim and O is allowed to attack this claim, thereby forcing P to defend it. There are rules governing this game of attacking and defending and these rules are related to the logical operators. The basic idea is that a sentence `S` logically follows from a set of sentences `Premises`, if P has a winning strategy to defend `S` on the assumption that O is committed to the sentences in `Premises`.

Suppose that O is committed to the sentence `C` and that P has claimed the sentence `A → (B ∨ C)`. The rules that define the logical operators (see section 2.2) specify how such a claim can be attacked. For the present example they imply that O must attack this claim by claiming `A`. This creates for P the obligation to claim `B ∨ C` (or to attack `A`). The sentence `B ∨ C` can be accepted by O, in which case P has succeeded in defending his original claim. However, O can also attack `B ∨ C`. In that case P must claim either `B` or `C`. In our example, P would be wise to claim `C`, because O is committed to that sentence and is therefore not allowed to attack it. If P claims `C`, he wins the dialogue and his original claim holds good. If P defends `B ∨ C` by claiming `B`, however, O can attack `B` and then P loses the dialogue because he has no way to defend this claim. The following table illustrates the first version of this brief dialogue.[8]

[7] Lorenzen and Lorenz 1978.
[8] The example does not follow the syntax of Lorenzen and Lorenz.

P	**O**
claim: A → (B ∨ C)	claim: A
claim: B ∨ C	? B ∨ C
claim: C	is committed to C and loses the dialogue

The second version of the argument would run as follows:

P	**O**
claim: A → (B ∨ C)	claim: A
claim: B ∨ C	? B ∨ C
claim: B	? B
has no additional defense and loses the dialogue	

As the different outcomes of the two dialogues concerning the same claim illustrate, the validity of a claim, given the commitments of the opponent, does not guarantee that the proponent wins the dialogue. However, it does guarantee that the proponent has a winning strategy (cf. version 1). It would be more in the spirit of Lorenzen and Lorenz to turn this around and say that a claimed sentence logically follows from the commitments of the opponent, if the proponent has a winning strategy. Whether he actually uses that strategy in a dialogue does not matter.

2.2 Dialectical characterization of logical operators

Lorenzen and Lorenz do not only give a dialectical characterization of valid conclusions; the meanings of the logical operators are also defined in terms of their dialectical use. I will illustrate this by means of the dialectical characterization of the operators of propositional logic.[9]

CONJUNCTION

If P claims A & B, O can attack this claim by ?l and ?r. ?l may be read as 'Is the left conjunct true?' and ?r as 'Is the right conjunct true?' This attack imposes on P the duty to defend the conjunction by claiming respectively A or B.

[9] Lorenzen and Lorenz 1978, 38.

P	O	P
A & B	?l	A
	?r	B

DISJUNCTION

If P claims A ∨ B, O can attack this claim by ?. This attack imposes on P the duty to defend the disjunction by claiming either A or B.

P	O	P
A ∨ B	?	A
		B

IMPLICATION

If P claims A → B, O can attack this claim by claiming A. This attack imposes on P the duty to defend the implication by claiming B, or by attacking A.[10]

P	O	P
A → B	A	B

NEGATION

If P claims A, O can attack this claim by claiming ~A. If this happens, P has lost the dialogue game. However, O is only allowed to make this attack if he was not committed to A.

P	O
A	~A

2.3 Some characteristics of the Dialogische Logik

There are four characteristics of the approach of Lorenzen and Lorenz to which I want to draw the reader's attention, because they are important in relation to the other work that will be discussed.

a) *The dialogue steps correspond approximately to the steps within a single argument.* If the dialogue games are compared to proofs in syntactic renderings of logic, a dialogue move together with the

[10] If O succeeds in defending A, P still has the duty to defend the implication by claiming B.

answer to it are the counterpart of a proof step. For instance, in the proof theory of propositional logic it is possible to derive $A \vee B$ from A in one step. The dialogical version of this step is that the claim that $A \vee B$ is questioned and then defended by claiming A.

b) This correspondence can be explained by the fact that the traditional proof steps are based on the meanings (semantics) of the logical operators, while these same meanings are in the view of Lorenzen and Lorenz defined by the dialogue rules that are attached to them. *The dialogue rules reflect the logical meanings of the operators, or the other way round.*
c) *To determine whether a sentence follows from other sentences, it is necessary to consider all possible dialogues.* It is possible to make mistakes in arguing for a conclusion and as a consequence it is impossible to define the validity of a conclusion given a set of premises in terms of the actual reasoning behavior of dialogue parties. That is why the definition of logical validity makes use of all possible dialogue games, by working with the notion of a winning strategy.
d) *The dialogue games assume a fixed set of commitments (premises).* This is a consequence of the fact that the dialogues aim at characterizing the notion of logical consequence. It does not matter whether the conclusion of a dialogue or a winning strategy is true or false; the only thing that matters is whether the conclusion follows from a set of premises. That is why the notion of a winning strategy presupposes a set of premises for which this strategy exists. Winning strategies are relative to a set of commitments, just like valid conclusions are relative to a set of premises.

This ends the description of the seminal work of Lorenzen and Lorenz, which deals with the dialectical characterization of the logical operators and of logical validity. In the next section we will see that dialectics can also be used to model a quite different aspect of reasoning, namely its defeasibility.

3. DEFEASIBILITY AND DIALECTICS

Most legal reasoning is based on the application of rules and principles. This even holds for case-based reasoning, because the decision in an old case is only relevant for a new case if one employs the principle that similar cases are to be treated similarly.[11] Moreover, the identification of the relevant factors in a case presupposes principles.[12]

Normally, a rule will be applied and its conclusion follows, if its conditions are satisfied. Sometimes, however, a rule should not be applied, even though its conditions are satisfied. If such a situation occurs, the conclusion of the rule does not follow. For instance, the rule that thieves are punishable is normally applied if somebody is a thief. The conclusion that this person is punishable follows 'by default'. However, if this person turns out to be insane, the rule should not be applied and the conclusion that this insane person is punishable does not follow.

Principles only lead to provisional conclusions, and only after balancing the reasons based on all relevant principles can the definitive conclusion be drawn. For instance, thieves ought to be punished and the fact that somebody is a thief is a reason why this person ought to be punished. As long as no other relevant information is considered, the conclusion should be that this person ought to be punished. If this person turns out to be a minor, however, there is also a reason why this person ought not to be punished. Only after weighing the reasons for and against punishing, the conclusion can be drawn whether this minor thief ought to be punished. The result of this weighing of reasons may be that our minor thief ought not to be punished.

In both cases, when the application of a rule is blocked and when a reason based on a principle must be weighed against other reasons, the addition of new information (an exception to a rule, or the applicability of a colliding principle) can take away the justification of a conclusion that was previously justified.[13] As my use of the word 'new' in the previous sentence already indicated, defeasibility of arguments is strongly connected with a procedural view of reasoning. In this respect, defeasibility differs from the notion of non-monotonicity, with which it is sometimes identified. (Non-)monotonicity is a characteristic of a system of logic. If a logic is monotonic, the valid conclusions of a theory are a subset of the valid conclusions of every superset of this theory. This definition does not involve the notion of time, let alone of a procedure. Defeasibility, on the contrary, becomes relevant with an increase of information over time. At a certain moment in time, when a particular amount of information is available, it is justified to draw some conclusions. At a later moment, when more information has become available, not all of these previously justified conclusions can be justified anymore, either because the rule on which they are based should not

[11] See chapter 3, section 13.

[12] Kaptein 1995.

[13] See chapter 1.

be applied, or because new reasons against the conclusion have become available.[14]

Although defeasibility is connected with the idea of time and therefore also with the idea of a process, it does not automatically lead to the notion of a procedure, let alone a dialectical procedure. For instance, the acquisition of knowledge by a single person over time will involve the defeat of previously drawn conclusions. Often, however, the defeat of an argument and its conclusion will be based on new information introduced by one's opponent in a debate. That makes it particularly attractive to use a dialectical way of characterizing defeasible reasoning.

3.1 Battles of arguments

Such a dialectical way of characterizing defeasible reasoning has recently become rather popular. Several authors have modeled defeasible reasoning as a battle of arguments.[15] Given a set of premises and some underlying logic, it is possible to formulate a number of arguments that lead to different conclusions.

Arguments can be in conflict in basically two ways.[16] First, it is possible that the conclusions of two arguments are incompatible.[17] This would be the case if there are conflicting applicable principles. Then, the weaker of the two arguments is defeated.[18] It is also possible that an argument directly attacks another argument, without having an incompatible conclusion. An argument may, for instance, lead to the conclusion that a rule employed in another argument suffers from an exception, without saying anything about the conclusion of that other argument. In that case the attacked argument is defeated.

[14] The temporal aspect of defeasible reasoning is emphasised in Verheij's CumulA-model. Verheij 1996, 107f.

[15] Proponents of this view are Loui 1987, Pollock 1987 and 1994, Vreeswijk 1993, Dung 1995, Verheij 1996 and 2003 (DL) and in the field of AI and Law, Gordon 1994 and 1995, Sartor 1994 and Prakken 1997.

[16] The following characterization of defeat abstracts from many different concrete logics and does not necessarily conform to any one of them, although - I think - it captures the spirit of most of them.

[17] The notion of incompatibility is left open to further definition. Logical inconsistency is an obvious candidate to be a form of incompatibility. The relation between incompatibility and inconsistency is discussed more elaborately in chapter 5, section 3.

[18] Which argument, if any, in a conflict is the weaker, needs further specification in a domain theory.

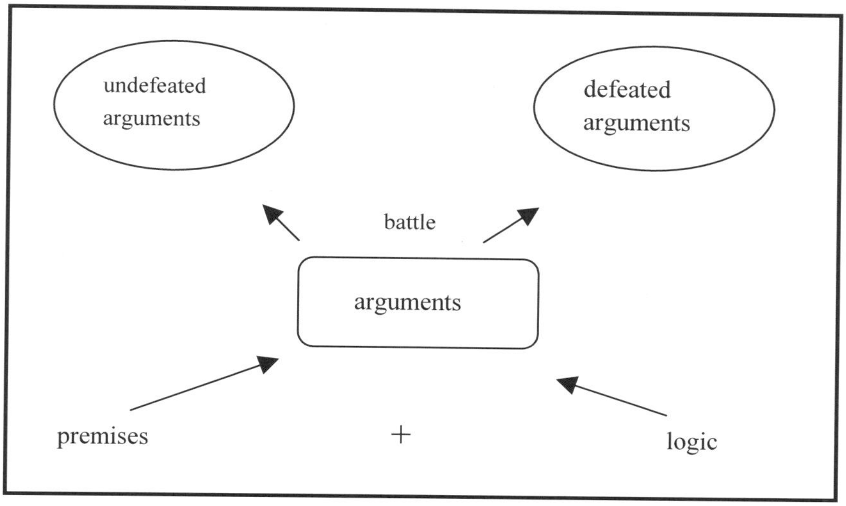

The picture is complicated a little because an argument can only defeat another argument if it is itself undefeated. As a consequence, the question whether an argument is defeated can only be answered by considering sets of arguments. One set consists of defeated arguments, the other of undefeated arguments.[19] The basic idea behind this approach is that the set of conclusions that can validly or justifiably be drawn from a set of premises by means of the underlying logic consists of the conclusions of the undefeated arguments.[20] Take, for instance, the following example[21]:

I. Mary testified that John is a thief.
II. It is well-known that Mary often lies.
III. John is a minor.
IV. John is a repeat-offender.

Moreover, the following principles are valid:

[19] The variant where a battle of two arguments remains undecided is also possible. In that variant the arguments and their conclusions are divided into three categories: justified, defensible and overruled. Cf. Prakken and Sartor 1996.

[20] In the case of defeasible argumentation, the notion of the validity of an argument becomes ambiguous. Defeasible arguments are not valid in the traditional semantic sense that the truth of the premises guarantees the truth of the conclusion. They may still be valid in the sense that their conclusions are justified by their premises. Those who want to stick to the semantic notion of logical validity must choose another term for the goodness of defeasible arguments. That is why I wrote about conclusions that can validly *or justifiably* be drawn. See also chapter 1, section 5 on the nature of logic.

[21] For the sake of a clear presentation, I made some sacrifices on logical precision.

a) Somebody is a thief, if there is a testimony to that effect.
b) Testimonies of persons who are well-known liars should not be taken into account.
c) Thieves ought to be punished.
d) Minors ought not to be punished.
e) The fact that somebody is a minor is considered to be a stronger reason against punishing this person, than the fact that this person is a thief is a reason for punishing.
f) If somebody is a repeat-offender, his or her minority is disregarded.
g) Normally, nobody should be punished.
h) If somebody is a thief, there is an exception to principle g.

Given these facts and principles, the following arguments are possible:

1. Mary testified that John is a thief. Therefore John is a thief. Therefore John ought to be punished. For the same reason, there is an exception to principle g.
2. It is well-known that Mary often lies. Therefore Mary's testimony ought to be disregarded.
3. John is a minor, therefore John ought not to be punished.
4. John is a repeat-offender. Therefore his being a minor ought to be disregarded.
5. Being a minor outweighs being a thief. Therefore argument 3 defeats argument. 1.
6. Nobody should be punished. Therefore John should not be punished.

Argument 4 defeats argument 3. As a consequence argument 3 cannot defeat argument 1 anymore, as it would in principle do because of argument 5. It seems therefore that John ought to be punished, because he is a thief and there is an exception to principle g. However, the argument leading to the conclusion that John is a thief is defeated because it is well-known that Mary often lies. As a consequence it turns out that argument 6 is not defeated and that John ought not to be punished. The arguments are divided as follows:

Undefeated	Defeated
2) It is well-known that Mary often lies. Therefore Mary's testimony ought to be disregarded.	1) Mary testified that John is a thief. Therefore John is a thief. Therefore John ought to be punished. Also therefore, there is an exception to principle g.
4) John is a repeat-offender. Therefore his being a minor ought to be disregarded.	3) John is a minor. Therefore John ought not to be punished.
6) Nobody should be punished. Therefore John should not be punished.	5) Being a minor outweighs being a thief. Therefore argument 3 defeats argument. 1.

3.2 Static dialectics

In Prakken and Sartor 1996, the above view of defeasible reasoning as a battle of arguments is cast in a dialectical shape. The conclusion of an argument holds as long as no defeating counterargument is produced. If such a counterargument is produced, the original conclusion can be reinstated by producing a counter$_2$argument. A counter$_3$-argument would then defeat the conclusion again and so on.

One can imagine a debate between two parties where each party is allowed to defend some thesis by providing an argument that has this thesis as its conclusion. Moreover, they are also allowed to produce counterarguments to their opponent's arguments. For instance, the public prosecutor (PP) adduces argument 1 to the effect that John ought to be punished. This argument would defeat basic argument 6 to the effect that John ought not to be punished. The defense produces counterargument 3 in combination with argument 5 to the effect that argument of the PP does not hold. This counterargument reinstates basic argument 6. The PP counterattacks with argument 4, thereby reinstating argument 1. Then the defense comes with argument 2, thereby reinstating argument 6.

Given a set of premises and a system of logic, there may be a winning strategy to defend a particular conclusion. In the above example, for instance, there is a winning strategy for the conclusion that John ought not to be punished. Valid conclusions can then be defined as conclusions for which a winning strategy obtains. This is the counterpart in non-monotonic logic of the definition of the logical operators in terms of dialogues.

Notice that this kind of dialectics assumes a fixed set of premises and implicitly (because of the notion of a winning strategy) deals with all arguments that are possible given these premises. In fact, there is a clear parallel with the way in which Lorenzen and Lorenz employed dialectics. In both cases, the purpose of the dialectics is to clarify the notion of logical validity. This explains that a fixed set of premises is assumed and that all possible dialogues are taken into consideration.

Nevertheless there are also important differences. The battle of arguments approach is not committed to a particular logic. The notion of validity with which it is concerned is not the validity of an argument within such a system of logic, but rather the status of an argument on the basis of a framework that deals with the battle of arguments. This framework presupposes the internal validity of arguments. As a consequence, the dialogue steps deal with arguments as a whole and not with the steps of a logical proof, unless the steps of the logical proofs may define subarguments, which are in their turn relevant for when one argument defeats another one. Moreover, the dialogues do not characterize the meanings of logical operators, but rather a theory of when one argument defeats another argument.

Because this form of dialectics assumes a fixed set of premises and takes all possible dialogues into account, the notion of time plays no role in it. That is why I propose to call this form of dialectics *static*.

3.3 Dynamic dialectics

As the above discussion of static dialectics illustrates, modeling defeasibility as a battle of arguments does not automatically lead to a dynamic approach. However, Prakken developed a four-layered model of legal argument, in which dynamics plays a crucial role.[22] The four layers in Prakken's model consist of a system of logic, a dialectical layer, a procedural layer and a strategical layer. Given a set of premises, the logic determines the set of possible arguments. The dialectical layer then sorts out the arguments into the defeated and the undefeated ones. The procedural layer determines how the set of premises, which functions as input to the logic and the argumentation framework, can evolve in time. The procedural rules of the third layer regulate how an actual dialog can be conducted. These rules allow dialogue parties for instance to add new premises, or to retract premises that turn out to be indefensible. The fourth layer deals with strategy, which argument moves that are allowed by the third layer should be made to reach the arguers goals.

[22] Prakken 1997, 270f.

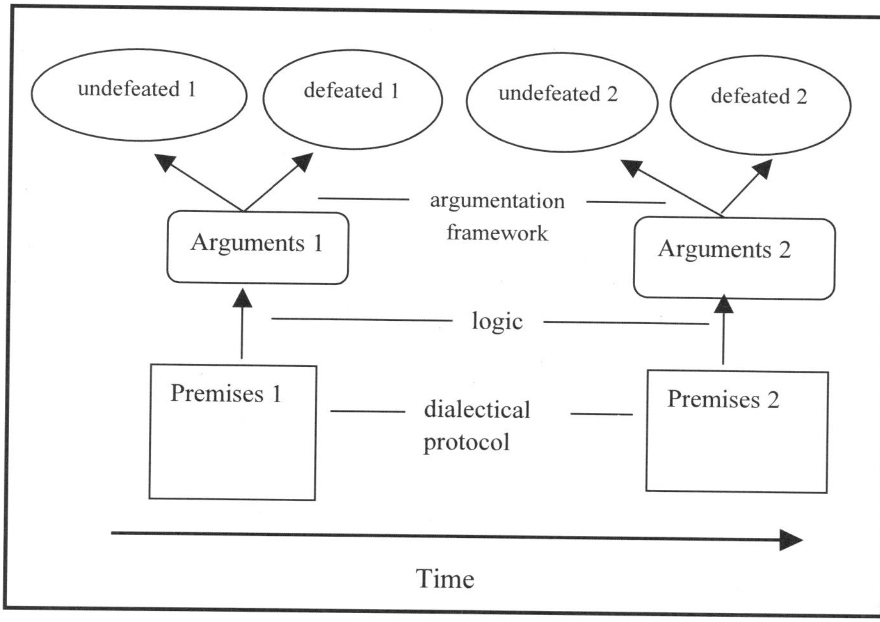

This model crucially differs from the one described above, where the dialectics only functions as a means to characterize valid conclusions in defeasible reasoning. The principal differences are that the present model takes the factor of time into account and that it has a non-deterministic element because the dialectical protocol allows dialogue parties to change the set of premises. Which changes will be made is up to the parties and as a consequence the valid conclusions at one point in time do not determine the valid conclusions at a later point in time.[23]

To highlight the difference between static dialectics and the present model, dialectical models that incorporate players and time will be called *dynamic dialectical*. Such dynamic models are negatively characterized by not assuming a fixed set of premises and consequently also by not dealing with all possible arguments.[24] Therefore their main purpose will not be the

[23] An exception must be made in case the dialectical protocol does not allow changes in the premises that change the set of valid conclusions. Such a protocol would make little sense, however, because the whole point of having a dialogue is to introduce some indeterminism.

[24] Dynamic dialectics may deal with all possible arguments at a particular stage of the argumentation.

characterization of logically valid arguments, or of conclusions that are justified relative to a set of premises.

4. VARIATIONS ON THE DIALECTICAL THEME

In the literature, several functions for dialectical systems have been mentioned. I will discuss three of them.

4.1 The HYPO-system

A well-known example of a static dialectical system is Ashley and Rissland's HYPO.[25] HYPO is a static system because it uses a fixed set of cases as the premises from which arguments can be constructed. It is a dialectic system because it generates three-ply arguments, where the first ply is the basic argument, the second ply an attack on the basic argument, and the third ply an attack on the second ply. The argument of the third ply, so to speak, reinstates the argument of the first ply.

Although HYPO is not primarily interested in establishing the validity of a conclusion given the current case and the cases from its case base, it exhibits interesting similarities to systems that deal dialectically with defeasible arguments. For instance, HYPO considers all possible arguments given the cases that are at its disposal. This is done by sorting the cases in a Claim Lattice on the basis of their similarity to the current case. Since arguments are closely related to the position that cases take in this Claim Lattice, the generation of the Claim Lattice is comparable to the generation and comparison of all possible arguments. Moreover, the three argument plies where each ply attacks the argument of the previous ply is very similar to the battle of argument model of defeasible reasoning.[26]

4.2 Dialectics as models of bounded rationality

Because humans sometimes reason irrationally, systems that aim to characterize valid reasoning dialectically tend to consider all possible arguments rather than arguments that were actually produced by human reasoners. Nevertheless it is possible to use actual, rather than all possible,

[25] Rissland and Ashley 1987; Ashley 1991.

[26] A logical analysis of the HYPO reasoning mechanism that can easily be translated into the battle of arguments-model, can be found in Hage 1997 (RwR), 185f. See also Prakken and Sartor 1997 (RP), Bench-Capon 1997 and Roth 2003.

dialogues to model rationality. Loui and Norman (1995) have presented a theory in which dialogues are used to model rationality, in particular bounded rationality.

Their model can be seen as a variation of the layered model of Prakken that was presented in section 3. Prakken considered changes in the set of premises over time. Every stage in the process is characterized by a set of premises. Given a system of logic, the premises of a particular stage make a number of arguments possible. Consequently, a stage is also characterized by a set of arguments. An argumentation framework determines for every stage and the set of arguments that characterizes it, which conclusions can validly be drawn.

The model of Loui and Norman differs from Prakken's model because stages are not characterized by sets of premises, but rather by the sets of arguments that were *actually* adduced. In fact, Loui and Norman assume a fixed set of premises and consider only the arguments that, given some system of logic, are created given those premises. Remember that Prakken considered all arguments that were made possible by the premises of a stage. Since humans are not capable to generate all arguments that can be based on their beliefs, they must work with the arguments that they have actually thought of.[27] If one's belief or behavior is in agreement with what one has actually considered, it is in some sense rational. The logical counterpart of this form of bounded rationality is that the battle of arguments only takes place between the arguments that were actually produced in a dialogue, and this is precisely what Loui and Norman propose.

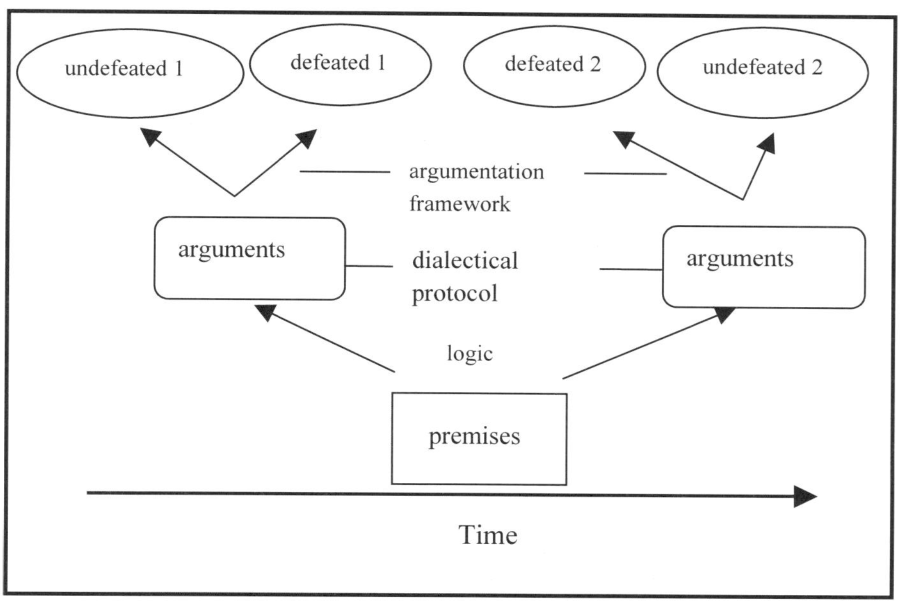

Verheij has proposed a system, CumulA, which is similar to that of Loui and Norman in that it makes use of argument stages.[28] It has the additional feature that not only the set of arguments, but also the set of premises is allowed to vary over time. Consequently it combines features of Prakken's layered model and the system of Loui and Norman. CumulA does not incorporate dialogue protocols, however.

4.3 Dialectics as a theory of rational acceptance

In his logical system DefLog, Verheij has extended the use of dialectics to make it deal with topics that are usually dealt with by means of belief revision.[29] Where most authors treat arguments as the entities that compete, Verheij takes statements as the relevant basic entities. A theory consists of a set of sentences that express these statements. The language in which these sentences are expressed knows only two logical operators, namely an operator for *primitive implication* and an operator for *dialectical negation*. A primitive implication can be used for modus ponens like arguments, while the dialectical negation indicates that the thus negated sentence is defeated.

A theory consists of a number of statements that are prima facie justified. It is, however, possible that some statements in the sentences are attacked by the theory as a whole. This is the case if repeated application of modus ponens arguments based on the primitive implications leads to the conclusion that a statement in the theory is defeated. A dialectical interpretation of a theory divides the theory into two sets of statements. The first set consists of the justified assumptions. This set should be conflict free in the sense that no statements in the set are attacked by this set. The other set consists of statements that are all attacked by the first set. Intuitively such a dialectical interpretation can be interpreted as a correction on the original theory in which the subset of statements is selected that is justified in the light of the original theory.[30] The justified conclusions of the original theory are then the conclusions that follow from the justified subset resulting from the dialectical interpretation of the theory.

[28] Verheij 1996.

[29] Verheij 2003 (DL) and Verheij 2005.

[30] Notice the analogy with the notion of integrated coherence as exposed in chapter 2.

5. TRUTH AND JUSTIFICATION; A PHILOSOPHICAL DIGRESSION

Dynamic dialectical systems can be subdivided into systems whose dialogue protocol largely reflects the system's underlying logic and systems where the dialogue protocol is to a large extent inspired by the domain on which the system is to operate. These latter dynamic dialectical systems, I will call *dialogical.* The transition between merely dialectical systems and dialogical ones is a gradual one.

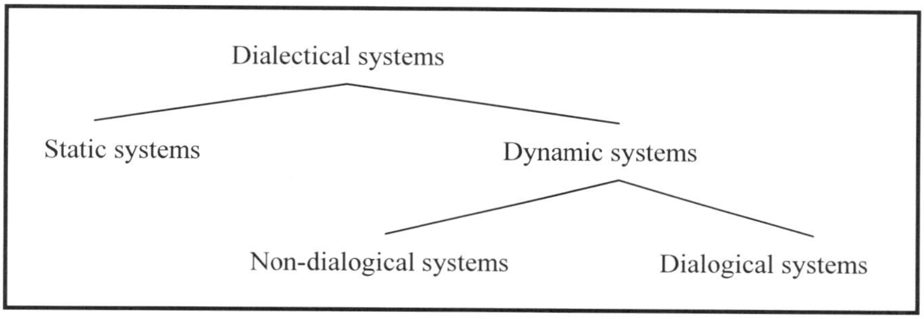

Dialogical versions of legal reasoning systems are inspired by two phenomena. The first is that legal issues often arise in disputes between two parties, that is, in dialogues. Dialogical systems mimic, so to speak, legal practice.

Next to this practical source of inspiration there is more theoretical one, exemplified in Gordon's work on the Pleadings Game. A major source of inspiration for Gordon was Alexy's theory of legal reasoning[31], which was, to my knowledge, the first dialogical theory of legal reasoning. Alexy was, in turn, inspired by the revival of the rhetorical approach to argumentation[32] and by dialogical approaches to truth[33] and justification.[34] I will say somewhat more about this German work and its philosophical background, because it is essential for a good understanding of the differences between dialogical approaches to legal reasoning and dynamic dialectical approaches that are not dialogical.

[31] Alexy 1978,
[32] E.g. Perelman and Olbrechts-Tyteca 1969.
[33] Habermas 1973.
[34] E.g. Schwemmer and Lorenzen 1973.

5.1 Habermas' consensus theory of truth

Many philosophers endorse a realist ontology and the correspondence theory of truth.[35] They assume that there is a world independent of our knowledge of it and that an assertive sentence is true if the state of affairs expressed in it obtains in that independent world and false if it does not obtain. These views taken together lead to well-known problems concerning truth and knowledge. The truth of sentences, or, in general, all representations of reality, depends on a relation between these representations and reality. All we humans have are representations of this reality, for instance in the form of sensory perceptions and we are unable to grasp directly the reality beyond the representations. Everything we can say or believe about that underlying reality is itself again a representation. Truth in the sense of correspondence is not something we can ascertain.

This insight has led Habermas to the conclusion that if we discuss the truth of a sentence, we are not really concerned with the correspondence of this sentence with reality, but rather with whether this sentence rightly claims what it does claim.[36] This rightness, Habermas continues, does not depend on an inaccessible relation between this sentence and reality, but rather in the possibility of upholding the sentence in a critical discussion. In this way, Habermas arrives at his consensus theory of truth: a sentence is true if it can be upheld in a completely rational discussion.

Notice that it is not an actual consensus that decides about the truth of a sentence, but the hypothetical consensus that would be achieved if a discussion were fully rational. Habermas discusses a number of demands on discussions that are necessary to safeguard their rationality. Amongst these are the demands that:

1. All potential participants in a discussion must have equal chances to participate. They must any time be able to open and continue discussions.
2. All participants must have equal chances to offer interpretations, statements, recommendations, explanations and justifications, and to question them.
3. All participants should have equal chances to use representative speech acts, namely to express attitudes, feelings and intentions.
4. All participants should have equal chances to use regulative speech acts, such as to command and to resist, to permit and to forbid.

[35] E.g. Devitt 1991 and Searle 1995.

[36] Habermas 1973.

Habermas' theory resembles the work of Lorenzen and Lorenz and dialectical renderings of defeasible reasoning, which also operate with the outcome of rational discussions. Still there is a difference, because the work of Lorenzen and Lorenz and, for instance, Prakken and Sartor, assumes a finite set of premises and considers argument strategies that enable one to win a discussion against all possible opposition, where the possible forms of opposition can be constructed on the basis of the premises and the logic. The rationality is, in the views of Lorenzen and Lorenz and in the battle of arguments-theoreticians, embodied in the demand to consider all dialogues.

Rational discussions in the sense of Habermas do not have a fixed set of premises. This has two consequences. First, the rationality of the discourse cannot be maintained by considering all possible arguments, because the set of all possible arguments is indeterminate. As an alternative, Habermas uses constraints on the settings of the dialogue.

Second, a dialogue according to Habermas has no fixed outcome, because its purpose is not to characterize logical validity, which is relative to a set of premises and a matter of form, but to define truth, which is absolute and a matter of content. This difference explains the difference in determinacy. Moreover, it is relevant for the difference between dialogical and other dialectical versions of legal reasoning systems. The latter only deal with the validity or rationality of (legal) reasoning, while the former tend to focus on the correctness of the outcome of legal discussions. Very briefly stated, dialogues deal with content, while other forms of dialectics deal with form.

That dialogues deal with content explains why Habermas places constraints on dialogues that lead to truth. These constraints are meant to ensure that everything that may be relevant for the outcome of the discussion will be adduced. Comparable constraints are lacking in static dialectical systems, where the set of premises is not only fixed, but its contents and origin are irrelevant.

5.2 Overcoming foundationalism

Where the concern of Habermas was semantic or ontological, the so-called Erlangen Schule was concerned with the justification of ethical and empirical 'knowledge'. The traditional model of justification holds that some thesis is justified if it can be derived (usually: deduced) from justified premises. This view of justification suffers[37] from an unbounded recursion. It presupposes a basis of justified premises, the justification of which does not

[37] Amongst others. See chapter 1, section 2.5.

depend on derivation from other justified premises. The problem, which is typical for all 'foundationalist' theories of knowledge[38], is that such a basis can only be found by dogmatizing some premises.

The solution to this problem that was proposed by Schwemmer, a member of the school of Erlangen, is that the basis of justification is only assumed as long as it is not brought up for discussion. For instance, it is possible to justify C by means of an argument on the basis of the premises $A \rightarrow C$ and A. As long as these premises are not questioned, the justification succeeds and C is considered to be justified. But it remains possible to question A, $A \rightarrow C$, or both, and when this happens, these premises must be justified. Such a justification makes in turn use of premises that are temporarily assumed, but that can always be questioned and brought up for discussion.[39]

Schwemmer's solution to the problem of foundationalism rests on the exchange of content for form. The content that is abandoned consists of the premises that would have to be accepted dogmatically. The form that comes in its place is the procedure that allows an audience to question the assumptions of some particular justification. This exchange of content for form is similar to the way in which Habermas replaced reality as the basis for truth by consensus in a rational discussion. Nevertheless there is an important difference. Habermas' insistence on the rationality of discussions, which related his work to that of Lorenzen and Lorenz and of the battle of arguments-theoreticians, and which is embodied in constraints on rational discussions, is abandoned in Schwemmer's solution. It is the *actual* questioning of assumptions that creates the obligation to extend the justificatory chain, not the mere possibility of questioning the premises. Indeed, if it were the (absence of the) possibility of challenging the premises that counts for justification, the unbounded recursion, which Schwemmer attempted to circumvent, would re-occur.

[38] Cf. Lehrer 2000, 45f.

[39] Alexy 1978, 181 on Schwemmer; see also Hage 1997 (Leg), 126f. This approach to justification has some similarities with Popper's views on falsification (Popper 1972). A theory may be falsified because conclusions that are deduced from it are considered to be false. Such a falsification presumes that the 'data' against which the theory is tested are correct themselves. Such a presumption can never be more than another falsifiable hypothesis, however. In a sense it depends on the scientific dialogue which theories are temporarily assumed to be data and are assumed to be fit to test other theories against.

5.3 Law as reason-based fact

The question might well be raised why the ideas of Habermas and Schwemmer, which are not so familiar outside Germany, have had such a strong influence in the fields of legal theory and of Law and AI. Part of the answer will probably be that dialogues were already familiar in the law, so that the theoretical framework proposed by Habermas and Schwemmer struck a familiar chord, which facilitated its acceptance.

To see another part to the answer, we must return to the ontology sketched above. According to this realistic ontology, reality is independent of our knowledge of it. For instance, Mount Everest would also have existed and would be snow-covered, if no conscious being had existed and no-one would have known about it. This realistic picture may be correct for brute facts such as the existence of Mount Everest and its being snow-covered, but it is certainly not correct for large parts of reality that consist of so-called reason-based, or institutional facts.[40] The existence of money, of football matches, of governments, of statutory laws and of legal obligations is certainly not independent of human minds. All of these are 'built' (constituted) on top of other facts or entities, which are the reasons for their existence. The connection between reason-based facts and the facts that are the reasons for their existence is created by rules that are adopted by humans. For instance, the rule that one ought to repair tortuously caused damages makes that the fact that John tortuously damaged Jennifer's car into the reason why John ought to repair the damages to Jennifer's car.

Reason-based facts are facts that are built on top of other facts, which are either brute, or reason-based themselves. The distinction between brute facts and reason-based facts has profound implications for the distinction between truth and knowledge. The presence of brute facts may be observed directly[41], or it may be inferred from other facts that provide evidence for their presence (e.g. smoke provides evidence for fire). In both cases, there is an independent standard for the correctness of our knowledge, that is, whether these brute facts actually obtain. Even if our knowledge is based on evidence and therefore on a rule that allows us to consider these particular facts as evidence, the rule can be tested by comparing the outcome of its application

[40] Cf. Anscombe 1957, MacCormick and Weinberger 1986, Ruiter 1993, Searle 1995 and Hage 1987 and 1997 (RwR). See also chapter 6, section 6.

[41] I presently presuppose an empiricist epistemology with respect to brute facts, and argue for an idealistic epistemology with respect to reason-based facts on the basis of it. The argument for an idealistic epistemology becomes even stronger when the empiricist assumption with respect to brute facts is replaced by an idealistic one.

with what can be observed to be really the case. The truth of a sentence that describes a brute fact is independent of our way of knowing this fact.

Our knowledge of reason-based facts can, on the contrary, only be based on our knowledge of their underlying reasons. If we want to know whether John ought to repair the damage to Jennifer's car, we must apply the rule about tort to the facts of their case to (re-)construct the legal consequences of the case. Moreover, there is no independent standard to establish whether our construction was correct. The only available test is to re-apply the legal rules. It is not possible to test the rules by means of our observation whether the legal consequences established by means of the rule 'really' obtain. In other words, the distinction between truth and knowledge, which characterizes brute facts, is absent in the case of reason-based facts. If the best procedure to obtain knowledge about reason-based facts has been followed, it makes little sense to ask the question whether this 'knowledge' is true. (This only holds for the step from the brute facts to the reason-based facts. Knowledge about reason-based facts always has a component of knowledge about brute facts and for this knowledge it may remain possible to ask whether it is correct.)

The second part of the reasons why dialogical, or, more generally, procedural, approaches to the law are so popular is, in my opinion, that the law in actual cases consists of reason-based facts, facts that are the result of the application of legal rules. It is only possible to establish these facts by applying the rules. In other words, it is only possible to establish what the law in a concrete case is by means of a procedure. Legal dialogues are obvious examples of such procedures. In section 7, after a discussion of Gordon's Pleadings Game, I will return to this procedural view of the law.

6. GORDON'S PLEADINGS GAME

A recurring theme in legal theory is how legal consequences in a particular case can be justified.[42] Just like other foundational enterprises, this one suffers from what has come to be known as the *Münchhausen trilemma*, after the legendary baron who pulled himself by his hairs out of the swamp.[43] A full justification of the legal consequences would be the result of a valid argument with justified premises. As we have seen above, the demand that the premises from which the argument starts are justified creates problems.

[42] E.g. Larenz 1983, MacCormick 1978, Alexy 1978, Aarnio e.a. 1981, Aarnio 1987, Peczenik 1989 and Hage 1997 (Leg).

[43] Albert 1968, 11f.

Either this demand evokes a boundless recursion (infinite regress) of founding arguments, or the justifying chain of arguments is circular, or some premises are assumed by denying that they need additional justification (by making them into dogmas).

To evade this trilemma, Alexy proposed to take a procedural approach to legal justification.[44] Building on ideas of Habermas[45], Schwemmer and Lorenzen[46] and Perelman[47], he considers a conclusion to be justified if its proponent has convinced its opponent in a dialogue that satisfies certain constraints. These constraints derive both from general considerations about dialogues and from special demands from the legal domain. Following Alexy, similar proposals have been made by Aarnio[48] and Peczenik.[49] The purpose of the dialogues is in this case to establish a set of premises shared by the proponent and the opponent of a thesis, from which the thesis can validly (in the case of Alexy: deductively) be derived. If it is not possible to establish such a common basis, the thesis cannot be justified. The finding of a common basis is in the law facilitated by the fact that a number of premises are accepted by default, because they are part of established law.

The ideas of Habermas and Schwemmer influenced Alexy, while Alexy's views have been used by Gordon to develop his Pleadings Game.[50] Through this work these ideas effectively entered into the field of Artificial Intelligence and Law.[51] However, the purpose of the Pleadings Game is not legal justification, but rather to establish the legal and factual issues that separate the parties in a legal conflict. Nevertheless, the topic with which the Pleadings Game deals is very similar to that of legal justification, namely the establishment of the premises for legal justification. Where Alexy aims at the justification of a legal judgment by finding a common set of premises from which the judgment follows, the Pleadings Game aims at finding premises about which parties disagree and that explain their disagreement about what should be the outcome of their case.

There is another difference. Whereas Alexy takes his starting point in the approach of Habermas, with strict constraints on the procedure to guarantee a rational outcome, Gordon assumes only a few of the Alexyan constraints,

44 Alexy 1978.

45 Habermas 1973.

46 Schwemmer and Lorenzen 1973.

47 Perelman and Olbrechts-Tyteca 1969.

48 Aarnio 1987.

49 Peczenik 1989. See also Feteris 1994 and Hage 1997 (Leg).

50 Gordon 1994 and 1995. Gordon also described the Trial Game, which will be left out of consideration here.

51 Gordon 1991, 1994 and 1995. See also Hage 1987 and Hage e.a. 1992 and 1994.

with the effect that his procedure is more like Schwemmer's that takes actual rather than rational consensus as crucial. In particular, Gordon skips all the argument forms, the justification rules, the rules for transition between discussion types, the rules and forms of internal and external legal justification and the special legal forms of reasoning, which Alexy poses as constraints on legal discussions.[52] The constraints assumed by Gordon are[53]:

1. No party may contradict himself.
2. A party who conceded that a rule is valid must be prepared to apply the rule to every set of objects that satisfy its antecedents.
3. An argument supporting an issue may be asserted only when the issue has been denied by the opponent.
4. A party may deny any claim made by the opponent, if it is not a necessary consequence of his own claims.
5. A party may rebut a supporting argument for an issue he has denied.
6. A party may defeat the rebuttal of a supporting argument for one of his own claims, if the claim is an issue.

Because of the purpose of the dialogues, the establishment of a set of premises, or rather the differences in the relevant premises that the parties are willing to accept, the dialogue rules are not aimed at defining logical operators. However, the rules of the Pleadings Game reflect the defeasible nature of legal reasoning and in this respect they are similar to the rules for dialectical approaches to defeasible reasoning.

The purpose of the Pleadings Game makes it differ from the work of Lorenzen and Lorenz and from static dialectical approaches in that the set of premises is not fixed and in that it is not necessary to survey the set of all possible arguments. The Pleadings Game is a mediating system rather than a conflict resolution system; it is left to the parties in a dialogue to establish about which premises they agree and about which they disagree. The validity of the arguments on the basis of these premises is left to the mediating system.

These characteristics make the Pleadings Game into a dynamic dialectical system. The dialogues take place and are not merely simulated, during a process that stretches out in time and that is non-deterministic, because the players are within certain confines free to introduce facts and rules into the dialogue. Only those argument moves are allowed in the Pleadings Game which are relevant from a logical point of view. All dialogue moves have a set of preconditions that are inspired by the logical status of the dialogue and the way in which the move changes this status. In

[52] Alexy 1978, 361f.
[53] Gordon 1994, 243.

other words, the procedural rules of the Pleadings Game by and large reflect the logic that underlies the game. Domain-related rules that impose additional constraints on the dialogue, such as the rules of legal justification and the obligatory legal forms of reasoning that were adopted by Alexy, are lacking. That is why I think that, on the sliding scale from non-dialogical to dialogical dynamic systems, the Pleadings Game is relatively near the pole of non-dialogical systems.

7. THE PROCEDURAL AND RHETORICAL NATURE OF THE LAW

In their paper *Hard Cases: A Procedural Approach*, Hage e.a. argued for a perspective on the dialectical approach in which dialogues do not only have a function in the establishment of premises, but also in the constitution of law in concrete cases.[54] This perspective formed the starting point for the thesis of Lodder.[55] Two key ideas play a central role in this connection: the *purely procedural* nature of the law in concrete cases and the *rhetorical* nature of this procedure.

The purely procedural nature of the law means that what is the law in a particular case is not something that is given independent of the procedure that leads to a decision about the law in a concrete case. This procedural nature is a direct consequence of the fact that the law in concrete cases is reason-based. There is no standard for the outcome of a legal case otherwise than that this outcome is the result of a rule-applying procedure.

Procedures can also play a role if there is an independent standard. In the presence of a standard, we can distinguish between perfect and imperfect procedures. Perfect procedures are guaranteed to lead to outcomes according to the standard. An example is to divide a cake in equal pieces by using a good scale to weigh the pieces. Imperfect procedures should also lead to outcomes in accordance with the standard, but they cannot guarantee the correctness of their outcomes. Criminal procedures, for instance, cannot guarantee that they will lead to the conviction of all, but only criminals.[56] Pure procedures do not have an independent criterion to measure their outcome against. Lotteries are examples of such pure procedures. Their

[54] Hage e.a. 1994.

[55] Lodder 1998 and 1999. The logical systems presented in Hage e.a. 1994 and in Lodder's thesis reflect this theoretical position only to a limited extent, however.

[56] Rawls 1972, 85f.

outcome is correct if the correct procedure was followed, no matter what the outcome is.

The application of rules, legal rules included, is not merely a logical operation, but rather a kind of action that may or may not be performed.[57] There can be reasons against the application of a rule that are not mentioned in the conditions of the rule. For instance, a superior rule with an incompatible conclusion may be applicable. Whether a rule is actually applied depends not only on whether the conditions of the rule are satisfied, but also on whether exceptional circumstances are *known*. Exceptions that obtain, but are unknown, cannot influence the application of the rule and the rule will be applied and will generate its legal consequence.

Moreover, the decision whether a rule is applicable to a concrete case depends on whether the case can be classified in terms of the rule conditions. This classification depends on classificatory rules, many of which are not given before the concrete case to which they are to be applied. For instance, the classification of illegally copying software as appropriating somebody else's good, may ask for a classificatory rule that was never formulated before. It depends on a concrete procedure whether such a rule is accepted as part of the law.

Clearly the actual procedure involved in the application of a rule is relevant for the legal consequences that hold in a concrete case. That is why there is no independent standard for the evaluation of legal conclusions and why the law in concrete cases is purely procedural. This procedural nature of the law would not be important if the procedure could only have one outcome. If the facts and the law are fixed in a case, even if the available information is incomplete in the sense that potentially relevant information is not taken into account, the outcome of the law applying procedure might also be fixed.[58] However, the input of the procedure is not fixed. The law-applying procedure allows for both changes in the recognized facts and changes in the law. By producing a convincing argument (in the psychological sense), a dialogue party can add rules and/or exceptions to the available legal rules, with the effect that the same body of facts leads to more or less legal consequences. Similarly it is possible to change the body of available facts by changing the rules for classification and/or proof.[59]

[57] Hage 1997 (RwR), 123.

[58] This is the case if the procedure that leads from the facts and the law to the legal consequences in a concrete case allows no external influence on the outcome. An example of external influence that should be excluded is that dialogue parties only come up with the 'wrong' arguments.

[59] These a-rational aspects of legal argumentation are emphasized in Lodder 1999.

This possibility of modifying the law during a procedure by convincing one's opponent defines the *rhetorical nature* of the law. The rhetorical nature of the law means that the procedure is concerned with convincing an audience of some thesis (about the outcome of a case). Conviction, in opposition to validity, depends on what actually happens. An audience may be convinced (persuaded some would say) by arguments that are not logically forcing, or that ultimately rest on premises that had not been accepted by the audience before the procedure. The procedural and the rhetorical nature of the law make that the legal consequences in a concrete case are the outcome of a correct procedure, whatever this outcome may be. *In this respect* the law in concrete cases is comparable to the outcome of a lottery.

The change of perspective that results from considering law as a pure rhetorical procedure has several implications. First, the procedural rules (dialectical protocols) become more important. The dialogue rules in systems that focus on the modeling of defeasible reasoning tend to be confined to ensuring that both parties have full opportunity to attack the arguments of their opponent. The ways in which attacks are made possible depends on the (non-monotonic) logic that is modeled by the system. For instance, systems may allow questioning premises, adducing reasons against the application of a rule, or adducing reasons for an incompatible conclusion. In other words, the dialogue rules are strongly related to the logic they model. This is clearly illustrated by the rules of Gordon's Pleadings Game, described in section 6.

If the emphasis shifts from modeling a logic to the establishment of law in concrete cases, other procedural rules become important. An example is the exclusionary rule, which forbids adducing evidence in a criminal procedure that was obtained illegally. Another example, also from criminal law, is that arguments based on analogical rule application are forbidden.[60] Even more fundamental is that in legal procedures, the parties are committed to the law, not only in the sense that they are forced to accept the valid rules of law, but also in the sense that they ought to apply these rules where relevant. In general it holds that if the function of a procedure is to establish the law, the nature of the procedure is not (primarily) a matter of logic, but it is a matter of law itself. In the following sections I will discuss some of the consequences of the shift from merely dynamic dialectical systems to law-establishing dialogue systems

[60] Kloosterhuis 1995.

8. THE ROLE OF LEGAL RULES IN LAW-ESTABLISHING DIALOGUES

The idea that law is purely procedural is somewhat counter-intuitive, to say the least. Clearly there are some hard cases, the outcome of which is uncertain and which can be argued in several ways. But just as clearly, there are cases about which every sensible lawyer will agree how they should be solved. This strongly suggests that the law is not purely procedural, but rather has an imperfect procedure.

This line of reasoning is strengthened by the observation that a purely procedural view of the law leaves little room for the rules of law that apparently determine the legal consequences of concrete cases. If the parties to a dialogue are free, within the confines of the dialogue rules, to determine the outcome of the dialogue, how can the role of legal rules be accounted for?

To meet these objections, I propose to distinguish between two views of purely procedural law. The one view, which seems wrong, is that the parties in a dialogue are completely free to use or not use the legal rules that are applicable to their case. According to this view, the dialogue rules leave the contents of the dialogue completely open. The other view, which is in my opinion correct, is that the rules of legal dialogues somehow force the parties in a dialogue to take the pre-existing legal rules into account. In the remainder of this section I will illustrate how dialogue rules might accomplish that.

First, I want to distinguish between civil cases in which parties are, at least according to Dutch law, to a large extent free to determine which facts will be taken into account and, for instance, criminal cases, in which one of the purposes of the procedure is to find the truth. In civil cases, the facts are, so to speak, at the disposal of the parties, while the law is not. In criminal cases, neither the facts nor the law is at the disposal of the parties. Because in civil cases both phenomena - aspects that are and aspects that are not at the disposal of the parties - play a role, I will continue my discussion with them. The part of the discussion devoted to the law in civil cases will grosso modo also be applicable to the law and the facts in criminal cases.

Since the parties in a dialogue are free to dispose of the facts of the case, precisely those facts are assumed to obtain that are accepted by both parties in the dialogue. The cause of this acceptance may be that some party is forced to accept (the absence of) certain facts as a consequence of her acceptance of other facts, of the burden of proof, or a decision of the arbiter (see section 10). Given these, sometimes severe, constraints, the facts of the case are the result of the dialogue between the parties and are not determined by independent law.

To account for the fact that the law is something that is, to some extent, given independent of what the dialogue parties want it to be, it is necessary to add a third party to the procedure. It will not do to add rules of law to the commitments of the dialogue parties, because if the parties do not use the rules to which they are committed, commitment to the law has few or no effects. It is crucial that somehow the application of valid rules of law is secured and for this purpose an independent 'guardian of the law' is necessary. The role of the judge in actual legal procedures springs to mind as an example of such an independent guardian of the law. It is her task to apply the valid rules (and principles ..., etc.) of the law to the case at hand. The role of this judge in legal procedures can be modeled as a third party in what now becomes a trialogue. The trialogue can in turn be modeled as three interrelating dialogues between the three parties involved in the procedure.

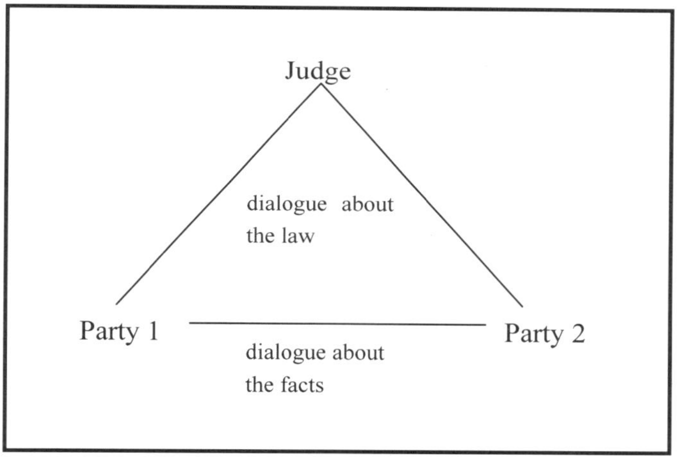

The two 'normal' parties have a dialogue about the facts of the case. The judge is committed to precisely those case facts to which both parties are, or become, committed. Moreover, both of the normal parties have a dialogue with the judge about the legal consequences of the case. The outcome of the trialogue consists of the commitments of the judge at the end of the procedure.

This sketch of trialogues leaves much to be specified. For instance, it must be defined how the three dialogues interrelate in time and in content. Moreover, it is still unclear how the judge must fulfill her task to safeguard the law. However, the sketch gives an impression how commitment to an independent law can be combined with a fully procedural view of the law.

Notice, by the way, how this trialogue model reflects a characteristic of civil law, namely that the parties to a civil dispute are free to dispose of their rights, including the right to enforce their legal position. If procedures are used to establish the law, the nature of the procedures must reflect the law and not only some system of logic. In the present example this is shown in the dialogue between the parties about the facts of the case and the commitment of the judge to the facts about which the parties agree.

9. REASONING ABOUT DIALOGUE RULES AND DIALOGUE MOVES

A dialogue can be considered as a sequence of dialogue moves. Dialogues are regulated by a set of dialogue rules, which must fulfill several roles. Amongst these roles, two important ones are to determine which party can/may make which dialogue moves at which moment and to determine which party is committed to which sentences, c.q. has won the dialogue. Rules that determine the commitments of the dialogue parties will reflect the logic that underlies the dialogue game. For instance, in Gordon's Pleadings Game, the commitment rules, which regulate the effects of dialogue moves, reflect Gordon's adapted version of conditional entailment.

The rules that determine which moves are possible at which moment may be influenced by the underlying logic too, but they can also to a large extent be determined by the domain of the dialogues, for instance by the law. I already mentioned rules that disallow to defend claims by adducing illegally obtained evidence, or by applying criminal laws analogously. Other feasible rules would be rules that forbid to question sentences that were decided upon by the arbiter (see section 10), or rules that confine the possibility of attacking claims in time. In theory, large parts of procedural law can be incorporated in the rules of some dialogue game.[61]

Because dialogue rules can to a large extent determine the outcome of dialogues, the rules for law-establishing dialogues will be specified by the law itself. Since every legal system has its own procedural rules, even several sets for different parts of the law, it seems hard to develop a general dialogical model for the establishment of the law. Nevertheless, it is possible to develop such a general model, by treating the dialogue rules as domain knowledge and by modeling legal procedures by means of a kind of second-order rules. A dialogue move is on this view possible if it is explicitly made possible by a (domain dependent) dialogue rule to which both parties are committed. At the beginning of a dialogue, both parties are committed to a set of first-order dialogue rules that are part of the legal system in question.

[61] Leenes 1999 deals amongst others with the legal constraints on dialogues.

The second order rules that are incorporated in the dialogue system dictate that the possibility of making dialogue moves depends on the first-order dialogue rules.

This approach has the additional advantage that it becomes possible for the parties to debate on the first-order dialogue rules. These rules are rules of law, just like, for instance, rules of criminal law and of civil law. To some extent these rules may be subject of the dialogue of the parties, for instance in the form of a discussion about their interpretation, which can be seen as discussion about which rules are valid.[62] This means that the procedural rules are subject of the dialogue too. Because the procedural rules govern the dialogue, a dialogue can change its own rules.[63]

Not only the dialogue rules may be subject of the discussion; individual moves may be the topic of an argument, too. The possibility of arguing about individual dialogue moves is important for law-establishing dialogues, because the outcome of the dialogue counts as law. Allowing or disallowing a move may therefore make the difference between winning and losing a legal case. If a dialogue move is disallowed, this disallowance can take two shapes. First, it may be that a (computer-implemented) dialogue system ignores the move completely, except for sending a message to the party who made the move that the move was illegal. Severe violations of the dialogue rules, such as ignoring ones own commitments, should be treated in this way. Second, the dialogue system may 'allow' the move, which is then in some sense possible, but the other party may claim that the move was illegal.[64] If this claim is upheld, the illegal move will be ignored. For instance, if some party adduces illegal evidence, this move may be claimed to be illegal. If this claim turns out to be correct, the move in which the illegal evidence was adduced must be withdrawn.

10. THE BURDEN OF PROOF AND THE ROLE OF THE ARBITER

Since the parties in a legal procedure usually have opposing interests, allowing the parties to establish the facts of a case amongst themselves

[62] Hage 1997 (RwR), 197f.

[63] Vreeswijk 2000 described a way of modeling the change of dialogue rules during the dialogue.

[64] This distinction between impossible and illegal moves corresponds to the legal distinction between acts in the law that are void and that are voidable. The distinction is given explicit attention in Lodder 1999, 35.

involves a danger. The opponent of the claim with which the dialogue begins has an interest in denying everything the proponent claims and in opposing every attempt to get her committed to anything. The law knows several means to limits the effects of such a destructive strategy. The first means is to have initial commitments for both parties to some facts that are assumed by default, for instance facts that are generally known to obtain.

The second means is to assign the burden of proof for particular facts to one of the parties. By assigning some dialogue party a burden of proof, a default decision is made about the presence of facts: some facts are assumed (not) to obtain, unless the party that has the burden of proof proves otherwise. In this way it becomes possible to add facts so that the possibility arises to determine the legal consequences of the case.

The burden of proof may be more or less severe. Freeman and Farley distinguish five levels of support that can be given to a claim[65]:

- *scintilla of evidence*, where there is at least one defensible argument for the claim;
- *preponderance of evidence*, where there is at least one defensible argument that outweighs all arguments of the opponent for the opposite conclusion;
- *dialectical validity*, where there is at least one credible, defensible argument for the claim and where all arguments of the opponent for the opposite claim are defeated;
- *beyond a reasonable doubt*, where there is at least one strong, defensible argument for the claim and where all arguments of the opponent for the opposite claim are defeated;
- *beyond a doubt*, where there is at least one valid, defensible argument for the claim and where all arguments of the opponent for the opposite claim are defeated.

Since the work of Freeman and Farley is based on a static dialectical theory, where the set of premises is fixed, their theory about the burden of proof does not help against an opponent who refuses to co-operate in establishing the facts. Although it specifies the amount of proof that is available given a set of premises, which is useful for a division of the burden of proof between the dialogue parties, it leaves the question open where the basic facts of the case, from which the other ones must be proven, come from.

Here is where the arbiter has her role.[66] She can make decisions about (factual) issues that bind the dialogue parties. Such a decision can be

[65] Freeman and Farley 1996.

straightforward, when some fact is decided to obtain, whether the parties agree or not. It may also be somewhat more circumspect, such as when one of the parties is assigned to the burden to prove (the absence of) some facts.

The role of an arbiter is unavoidable in law-establishing dialogues.[67] It is, however, a problematic role, because a decision of the arbiter on an issue makes a dialogue about this issue superfluous. The idea of having an arbiter is against the very spirit of dialogue games.[68] Nevertheless, arbiters are unavoidable and the best way to cope with them is to limit their role. How this should be done is beyond the scope of this chapter.[69]

11. MEDIATING SYSTEMS

If the law is seen as having a rhetorical nature, the natural role for dialogical systems is that they support legal dialogues, rather than to assess their rationality. Systems that fulfill such a supporting role are called 'mediating systems'. In the recent literature on Artificial Intelligence and Law, four such mediating systems have been proposed. One of them is the ZENO argumentation framework by Gordon and Karacapilidis[70], another one the Room 5 system by Loui et al.[71], the third one is the DiaLaw system by Lodder[72] and the fourth is Verheij's Argumed.[73]

The ZENO argumentation framework makes use of a discussion model that contains messages that are exchanged by the participants in a discussion.

---

[66] To avoid misunderstandings, it may be useful to point out that the arbiter is not necessarily the same person as the judge who was introduced in the previous section in connection with legal issues. The roles of the arbiter and the judge are not the same. In actual legal procedures, the two roles tend to be merged in the person of the judge.

[67] In merely dialectical systems, an arbiter is superfluous, because if a claim cannot be proven, it is invalid. In systems as the Pleadings Game, the role of the arbiter only becomes important when the pleadings game has finished. The arbiter may have to decide about the remaining issues. Gordon assigns this function of the arbiter to the Trial Game.

[68] For this reason, the role of the arbiter is not implemented in Lodder's DiaLaw system. See Lodder 1999, 29.

[69] In Hage e.a. 1994 the proposal was made to allow a call to the arbiter only if there is no winning strategy for or against the issue at stake. This limitation of the role of the arbiter does not go far enough, because it allows a call to the arbiter at the beginning of almost every dialogue about the facts of a case.

Prakken 2001 tries to model the role of judges in Dutch civil procedure in a formal dialogue game.

[70] Gordon and Karacapilidis 1997.

[71] Loui e.a. 1997.

[72] Lodder 1998 and 1999.

[73] Verheij 2003 (AAA) and 2004.

The contributions to the discussion can be given informally and are interpreted and formalized by a human mediator. The results of this interpretation and formalization are called marked messages. These are stored in the discussion model. The content of the discussion model can be modeled as a dialectical graph. In such a graph, the positions of the different parties in the discussion and the support and attack relations between them are modeled in the form of a tree. The root of the tree represents the issue at stake and the branches indicate lines of argumentation leading to different solutions for the issue. Given such a tree it is possible to define several levels of support for the solutions to the issue. Gordon and Karacapilidis distinguish five such levels, namely *scintilla of evidence*, *preponderance of the evidence*, *no better alternative*, *best choice* and *beyond a reasonable doubt*.[74] Positions taken by the parties are labeled as *in* or *out*, depending on whether they meet the level of proof that is selected for the issue. For instance, there is a *scintilla of evidence* for a particular position if there is at least one position, labeled as *in*, which supports the position at stake.

The Room 5 system by Loui et al. is similar to the ZENO-system in that it provides an environment for humans to conduct structured legal discussions. Its logical support is somewhat less than that of ZENO, but this is compensated by a facility for retrieving federal decisions on past cases.

Where the ZENO argumentation framework supports decision making processes in general, Lodder's DiaLaw aims at characterizing legal justification. A legal solution for a case is justified if the parties in a legal dialogue reach an agreement about this solution. The DiaLaw system supports legal dialogues by enforcing the dialogue protocol and by keeping track of the commitments of the parties in the dialogue.[75] As a consequence, it has reason-based logic[76] as its underlying logic. However, this logic is not used to evaluate the validity of arguments proposed by the dialogue parties, but rather to enable one party in a dialogue to force his opponent to accept what he was logically already committed to. In fact, it is one of Lodder's main claims that moves in dialogues need not lead to arguments that are valid according to some system of logic.[77] Let me use an example to illustrate this. Suppose that A has the position that O.J. murdered his wife. When challenged to defend this position, he adduces the argument that O.J. was found next to his wife's body with a smoking gun in his hand. If this

[74] As these alternatives suggest, the ZENO framework uses results from the work of Freeman and Farley (1996) to define the level of support or positions.

[75] The DiaLaw system is a strongly improved and implemented version of the dialogical variant of reason-based logic that was proposed in Hage e.a. 1994.

[76] Verheij 1996 and Hage 1996 and 1997. See also chapter 3.

[77] Lodder 1997, 1998 and 1999.

argument is accepted as providing sufficient support, A's position that O.J. murdered his wife counts as justified, despite the fact that there is no 'logical' relation between the positions that O.J. was found next to his wife's body with a smoking gun and that he murdered his wife.

Although justifying arguments need not be logically valid, logic plays a role in DiaLaw through the mechanism of forced commitment. If A's opponent has accepted that O.J. was found with a smoking gun and he has also accepted the rule of evidence that if somebody is found with a smoking gun next to a corpse, the person with the gun may be assumed to have committed the murder, he must accept that O.J. committed the murder, unless he can justify the position that there is an exception to the rule.

Verheij's Argumed system[78] is an argument assistance system based on Verheij's logic for defeasible reasoning DefLog (see section 4.3). The program provides the user with a graphical interface by means of which he can make the logical structure of arguments explicit. This logical structure is modeled by the logical means of DefLog, which means that statements can either support or attack each other. The ArguMed system keeps track of which statements are justified or defeated:

- A statement is justified if and only if
  - it is an assumption against which there is no defeating reason, or
  - it is an issue for which there is a justifying reason.
- A supporting reason is justifying if and only if the reason and the conditional underlying the corresponding supporting argument step are justified.
- An attacking reason is defeating if and only if the reason and the conditional underlying the corresponding supporting argument step are justified.

The ZENO framework, the Room 5 system, DiaLaw and Argumed have in common that they support human discussants by structuring their discussion and by providing logical tools to maintain a minimum level of rationality. They differ from systems as proposed by Loui and Norman[79] and Prakken and Sartor in that their purpose is not to provide a standard for the evaluation of the rationality of a dialogue, but rather to support discussants in having a rational dialogue. Although these purposes are not in opposition, there is a shift in emphasis that places ZENO, Room 5, DiaLaw and Argumed nearer to the dialogical pole on the gliding scale from dialectics to dialogues.

[78] Verheij 2003 (AAA). This paper also describes the Argue! system, which I will not discuss here. See also Verheij 2005.

[79] Loui and Norman 1995.

12. CONCLUDING OBSERVATIONS

When the several systems for legal dialectics and dialogues are compared, it is possible to make a number of distinctions. In the course of this chapter I have mentioned a number of systems, without mentioning whether they were implemented or not. In fact, most of the mentioned systems are logical systems, which give a dialectical characterization of logical consequence. The Pleadings Game, ZENO, Room 5, DiaLaw and ArguMed, are computational systems, however.

A second distinction is between conflict resolution systems and mediating systems. Logical issues, if cast in a dialectical form, become a kind of conflicts. The systems of Lorenzen and Lorenz and those of the battle of argument-theoreticians, are systems that decide how these conflicts are to be resolved. Mediating systems, on the contrary, do not resolve conflicts. They rather help humans to resolve their conflicts themselves, by providing an environment for structured discussion.

Another distinction is also based on the function of the systems. Some systems are intended to give a dialectical characterization of a particular form of logic. The system of Lorenzen and Lorenz, to take a typical case, aims at a dialectical characterization of intuitionistic logic. The battle of arguments-theorists (e.g. Prakken and Sartor) aim at the characterization of non-monotonic logics. Other systems aim at the establishment of the premises of legal arguments either as a basis for legal justification[80] or as identification of the issues between parties in a legal debate (Gordon). Battles of arguments can also be used to model some form of bounded rationality (Loui and Norman). Finally, there are systems the purpose of which is to determine the law in actual cases (Hage, Leenes and Lodder).

A fourth distinction is between static and dynamic systems. Mediating systems are by nature dynamic ones, but not all dynamic systems are mediating systems. For instance, the system of Loui and Norman works with argument stages and is in that sense dynamic. Nevertheless, it operates with a fixed set of premises, which is atypical for dynamic systems. It is in a sense intermediate between static systems and mediating systems.

Verheij's CumulA[81] is dynamic in that both the set of premises and the set of arguments can change in time. It is not a mediating system, first because it is not implemented and second because it has no dialogue protocol that specifies how the sets of premises and arguments may change.

[80] Aarnio e.a. 1981.

[81] Verheij 1996.

All of these systems deal with some form of rationality. A major dividing line between them can be based on the question what kind of rationality they aim to model. Some systems deal with the rationality of argument *forms*. The work of Lorenzen and Lorenz and the battle of arguments-theories, falls in this category. These systems typically assume a fixed set of premises and regard all possible arguments based on these premises. The question with which they deal is whether some conclusion follows from the premises and this is the case if, in a dialectical setting, there is a winning strategy to defend the conclusion. Actual dialogues, for which human players are needed who must make choices between several possible dialogue moves, do not play a role in this connection. These are the systems that I called non-dialogical.

Other systems deal with the rationality of the outcome of dialogues. They are concerned with content, not merely with form. Typically they do not assume a fixed set of premises; the rationality of the outcome depends in part on the way in which the premises of the argument were established. They do not consider all possible arguments, but are rather concerned with actual dialogues that lead to a particular conclusion. For this reason, the systems cannot provide the dialogue moves themselves, but depend on human players. Implementations of such systems will be mediating systems, rather than reasoning systems. These are the systems that I called dynamic dialectical.

The category of dynamic systems can be subdivided into logic-related systems and law-related systems, although I want to emphasize that this distinction is a matter of degree. Logic-related systems have dialogue rules that reflect primarily the logic that underlies the dialogue system. Notice that all dialogue systems that have anything to do with reasoning must have some underlying logic and that the dialogue rules of such systems must reflect these underlying logics. For some systems it holds that almost all dialogue rules reflect the underlying logic and that there are few other rules. The Pleadings Game of Gordon falls in this category. The law-establishing systems (Hage, Leenes, Lodder) must incorporate legal rules in the dialogue rules, because otherwise the outcome of the dialogues could not be called law.

Law-establishing systems must both make sure that the dialogues take the law into account and that the dialogues are not frustrated by a non-cooperating party. To accommodate for these needs, the roles of a judge and of an arbiter are introduced in the dialogue game. These introductions change dialogues into procedures that involve more parties.

The following tables provide an overview of some of the distinctions made above:

SYSTEMS WITH FIXED PREMISES (deal with rationality of form)	
Static dialectical systems (deal with full rationality)	**Non-dialogical dynamic systems (1) (deal with bounded rationality)**
Systems that consider all possible arguments given some logic	Systems that consider only arguments that were actually adduced
a. Lorenzen and Lorenz 1978 b. Prakken and Sartor 1996	a. Loui and Norman 1995 b. Prakken 1995

SYSTEMS WITH DYNAMIC PREMISES (deal with rationality of content; mediating systems)	
Non-dialogical dynamic systems (2)	**Dialogical systems (law-establishing dialogs)**
Systems with a dialogue protocol that is largely logic-based	Systems with a dialogue protocol that is also domain-based
a. Gordon's Pleadings Game 1994, 1955 b. Hage, Leenes and Lodder 1994, the formal part c. Verheij's CumulA 1996 d. Lodder's DiaLaw 1998, 1999 e. Verheij 2003 (DL and AAA) and 2005.	a. Alexy's Theorie der juristischen Argumentation 1978 b. Hage, Leenes and Lodder 1994, the informal part

Chapter 9

LEGAL REASONING AND LEGAL INTEGRATION

1. INTRODUCTION

Asking the right question is half of the answer. This valuable insight is not only applicable to problems in our daily lives, but also – and maybe even more – in scientific research. Jurisprudence is no exception here and many a jurisprudential discussion has benefited from somebody asking the right questions. In the author's opinion, the main virtue of legal theory in its old fashioned sense of applying techniques from analytical philosophy to jurisprudential issues is that it helps asking the right questions. Given the right questions, 'ordinary' legal knowledge often suffices to answer them. The purpose of this chapter is to illustrate this general point by showing how techniques from modern legal logic can benefit the actual discussion about European legal integration.

In 1997 Pierre Legrand published an eloquent argument against the introduction of a European Civil Code as a means to achieve integration of European private law.[1] His argument rests on two pillars. One is that integration is not desirable. The other one is that integration cannot be achieved by means of a uniform European Civil Code. Legrand criticizes the proposal in favor of a European Civil Code on four grounds, one of which (the relevant one for our purposes) is that such a code 'would fail to effect the universal reach for which it stands'. The presence of one and the same

[1] Legrand 1997.

code cannot lead to the same law if this code is to operate within two fundamentally different legal cultures, namely the cultures of civil law and of common law.

Legrand writes in this connection about two different *mentalités*. On the one hand there is the mentalité of the civil law tradition. According to Legrand, using an analysis of Pitkin, the civil law tradition takes abstract rules as the starting point for decision making and sees decision making as 'deductive in the sense that the rules that structure it are posited prior to the practices that apply it'.[2] The common law tradition, on the contrary, takes its starting point in concrete cases. When reference is made to an old case in order to decide a new one, the old case is not abstracted into a general rule, but is rather taken integrally, that is with all its factual details in place. Legrand quotes Samuel in this connection: 'legal development is not a matter of inducing rules, terms or institutions out of a number of factual situations. Rather it is a matter of pushing outwards from within the facts themselves.'

These descriptions of the civil law tradition and the common law tradition are highly abstract. Legrand takes the effort to describe the supposed differences more extensively, but his argument retains its highly abstract level all the time. Maybe an example can make the same point in a more down to earth fashion.

2. THE CASE OF THE MURDEROUS SPOUSE

A rich old lady was nursed by a poor young man. After some time the two married without making any special arrangements about their properties. According to the Dutch law, this meant that their properties were joined together and became their common property.

Not long after their marriage the young man allegedly murdered his wife. He was punished for the murder, but that is not the issue at stake. The issue was whether he could receive half of the marital estate because the marriage had ended. That he could not *inherit* the other half was clear, because of a statutory rule stating that somebody cannot inherit from a person he murdered. The Dutch legislation does not contain a special rule for the division of the marital estate in case a husband murders his wife, however.

The seemingly innocent observation that the Dutch legislation does not contain a special rule for the division of the marital estate in case a husband

2 Compare in this connection also Smits 2002, 82 on the syllogistic nature of legal reasoning in the civil law tradition.

murders his wife, gives rise to a difficult discussion. It is clear that the Dutch law does not contain a *written* rule that deals explicitly with the division of the marital estate in case one spouse murdered the other one. It is less clear that the Dutch law does not contain any rule dealing with this issue. If one assumes that a legal system has a rule for a particular type of situation if it has a solution for that kind of situation, one might well argue that there many cases which lack a suitable written rule, but which are nevertheless governed by some legal rule. The presence of a legal rule is then identified with the existence of a legally correct solution for a particular type of case. This view is defensible, but has the disadvantage that it diffuses the difference between, on the one hand, rules that were made to deal with some type of case and, on the other hand, the legal solutions for types of cases, which are sometimes based upon rules in the just mentioned sense.[3] When I use the expression 'rule' in this chapter, I refer to rules that were explicitly made and not to legal solutions for types of cases.

Let us concede to Legrand that in common law style reasoning there is ample room to deal with a case like the one of the murderous spouse in a proper way and that it is relatively easy to decide that the murderer should not receive half of the marital estate. If we may believe Legrand, such a solution would be hard to reach in a civil law tradition, however. There is in Dutch law only one rule that is by and large relevant and it states that if a marriage ends, the marital community of properties is divided between the partners. (If one of the partners has deceased, her portion is taken by her inheritors). This rule determines which facts of the case are relevant and these facts are merely that the marriage has ended (by the dead of one of the spouses). That the marriage ended because one spouse killed the other is not relevant, because the rule in question does not mention this fact. The relevant rule selects which facts are relevant and because the rule was 'posited prior to the practices that apply it' it could not take into account that the remaining spouse murdered the deceased one. On civil law style reasoning this would mean, at least according to Legrand, that the murderer would receive half of the marital estate.

Legrand might escape this conclusion by resorting to the view that rules are what I called 'legal solutions for types of cases'. On this broad view of rules, civil law systems might have a suitable rule for this type of case, although an unwritten one. Such a rule would be adapted to the needs of the

[3] This is approximately the same distinction as the one made by Kelsen between 'Rechtsnormen' and 'Rechtssätze' (Kelsen 1960, 73f.) and by Alchourrón and Bulygin (1981) between the expressive and the hyletic conception of norms. See also chapter 1, section 3 on Case Legal Consequence Pairs.

case at hand and would lead to the conclusion that the murderous spouse would not receive half of the marital estate. However, if Legrand would take this way out, his argument about the difference in mentality between the common law system and the civil law system loses its edge, because then rules would not be posited prior to the cases to which they are to be applied.

Let us therefore assume that the difference between civil law and common law really operates in the way Legrand suggests. Then Legrand would be right that the difference in *mentalité* between the civil law and the common law tradition would devastate the effects of a common civil code. I will argue, however, that the difference does not operate in this way and that, as a consequence, Legrand's argument is not as strong as it might seem at first sight. Later in this chapter I will return to the case of the murderous spouse and the way it was really dealt with in the Dutch civil law tradition. But first I must set out the path of the chapter.

I will argue that Legrand's argument hinges on the issue whether the law is an open system. In fact, his argument can be interpreted as stating that in a case-based system, the law is necessarily open, while in a rule-based system it is necessarily closed. This difference between a case-based approach and a rule-based approach makes that the introduction of a European civil code would not lead to uniform private law.

Legrand's argument might also be interpreted differently, namely as stating that common law systems just *happen* to be more open, without endorsing the view that this openness derives from common law systems being case-based. On this interpretation, the argument of this chapter loses much of its force, but the same counts for Legrand's argument, because it would not have presented any reason *that*, let alone *why* common law systems happen to be more open. So the argument of this chapter has two versions, directed against two interpretations of Legrand's theory. If Legrand does not presuppose that the difference in style of reasoning between the common law tradition and the civil law tradition stems from the difference between case-based reasoning and rule-based reasoning, his own argument is unfounded. However, if his argument is based on the assumption that the difference in style of reasoning between the common law tradition and the civil law tradition stems from the difference between case-based reasoning and rule-based reasoning, this chapter shows his assumption to be misguided. In both cases, Legrand's argument is refuted.

After a brief discussion of what the open nature of the law amounts to, I will elaborate Legrand's argument to show why the law might be open in common law and closed in civil law. I then resume my argument against Legrand by showing how the logic of rule application allows a civil law system to be open too. In this connection I will draw from recent results in the field of legal logic and in particular the analysis of legal reasoning by means of so-called non-monotonic logics. The conclusion here will be that the mere fact that a civil law system works with rules instead of cases, does not imply that such a system must be closed. It depends on other factors how open a rule-based legal system will be.

With this conclusion, Legrand's main argument has been refuted. What remains to be done is to show how a civil law system may be more or less open and say a little about the reasons that play a role in this connection. The same reasons are, I will argue, also relevant for common law systems.

3. THE LAW AS AN OPEN SYSTEM

One of the advantages of having a legal system, as opposed to deciding all cases on grounds of fairness, is that a legal system offers a higher degree of predictability of the outcomes. By indicating which facts of a case are legally relevant and in which way they lead to a particular outcome, it becomes easier to predict what the outcome of a case will be and this predictability makes social interaction easier. Fuller has even argued that a minimum amount of predictability is necessary for the very existence of a legal system.[4]

At the same time the limitation of legally relevant facts makes it sometimes impossible to take facts into account that seem relevant if one would not limit one's view to what is deemed relevant by the law. Legal reasoning is not only applying the relevant law to a case, but also a special case of practical reasoning, in the sense of deciding what to do.[5] From this perspective, the limitation of facts that can be taken into account as relevant for the decision at stake to only a pre-established set, is against the nature of the law, because it is not rational to leave potentially relevant facts out of consideration. Here we encounter a fundamental tension with which every legal system has to cope and it is this tension that is reflected in the issue to what extent a particular legal system is open.

A legal system is more open in the sense that is relevant here, to the extent that it allows more facts to be recognized as legally relevant that prima facie seemed to be irrelevant. As said, one of the points of having a legal system is that it distinguishes between facts that are relevant and facts that are not relevant for the solution of particular cases. Moreover, this distinction between relevant and irrelevant facts should be made before the cases arise to which the distinction is to be applied. If every case should be

4 Fuller 1969, 33f.

5 Alexy 1978, 263 and 1999, 374-384.

decided on all facts that are ex post deemed relevant, one might have a reasonable way to deal with these cases - although even this reasonableness can be disputed - but it is not a legal way. Having a legal system implies by definition an a priori determination of what counts as relevant in the eyes of the law.[6]

The question at stake concerning the openness of a legal system is how strict this determination is. If it is not strict at all, in a degree that the a priori determination of what counts as legally relevant has no practical meaning, the system in question is not a legal system anymore. If the determination is very strict, in the sense that it does not allow any exceptions, the legal system in question is closed. It is questionable whether such a closed system can function, given that the law is used to decide what should be done all things considered.[7] In reality, all legal systems are to some extent open. They allow some exceptions to the a priori determination of what counts as legally relevant, but they do not allow unlimited exceptions. The degree of openness of a legal system depends on the extent to which it allows exceptions.

If we may believe Legrand, a common law system allows principally more exceptions to the a priori determination of what is legally relevant, than a civil law system. In order to evaluate this claim, we must take a closer look at both the 'logic' of case-based reasoning and the 'logic' of rule-based reasoning. In the next section I will introduce some logical distinctions by means of which this closer look can be taken.

4. OF REASONS AND THEIR LOGIC[8]

If we have a suitable conceptual framework, the differences between common law style reasoning and civil law style reasoning are easier to understand. In this section I will try to develop such a framework in the form of reason-based logic. Reason-based logic is one example of so-called non-monotonic logics that have been developed in research on artificial intelligence to deal with rules of thumb and exceptions. In contrast to other non-monotonic logics, reason-based logic has been developed especially to deal with the peculiarities of reasoning with legal rules and principles.[9]

6 Fuller 1969, 49f. and Radbruch 1973, 164f.

7 Hage and Peczenik 2000.

8 The sections 4 to 6 exhibit a large overlap with parts of chapter 3. This overlap could only be avoided at the cost of seriously interrupting the argument line of the present chapter.

9 Verheij 1996, Hage 1996 and 1997 (RwR). See also chapter 3.

4.1 Reasons

A central notion in reason-based logic is that of a reason. I take all reasons to be facts, namely those parts of reality that make true sentences true. For instance, if the sentence 'It is raining' is true, it is made true by the fact that it is raining. I take everything denoted by a true that-phrase as a fact. This implies that I allow facts without a material basis, such as the fact that five is bigger than three and facts that are only possible on the basis of rules, such as the fact that courts have the power to sentence and the fact that a debtor ought to pay his debts. Clearly I thereby allow the presence of facts that can only obtain within the context of a legal system.

Some facts are relevant for the presence of other facts. For instance, the fact that John owns a book is relevant for the fact that he is permitted to tear the book in pieces. This kind of relevance is expressed by the word 'reason'. The fact that John owns the book is the reason why he is permitted to tear it apart and the fact that Lea is imprisoned is the reason why she cannot cast a valid vote.[10]

The word 'reason' can be used in other senses too, but the sense used above is the sense of 'reason' that I am interested in here. Reasons in this sense are *facts which make that other facts obtain or do not obtain.* I will call the fact for which a reason 'pleads', the *conclusion* of the reason. So the fact that John owns a book is the conclusion of the reason that Gerald transferred the ownership of this book to John.

Reasons can be subdivided into decisive reasons and contributive reasons. A *decisive reason* guarantees the presence of the fact for which it is a reason, or the absence of the fact against which it is a reason. For instance, the facts that there are two dogs, three cats and no other animals in the room are together a decisive reason for the fact that there are five animals in the room. Similarly, the fact that the only force that operates on a body is gravitational, is a decisive reason why this body is accelerated in the direction of the gravitational force.

Contributive reasons, on the contrary, do not guarantee the facts for which they 'plead'. They merely contribute to their presence. For instance, if Jane promised to visit Geraldine, this is a contributive reason why she should visit Geraldine. Whether she should visit Geraldine all things considered, depends on the presence of other reasons.

[10] Sometimes a reason consists of more than one fact. For instance, the facts that Frank committed a tort and thereby caused damages are together a reason why Frank is liable for the damages. Neither one of these facts would, taken on its own, be a reason, but in combination they are a reason for the existence of liability.

First, if there is a decisive reason why she should not visit Geraldine, then she should not visit Geraldine. Second, if there are contributive reasons not to visit Geraldine and if these reasons against visiting outweigh the reasons for visiting, she should not visit Geraldine either. However, if there are no reasons against visiting Geraldine, or if the reasons against visiting are outweighed by the totality of reasons for visiting, Jane should visit Geraldine.

A crucial aspect of contributive reasons is that *they have to be weighed* against contributive reasons pleading in a different direction. This weighing often boils down to taking a decision which set of reasons outweighs the other set. Sometimes, but not always, this decision can itself be guided by reasons. For instance, if two sets of reasons have been weighed before, the outcome of the earlier decision can count as a precedent for the new decision. (The same reasons must be weighed in the same way.)[11] There may also be reasons concerning the weight or even the relevance of other facts as reasons. Take for instance the following example[12]:

A small supermarket had to dismiss one of its employees for financial reasons. For this dismissal, the allowance of a judge was necessary. One of the employees, called Mary, had been longer in service and this is a reason for the judge not to permit to dismiss her. The other employee, called Richard, had better papers for the job and this is a reason not to dismiss him. Since it is clear that one of the employees has to be dismissed for financial reasons, a reason against permitting the dismissal of Richard is also a reason for permitting the dismissal of Mary.

The judge decided that, although Richard had better papers for the job, Mary was still sufficiently qualified, so that the better papers did not count for much. The fact that Mary had been longer in service should therefore tip the balance of reasons. Notice that the fact that Mary was suitable for the job was not considered as a reason not to dismiss her, but only as a reason why the seniority of Mary outweighs the better papers of Richard.

4.2 Rules

Rules are usually assumed to have a conditional structure. They consist of a condition part and a conclusion part and the point of rules is that if their conditions are satisfied, their conclusions obtain. Take for instance the main Dutch rule of tort law, which states effectively that if somebody commits a tort and this tort can be attributed to its actor, the actor is liable for the

[11] This theme is elaborated in chapter 5.

[12] Kantongerecht Rotterdam, June 12th, 1985, Praktijkgids 1985/2349.

damages caused by his act. Formulated in this way, the rule has two conditions that are necessary for its conclusion to obtain.

If a rule applies to a case, the conclusion of the rule holds for this case. In terms of reasons, we might say that the application of a rule to a case is a decisive reason for the rule conclusion to hold. This leaves the question unanswered, however, *when* a rule applies to a case. The standard situation when a rule applies is when the case satisfies the conditions of the rule. So, to stick with out analysis of the Dutch rule of tort law, if A committed a tort and this tort can be attributed to A, the rule applies to A's case and the conclusion follows that A is liable for the damages caused by his act. This standard situation is the one intended by the legislator who formulated the rule this way. It is also the normal situation in which the rule applies.[13]

4.3 Principles

Legal principles come in at least two main types. On kind of principles resembles rules in the sense that they exhibit the same conditional structure that is also characteristic for rules. I will call them *rule-like principles*. The principles of the other kind function like goals and for this reason I will call them goal principles or, briefly, *goals*.

Typical examples of rule-like principles are the principles that nobody can transfer a right that he has not got himself (nemo plus principle), the principle of the rule of law (the government has no power unless it was explicitly assigned by (written) law) and the principle that any act that violates a criminal law is tortuous. Rule-like principles differ from rules in that their application to a case does not generate a decisive reason for their conclusion, but merely a contributive reason.[14] As a consequence, the conclusion of a principle still needs to be balanced against other reasons, if there are any. For instance, a violation of a criminal law is in principle tortuous, but if there were sufficiently urgent reasons to commit this violation (a matter of balancing), the violation was justified and the act was not tortuous. In the rest of this chapter I will disregard rule-like principles.

Goal principles state goals that the law strives to realize as much as possible, within the confines of what is physically and legally possible.[15] Examples are human rights, but also governmental policies (e.g. full

[13] In section 6, I will discuss some less normal situations.

[14] In chapter 3 I wrote about abstract reasons instead of principles. Abstract reasons and principles can be translated into each other as follows: The validity of the principle 'If a then b' boils down to it that a is an abstract reason for b and the other way round.

[15] Alexy 1996 and 2000.

employment) and legal principles such as party autonomy and consumer protection in contract law. Goals are related to rule-like principles in the sense that they are merely the basis of contributive reasons. If some regulation or decision contributes to a goal, this is a contributive reason to adopt this regulation or to take this decision. This contributive reason still needs to be balanced against possible contributive reasons against the regulation or decision.

For instance, that the prohibition to publish a photograph of a recently released prisoner promotes the privacy of this prisoner is a contributive reason to prohibit the publication. This reason still needs to be weighed against a contributive reason for allowing the publication, based on another goal, namely the freedom of the press.[16]

5. THE SUBSUMPTION MODEL OF RULE-BASED REASONING

According to Legrand, rule-based reasoning allows much less leeway to adapt the law to the needs of the case at hand. Legrand sees rule-based decision making as 'deductive in the sense that the rules that structure it are posited prior to the practices that apply it'.

This phrasing is somewhat ambiguous. On the one hand it may merely mean that legal decision making can be divided into two stages. In the first stage a rule is formulated, based on the sources of the law and the needs of the case at hand, while in the second stage this rule is applied deductively to the case. This view has often been defended in the literature, under the headings of the distinction between heuristics and legitimation[17], secondary and primary justification[18], or internal and external evaluation of law application.[19] [20]

On the other hand it may mean that pre-given rules are processed in a blind way, more or less like if it were done by a computer program, without taking the needs of the case at hand into consideration. It seems that Legrand has this way of 'deductive' rule application in mind, because otherwise the rest of his observations are not to the point. Let us call this view of rule

[16] Cf. Alexy 1996, 84f.

[17] Nieuwenhuis 1976.

[18] Alexy 1978, 273 and MacCormick 1978, 101f.

[19] Wróblewski 1992, 62f.

[20] This view also seems to treat rules as legal solutions for types of cases as discussed in section 1.

application the *subsumption model.* According to this subsumption model the logic of rule application is the following:

1. Determine whether the facts of the case at hand satisfy the conditions of the rule.
2. If the answer is affirmative, the rule applies and the rule consequences are attached to the case.
3. If the answer is negative, the rule does not apply and the rule consequences are not attached to the case.

The only step in this model that allows some leeway to adapt the legal consequences to the needs of the case in question is the first one, because it requires interpretation of the rule conditions and classification of the case facts.[21]

As a model of how reasoning with rules works, the subsumption model is not correct. In particular it cannot account for the possibilities to make exceptions to rules and to apply rules analogously. Clearly there have been attempts in the literature on law and logic to fit exceptions and analogous rule application into the subsumption model[22], but the upshot of these attempts has always been that the rule does not run as it seems to run given its wordings. Either it contains an additional condition that is not satisfied by the case at hand (to account for exceptions), or its conditions are actually more general than the wordings suggest (to account for analogous application). Such attempts to argue that rules do not run as they seem to run at first sight are not to be recommended, because they misinterpret what goes in on legal reasoning to make the reasoning fit a preconceived, but wrong model.[23]

It is therefore better to replace the subsumption model of rule application by a more realistic one. In this connection I want to propose the reason-based model of rule application.

[21] Arguably, an important objection against the subsumption model, apart from that it is not faithful to legal practice, is that it places a too heavy burden upon legal interpretation, thereby leading to 'interpretations' that can only with the greatest difficulty be called so.

[22] See for instance Zippelius 1974, 41 and 69.

[23] A more extensive discussion of these matters can be found in Hage 1997 (RwR), 4f.

6. THE REASON-BASED MODEL OF RULE APPLICATION

The reason-based model of rule application has as its starting point two assumptions. The first one is that if a rule applies to a case, its conclusion is attached to that case as a legal consequence.[24] For instance, if the rule that he who commits an attributable tort is liable for the damages caused by the tort, applies to a case, the tortfeasor is liable for the damages caused by his tort.

The second assumption is that whether a rule applies depends on a balance of reasons for and against application. To elaborate the same example, this means that whether the rule that he who commits an attributable tort is liable for the damages caused by the tort, applies to a case, depends on both the contributive reasons pleading for application and the contributive reasons against application and therefore *not merely on whether the rule conditions are satisfied.*

The first assumption is not really different from the subsumption model, but the second one makes a crucial difference, because

1. it allows reasons against the application of a rule that compete with reasons for application, and
2. it does not state in an a priori fashion which facts count as reasons for or against application.

In particular the second characteristic of the reason-based model makes that reasoning with rules according to this model is very well compatible with a relatively open system of the law. Let me elaborate a bit on the reason-based model of rule application, to justify this claim.

Although the reason-based model as described above does not specify which facts count as reasons for and against application of a rule, there are very plausible ways to extend this model. I will discuss three of such extensions.

6.1 The first extension of the reason-based model of rule-application

The first extension is to assume that if the facts of a case satisfy the conditions of a rule - I will say that the rule is *applicable* to the case - this is merely a *contributive* reason why the rule applies.[25] Again, this looks similar

[24] This might be interpreted as 'all or nothing application' in the sense of Dworkin 1978, 24.

[25] Notice that the applicability of a rule is not the same as its application. The point of the reason-based model is that applicability is merely a contributive reason for application.

to the subsumption model, but there is a crucial difference, because on the subsumption model, the applicability of the rule is a *decisive* reason to apply the rule. What does this difference mean?

First, it means that even if a rule is applicable, there may still be reasons against applying the rule, reasons which may, but need not, outweigh the applicability of the rule as a reason for application. This might, for instance, be the case, if application of the rule would be against the purpose of the rule.

Fuller gave an example of a prohibition to sleep in the railway station, which was motivated by the desire to retain tramps from spending their night on the station.[26] It would be against the purpose of this rule to apply it to the traveler who dozed away a few minutes while waiting on a late train, because this would not contribute to the goal of retaining tramps from spending their nights on the station.

If application of a rule to a case would be against the rule's purpose, this is normally a contributive reason against application of the rule. Normally a rule is not applicable to cases where application would be against the rule's purpose. If the rule is nevertheless applicable, there are both a reason for and a reason against applying the rule to that case. The demands of legal certainty plead for the conclusion that the applicability of the rule outweighs the fact that application would be against the rule's purpose, but this demand is not decisive (merely a contributive reason why applicability outweighs its competitor) and the balance of reasons might be that the reason against application of the rule outweighs the reason for application. The rule does not apply then, and does not attach its conclusion as a legal consequence to the case.

Second, it means that there can be a decisive reason against application of the rule, and such a decisive reason by definition brings about that the rule does not apply, even if it is applicable. A decisive reason against application of an applicable rule obtains, for instance, if another rule with an incompatible conclusion is also applicable to the case and this second rule has precedence over the first rule. In Dutch rental law, the rules concerning the rent of business accommodations are sometimes in conflict with the general rules about rent and if such a conflict occurs, the more specific rules concerning the rent of business accommodations have precedence over the general rules about rent. The applicability of a rule that has precedence over another rule is normally a decisive reason against applying the latter rule.

Third, the first extension means that if a rule is applicable and there exists therefore a contributive reason for applying the rule and there is no

[26] Fuller 1958.

reason, either contributive or decisive, against application, the rule certainly applies and its consequence is attached to the case. *This is the normal situation and in this situation the reason-based model and the subsumption model of rule application lead to the same results.* It is this kind of situation that lends some plausibility to the subsumption model, because the shortcomings of that model are not relevant in the normal situation.

6.2 The second and third extension to the reason-based model of rule-application

The second extension to the reason-based model of rule application is that *if a rule is not applicable to a case, this is a contributive reason against applying the rule to this case.* At first sight this extension seems superfluous, because if a rule is not applicable, there seems to be no reason for applying it, so the issue of application seems not to arise at all. The relevance of the second extension only becomes clear in the light of the third extension of the reason-based model of rule application.

This third extension is that *there can be other reasons for applying a rule than only the applicability of the rule in question.* The reason-based model itself does not specify what these other reasons might be; it only leaves the possibility open that there are other reasons for application.

Reasons to apply a rule to a case, even if its conditions are not satisfied, will usually be based on application of principles or goals that led the legislator to make the rule in the first place. This means that the case belongs to a type that is similar to those for which the legislator had the rule in mind. The cases to which the rule is applied although the rule conditions are not satisfied, will therefore normally resemble cases to which the rule is applicable. That is why we normally speak of *analogous application* of a rule if a rule is applied to a case in which it is not applicable.[27]

The reasons to apply a rule analogously must always be weighed against the non-applicability of the rule as a reason against application. Legal certainty provides again a contributive reason why the non-applicability outweighs the reasons for analogous application, but in the end the conclusion may nevertheless be that the rule should be applied analogously.

[27] A more extensive discussion of analogous rule application can be found in Verheij and Hage 1994 and in Hage 1997 (RwR), 118f.

7. THE TWO-LAYER MODEL OF THE LAW

An important question to be raised about legal reasoning is why rules lead to decisive reasons. The presence of a decisive reason means that contributive reasons for the opposite conclusion are not even taken into account, which is at first sight irrational. An attractive answer to this question has been offered by Raz, who compared rules[28] with decisions. Decisions are, ideally, based on weighing the contributive reasons for and against a particular course of action. Having taken the decision, the decision maker does not need to weigh the contributive reasons again. Instead she can rely on the decision that comes instead of the original contributive reasons that went into the decision.[29]

Analogously, rules come instead of the contributive reasons that went into the decision to make them. Rules 'mediate between deeper-level considerations and concrete decisions. They provide an intermediate level of reasons to which one appeals in normal cases where a need for a decision arises. Reasons on that level can themselves be justified by reference to the deeper concerns on which they are based'.

Moreover, the force of rules '… is completely exhausted by those underlying considerations. Contrariwise, whenever one takes a rule or directive as a reason one cannot add to it as additional independent factors the reasons which justify it'. So, rules can be seen as a kind of summaries of the reasons that went into making them. But there is more, because 'through the acceptance of rules setting up authorities, people can entrust judgment as to what is to be done to another person or institution…'.[30]

Given this account of the relation between rules and the contributive reasons underlying them, the reason-based logic of rules as described above can easily be explained and justified. If a rule applies in a case, this is a reason to decide the case in accordance with the rule. The contributive reasons pleading for or against this decision have lost their force because they were summarized in the rule. There is no need to weigh reasons anymore and the rule decides the case. That is why application of a rule leads to a decisive reason.

[28] Actually Raz's discussion is confined to reasons for action and as a consequence also to rules that prescribe behavior (mandatory norms). There is no fundamental reason to restrain Raz's argument to behavior guiding rules, however.

[29] Raz 1975, 65f.

[30] Raz 1986, 58/9.

However, a rule only replaces the reasons that went into it. Possible other reasons that were not taken into account in making the rule still have force.[31] If in an actual case such reasons are present, the case cannot be decided anymore by means of the rule alone. Instead the contributive reasons for and against the projected solution have to be weighed. If the outcome of this weighing process is that another decision than that suggested by the rule should be taken, there is an exception to the rule and the rule does not apply.[32]

I will adapt a rule from Dutch private law to illustrate this point. The rule at stake is to be found in article 3:86 of the Dutch Civil Code and deals (amongst others) with the situation that somebody, acting in good faith, obtained through transfer a moveable property from another person, who did not have the power to transfer (in general: not the owner). The rule runs (approximately) that if the property was not stolen and if the receiving person acted in good faith and had to pay for the transferred property, he would become the new owner.

This rule balances the interests of the original owner (he loses his property only in special circumstances) and the receiving party who acted in good faith (who gains property when he most 'deserves' it). Suppose, however that (contrary to reality) the legislator who made this rule did not consider the situation in which the original owner lost his property not because of theft, but because of embezzlement. Then, in case of embezzlement, the rule must temporarily be left out of consideration and all reasons for and against the conclusion that the receiving party has gained ownership must be balanced again. However, the rule's applicability is an additional reason that must be taken into account, because of legal certainty. It is the balance of all these reasons, including the rule's applicability that determines whether the original owner retains his property or whether the receiving party gains ownership.

Raz does not agree without reservations with the last point that if the outcome of the weighing process is that another decision than that suggested by the rule should be taken, the rule does not apply. In his discussion of the case that there are reasons which the authority (the rule maker) was meant to reflect correctly but failed to reflect, Raz writes that these reasons 'are none the less among the reasons which justify holding the directives binding'. Raz justifies this strange seeming view by pointing out that 'An authority is

[31] Such reasons include both reasons pleading directly for or against the rule's conclusion and reasons that regard the (relative) relevance of the reasons that went into the rule. These last reasons were not mentioned in Hage 1997 (RwR).

[32] Sometimes this takes the form of reviewing a rule against legal principles. See in this connection Hage 1999 (TLR).

justified, according to the normal justification thesis, if it is more likely than its subjects to act correctly for the right reasons … If every time a directive is mistaken … it were open to challenge as mistaken, the advantage gained by accepting the authority as more reliable and successful guide to right reason would disappear'.[33] Having written this, Raz continues with a distinction between clear (easily recognizable) errors and big errors (errors with big consequences) and suggests thereby that if the authorities made a clear error, this would be a reason for making an exception to the rule, while errors that are not clear (but possibly big) do not justify making an exception.

This is not the occasion to have a full discussion with Raz. Suffice it to say that Raz's theory about the relation between contributive reasons and rules provides jurisprudential underpinnings, both for the reason-based account of the logic of rules and for the view that rules have some independent authority, next to the reasons that went into them.

8. THE REASON-BASED MODEL OF RULE APPLICATION AND THE OPEN NATURE OF THE LAW

Having introduced the reason-based model of rule application, I am in a position to establish whether this model allows more ways to introduce new relevant facts than the subsumption model. I will do so by following the steps of the reason-based model and consider for each step whether it gives new opportunities to introduce relevant facts. According to the reason-based model of rule application, the following steps must be taken:

1) Determine whether the facts of the case at hand satisfy the conditions of the rule.
2) If the facts satisfy the rule conditions, there is a contributive reason to apply the rule. Then it must be determined whether there are reasons against application of the rule.
   a) If there is a decisive reason against application, there is an exception to the rule and the rule does not apply.
   b) If there are no reasons against application of the rule, the rule applies and its conclusion is attached to the case as legal consequence.

[33] Raz 1986, 61.

c) If there are one or more contributive reasons against application, these reasons must be balanced against the reasons for application, including the applicability of the rule.
   i) If the contributive reasons for application outweigh the contributive reasons against application, the rule applies and its conclusion is attached to the case as legal consequence.
   ii) If the contributive reasons against application outweigh the contributive reasons for application, there is an exception to the rule, the rule does not apply and its conclusion is not attached to the case as legal consequence.

3) If the facts do not satisfy the rule conditions, there is a contributive reason not to apply the rule. Then it must be determined whether there are reasons to apply the rule analogously.
   a) If there are one or more contributive reasons for analogous application, these reasons must be balanced against the reasons against application, including the non-applicability of the rule.
      i) If the contributive reasons for analogous application outweigh the contributive reasons against application, the rule applies (analogously) and its conclusion is attached to the case as legal consequence.
      ii) If the contributive reasons against application outweigh the contributive reasons for analogous application, the rule does not apply and its conclusion is not attached to the case as legal consequence.
   b) If there are no reasons for analogous application of the rule, the rule does not apply and its conclusion is not attached to the case as legal consequence.

The first step is to determine whether the facts of the case at hand satisfy the conditions of the rule. Although this step requires interpretation of the rule (or classification of the case facts) and for this reason provides some leeway to introduce new relevant facts, it is not new in comparison to the subsumption model. Therefore the first step of the reason-based model does not make a difference with the subsumption model.

If on the first step, the rule was found to be applicable, the second step of the reason-based model is to determine whether there is a decisive reason against application of the rule. The reason-based model as such does not determine what would amount to a decisive reason against application of the rule and therefore provides ample room to introduce new relevant facts. However, decisive reasons are much less frequent than contributive ones and it is not probable that a legal system will recognize many decisive reasons against the application of an applicable rule. A conflict with another applicable rule, as mentioned above, is the most plausible candidate.

Whether such a conflict occurs, depends solely on the interpretation of the other rule and/or the classification of the case facts and here we do not find additional leeway in comparison to the subsumption model.

However, if there is a conflict, a decision needs to be taken which rule has precedence over the other. A legal system may have precedence 'rules' that deal with this issue (such as Lex Specialis), but these precedence 'rules' are better regarded as rule-like principles than as rules in the strict sense used here. For instance, even if one of two conflicting rules is more specific than the other, this is no more than a contributive reason why this rule has precedence. There may also be contributive reasons why the other rule has precedence (for instance that the other rule is more recent, or stems from a higher court) and legal systems usually have no limits on possible contributive reasons concerning which rule in a conflict set has precedence. So the issue of precedence in case of a rule conflict provides the opportunity to introduce new relevant facts.

If on the first step, the rule was found to be applicable and the second step did not lead to a decisive reason against application of the rule, the third step of the reason-based model is to determine whether there are contributive reasons against application of the rule. The reason-based model does not specify what can count as a contributive reason against application of a rule and it is completely up to the legal system in question what kinds of contributive reasons against application of an applicable rule it recognizes. Moreover, if there are such contributive reasons against application, it is also up to the legal system to determine how these reasons are to be weighed against the rule's applicability and possible other reasons pleading for application of the rule. In other words, there is plenty of leeway here to introduce new relevant facts.

If on the first step, the rule was found not to be applicable, the second step of the reason-based model is to determine whether there are contributive reasons to apply the rule analogously. Again, the reason-based model itself does not specify what can count as a contributive reason for analogous application of a rule and it is completely up to the legal system in question what kinds of contributive reasons for analogous application of a rule it recognizes. Moreover, if there are such contributive reasons for analogous application, it is also up to the legal system to determine how these reasons are to be weighed against the rule's non-applicability and possible other reasons against application of the rule. In other words, here is plenty of leeway to introduce new relevant facts too.

To summarize, the reason-based model of rule application allows the introduction of new relevant facts into the law that are lacking in the subsumption model, when a decision needs to be made:

1. which of two conflicting rules has precedence over the other;
2. whether there are contributive reasons against the application of an applicable rule;
3. whether there are reasons to apply a non-applicable rule analogously;
4. in case there are both contributive reasons for and against application of a rule, whether the reasons for application outweigh the reasons against application, or the other way round.

9. THE REASON-BASED MODEL OF CASE-BASED REASONING

To evaluate Legrand's claim that the case-based style of reasoning allows more possibilities to introduce new relevant facts into the law, we must compare the above reason-based model of rule application with a similar reason-based model of case-based reasoning. To that purpose I will outline a logical model of case-based reasoning based on the same conceptual framework of contributive reasons, decisive reasons and principles.

Cases can be used in legal reasoning in two main ways. One of them, prevalent in the civil law tradition, is to extract some kind of rule from the case and use this rule more or less like statute-based rules. The other one, prevalent in the common law tradition, is for reasoning by analogy. Reference to an old case is made to argue that the decision in a new case should be similar, because the old and the new case are similar. I will call this latter form of using cases *case-based reasoning.*

A crucial difference between the reason-based models of rule-based reasoning and case-based reasoning is that while rule-based reasoning turns around the fact that the application of a rule leads to a *decisive* reason for the rule conclusion, a similar phenomenon is lacking in case-based reasoning.

The reason for this being, if we follow Raz's analysis, that rules have a particular element of authority that is lacking in cases. This does not mean that there is no element of authority involved in cases. In fact, the binding force of cases in systems where some form of stare decisis holds, illustrates the contrary. The crucial difference is that where rules are framed with the purpose of laying down authoritatively which facts count as relevant, cases are not.

Nevertheless, stare decisis presupposes that if two cases are legally completely identical, the decision of the one case should also hold in the other one. It is only that cases by themselves, otherwise than rules, do not state what is relevant in them.

Because case-based reasoning is not based on decisive reasons the way rule-based reasoning is, the facts of a case do not include decisive reasons, but only contributive reasons for and against a possible conclusion. Let us assume that case-based reasoning involves two cases, which are treated as analogous or not with regard to a particular conclusion. Let us call the cases O(ld) and N(ew) and assume that in case O a decision D was taken. The issue at stake is whether decision D should also be taken in case N and to what extent O provides authority for doing so.

Both cases contain, trivially, zero or more facts that are relevant for the decision D. Some of these facts (again zero or more) are contributive reasons that plead for D and some are contributive reasons that plead against D. Other facts (zero or more) are indirectly relevant, for instance by influencing the (degree of) relevance of the facts that are contributive reasons.[34]

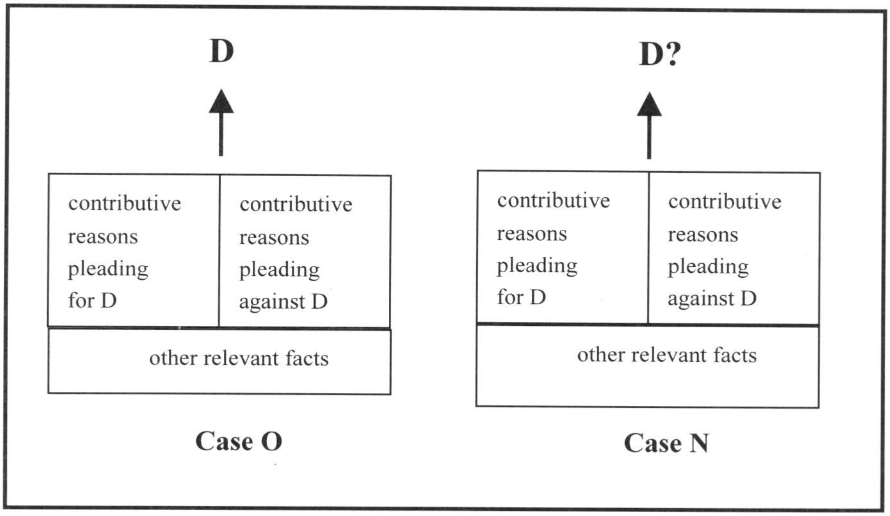

Stone has argued extensively that there is lot of leeway for judicial choice in a system of precedent.[35] Given the logical apparatus indicated above, it is possible to indicate three choices that must be made before case-based reasoning is actually possible.

The *first decision* that must be made is which facts are in some way relevant for the conclusion that is at stake. This decision must be made for both cases. The motivation given for the judgment in the old case may be

[34] The ways in which other relevant facts can be relevant are quite diverse and it is beyond the scope of this paper to elaborate on this issue. The interested reader is referred to Roth 2003.

[35] Stone 1968, 267f.

helpful in this connection, but it is not decisive. The determination which facts are relevant for the issue at stake is both crucial for the outcome of the case-based reasoning process and at the same time hardly guided by the cases themselves. It presupposes some a priori understanding of what is legally relevant.[36]

All facts that are relevant for some conclusion have their relevance because they belong to a type of fact that is normally relevant for this kind of conclusion. For instance, the fact that John damaged Jane's car is relevant for the conclusion that he ought to pay for the damages, because damaging is (under certain circumstances) a tort and torts are relevant for liability. There is for all relevant facts one particular level of description that brings out their relevance for the issue at stake.

The *second decision* that must be made concerns the level of abstraction at which the relevant facts are to be described. Take, for instance, the famous case of Donoghue vs Stevenson[37] that deals with the liability of the producer of a bottle of ginger beer that contained a decomposed snail. Is the relevant fact that the product was an opaque bottle of ginger beer, or that it was an opaque bottle of beverage, or any bottle of beverage, or any container of commodities for human consumption?[38]

Third, the logical role of the facts in the old case must be determined. Given the coarse categorization of possible logical roles described above, three roles are possible, namely those of contributive reason for the decision, contributive reason against the decision and otherwise relevant facts. The precise logical role of a fact is important for the treatment of this fact in case-based reasoning. Suppose, for instance, that a fact was relevant in the old case because it pleaded for the decision taken in that case. If this fact is absent in the new case, this is probably a reason to distinguish between the cases, because the support for the decision is, at least in one respect, less strong in the new case than in the old case. If the same fact pleaded against the decision taken in the old case, the absence of this fact in the new case is probably not a reason to distinguish the cases, because the support for the decision is even stronger in the new case, since a reason against that decision is lacking.

[36] By stating that the determination of the relevant case facts requires an a priori understanding of what is legally relevant, I do *not* mean to say that relevancy is established a priori. It may very well be that the recognition of some facts as legally relevant is the outcome of persuasive reasoning in connection with the new case that is to be decided and therefore originates after the new case. My point here is that the recognition of relevance is not justified by either the old or the new case.

[37] 1932, A.C. 562.

[38] Stone 1968, 269.

Consider the following example: In case Old, the defendant hit the plaintiff on purpose, while in case New he hit the plaintiff by accident. Let us assume that the intention to hit is a reason for the liability of the defendant. If in the Old case the defendant was held liable, the fact that the intention to hit was lacking in the New case is a reason to distinguish the cases. If, however, in the Old case the defendant was not held liable, the difference between the cases is not a reason to distinguish them, but rather a reason to argue a fortiori.

The same counts for a fact in the old case that increased the importance of some reason for the conclusion that was actually taken or decreased the importance of a reason against the actual decision. If such a fact is lacking in the new case, that is a reason to distinguish the cases. If, however, in the new case a fact is lacking that decreased the importance of a reason for the conclusion or increased the importance of a reason against the conclusion, this is not a reason to distinguish the cases.

Take for instance the case about the supermarket, discussed in section 4.1. In this case the fact that one person was suitable for her job decreased the relevance of her not having the required papers. The conclusion in this case was that she should not be dismissed. As a consequence, if in a new case the person in question is not very suitable for his job, the cases are distinguishable. Had the conclusion in the old case been that the person in question should be dismissed despite her suitability, the cases are not distinguishable.[39]

To summarize, the reason-based model of case-based reasoning requires decisions concerning:

1. which facts are relevant,
2. under which categorization they are relevant and
3. their logical role.

On the basis of these decisions it is possible to determine on logical grounds whether the old case provides support for deciding the new case in the same way. Such support is present if both

- all reasons that were present in case O that plead for D are also present in case N, with at least the same importance;
- all reasons that are present in case N that plead against the decision were also present in case O, with at least the same importance.[40]

[39] More examples of this style of reasoning can be found in Roth 2003.

[40] These findings are argued extensively and elaborated in Hage 2001 (FLC). See also chapter 5.

It should, however, be noted that the presence of this support is not sufficient to decide the new case. If case O is relevant for the decision in case N, this is a contributive reason to decide case N in the same way case O was decided. This contributive reason still has to be weighed against possible contributive reasons for a different decision than was taken in O.

10. COMPARING CASE-BASED AND RULE-BASED REASONING

Let us return from our digression into the logic of case-based reasoning and focus again on the differences between case-based reasoning and rule-based reasoning and the relevance of these differences for the issue to what extent a legal system is open. In section 8 I distinguished four ways in which the reason-based model of rule application allows the introduction of new relevant facts, namely when decisions had to be taken:

1. which of two conflicting rules has precedence over the other;
2. whether there are contributive reasons against the application of an applicable rule;
3. whether there are reasons to apply a non-applicable rule analogously;
4. in case there are both contributive reasons for and against application of a rule, whether the reasons for application outweigh the reasons against application, or the other way round.

The question that we must answer now is how these possibilities relate to the corresponding possibilities in case-based reasoning. From the three decisions required by the case-based reasoning model, the first two, the decisions concerning which facts are relevant and under which categorization they are relevant, allow the introduction of new relevant facts.

It is remarkable that the rule-based model is much more specific about when decisions concerning relevance have to be made. The reason for this is that the rule-based model of legal decision making is more structured than the case-based model. This difference in specificity makes a thorough comparison difficult, but the lesser specificity of the case-based model suggests that it allows more leeway for the recognition of new relevant facts, precisely as Legrand suggested. But let us take a closer look at the issue at stake and try to do so by paying special attention to the following question:

> *Can there be facts that are intuitively relevant for the solution of a case, which the rule-based model nevertheless disallows to be taken into account?*

Answering such a question in abstract is not so easy, but let me try. Suppose that we have a case C and that the issue at stake is whether decision D should be taken. Then there are four possibilities which I will discuss in turn:

a. There is an applicable rule R with conclusion D.
b. There is an applicable rule R with a conclusion that is incompatible with D.
c. There are two applicable rules, one with conclusion D and one with a conclusion that is incompatible with D.
d. There is no applicable rule that deals with the issue D.

Ad a.

If there is an applicable rule R with conclusion D, the normal outcome of the case should be D. Additional relevant facts F are only really relevant if they plead against this conclusion. Is it possible to conclude that not-D on the basis of these additionally relevant facts? The answer is a plain *yes*. The 'only' thing that is necessary is to make an exception to the rule R, because F outweighs the applicability of R. Logically, there is no problem to take F into account on the rule-based model. Whether F is considered to be sufficiently important to make an exception to R is an issue that cannot be dealt with by means of logic alone. That is a matter of the legal system in question, but the above shows that, otherwise than Legrand suggests, it is not a matter that is decided purely by the fact that the system belongs to the civil law tradition.

Ad b.

This situation is exactly the mirror of the previous. Now F is only really relevant if it pleads for D. Again the central question is whether F is sufficiently important to make an exception to R, and again this question cannot be answered purely on the basis of the civil law tradition of the legal system.

Ad c.

If there are two conflicting rules that are both applicable to a case, the issue at stake is to which rule an exception must be made because of the applicability of the other rule. In other words, it must be decided which of the two rules has precedence over the other.

Sometimes there is an applicable rule that deals with this question. For instance, article 7a:1623b, section 5 of the Dutch Civil Code states explicitly that the terms for giving notice for a contract of rent of housing replace the terms for rent contracts in general. If new relevant facts should play a role in such a case, it must be by making an exception to such a priority rule.

More often a conflict of rules is governed by principles that deal with their preference. The Lex Specialis 'rule' is such a principle that gives a contributive reason why the more specific rule has precedence. New relevant facts can in this case play a role when they are either contributive reasons that plead in the different direction than such a principle (for precedence of the other rule), or reasons to balance the reasons concerning precedence in some way.

If there is neither a rule nor a principle dealing with the precedençe of the conflicting rules, new relevant facts can play a role through being reasons for giving either one of the conflicting rules precedence. (This situation is not essentially different from the previous one.)

Ad d.

If under a rule-based system a case arises for which there is no rule, the case must be decided by reasons that are not based on a rule. *Logically* there is no objection against declaring any fact legally relevant, so this situation does not pose any objections against assigning facts legal relevance.

Summarizing, we find that in neither one of the four distinguishable cases, there are logical objections against assigning legal relevance to a fact or set of facts. So the answer to the question whether there can be facts that are intuitively relevant for the solution of a case, but which the rule-based model disallows to be taken into account, is negative. The rule-based model *as such* does not pose any limitations to the recognition of legal relevance.

11. THE CASE OF THE MURDEROUS SPOUSE REVISITED

The above discussion about the possibilities of rule-based reasoning and case-based reasoning has been rather abstract. Let us reconsider the case of the murderous spouse to see what the outcome of that discussion means in legal practice. To that purpose we will first look how that case might be handled under a system of case-based reasoning and then consider how the Dutch courts, who operated under a system of rule-based reasoning, actually dealt with it. Remember that the case ran as follows:

> A rich old lady was nursed by a poor young man. After some time, the two married, without making any special arrangements about their properties. According to the Dutch law, this meant that their properties were joined together and became their common property. Not long after their marriage the young man murdered his wife. The legal issue at stake was whether he could receive half of the marital estate because the marriage had ended.

The treatment of the case as if it were handled under a system of case-based reasoning is only possible if an initial difficulty is overcome, namely that the

Dutch system works primarily with rules and case law is mainly used for the interpretation of statutory rules. The most relevant antecedent legal material is a statutory rule stating that he who was convicted for killing, or for trying to kill, the deceased, is not worthy to inherit from the deceased.[41] Implicitly this rule means that such a person does not inherit. To use this rule for case-based reasoning, we will treat it as if it were a case and assume that in this case it was decided that the murderer of the deceased, who would normally inherit, in fact did not receive the estate.

To use this case as a possible precedent, it is necessary to establish which facts of the case are relevant, under which categorization they are relevant and what their logical role is. The origin of our hypothetical case in a statutory rule makes it easier than normal to determine which facts in the old case are relevant, because our hypothetical case does not contain any irrelevant facts. But this origin does not provide any help in determining which facts of the new case are relevant. Does it matter that the potential inheritor nursed the deceased, or that he married her only recently? Obviously it is relevant that the murderer actually married the deceased, because otherwise the issue could not arise whether he was entitled to half of their estate because their marriage ended, but is it also relevant that he was married to the deceased as an independent reason why he should receive half of the estate?

The second issue, concerning the categorization under which the relevant facts are relevant, is completely open. Does the murderer in the old case not inherit because he murdered the deceased, or because he inflicted some wrong on the deceased, or because he inflicted some serious wrong on the deceased, or because he inflicted a wrong that merely causally contributed to the deceased's dying, without necessarily amounting to murdering the deceased? Is the fact that the murderer was married to the deceased relevant because being married is a close relationship, or because it is a legally recognized relationship?

The third issue is relatively easy to decide for the old case. The fact that the potential inheritor murdered the deceased is a reason why he should not inherit. Presumably this is also a reason why he should not receive half of the marital estate. But what is the role of the fact that the murderer was married to the deceased? Is not this also a reason why he should receive half of the estate? And is the fact that they were married only recently a reason to make this last reason relatively less important, or is it (also) a reason why the fact that the potential inheritor murdered his wife is a stronger reason why he should not receive half of the marital estate?

[41] Article 4:3 section 1 sub a of the Dutch Civil Code.

The desirable conclusion that the murderous spouse does not receive half of the marital estate can be reached by assuming that in the old case the reason why the murderer did not inherit were that

- receiving a heritage is drawing a benefit from the deceased's passing away;
- he murdered the deceased;
- the fact that he murdered the deceased was a reason against his inheriting that outweighed the reason(s) why he should inherit.

There should also be assumptions about the new case, namely that:

- Receiving half of the marital estate is drawing a benefit from the deceased's passing away.
- The fact that the murderer was married to the deceased as a reason for letting him receive half of the estate does not outweigh the fact that he murdered the deceased as a reason why he should not receive half of the estate.

Given these assumptions about the cases, the two cases are completely analogous and this is a reason why the conclusion of the first case, that the murderer should not draw a benefit from his murdering the deceased (at this level of abstraction), should also hold for the new case.

Apparently the case-based style of reasoning provides sufficient leeway to reach a desirable conclusion. What about the rule-based style of reasoning?

The Court of Justice that decided the case had the problem that the Dutch law does not contain any other rule about the subject than the general rule stating that when a marriage ends, the marital estate is divided equally between the former spouses, which implies that if the marriage ends by the death of one of them, the division takes place between the surviving spouse and the inheritors of the deceased one. No word in this regulation about the possibility that the one spouse murdered the other one. So if the Court were to apply the applicable rule, the result would be that the murderous spouse received half of the marital estate.

That is not what happened in fact, however. The Court found that there is a legal principle underlying the rule of article 4:3 section 1 sub a of the Dutch Civil Code, the rule that a murderer is not worthy to inherit from the person he murdered.[42] This principle runs - according to the Court - that a murderer should not profit from his murder. By applying this principle to the case of the murderous spouse, the Court found that the rule about the

[42] HR December 7 1990; NJ 1991, 593.

division of the marital estate should not be applied in case the one spouse murdered the other one. In other words, the actual outcome of the case of the murderous spouse under a system of rule-based reasoning is exactly the same as the outcome would presumably be under a system of case-based reasoning and – although with a different logical construction – for essentially the same reason as under case-based reasoning.

In the case of the murderous spouse, the alleged rigidity of a system of rule-based reasoning turned out not to be as limiting as Legrand would like us to believe. Of course, this is only one example, but this example illustrates a point that was made theoretically above, namely that any fact that can be recognized as legally relevant under a system of case-based reasoning can also be recognized as relevant under a system of rule-based reasoning. Case-based reasoning and rule-based reasoning make use of different logical constructions, but this difference in form needs not lead to a difference in content. Everything that is possible under a system of case-based reasoning is also possible under a system of rule-based reasoning, although not always in precisely the same way.

12. THE POSSIBLE AND THE ACTUAL

We have found that the differences between case-based reasoning and rule-based reasoning are merely differences in form and that these differences need not lead to any differences in the outcomes of actual cases. Everything that is possible under a system of case-based reasoning is also possible under a system of rule-based reasoning. To the extent that Legrand's argument is based on the different possibilities offered by case-based reasoning and by rule-based reasoning, his argument is mistaken.

However, Legrand might try to rescue his position by pointing out that there is a difference between what is legally possible and what actually happens. Maybe systems based on case-based reasoning contingently allow the introduction of new relevant facts more easily than systems based on case-based reasoning. The attribution of this difference, if it exists, to the nature of case-based reasoning and rule-based reasoning would be less happy then, but that does not take the difference away.

Suppose that Legrand is right in the sense that there are differences in legal mentality concerning the issue how easy prima facie irrelevant facts are recognized as legally relevant nevertheless. It might even be the case that systems based on precedent just happen to be more open in this sense than rule-based systems. Whether this is so should be established by empirical research, however and cannot be argued on a priori grounds purely by considering the inherent nature of case-based reasoning and rule-based reasoning. That is the outcome of our logical investigations of the previous sections.

Suppose, however, that empirically Legrand turns out to be right and that there is a difference in how open legal systems are (which is well possible) and that this difference coincides with whether a legal system is precedent-based or rule-based (which is not obvious). Does it follow from this finding that the enterprise of obtaining legal integration by means of a European civil code is doomed to fail?

That does *not* follow, because, if my argument in this chapter is correct, the differences are not intrinsically tied to the different logical bases of the legal systems in question, but are merely coincidental, presumably the outcome of historical developments which were different for different legal systems.[43] But differences that have grown historically can also disappear historically and the introduction of a European civil code might be a factor that contributes to the disappearance of these differences. Whether this is the case and whether this is desirable cannot be established on logical grounds and falls outside the scope of this chapter.

13. CONCLUSION

I started this chapter with the truism that asking the right question is giving half of the answer. Legrand argued against the introduction of a European Civil Code on the ground that the presence of one and the same code cannot lead to the same law if this code is to operate within two fundamentally different legal cultures, namely the cultures of civil law and of common law. Common law systems would, in my terminology, be more open than civil law systems. I hope to have shown how the issue raised by Legrand can be formulated quite sharply by means of logical models of rule application and case-based reasoning. Moreover, I have argued by means of an alternative model of rule application that, although there are logical differences between precedent-based systems and rule-based systems, these differences need not lead to differences in the recognition of new relevant facts. In other words, the differences between common law systems and civil law systems need not lead to differences concerning how open the systems in question are. Therefore, the reasons adduced by Legrand that are based on the difference between the mentality of common law systems and the mentality of civil law systems fail to achieve their purpose.

[43] A brief description of these different developments can be found in Smits 2002, chapter 3.

It is not impossible, however, that legal systems differ concerning the issue how open they are. Because these differences are not necessarily tied to differences in the logical bases of these systems, there are no logical reasons why such differences, where they exist, could not be overcome. The introduction of a European Civil Code might be among the causes why the differences in openness of legal systems can disappear.

Bibliography

Aarnio e.a. 1981
A. Aarnio, R. Alexy and A. Peczenik, The Foundations of Legal Reasoning, *Rechtstheorie* 12 (1981), 133f, 257f, and 423f.

Aarnio 1987
A. Aarnio, *The Rational as Reasonable. A Treatise on Legal Justification.* Dordrecht: Reidel 1987.

Albert 1968
H. Albert, *Traktat über kritische Vernunft*, Tübingen: Siebeck 1968.

Alchourrón and Bulygin 1971
C.E. Alchourrón and E. Bulygin, *Normative Systems*, Wien: Springer 1971.

Alchourrón and Bulygin 1981
C.E. Alchourrón and E. Bulygin, *The Expressive Conception of Norms*, in Hilpinen 1981, 95-124.

Alchourrón 1993
C.E. Alchourrón, *Philosophical Foundations of Deontic Logic and the Logic of Defeasible Conditionals*. In Meyer and Wieringa 1993, 43-84.

Aleven 1997
V. Aleven, *Teaching case-based argumentation through a model and examples*. PhD-thesis Pittsburgh 1997.

Aleven 2003
V. Aleven, Using background knowledge in case-based legal reasoning: A computational model and an intelligent learning environment, *Artificial Intelligence* 150 (2003), 183-237.

Alexy 1978
R. Alexy, *Theorie der juristischen Argumentation*. Frankfurt am Main: Suhrkamp 1978.

Alexy 1979
R. Alexy, Zum Begriff des Rechtprinzips, *Rechtstheorie*, Beiheft 1 (1979), 59-87.

Alexy 1996
R. Alexy, *Theorie der Grundrechten*, 3e Auflage, Frankfurt a/M: Suhrkamp 1996.

Alexy and Peczenik 1990
R. Alexy, and A. Peczenik, The Concept of Coherence and Its Significance for Discursive Rationality, *Ratio Juris* 3 (1990), 130-147.

Alexy 1999
R. Alexy, The Special Case Thesis, *Ratio Juris*, vol. 12 (1999), 374-384.

Alexy 2000
R. Alexy, On the Structure of Legal Principles, *Ratio Juris* 13 (2000), 294-304.

Alexy 2003
R. Alexy, On Balancing and Subsumption. A Structural Comparison, *Ratio Juris* 16 (2003), 433-449.

Alston 1992
W.P. Alston, *Foundationalism*, in Dancy and Sosa 1992, 144-147.

Anscombe 1957
G.E.M. Anscombe, *Intention*, Oxford: Basil Blackwell 1957.

Ashley 1990
K.D. Ashley, *Modeling Legal Argument: Reasoning with Cases and Hypotheticals*, Cambridge: MIT-Press 1990.

Ashley 1991
K.D. Ashley, Reasoning with cases and hypotheticals in HYPO. *International Journal of Man-Machine Studies* 34 (1991), 753-796.

Ashley 1992
K.D. Ashley, Case-Based Reasoning and its implications for Legal Expert Systems, *Artificial Intelligence and Law* 1 (1992), 113-208.

Audi 1998
R. Audi, *Epistemology, a contemporary introduction to the theory of knowledge*, London: Routledge 1998.

Austin 1975
J.L. Austin, *How to do things with words*, 2nd ed. edited by J.O, Urmson and M. Sbisa, Oxford: University Press 1975. (1st edition 1962)

Bankowski 1995
Z. Bankowski, I. White and U. Hahn., *Informatics and the Foundations of Legal Reasoning*, Dordrecht: Kluwer 1995

Barth and Krabbe 1982
E.M. Barth and E.C.W. Krabbe, *From Axiom to Dialogue*. New York: Walter de Gruyter 1982.

Barwise and Perry 1983
J. Barwise and J. Perry, *Situations and Attitudes*, Cambridge: MIT Press 1983.

Bayón 2001
J.C. Bayón, *Why is legal reasoning defeasible?*, in Soeteman 2001, 327-346.

Bench-Capon e.a. 1992
T.J.M. Bench-Capon, P.E.S. Dunne and P.H. Leng, A dialogue game for dialectical interaction with expert systems, *Proceedings of the 12th Expert Systems Conference*, Avignon 1992.

Bench-Capon 1997
T.J.M. Bench-Capon, *Arguing with cases*, in Oskamp e.a. 1997, 85-100.

Bench-Capon and Rissland 2001
T.J.M. Bench-Capon and E.L. Rissland, *Back to the Future: Dimensions Revisited*, in Verheij 2001, 41-52.

Bench-Capon and Sartor 2001
T.J.M. Bench-Capon and G. Sartor, Theory based explanation of case law domains, *Proceedings of the 8th International Conference on Artificial Intelligence and Law*, ACM Press, New York 2001, 12-21.

Bench-Capon e.a. 2002
T.J.M. Bench-Capon, T. Daskalopulu and R. Winkels (eds.), *Proceedings Jurix 2002*, Amsterdam: IOS Press 2002.

Bench-Capon and Sartor 2003
T.J.M. Bench-Capon and G. Sartor, A Model of Legal Reasoning with Cases Incorporating Theories and Values, *Artificial Intelligence* 150 (2003), 97-143.

Bender 1989 (CSCT)
J.W. Bender (ed.), *The Current State of the Coherence Theory*, Dordrecht: Kluwer 1989.

Bender 1989 (CJK)
J.W. Bender, *Coherence, Justification, and Knowledge: The Current Debate*, in Bender 1989 (CSCT), 1-14.

Blackburn and Simmons 1999
S. Blackburn and K. Simmons (eds.), *Truth*, Oxford: University Press 1999.

Bracker 2000
S. Bracker, *Kohärenz und juristische Interpretation*. Baden-Baden: Nomos 2000.

Breuker 2000
J. Breuker e.a. (eds.), *Proceedings of the Thirteenth Jurix Conference*, Amsterdam: IOS Press 2000.

Brewka and Gordon 1994
G. Brewka and T. F. Gordon, How to buy a porsche, an approach to defeasible decision making. In *Working Notes of the AAAI-94 Workshop on Computational Dialectics*, *Seattle*, Washington 1994, 28-38.

Brouwer e.a.1992
P.W. Brouwer e.a. (eds.), *Coherence and Conflict in Law*, Deventer: Kluwer 1992.

Brouwer e.a.1999
P.W. Brouwer e.a. (red.), *Drie dimensies van recht*, Den Haag: BJu, 1999.

Brozek 2004
B. Brozek, *Defeasibility of legal reasoning*, Zakamyce: Kantor 2004.

Bulygin 1999
E. Bulygin, *True or false statements in normative discourse*, in Egidi 1999, 183-191.

Bulygin 2003
Eugenio Bulygin, Review of Jaap Hage's Law and Defeasibility, *Artificial Intelligence and Law* 11 (2003), 245-250.

Burg 2000
E. Burg, *The Model of Principles. The quest for rationality in the implementation of conflicting principles.* PhD-thesis, Amsterdam 2000.

Chiassoni 2001
P. Chiassoni (ed.), *The Legal Ought*, Torino: G. Giapichelli Editore 2001.

Chisholm 1989
R.M. Chisholm, *Theory of Knowledge* (3rd ed.), Englewood Cliffs: Prentice-Hall 1989.

Cliteur e.a. 1997
P.B. Cliteur, B.C. Labuschagne en C.E. Smith, *Rechtsfilosofische stromingen van de twintigste eeuw*. Deventer: Gouda Quint 1997.

Dancy and Sosa 1992
J. Dancy and E. Sosa, *A Companion to Epistemology*, Oxford: Blackwell 1992

Davidson and Harman 1972
D. Davidson and G. Harman (eds.), *Semantics of natural language* (2nd ed.), Dordrecht: Reidel 1972

Den Haan 1996
N. den Haan, *Automated Legal Reasoning*. PhD-thesis, Amsterdam 1996.

Devitt 1991
M. Devitt, *Realism and Truth*, 2nd edition, Oxford: Basil Blackwell 1991.

Donnellan 1966
K.S. Donnellan, Reference and Definite Descriptions, *The Philosophical Review* LXXV (1966), 281-304. Also in Schwartz 1977, 42-65.

Dworkin 1978
R. Dworkin, *Taking Rights Seriously*, 2nd ed., London: Duckworth 1978.

Dworkin 1985
R. Dworkin, *A matter of principle*. Clarendon Press, Oxford 1985.

Dworkin 1986
R. Dworkin, *Laws Empire*, London: Fontana 1986.

Dung 1995
P.M. Dung, On the acceptability of arguments and its fundamental role in nonmonotonic reasoning, logic programming and n-person games, *Artificial Intelligence* 77 (1995), 321-357.

Edwards 1988
W. Edwards, *Summing up: The society of Bayesian trial lawyers.* In Tillers and Green 1988, 337-342.

Egidi 1999
R. Egidi (ed.), *In Search of a New Humanism*, Dordrecht: Kluwer 1999.

Fahrenbach 1973
H. Fahrenbach (ed.), *Wirklichkeit und Reflexion, Festschrift für W. Schulz*, Pfullingen 1973.

Feteris 1994
E.T. Feteris, *Redelijkheid in juridische argumentatie* (Rationality in legal argumentation), Zwolle: Tjeenk Willink 1994.

Fiedler 1986
H. Fiedler, *Formalisierung im Recht und Ansätze juristischer Expertensysteme*, München 1986.

Folgelklau and Spaak 2003
A. Folgelklou and T. Spaak (eds.), *Festskrift till Ake Frändberg*, Uppsala: Iustus Förlag 2003

Freeman and Farley 1996
K. Freeman, and A.M. Farley, A Model of Argumentation and Its Application to Legal Reasoning. *Artificial Intelligence and Law* 4 (1996), 163-197. Also in Prakken and Sartor 1997, 7-41.

Fuller 1958
L.L. Fuller, Positivism and Fidelity to Law: A Reply to Professor Hart, *Harvard Law Review*. vol. 71 (1958), 630-672.

Fuller 1969
L.L. Fuller, *The Morality of Law*, 2nd ed., New Haven: Yale University Press 1969.

Gabbay and Guenther 2001
D. Gabbay and F. Guenthner (eds.), *Handbook of Philosophical Logic* (2nd ed.), volume 4. Dordrecht: Kluwer 2001.

Geach and Black 1980
P. Geach and M. Black (eds.), *Translations from the Philosophical Writings of Gottlob Frege* (3rd ed.), Oxford: Basil Blackwell 1980.

Geffner and Pearl 1992
H. Geffner and J. Pearl, Conditional entailment: bridging two approaches to default reasoning, *Artificial Intelligence* 53 (1992), 209-244.

Ginsberg 1987
M.L. Ginsberg (ed.), *Readings in Nonmonotonic Reasoning*, Los Altos: Morgan Kauffman 1987

Gordon 1986
Th. F. Gordon, *The Role of Exceptions in Models of the Law*, in Fiedler 1986, 52-59.

Gordon 1991
Th. F. Gordon, An abductive theory of legal issues, *International Journal of Man-Machine Studies* 35 (1991), 95-118.

Gordon 1994
Th. F. Gordon, The Pleadings Game: An Exercise in Computational Dialectics, *Artificial Intelligence and Law* 2 (1994), 239-292.

Gordon 1995
Th. F. Gordon, *The Pleadings Game, An Artificial Intelligence Model of Procedural Justice*, Dordrecht: Kluwer 1995.

Gordon 1997
Th. F. Gordon and N. Karacapilidis, The Zeno Argumentation Framework, *Proceedings of the Sixth International Conference on Artificial Intelligence and Law*. New York: ACM 1997, 10-18.

Grayling 1997
A.C. Grayling, *An Introduction to Philosophical Logic* (3rd. ed.), Oxford: Blackwell 1997.

Grütters e.a. 1992
C.A.F.M. Grütters, , J.A.P.J. Breuker, H.J. Van den Herik, A.H.J. Schmidt, and C.N.J. de Vey Mestdagh (eds.), *Legal Knowledge Based Systems: Information Technology and Law, JURIX '92*, Lelystad: Vermande 1992.

Haack 1978
S. Haack, *Philosophy of Logics*, Cambridge: Cambridge University Press 1978.

Haack 1993
S. Haack, *Evidence and Inquiry. Towards Reconstruction in Epistemology*. Oxford: Blackwell 1993.

Haack 1999
S. Haack, *A Foundherentist Theory of Empirical Justification*, in Pojman 1999, 283-293.

Habermas 1973
J. Habermas, *Wahrheitstheorieën*, in Fahrenbach 1973, 211-265.

Hage 1987
J.C. Hage, *Feiten en betekenis. Een verhandeling over ontologie en praktische rede.* (Facts and Meaning; a treatise on ontology and practical reason.) PhD-thesis Leiden 1987.

Hage e.a. 1992
J.C. Hage, G.P.J. Span and A.R. Lodder, *A Dialogical Model of Legal Reasoning*, in Grütters e.a. 1992, 135-146.

Hage e.a. 1994
J.C. Hage, R. Leenes and A. Lodder, Hard cases; a procedural approach, *Artificial Intelligence and Law* 2 (1994), 113-167.

Hage 1996
J.C. Hage, A Model of Legal Reasoning and a Logic to Match. *Artificial Intelligence and Law* 4 (1996), 199-273. Also in Prakken and Sartor 1997, 43-117.

Hage 1997 (RwR)
J.C. Hage, *Reasoning with rules*, Dordrecht: Kluwer 1997.

Hage 1997 (Leg)
J.C. Hage, *Legitimatietheorieën*, (Theories of legitimation), in Cliteur e.a. 1997, 243-282.

Hage 1999 (RC)
J.C. Hage, *Rule Consistency*, in Van den Herik 1999, 47-60.

Hage and Verheij 1999
J.C. Hage and H.B. Verheij, The law as a dynamic interconnected system of states of affairs: a legal top ontology. *International Journal of Human-Computer Studies* 51 (1999), 1043-1077.

Hage 1999 (TLR)
J.C. Hage, *Twee lagen van het recht* (Two layers of the law), in Brouwer e.a. 1999, 197-217.

Hage 1999 (MNDL)
J.C. Hage, *Moderately Naturalistic Deontic Logic*, in McNamara and Prakken 1999, 55-72.

Hage 2000 (RC)
J.C. Hage, Rule Consistency, *Law and Philosophy* 19 (2000), 369-390.

Hage 2000 (GTE)
J.C. Hage, *Goal-based Theory Evaluation*. In Breuker 2000, 59-72.

Hage 2000 (CRN)
J.C. Hage, Consistency of Rules and Norms. *Information & Communications Technology Law* 9 (2000), 219-240.

Hage 2000 (DM)
J.C. Hage, Dialectical Models in Artificial Intelligence and Law, *Artificial Intelligence and Law* 8 (2000), 137-172.

Hage and Peczenik 2000
J.C. Hage and A. Peczenik, Law, Morals, and Defeasibility, *Ratio Juris* 13 (2000), 305-325.

Hage 2001 (LL)
J.C. Hage, *Legal Logic. It's Existence, Nature and Use*, in Soeteman 2001, 347-373.

Hage 2001 (FLC)
J.C. Hage, Formalizing legal coherence. *Proceedings of the 8th International Conference on Artificial Intelligence and Law*, New York: ACM 2001.

Hage and Peczenik 2001
J.C. Hage and A. Peczenik, *Legal internalism*, in Chiassoni 2001, 141-170.

Hage and Sartor 2003
J.C. Hage and G. Sartor, Legal Theory Construction, *Associations* 7 (2003), 171-184.

Hage 2003 (LRI)
J.C. Hage, Legal Reasoning and Legal Integration, *Maastricht Journal of European and Comparative Law* 10 (2003), 67-97.

Hage 2003 (LD)
Jaap Hage, Law and Defeasibility, *Artificial Intelligence and Law* 11 (2003), 221-243.

Hage 2004
J.C. Hage, Law and Coherence, *Ratio Juris* 17 (2004), 87-105.

Hale and Wright 1997
B. Hale and C. Wright, *A Companion to the Philosophy of Language*, Oxford: Blackwell 1997.

Hamblin 1970
C.L. Hamblin, *Fallacies*. London: Methuen 1970.

Hamner Hill 1987
H. Hamner Hill, A functional taxonomy of normative conflict. *Law and Philosophy* 6 (1987), 227-247.

Hare 1952
R.M. Hare, *The Language of Morals*, Oxford: University Press 1952.

Hare 1963
R.M. Hare, *Freedom and Reason*, Oxford: University Press 1963.

Hare 1981
R.M. Hare, *Moral Thinking. Its Levels, method and point*, Oxford: Clarendon Press 1981.

Hart 1949
H.L.A. Hart, The Ascription of Responsibility and Rights. *Proceedings of the Aristotelian Society*, 49 (1949), 171-194.

Hart 1961
H.L.A. Hart, *The Concept of Law*, Oxford: Clarendon Press 1961.

Hilpinen 1981
R. Hilpinen (ed.), *New Studies in Deontic Logic. Norms, Actions, and the Foundation of Ethics*, Dordrecht: Reidel 1981.

Honderich 1995
T. Honderich (ed.), *The Oxford Companion to Philosophy*, Oxford: University Press 1995

Israel 1980
D.J. Israel, What's wrong with non-monotonic logic?, *Proceedings of the First Annual Conference on Artificial Intelligence*, Stanford 1980, 99-101. Also in Ginsberg 1987, 53-55.

Jones 1995
O.R. Jones, *Supervenience*, in Honderich 1995, 860.

Kaptein 1995
H. Kaptein, *The redundancy of precedent and analogy. Or Eat s**t, five billion flies can't be wrong*, in Van Eemeren 1995, 122-137.

Keeney and Raiffa 1993
R.L. Keeney and H. Raiffa, *Decision with Multiple Objectives. Preferences and Value Tradeoffs* (2nd ed.), Cambridge: University Press 1993.

Kelsen 1960
H. Kelsen, *Reine Rechtslehre* (2e Auflage), Wien: Franz Deuticke 1960.

Kelsen 1979
H. Kelsen, *Allgemeine Theorie der Normen*, (K. Ringhofer and R. Walter eds.), Wien: Manz-Verlag 1979.

Kim and Sosa 1995
J. Kim and E. Sosa, *A Companion to Metaphysics*, Oxford: Blackwell 1995.

Kirkham 1992
R.L. Kirkham, *Theories of Truth*, Cambridge: MIT Press 1992.

Kloosterhuis 1995
H. Kloosterhuis, *The study of analogy argumentation in law: four pragma-dialectical starting points*, in Van Eemeren 1995, 138-145.

Kress 1996
K. Kress, *Coherence*, in Patterson 1996, 533-552.

Kripke 1972
S.A. Kripke, *Naming and Necessity*, in Davidson and Harman 1972, 253-355.

Lambert 1995
K. Lambert, *Meinong, Alexius*, in Kim and Sosa 1995, 305–307.

Larenz 1983
K. Larenz, *Methodenlehre der Rechtswissenschaft* (5th ed.), Berlin: Springer 1983.

Leenes e.a. 1994
R.E. Leenes, A.R. Lodder and J.C. Hage, A Dialogue Game for Legal Arguments. *Law, Computers & Artificial Intelligence* 3 (1994), 211-226.

Leenes 1999
R.E. Leenes, *Hercules of Karneades*, PhD thesis, Enschede 1999.

Legrand 1997
P. Legrand, Against a European Civil Code, *Modern Law Review* 60, (1997), nr. 1.

Lehrer 2000
K. Lehrer, *Theory of Knowledge* (2nd ed.), London: Routledge 2000.

Lindahl 1977
L. Lindahl, *Position and Change. A Study in Law and Logic*. Dordrecht: Reidel 1977.

Lindahl 1992
L. Lindahl, *Conflicts in Systems of Legal Norms: A Logical Point of View*, in Brouwer 1992, 39-64.

Lindahl and Odelstad 2004
L. Lindahl and J. Odelstad, Normative Positions Within an Algebraic Approach to Normative Systems, *Journal of Applied Logic* 2 (2004).

Lloyd 1979
D. Lloyd, *Introduction to jurisprudence*, 4h ed. with M.D.A. Freeman as co-editor. London: Stevens and Sons 1979.

Lodder and Herczog 1995
A. Lodder and A. Herczog, DiaLaw: A Computational Framework for Dialectical Reasoning. *Proceedings of the Fifth International Conference on Artificial Intelligence and Law*, New York: ACM 1995, 146-155.

Lodder 1997
A. Lodder, *Procedural arguments*, in Oskamp 1997, 21-32.

Lodder 1998
A. Lodder, *DiaLaw. On Legal Justification and Dialog Games*. PhD-thesis Maastricht 1998.

Lodder 1999
A. Lodder, *DiaLaw. On Legal Justification and Dialogical Models of Argumentation*, Dordrecht: Kluwer 1999.

Lorenzen and Lorenz 1978
P. Lorenzen and K. Lorenz, *Dialogische Logik*, Darmstadt: Wissenschafliche Buchgesellschaft 1978.

Loui 1987
R.P. Loui, Defeat among arguments: a system of defeasible inference. *Computational Intelligence* 2 (1987), 100-106.

Loui and Norman 1995
R.P. Loui and J. Norman, Rationales and Argument Moves. *Artificial Intelligence and Law* 3 (1995), 159-189.

Loui 1997
R.P. Loui et al., Progress on Room 5. *Proceedings of the Sixth International Conference on Artificial Intelligence and Law*, New York: ACM 1997, 207-214.

Lukaszewicz 1990
W. Lukaszewicz, *Non-Monotonic Reasoning; formalization of commonsense reasoning*. London: Ellis Horwood 1990.

MacCormick 1972
D.N. MacCormick, *Legal Obligation and the Imperative Fallacy*, in Simpson 1972, 100-130.

MacCormick 1978
D.N. MacCormick, *Legal Reasoning and Legal Theory*, Oxford: Clarendon Press 1978.

MacCormick 1995
D.N. MacCormick, *Defeasibility in law and logic*, in Bankowski 1995, 99-118.

MacCormick and Weinberger 1986
D.N. MacCormick and O. Weinberger, *An Institutional Theory of Law*, Dordrecht: Reidel 1986.

McNamara and Prakken 1999
P. McNamara and H. Prakken (eds.), *Norms, Logics and Information Systems*, Amsterdam: IOS Press 1999.

Mazzarese 1991
T. Mazzarese, 'Norm Proposition': Epistemic and Semantic Queries, *Rechtstheorie* 22 (1991), 39-70.

Mazzarese 1999
T. Mazzarese, *"Norm proposition". A Tentative Defense of a Skeptical View*, in Egidi 1999, 193-204.

McCarty 1997
L.T. McCarty, Some Arguments about Legal Arguments. *Proceedings of the Sixth International Conference on Artificial Intelligence and Law*, New York: ACM 1997, 215-224.

Meyer and Wieringa 1993
J.-J.Ch, Meyer and R.J. Wieringa (eds.), *Deontic Logic in Computer Science*, Chicester: John Wiley 1993.

Miller 2003
A. Miller, *An Introduction to Contemporary Metaethics*, Cambridge: Polity Press 2003.

Moser 1989
P. K. Moser, *Lehrer's Coherentism and the Isolation Objection*, in Bender 1989 (CSCT), 29-37.

Neurath 1932/3
O. Neurath, *Protocol Sentences*, in Ayer 1959, 199-208. Originally (in German) in *Erkenntnis* 1932/3, 204-214.

Nieuwenhuis 1976
J.H. Nieuwenhuis, Legitimatie en heuristiek van het rechterlijk oordeel, *Rechtsgeleerd Magazijn Themis* (1976), 494-515.

Nitta e.a. 1993
K. Nitta, S. Wong and Y. Othake, A Computational Model for Trial Reasoning. *Proceedings of the Fourth International Conference on Artificial Intelligence and Law*, New York: ACM Press 1993, 20-29.

Nitta e.a. 1995
K. Nitta, M. Shibasaki, T. Sakata, T. Yamaji, W. Xianchang, H. Ohsaki, S. Tojo, I. Kokubo and T. Suzuki, New HELIC-II: A Software Tol for Legal Reasoning, *Proceedings of the Fifth International Conference on Artificial Intelligence and Law*, New York: ACM 1995, 287-296.

Odelstad and Lindahl 2002
J. Odelstad and L. Lindahl, *The Role of Connections as Minimal Norms in Normative Systems*, in Bench-Capon e.a. 2002, 31-40.

Oskamp e.a. 1997
A. Oskamp e.a. (eds.), *Proceedings of the Tenth Jurix Conference*, Amsterdam: IOS 1997.

Patarro 2001
E. Patarro, *Towards a Theory of Norms*, in Chiassoni 2001, 11-36.

Patterson 1996
D. Patterson (ed.), *A Companion to Philosophy of Law and Legal Theory*, Oxford: Blackwell 1996.

Peczenik and Uusitalo 1979
A. Peczenik and J. Uusitalo (eds.), *Reasoning on legal reasoning*, Vammala: Vammalan Kirsjapoino Oy 1979.

Peczenik 1989
A. Peczenik, *On Law and Reason*, Dordrecht: Kluwer 1989.

Peczenik 1997
A. Peczenik, *Jumps and Logic in the Law*, in Prakken and Sartor 1997 (LM), 141-174.

Peczenik and Hage 2000
A. Peczenik and J.C. Hage, Legal Knowledge about What?, *Ratio Juris* 13 (2000), 326-345.

Perelman and Olbrechts-Tyteca 1969
Ch. Perelman and L. Olbrechts-Tyteca, *The New Rhetoric; a Treatise on Argumentation*. Notre Dame: University of Notre Dame Press 1969.

Pojman 1999
L. Pojman (ed.), *The Theory of Knowledge: Classical and Contemporary Readings* (2nd ed.), Belmont: Wadsworth 1999

Pollock 1987
J.L. Pollock, Defeasible Reasoning, *Cognitive Science* 11 (1987), 481-518.

Pollock 1994
J.L. Pollock, Justification and defeat, *Artificial Intelligence* 67 (1994), 377-407.

Pollock 1995
J.L. Pollock, *Cognitive Carpentry*, Cambridge: MIT-Press 1995.

Pollock and Cruz 1999
J.L. Pollock and J. Cruz, *Contemporary theories of knowledge* (2nd. ed.), Lanham: Rowman and Littlefield 1999.

Popper 1972
K.R. Popper, *The Logic of Scientific Discovery*, London: Hutchinson 1972.

Prakken e.a. 1994
H. Prakken, A.J. Muntjewerff and A. Soeteman (eds.), *Legal knowledge based systems; the relation with legal theory*, Lelystad: Koninklijke Vermande 1994.

Prakken 1995
H. Prakken, From Logic to Dialectics in Legal Argument. *Proceedings of the Fifth International Conference on Artificial Intelligence and Law*, New York: ACM 1995, 165-174.

Prakken and Sartor 1996
H. Prakken, and G. Sartor, A Dialectical Model of Assessing Conflicting Arguments in Legal Reasoning, *Artificial Intelligence and Law* 4 (1996), 331-368. Also in Prakken and Sartor 1997, 331-368.

Prakken and Sartor 1997 (LM)
H. Prakken and G. Sartor (eds.), *Logical Models of Legal Argumentation*, Dordrecht: Kluwer 1997.

Prakken and Sartor 1997 (RP)
H. Prakken and G. Sartor, Reasoning with Precedents in a Dialogue Game, *Proceedings of the Sixth International Conference on Artificial Intelligence and Law,* New York: ACM 1997, 1-9.

Prakken 1997
H. Prakken, *Logical Tools for Modelling Legal Argument, A Study of Defeasible Reasoning in Law*, Dordrecht: Kluwer 1997.

Prakken and Sartor 1998
H. Prakken and G. Sartor, Modelling Reasoning with Precedents in a Formal Dialogue Game. *Artificial Intelligence and Law* 6 (1998), 231-287.

Prakken and Vreeswijk 2001
H. Prakken and G. Vreeswijk, *Logics for defeasible argumentation*, in Gabbay and Guenthner 2001.

Prakken 2001
H. Prakken, Modelling reasoning about evidence in legal procedure, *Proceedings of the Eight International Conference on Artificial Intelligence and Law,* New York: ACM 2001, 119-128.

Prakken e.a. 2003
H. Prakken, C. Reed and D. Walton, Argumentation schemes and generalisations in reasoning about evidence, *Proceedings of the 9th International Conference on Artificial Intelligence and Law*, Edinburgh, 2003. New York: ACM Press 2003.

Prakken and Sartor 2004
H. Prakken and G. Sartor,. The Three Faces of Defeasibility in the Law, *Ratio Juris* 17 (2004), 118-139.

Puntel 1983
L.B. Puntel, *Wahrheitstheorien in der neueren Philosophie*, Darmstadt: Wissenschaftliche Buchgesellschaft 1983.

Putnam 1975 (MLR)
H. Putnam, *Mind, Language and Reality; Philosophical Papers, vol. 2*, Cambridge: University Press 1975.

Putnam 1975 (MM)
H. Putnam, *The Meaning of 'Meaning'*, in Putnam 1975 (MLR), 215-271.

Quine 1953
W.V. Quine, *From a Logical Point of View*, New York: Harper & Row 1953.

Quine 1956
W.V. Quine, Quantifiers and Propositional Attitudes, *Journal of Philosophy* 53 (1956). Also in Quine 1976, 185-196.

Quine 1976
W.V. Quine, *The Ways of Paradox and other essays* (2nd ed.), Cambridge, Harvard University Press: 1976.

Quine 1986
W.V. Quine, *Philosophy of Logic* (2nd ed.), Cambridge: Harvard University Press 1986.

Radbruch 1973
G. Radbruch, *Rechtsphilosophie* (4th ed.), edited by E. Wolf und H-P Schneider, Stuttgart: Koehler Verlag 1973.

Ramsey 1931
F.P. Ramsey, *The Foundation of Mathematics*, London: Routledge and Kegan Paul 1931.

Ramsey 1999
F.P. Ramsey, *On Facts and Propositions*, in Blackburn and Simmons 1999, 106-107. Originally in Ramsey 1931.

Rawls 1972
J. Rawls, *A Theory of Justice*, Oxford: University Press 1972.

Raz 1975
J. Raz, *Practical Reason and Norms*, London: Hutchinson 1975.

Raz 1979
J. Raz, *The Authority of Law; Essays on Law and Morality*, Oxford: Clarendon Press 1979.

Raz 1986
J. Raz, *The Morality of Freedom*, Oxford: Clarendon Press 1986.

Raz 1994 (EPC)
J. Raz, *Ethics in the Public Domain. Essays in the Morality of Law and Politics*, Oxford: Clarendon Press 1994.

Raz 1994 (RC)
J. Raz, *The Relevance of Coherence*, in Raz 1994, 277-326.

Redondo 1999
C. Redondo, *Reasons for Action and the Law*, Dordrecht: Kluwer 1999.

Rissland and Ashley 1987
E.L. Rissland and K.D. Ashley, A Case Based System for Trade Secrets Law, *Proceedings of the First International Conference on Artificial Intelligence and Law*, New York: ACM 1987, 60-66.

Rissland and Skalak 1991
E.L. Rissland and D.B. Skalak, CABARET: rule interpretation in a hybrid structure, *International Journal for Man-Machine Studies* 34 (1991), 839-887.

Rissland, Skalak and Friedman 1996
E.L. Rissland, D.B. Skalak and M.T. Friedman, Bank XX: Supporting Legal Arguments through Heuristic Retrieval, *Artificial Intelligence and Law* 4 (1996), 1-71.

Ross 1957.
A. Ross, Tû-Tû. *Harvard Law Review* 70 (1957), 812.

Roth 2003
B. Roth, *Case-based reasoning in the law. A formal theory of reasoning by case comparison*. PhD-thesis, Maastricht 2003.

Royakkers 1996
L.M.M. Royakker, *Representing L∃g∀l Rules in Deontic Logic*, Tilburg 1996.

Ruiter 1993
D.W.P. Ruiter, *Institutional Legal Facts. Legal Powers and their Effects*, Dordrecht: Kluwer 1993.

Ruiter 1997
D.W.P. Ruiter, Legal validity qua specific mode of existence. *Law and Philosophy* 16 (1997), 479-505.

Rumelhart and McClelland 1986
D.E.Rumelhart, J.L. McClelland and the PDP Research Group, *Parallel Distributed Processing. Explorations in the Microstructure of Cognition. Volume 1: Foundations*, Cambridge: MIT Press 1986.

Sartor 1994
G. Sartor, A Formal Model of Legal Argumentation. *Ratio Juris* 7 (1994), 177-211.

Sartor 1995
G. Sartor, *Defeasibility in Legal Reasoning*, in Bankowski 1995, 119-158.

Sartor 2005
G. Sartor, *Legal Reasoning*, to appear in the Springer series of Treatises in Legal Theory.

Schauer 1991
F. Schauer, *Playing by the rules*. Oxford: Clarendon Press 1991.

Schwartz 1977
S.P Schwartz (ed.), *Naming, Necessity, and Natural Kinds*, Ithaca: Cornell University Press 1977.

Schwemmer and Lorenzen 1973
O. Schwemmer and P. Lorenzen, *Konstruktive Logik, Ethik und Wissenschaftstheorie*, Mannheim 1973.

Searle 1969
J.R. Searle, *Speech acts. An essay in the philosophy of language.* Cambridge: University Press 1969.

Searle 1979
J.R. Searle, *Expression and Meaning. Studies in the theory of speech acts*, Cambridge: University Press 1979.

Searle and Vanderveken 1985
J.R. Searle and D. Vanderveken, *Foundations of Illocutionary Logic*, Cambridge: University Press 1985.

Searle 1995
J.R. Searle, *The construction of social reality*, New York: The Free Press 1995.

Simpson 1972
A.W.B. Simpson, *Oxford Essays in Jurisprudence*, Oxford: 1972,

Skalak and Rissland 1991
D.B. Skalak and E.L. Rissland, Argument Moves in a Rule-Guided Domain. *Proceedings of the Third International Conference on Artificial Intelligence and Law*, New York: ACM 1991, 1-11.

Skalak and Rissland 1992
D.B. Skalak, and E.L Rissland, Arguments and Cases: An Inevitable Intertwining. *Artificial Intelligence and Law* 1 (1992), 3-44.

Smith 1994
M. Smith, *The Moral Problem*, Oxford: Blackwell 1994.

Smits 2002
J. Smits, *The Making of European Private Law*, Antwerpen: Intersentia 2002.

Soeteman 1989
A. Soeteman, *Logic in Law. Remarks on Logic and Rationality in Normative Reasoning, Especially in Law*, Dordrecht: Kluwer 1989.

Soeteman 2001
A. Soeteman (ed.), *Pluralism and law*. Dordrecht: Kluwer 2001.

Soeteman 2003
A. Soeteman, *Do we need a legal logic*? In Folgelklou and Spaak 2003, 221-234.

Sosa 1989
E. Sosa, *Equilibrium in Coherence?*, in Bender 1989 (CSCT), 242-250.

Stalnaker 1997
R. Stalnaker, *Reference and necessity*, in Hale and Wright 1997, 534-554.

Stone 1968
J. Stone, *Legal System and Lawyer's Reasoning*, Stanford: University Press 1968.

Strawson 1952
P.F. Strawson, *Introduction to Logical Theory*, London: Methuen 1952.

Strawson 1959
P.F. Strawson, *Individuals. An essay in descriptive metaphysics*, London: Methuen 1959.

Strawson 1971
P.F. Strawson, *Logico Linguistic Papers*, London: Methuen, 1971.

Thagard 1992
P. Thagard, *Conceptual Revolutions*, Princeton: University Press 1992.

Thagard and Verbeurgt 1998
P. Thagard and K. Verbeurgt, Coherence as constraint satisfaction. *Cognitive Science* 22 (1998), 1-24.

Thagard 1999
P. Thagard, Ethical Coherence, *Philosophical Psychology* 11 (1999), 405-422.

Tillers and Green 1988
P. Tillers and E.D. Green (eds.), *Probability and inference in the law of evidence: The uses and limits of Bayesianism.* Dordrecht: Kluwer 1988.

Toulmin 1953
S.E. Toulmin, *The Philosophy of Science. An Introduction*, London: Hutchinson 1953.

Toulmin 1958
S.E. Toulmin, *The Uses of Argument*, London: Cambridge University Press 1958.

Twining 1985
W.L. Twining, *Theories of evidence*: Bentham and Wigmore. Stanford, CA: Stanford University Press 1985.

Twining 1991
W.L. Twining, *Rethinking evidence*. Evanston: Northwestern University Press 1991.

Van den Herik e.a. 1999
H.J. van den Herik e.a. (eds.), *Proceedings of the Twelfth Jurix Conference*, Nijmegen: GNI 1999.

Van Eemeren e.a. 1995
F.H. van Eemeren *et al.* (eds.), *Proceedings of the Third ISSA Conference on Argumentation*, vol. IV, Special Fields and Cases, Amsterdam: Sic Sat 1995.

Verheij and Hage 1994
H.B. Verheij and J.C. Hage, *Reasoning by analogy; a formal reconstruction*. In Prakken e.a. 1994, 65-78.

Verheij 1996
H.B. Verheij, *Rules, Reasons, Arguments. Formal studies of argumentation and defeat*. Ph-D thesis Maastricht University 1996.

Verheij 1999
H.B. Verheij, *Logic, Context, and Valid Inference. Or: Can there be a Logic of Law?* in Van den Herik 1999, 109-121.

Verheij 2003 (DL)
H.B. Verheij, Deflog: on the Logical Interpretation of Prima Facie Justified Assumptions, *J. Logic Computat.* 13 (2003), 319-346.

Verheij 2003 (AAA)
H.B. Verheij, Artificial argument assistants for defeasible argumentation, *Artificial Intelligence* 150 (2003), 291-324.

Verheij 2005
H.B. Verheij, *Virtual Arguments. On the Design of Argument Assistants for Lawyers and Other Arguers*, Den Haag: T.M.C. Asser Press.

Von Wright 1963
G.H. von Wright, *Norm and Action*, London: Routledge and Kegan Paul 1963.

Von Wright 1991
G.H. von Wright, Is There a Logic of Norms?, *Ratio Juris* 4 (1991), 265-283.

Vreeswijk 1993
G.A.W. Vreeswijk, *Studies in Defeasible Argumentation*. PhD-thesis, Amsterdam 1993.

Vreeswijk 2000
G.A.W. Vreeswijk, Representation of Formal Dispute with a Standing Order, *Artificial Intelligence and Law* 8 (2000), 205-231.

Weinberger 1989
O. Weinberger, *Rechtslogik* (2nd ed.), Berlin: Duncker & Humblot 1989.

Wolenski 1979
J. Wolenski, *Context of discovery, context of justification and analysis of legal decision making*, in Peczenik and Uusitalo 1979, 115-120.

Wolenski 1982 (JL)
J. Wolenski, Was ist juristische Logik?, *Schriftenreihe Methodologie der marxistisch-leninistischen Rechtswissenschaft; Heft 10: Probleme des objektiven und subjectiven Rechts*, Leipzig 1982, 176-189.

Wolenski 1982 (DS)
J. Wolenski, Deontic sentences, possible worlds and norms, *Reports on Philosophy (of the Jagiellonian University)* 6, 65-73.

Wróblewski 1992
J. Wróblewski, *The Judicial Application of Law*, edited by Z. Bankowski and N. MacCormick, Dordrecht: Kluwer 1992.

Zalta 2002
Edward N. Zalta, The Stanford Encyclopedia of Philosophy (Spring 2002 edition), http://plato.stanford.edu/.

Zippelius 1974
R. Zippelius, *Einführung in die juristische Methodenlehre* (2nd ed.), München: Beck 1974.

Index

Law and Philosophy Library

1. E. Bulygin, J.-L. Gardies and I. Niiniluoto (eds.): *Man, Law and Modern Forms of Life*. With an Introduction by M.D. Bayles. 1985 ISBN 90-277-1869-5
2. W. Sadurski: *Giving Desert Its Due*. Social Justice and Legal Theory. 1985 ISBN 90-277-1941-1
3. N. MacCormick and O. Weinberger: *An Institutional Theory of Law*. New Approaches to Legal Positivism. 1986 ISBN 90-277-2079-7
4. A. Aarnio: *The Rational as Reasonable*. A Treatise on Legal Justification. 1987 ISBN 90-277-2276-5
5. M.D. Bayles: *Principles of Law*. A Normative Analysis. 1987 ISBN 90-277-2412-1; Pb: 90-277-2413-X
6. A. Soeteman: *Logic in Law*. Remarks on Logic and Rationality in Normative Reasoning, Especially in Law. 1989 ISBN 0-7923-0042-4
7. C.T. Sistare: *Responsibility and Criminal Liability*. 1989 ISBN 0-7923-0396-2
8. A. Peczenik: *On Law and Reason*. 1989 ISBN 0-7923-0444-6
9. W. Sadurski: *Moral Pluralism and Legal Neutrality*. 1990 ISBN 0-7923-0565-5
10. M.D. Bayles: *Procedural Justice*. Allocating to Individuals. 1990 ISBN 0-7923-0567-1
11. P. Nerhot (ed.): *Law, Interpretation and Reality*. Essays in Epistemology, Hermeneutics and Jurisprudence. 1990 ISBN 0-7923-0593-0
12. A.W. Norrie: *Law, Ideology and Punishment*. Retrieval and Critique of the Liberal Ideal of Criminal Justice. 1991 ISBN 0-7923-1013-6
13. P. Nerhot (ed.): *Legal Knowledge and Analogy*. Fragments of Legal Epistemology, Hermeneutics and Linguistics. 1991 ISBN 0-7923-1065-9
14. O. Weinberger: *Law, Institution and Legal Politics*. Fundamental Problems of Legal Theory and Social Philosophy. 1991 ISBN 0-7923-1143-4
15. J. Wróblewski: *The Judicial Application of Law*. Edited by Z. Bańkowski and N. MacCormick. 1992 ISBN 0-7923-1569-3
16. T. Wilhelmsson: *Critical Studies in Private Law*. A Treatise on Need-Rational Principles in Modern Law. 1992 ISBN 0-7923-1659-2
17. M.D. Bayles: *Hart's Legal Philosophy*. An Examination. 1992 ISBN 0-7923-1981-8
18. D.W.P. Ruiter: *Institutional Legal Facts*. Legal Powers and their Effects. 1993 ISBN 0-7923-2441-2
19. J. Schonsheck: *On Criminalization*. An Essay in the Philosophy of the Criminal Law. 1994 ISBN 0-7923-2663-6
20. R.P. Malloy and J. Evensky (eds.): *Adam Smith and the Philosophy of Law and Economics*. 1994 ISBN 0-7923-2796-9
21. Z. Bańkowski, I. White and U. Hahn (eds.): *Informatics and the Foundations of Legal Reasoning*. 1995 ISBN 0-7923-3455-8
22. E. Lagerspetz: *The Opposite Mirrors*. An Essay on the Conventionalist Theory of Institutions. 1995 ISBN 0-7923-3325-X

Law and Philosophy Library

23. M. van Hees: *Rights and Decisions.* Formal Models of Law and Liberalism. 1995 ISBN 0-7923-3754-9
24. B. Anderson: *"Discovery" in Legal Decision-Making.* 1996 ISBN 0-7923-3981-9
25. S. Urbina: *Reason, Democracy, Society.* A Study on the Basis of Legal Thinking. 1996 ISBN 0-7923-4262-3
26. E. Attwooll: *The Tapestry of the Law.* Scotland, Legal Culture and Legal Theory. 1997 ISBN 0-7923-4310-7
27. J.C. Hage: *Reasoning with Rules.* An Essay on Legal Reasoning and Its Underlying Logic. 1997 ISBN 0-7923-4325-5
28. R.A. Hillman: *The Richness of Contract Law.* An Analysis and Critique of Contemporary Theories of Contract Law. 1997 ISBN 0-7923-4336-0; 0-7923-5063-4 (Pb)
29. C. Wellman: *An Approach to Rights.* Studies in the Philosophy of Law and Morals. 1997 ISBN 0-7923-4467-7
30. B. van Roermund: *Law, Narrative and Reality.* An Essay in Intercepting Politics. 1997 ISBN 0-7923-4621-1
31. I. Ward: *Kantianism, Postmodernism and Critical Legal Thought.* 1997 ISBN 0-7923-4745-5
32. H. Prakken: *Logical Tools for Modelling Legal Argument.* A Study of Defeasible Reasoning in Law. 1997 ISBN 0-7923-4776-5
33. T. May: *Autonomy, Authority and Moral Responsibility.* 1998 ISBN 0-7923-4851-6
34. M. Atienza and J.R. Manero: *A Theory of Legal Sentences.* 1998 ISBN 0-7923-4856-7
35. E.A. Christodoulidis: *Law and Reflexive Politics.* 1998 ISBN 0-7923-4954-7
36. L.M.M. Royakkers: *Extending Deontic Logic for the Formalisation of Legal Rules.* 1998 ISBN 0-7923-4982-2
37. J.J. Moreso: *Legal Indeterminacy and Constitutional Interpretation.* 1998 ISBN 0-7923-5156-8
38. W. Sadurski: *Freedom of Speech and Its Limits.* 1999 ISBN 0-7923-5523-7
39. J. Wolenski (ed.): *Kazimierz Opalek Selected Papers in Legal Philosophy.* 1999 ISBN 0-7923-5732-9
40. H.P. Visser 't Hooft: *Justice to Future Generations and the Environment.* 1999 ISBN 0-7923-5756-6
41. L.J. Wintgens (ed.): *The Law in Philosophical Perspectives.* My Philosophy of Law. 1999 ISBN 0-7923-5796-5
42. A.R. Lodder: *DiaLaw.* On Legal Justification and Dialogical Models of Argumentation. 1999 ISBN 0-7923-5830-9
43. C. Redondo: *Reasons for Action and the Law.* 1999 ISBN 0-7923-5912-7
44. M. Friedman, L. May, K. Parsons and J. Stiff (eds.): *Rights and Reason.* Essays in Honor of Carl Wellman. 2000 ISBN 0-7923-6198-9
45. G.C. Christie: *The Notion of an Ideal Audience in Legal Argument.* 2000 ISBN 0-7923-6283-7

Law and Philosophy Library

46. R.S. Summers: *Essays in Legal Theory*. 2000 ISBN 0-7923-6367-1
47. M. van Hees: *Legal Reductionism and Freedom*. 2000 ISBN 0-7923-6491-0
48. R. Gargarella: *The Scepter of Reason*. Public Discussion and Political Radicalism in the Origins of Constitutionalism. 2000 ISBN 0-7923-6508-9
49. M. Iglesias Vila: *Facing Judicial Discretion*. Legal Knowledge and Right Answers Revisited. 2001 ISBN 0-7923-6778-2
50. M. Kiikeri: *Comparative Legal Reasoning and European Law*. 2001 ISBN 0-7923-6884-3
51. A.J. Menéndez: *Justifying Taxes*. Some Elements for a General Theory of Democratic Tax Law. 2001 ISBN 0-7923-7052-X
52. W.E. Conklin: *The Invisible Origins of Legal Positivism*. A Re-Reading of a Tradition. 2001 ISBN 0-7923-7101-1
53. Z. Bańkowski: *Living Lawfully*. Love in Law and Law in Love. 2001 ISBN 0-7923-7180-1
54. A.N. Shytov: *Conscience and Love in Making Judicial Decisions*. 2001 ISBN 1-4020-0168-1
55. D.W.P. Ruiter: *Legal Institutions*. 2001 ISBN 1-4020-0186-X
56. D.G. Lagier: *The Paradoxes of Action*. (Human Action, Law and Philosophy). 2003 ISBN 1-4020-1661-1

Volumes 56–63 were published by Kluwer Law International.

---

57. G. den Hartogh: *Mutual Expectations*. A Conventionalist Theory of Law. 2002 ISBN 90-411-1796-2
58. W.L. Robison (ed.): *The Legal Essays of Michael Bayles*. 2002 ISBN 90-411-1835-7
59. U. Bindreiter: *Why Grundnorm?* A Treatise on the Implications of Kelsen's Doctrine. 2002 ISBN 90-411-1867-5
60. S. Urbina: *Legal Method and the Rule of Law*. 2002 ISBN 90-411-1870-5
61. M. Baurmann: *The Market of Virtue*. Morality and Commitment in a Liberal Society. 2002 ISBN 90-411-1874-8
62. G. Zanetti: *Political Friendship and the Good Life*. Two Liberal Arguments against Perfectionism. 2002 ISBN 90-411-1881-0
63. W. Sadurski (ed.): *Constitutional Justice, East and West*. 2002 ISBN 90-411-1883-7
64. S. Taekema: *The Concept of Ideals in Legal Theory*. 2003 ISBN 90-411-1971-X
65. J. Raitio: *The Principle of Legal Certainty in EC Law*. 2003 ISBN 1-4020-1217-9
66. E. Santoro: *Individual Autonomy, Freedom and Rights*. 2003 ISBN 1-4020-1404-X
67. D. González Lagier: *The Paradoxes of Action*. (Human Action, Law and Philosophy). 2003 ISBN Hb-1-4020-1661-1
68. R. Zimmerling: *Influence and Power*. Variations on a Messy Theme. 2004 ISBN Hb-1-4020-2986-1

Law and Philosophy Library

69. A. Stranieri and J. Zeleznikow (eds.): *Knowledge Discovery from Legal Databases*. 2005 ISBN 1-4020-3036-3

70. J. Hage: *Studies in Legal Logic*. 2005 ISBN 1-4020-3517-9